THE TOY TRAIN DEPARTMENT

Electric Train Catalog Pages from the legendary
Sears Christmas Wishbooks of the 1950's and 1960's

Edited by Thomas W. Holland

Foreword by Richard P. Kughn
Chairman Emeritus, Lionel L.L.C.

Windmill Press

Copyright © 1996

WINDMILL PRESS
P.O. Box 56551
Sherman Oaks, California 91413

First Edition

Manufactured in the United States of America

All rights reserved. No part of this book may be reproduced in any form
or by any means, including electronic, photocopying or recording, or by any
information storage system, without written permission of the publisher,
except in the case of brief quotations used in critical articles and reviews.

Published by Windmill Press, P.O. Box 56551, Sherman Oaks, California 91413
Telephone (818) 995-6410   FAX (818) 995-3590

ISBN: 1-887790-00-4

LC: 95-78549

Publisher's Cataloging in Publication
(Prepared by Quality Books Inc.)

The toy train department : electric train catalog pages from
  the legendary Sears Christmas wishbooks of the 1950's and 1960's /
  edited by Thomas W. Holland.
  p. cm.
  ISBN: 1-887790-00-4

1. Railroads--Models--Catalogs--History. 2. Manufactures--
Catalogs. 3. Sears, Roebuck and Company--Catalogs.   I. Holland,
Thomas W., ed.

TF197.T69 1995   625.1'9
                                     QBI95-20396

*Front cover photograph: A young electric train fan is amazed by the wondrous toys
available in Sears' 1959 Christmas Wishbook.*
*Rear cover photographs: Sears Department Store, Canoga Park, California as it looked in 1964 (photo
courtesy Sears, Roebuck and Co.); A department store train display at Christmas circa. 1952*

THE CATALOG PAGES WITHIN THIS BOOK ARE REPRINTED
BY ARRANGEMENT WITH SEARS, ROEBUCK AND CO.
AND ARE PROTECTED UNDER COPYRIGHT.

NO DUPLICATION IS PERMITTED.

1950 - Pages 186 through 189 © 1950 Sears, Roebuck and Co.
1951 - Pages 215, 240 through 244 © 1951 Sears, Roebuck and Co.
1952   Pages 271 through 276 © 1952 Sears, Roebuck and Co.
1953 - Pages 241 through 246 © 1953 Sears, Roebuck and Co.
1954 - Pages 223, 261 through 266 © 1954 Sears, Roebuck and Co.
1955 - Pages 236 through 241 © 1955 Sears, Roebuck and Co.
1956 - Pages 271 through 277 © 1956 Sears, Roebuck and Co.
1957 - Pages 257 through 263 © 1957 Sears, Roebuck and Co.
1958 - Pages 249, 370 through 376 © 1958 Sears, Roebuck and Co.
1959 - Cover plus Pages 434 through 441 © 1959 Sears, Roebuck and Co.
1960 - Pages 435 through 445 © 1960 Sears, Roebuck and Co.
1961 - Pages 393 through 403 © 1961 Sears, Roebuck and Co.
1962 - Pages 436 through 443, 448 © 1962 Sears, Roebuck and Co.
1963 - Pages 177, 181 through 185 © 1963 Sears, Roebuck and Co.
1964 - Pages 214 through 218 © 1964 Sears, Roebuck and Co.
1965 - Pages 446 through 447, 486 © 1965 Sears, Roebuck and Co.
1966 - Pages 464 through 465 © 1966 Sears, Roebuck and Co.
1967 - Pages 521 through 523 © 1967 Sears, Roebuck and Co.
1968 - Pages 496, 521, 523 © 1968 Sears, Roebuck and Co.
1969 - Pages 515 through 518 © 1969 Sears, Roebuck and Co.

For Will and Emily

Acknowledgments

Many people worked behind the scenes to bring this book to fruition and I am most grateful for all the help I received.

Most importantly, I want to thank Sears, Roebuck and Company and their archivist Vicki Cwiok. Without their help this book simply would not have been possible.

Thanks also to Eleanor Holland, Doug Roth and Frank Thompson for their moral support and invaluable advice.

Tracking down all these rare catalog pages was a logistical ordeal and required the kind assistance of numerous people. I want to particularly thank catalog experts Jerry Harrington, Ed Osepowicz, Tim Goss, and Rich Hesson.

Al Summerfield, owner of Al's Train Shop in Burbank, California gave me lots of electric train marketing advice. Thanks to Betsy Annas for photographing the cover and Carolyn Porter and Alan Gadney who helped me with design and the complex job of reproducing the delicate old original catalog pages.

Also greatly appreciated was the interest and support of this project from Richard P. Kughn, Chairman and Chief Executive Officer of Lionel Trains, Inc. and Sheri Weitzman at the Lionel Railroaders Club.

Foreword

by Richard P. Kughn
Chairman Emeritus
Lionel L.L.C.

Since 1900, when Joshua Lionel Cowan first developed his electric gondola as an advertising gimmick for a store window display, the Lionel name has been at the forefront of the toy train business. An inventor and businessman, Joshua Cowan knew well the power of a good idea, and no less significant, the need for marketing and promotion to support it. When, in 1934, he teamed up with his good friend Walt Disney to create the infamous "Mickey & Minnie Mouse Handcar" that reportedly saved Lionel during the Depression, Cowan was probably also aware of the promotional appeal of the Disney characters that were in part responsible for sales of a quarter of a million units at a hefty one-dollar apiece.

Cowan was never one to rest on his laurels, however, and was always on the lookout for new ideas, new gimmicks, new techniques. And, at the same time, neither was the rest of the world standing still. As American cities grew and suburbs became a reality, so did the growth of the shopping center concept emerge as a significant landmark in retailing. I know this firsthand, having spent the majority of my career -- prior to purchasing Lionel Trains -- with one of the country's largest mall developers. In fact, to this day, I am still very much involved in this ever-changing industry.

One of the early leaders in retail trend-setting is still one of America's foremost department stores -- Sears, Roebuck & Company. It too had inauspicious beginnings in the heartland of rural America way back in the 1880's, but through the years expanded its interests nationwide, becoming the place "Where America shops for value." You may not know it, but Sears originated the concept of the mail order merchandise catalog, launching its first ever Sears catalog in 1896. The Sears catalog and its seasonal variation, the "great American Christmas Wishbook" continued to be the barometer of trends and mirror of American family life in the decades to come. Not coincidentally, much of Lionel's success, in particular during its post-World War II heyday, was due to the growth of retail department stores and the store catalog concept, as well as its own catalog. Both companies so faithfully created -- in their catalogs -- a reflection of the life and times of the American family tradition, it's not surprising that they formed this retailing bond. In fact, in postwar times, only the Sears catalog (and its retail "cousin", Montgomery Ward) were better known than Lionel.

Over the years, many Lionel products were offered in the Sears "Wishbook" catalog. That "Wishbook" is now part of Sears' lore (the catalog division of the retailing giant having been laid to rest in 1993), but Lionel carries on that tradition with its own catalog of over 250 toy train products to delight kids and kids at heart for years to come. In the Fifties, the focus was on trains that emulated the locomotives that passed by your street, carrying passengers to faraway places or freight to the industrial heartland. In the Sixties, military themes were among the highlights of Lionel's catalog, as well as its pages in the Sears Wishbook. And in 1995, Lionel offers everything -- and then some -- from die-cast steam locomotives with whistles and smoke to high tech power and control systems.

Whether you're of an age that you remember your first Sears Wishbook and the Lionel train in it that you hoped Santa would bring... or whether you've been "making tracks" with Lionel for some time now... or even if you've just discovered the magical world of Lionel model railroading, I know you will enjoy this look at Lionel's and Sears' illustrious past.

                                              Richard P. Kughn
                                              Chairman Emeritus
                                              Lionel L.L.C.

Introduction

When I was a kid I could hardly wait for the mailman to deliver our family's Sears Christmas Catalog. Everybody called it the "Wishbook" back then, and for good reason. Those pages were full of magic... enough toys and dolls and trains to make any child's head spin with delight. I studied every one of those pages to write up my annual Christmas list for Santa Claus. In fact, when I was really small I used to cut out the catalog's pictures and paste them to my list. I figured it was much easier than writing and surely faster for Santa. (By the way, I never received a fraction of all that I wanted.)

Today those old Sears Christmas catalogs have virtually disappeared. Disposable in their day, they were usually thrown in the trash after the holidays leaving only warm, happy memories behind. But most people today, particularly Baby Boomers like me who remember the joy those old catalogs brought them, are fascinated by the magical images and the fond memories they still conjure up.

The genesis of this book was my own interest in toy electric trains. When I was a kid in the 1950's and electric trains were in their heyday, my folks bought me an inexpensive Marx train set one Christmas. That lithographed tin outfit was my pride and joy and I ran it endlessly over my four-by-eight foot plywood railroad empire. In those days it seemed every boy I knew had electric trains too. Some had the higher quality and more expensive Lionel and American Flyer sets. A few kids had fancy layouts their dads had helped them build. A few even had illuminated passenger cars and big ZW transformers... my dream accessories... but it was usually their dads who were the primary railroaders in those families!

As the years went by I gradually forgot about my trains, but that Marx set, packed away in a beat-up cardboard box, somehow stayed with me during my career moves around the country. A few years ago a friend mentioned that he had pulled his old trains out of the attic to set up for his son at Christmas. With childlike glee my pal told me about his Lionel trains... how he had dusted them off, repaired electric cords and visited local train shops looking for new track. It sounded like fun and I rushed home to dig out my own old set. But it wasn't until I attended a huge local train show that I realized how many grown men were still playing with trains. These guys were reliving their happy childhood memories. They brought their families too, hoping the excitement would rub off. And there were electric trains for sale everywhere. I realized that it wasn't too late to possess those wonderful toys I wished I'd received as a child. I was hooked on trains, again.

As you will see in these pages dating from 1950 through 1969, Sears' marketing of toy electric trains reached its peak in the mid-to-late 1950's, taking up as many as nine full catalog pages. Although electric trains had been featured in Sears catalogs as early as the mid-1920's, they never sold better than in those booming postwar years.

But by 1960, the electric train market was already falling off despite the debut of smaller, less expensive HO-gauge trains. The big manufacturers like Lionel and Gilbert's American Flyer were being pushed out by Marx and Sears' own house brands. The deathblow came in the mid-1960's with the arrival of slot cars. Now kids could have fast, flashy sports cars streaking around the house, with hand-held controllers that allowed for more interaction with the toy. By 1965, not a single electric train was advertised in the Sears Christmas catalog, but pages and pages of slot cars certainly were.

During this time the big train companies suffered. Lionel had management troubles and even tried making slot cars themselves. Gilbert, makers of American Flyer trains, tried to capitalize on the nation's moon-bound space frenzy with their science kits and chemistry sets, but ultimately to no avail. Even Marx, whose low cost train sets had flooded the market, moved on to other more lucrative toy arenas.

Today, there is a growing re-interest in electric trains and in old toys in general. Lionel now owns American Flyer and the re-structured company is booming. New manufacturers and large-gauge "backyard" trains are creating a resurgence of excitement. Train meets draw thousands of people. The hobby is far from dying.

I hope the catalog pages in THE TOY TRAIN DEPARTMENT spark your interest as they did mine. Longtime collectors will surely benefit from the book's historical reference value, and if you're new to the hobby or have an old box of trains in the attic that need dusting off perhaps it will be the start of a wonderful new hobby.

Thomas W. Holland
Editor

The Sears Catalog

In a book about toy electric trains and their marketing in the Sears Christmas Wishbooks, it is ironic that the real railroads of the 1880's played a substantial role in the beginnings of Sears, Roebuck and Company.

The roots of the famous Sears Catalog began in 1886 when Richard W. Sears, then a railroad station agent for the Minneapolis and St. Louis Railway, in North Redwood, Minnesota, began selling watches and jewelry and later offered them through printed mailers which grew into catalogs. In those years the railroads literally moved America, taking people to work, settlers to new homes and delivering the clothing and supplies they would require. Thanks in large part to the railroad's ability to move things virtually anywhere in the country cheaply and quickly, Sears, Roebuck and Company grew into one of the nation's leading corporations.

In 1896 Sears produced its first large general merchandise catalog featuring 753 pages of merchandise targeted to America's farmers and their families with a variety of items for sale -- from apparel to plows -- in addition to watches and jewelry. The specialized Sears Christmas Catalogs -- nicknamed the "Wishbook" -- began in the mid-1930's. It became a holiday staple in virtually every American home.

Not realized at the time, of course, the Sears catalogs were recording the changing scene in America and represented the daily lives and work of thousands of Americans. Edgar Rice Burroughs, author of the famed "Tarzan" series, was at one time a copywriter for Sears catalogs. Jean Arthur, Lauren Bacall, Joan Caulfield, Anita Colby, Susan Heyward, Fredric March, Norma Shearer and Gloria Swanson all appeared on the pages of Sears catalogs as models in years past.

The famous Sears catalogs have been a barometer of the time, reflecting events, the way people lived and how they perceived their surroundings. For example, within months after the destruction of the U.S.S. Maine in Havana harbor in 1898, the catalog offered a complete "stereopticon lecture outfit" on that subject and the Cuban war.

Its easy to forget how far back the Sears catalog really does go. Sears sold the pioneers "Covered wagon covers" and in 1889, before the West was fully settled, the catalog stated: " Cash in full must accompany all orders from points in Washington, Oregon, California, Idaho, Nevada, Utah, Arizona, New Mexico, Montana and Wyoming -- if you live in one of the ten states and territories named." But C.O.D. orders were accepted from the more settled Eastern States.

Even wars and depressions are reflected in the catalog's pages. Song hits sold in the Spring 1918 catalog included "It's a Long Way to Berlin," "Keep the Home Fires Burning," and "Good-Bye Broadway, Hello France." And in the Fall 1942 catalog, Sears announced that its subsidiary, Allstate Fire Insurance Company, sold "the New U.S. Government War Damage Insurance Plan to protect homes and farms against war damage due to enemy attack or resistance by U.S. armed forces." In 1943 the catalog proclaimed: " Silvertone radios have gone to war. Tomorrow they will be back -- better than ever."

For anyone who recalls the Great Depression of the 1930's, perhaps the single most telling proof of its effect appeared in the 1933 Sears catalog which offered a book titled " Understanding the Stock Market" for 87¢. Called " a simple, yet thorough explanation of how the mysterious stock market operates," it had been marked down from $2.50.

Certainly, if anyone wishes to trace the rise of the automobile and the decline of the horse-drawn buggy, the Sears catalog documents the entire process. Taking note of the Tin Lizzie for the first time, the 1894 catalog listed automobile caps and books. But the horse still ruled the roads, with the catalog devoting eight full pages to such items as buggy boots, bridles, cruppers, harness, tops and whips. By 1929 the tables had turned. The buggy offering was down to half a page, and disappeared entirely thereafter. The catalog index, at the same time, listed 266 separate items under auto accessories.

In January 1993, Sears discontinued its catalog operation. But the old pages that still exist, such as those reproduced in this book, offer a rare peek through a window to the past, documenting virtually everthing about we Americans and our lives. For electric train hobbyists, the Sears Wishbook documents the toy's golden era in a way no other historical text can.

PLEASE NOTE:

The merchandise represented in these catalog pages is NOT AVAILABLE from Sears, Roebuck and Co.

The products presented here are strictly for historical purposes and are NOT FOR SALE.

This book is intended solely as a referencing source and is in no way to be construed as a current offering of Sears, Roebuck and Co.

SEARS CHRISTMAS CATALOG

1950

By 1950 Sears, Roebuck & Company's annual Christmas Wishbook catalog was already a fixture in most American homes. In these pre-shopping mall days, and with many people still living far from big city stores, the catalog business was booming. Spendable income was on the increase and toy trains were the Christmas gifts of choice.

Lionel Trains were "Sears' Best" and were prominently featured in 1950. A complete Union Pacific set led by Lionel's #2023 diesel was offered at a then-pricey $47.50. For those wanting the thrill of electric trains on a budget, Sears also sold tin lithographed Marx sets as well as their own house brand called Happi-Time.

Accessories were highlighted also, with such classics as the Operating Milk Car and Cattle Car shown. This was the only catalog of the period to illustrate the legendary Lionel ZW transformer.

  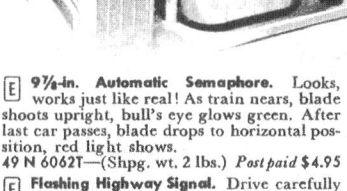 

Lionel Accessories

Both cars below have 8 solid steel wheels, die-cast trucks, knuckle-type electric couplers. Dummy hand brakes. No track.

A **Searchlight Car.** Realistically detailed. Powerful searchlight swivels freely, switches on and off by *REMOTE CONTROL!* Molded plastic platform; dummy G.M. Diesel generator 10 in. long. (Shpg. wt. 2 lbs.).
49 N 6067T—(Was $6.50.). Postpaid...$5.95

B **Operating Dump Car.** Ingenious gear action. Enameled aluminum body tilts up, side drops, load of coal slides into bin... *all by REMOTE CONTROL!* Die-cast frame. Dummy handbrake, railings. Dummy coal and plastic bin included. (Shpg. wt. 2 lbs.)
49 N 6059T—9½ in. long. Postpaid....$7.75

C **Conveyor Coal Loader.** Realistic dummy coal "flows" up endless rubber conveyor belt with multiple buckets, tips into waiting car. Car, track not included. General Motors Diesel-type housing encloses heavy duty self-lubricating electric motor. Heavy 10x 7½-inch die-cast base. Controller, wire leads and dummy coal included.
49 N 6070T—(Shpg. wt. 6 lbs.) Postpaid $11.95

D **11¾-inch Rotary Beacon.** Embossed lattice-work steel structure has platform on top, ladder on side. Powerful miniature searchlight revolves. Red and green fresnel-type lenses rotate over light on hardened steel pivots.
49 N 6042T—(Shpg. wt. 2 lbs.).. Postpaid $2.95

E **9⅞-in. Automatic Semaphore.** Looks, works just like real! As train nears, blade shoots upright, bull's eye glows green. After last car passes, blade drops to horizontal position, red light shows.
49 N 6062T—(Shpg. wt. 2 lbs.) Postpaid $4.95

F **Flashing Highway Signal.** Drive carefully ... railroad crossing ahead! Two red warning lights flash on and off alternately from one side to other when train nears, stop when last car passes. 9 in. high.
49 N 6049T—(Shpg. wt. 1 lb.). Postpaid $4.75

Lionel Electric Trains — Remote Control for 110-120-v. 60-cycle A.C.

$52.50 Cash Postpaid — Only $5.50 Down

Operating Dump Car and Unloading Bin. Dumps coal by REMOTE CONTROL. Side drops; load of coal slides out into the bin.

Operating Milk Car and Platform. Doors open by REMOTE CONTROL. Milk man comes out on platform and delivers milk cans.

Big "O"-gauge 6-unit Freight with smoke, whistle

• Magnificently scale-detailed 20-wheel die-cast steam turbine locomotive with new Magnetraction. Powerful 8-wheel drive... two six-wheel pony trucks... piston rod action... bright headlamp.
• Operating milk car... operating coal dump car... lighted caboose. All cars accurately detailed scale models of real cars with 8 solid steel wheels, die cast trucks, knuckle-type electric couplers.

Just like a real freight thundering down the rails puffing harmless, realistic smoke... whistle blowing ... bright headlamp gleaming! Run it fast or slow, forward or backward... couple and uncouple cars... operate milk or coal dump car... sound its deep-toned whistle... all by *REMOTE CONTROL* without touching track or train! 6-unit train 55 in. long; includes locomotive, tender with built-in whistle, plastic operating milk-car, metal oil car and operating coal dump car, lighted plastic caboose. 16 sections "O"-gauge track, milk platform, 7 milk cans, "coal," bin included.
79N05985T—Complete train. Transformer not included... order below. (Shpg. wt. 20 lbs.). Postpaid $52.50

PLUS LIONEL MAGNE-TRACTION

Oval track, 149 in. around

"027"-gauge Track, Switches, Crossover

G 49 N 6048T—**Remote Control Switches.** One right-hand, one left-hand switch, control panel, and connecting wire. (Shpg. wt. 3 lbs.). Postpaid......Pair $10.95
H 49 N 6035T—**90-degree Crossover.** 7⅜ inches square. (Ship. wt. 8 oz.). Postpaid.....Each $1.75
J 49 N 6003T—**Straight Track Section.** Length 8¾ inches. (Shpg. wt. 3 oz.). Postpaid. Each 25c
K 49 N 6004T—**Curved Track Section.** Length 9½ inches. (Shipping wt. 3 oz.). Postpaid Each 25c
L 49 N 6043T—**Magnetic Track Set.** For remote control uncoupling, unloading. Control panel and wire. (Shipping weight 1 pound.)........Postpaid $2.75

"O"-gauge Track, Switches, Crossover

M 49 N 6090T—**Remote Control Switches.** 1 left, 1 right-hand switch, control panel, connecting wire.(Wt.5 lbs.) Ppd. Pair $18.75
N 49 N 6060T—**90-degree Crossover.** 9½ inches square. (Shpg. wt. 8 oz.).....Each $2.50
P 49 N 6008T—**Straight Track Section.** Length 10 inches. (Shpg. wt. 4 oz.). Postpaid. Each 30c
R 49 N 6009T—**Curved Track Section.** Length 10⅞ in. (Shpg. wt. 4 oz.). Postpaid. Each 30c
S 49 N 6061T—**Magnetic Track Set.** For remote control uncoupling, unloading. Control panel, wires. (Shpg. wt. 1 lb.)..Postpaid $3.00

$13.95
$25.00

"TRAINMASTER" Transformers

Built-in *self-resetting automatic circuit breakers* protect against overloads and shorts. Red light signals short. For 110-120 volts 60-cycle A.C.

T **Type RW—110-watt.** Two variable-voltage circuits for running train; 4 fixed voltages for accessories. Two buttons: one blows whistle, one for reversing. U.L. approved. (Shpg. wt. 6 lbs.)
49 N 6088T.... Postpaid $13.95

U **Type ZW—275-watt.** Runs up to 4 trains at same time on different layouts. Two independently controlled variable-voltage circuits, each with its own built-in whistle and direction controls. Two variable-voltage accessory circuits. Durable molded case. (Shpg. wt. 14 lbs.)
79 N 06091T... Postpaid $25.00

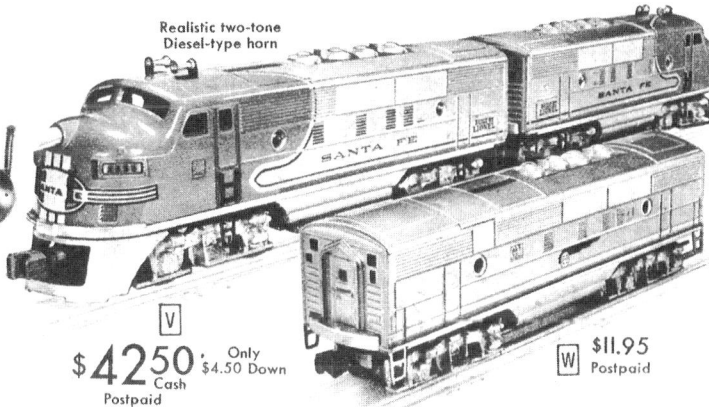

Realistic two-tone Diesel-type horn

$42.50 Cash Postpaid — Only $4.50 Down

$11.95 Postpaid

Santa Fe Twin Diesel with horn

V Now with sensational Magnetraction to give it greater pulling power! Millions have thrilled at the sight of the mighty Santa Fe F3 diesel. Now Lionel has reproduced this giant two-sectional General Motors locomotive in miniature ... even trainmen marvel at its blueprint accuracy! **Super-power twin motors** with wide speed range are mounted in first locomotive section; 4-wheel drive on each. Realistic deep-throated horn. Plastic cab magnificently detailed, including louvres, ladders, stanchions. Driver's compartment glassed-in with transparent plastic. Two simulated windshield wipers. **Illuminated number box;** gleaming headlamp. **Authentic markings.** For use with any Lionel electric train set.
79 N 06099T—Length 26½ in. overall. (Shpg. wt. 10 lbs.).....Postpaid $42.50

W **Santa Fe "B" Unit.** An exact copy! Couple it between the two halves of above locomotive to give an exceptionally long, streamlined effect.
49 N 6075T—13½ inches long overall. (Shpg. wt. 4 lbs.).....Postpaid $11.95

Easy Terms on page 283 — c PAGE 187.. LIONEL TRAINS

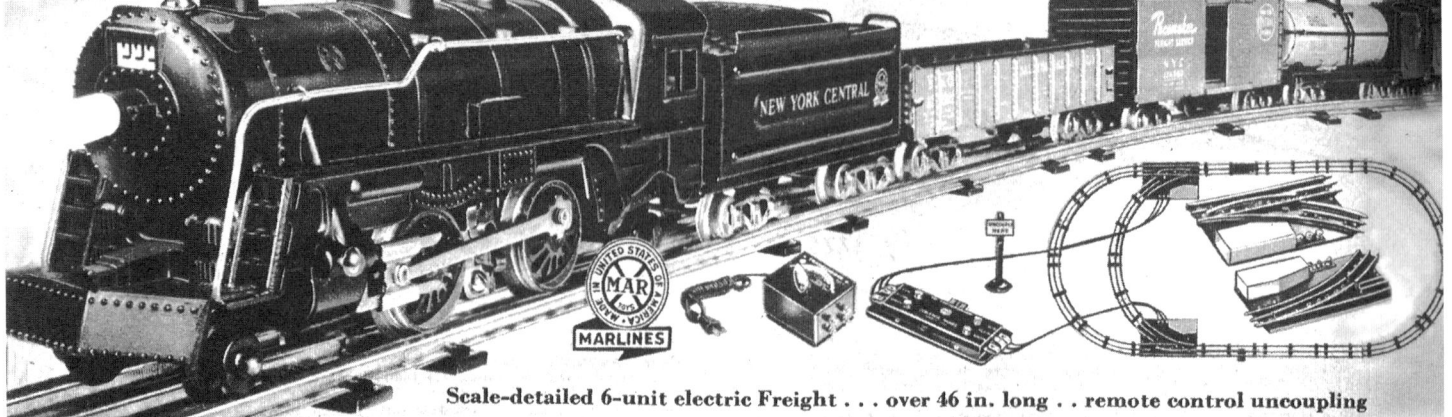

Scale-detailed 6-unit electric Freight... over 46 in. long...remote control uncoupling

Now a built-in circuit breaker protects transformer and equipment! Run train forward or backward, fast or slow... couple and uncouple cars... all by REMOTE CONTROL. Train is over 46 in. long. Lithographed, embossed metal cars are 3/16-inch scale model replicas of modern railroad stock, double trucks (8 wheels). Automatic uncoupling units on cars... *uncouple any car without touching it!*

$21.97 Cash
$2.50 Down with Remote Control Switches

PRICE CUT! Economy Train Set. 14 sections of track make oval 137 in. around.
79 N 05947—Shipping weight 10 lbs.. **$14.45**

Big 8-wheel scale-detailed die-cast locomotive has powerful 4-wheel drive, oilless bronze bearings, die cast wheels, piston rod action, bright headlamp. Set includes: Locomotive, tender, box car with sliding doors, oil car, gondola, caboose; new variable-speed 50-watt U.L. approved transformer with built-in circuit breaker (110-120-volt 60-cycle A.C.); track, etc.

De Luxe Train Set with pair of Remote Control Switches. Switches open, close by operating 4-button control panel. 16 sections of track (184-in. running length).
79 N 05949—Shipping weight 13 pounds. Only $2.50 down on Easy Terms....... Cash **$21.97**

New! HAPPI-TIME Electric Freight..12-wheel die-cast scale-model engine

Greatest value in our Train line!

[A] $19.89 Cash
Only $2.00 Down

Big 6-wheel drive scale-detailed 12-wheel die-cast locomotive... usually found only in sets selling for $25.00 and above! Pony trucks and guide wheels included. Realistic piston rod action. Powerful headlamp. New die-cast coal and water type tender! Train over 4-ft. long. Colorful embossed metal cars, 3/16-in. scale models of real freight cars. Double trucks (8 wheels). Couple and uncouple cars... run train fast or slow... forward or backward... all by REMOTE CONTROL! Set includes: Locomotive, tender, tank car, box car, highside gondola, caboose; 16 sections of track; UL approved 50-watt transformer (110-120 volt 60-cycle AC) built-in circuit breaker.
79 N 05948—Shpg. wt. 13 lbs... Reduced to...... **$19.89**

Was $9.79
$7.95
Price Reduced $1.84

[B] Save over 18% on this 5-unit 35½-inch Remote Control Freight Set! Same remote control of speed and direction as on our higher priced sets! Carefully detailed steam-type steel locomotive equipped with *REMOTE CONTROL*, oilless bronze bearings, die-cast wheels, piston rod action and bright headlamp. Metal tender; brightly lithographed 4-wheel freight cars: gondola, tank car and caboose.

Ten sections of track form oval 102 in. around. Underwriters' approved 50-watt transformer for 110-120-volt 60-cycle A.C. All necessary wires and track connectors included. *Was $9.79.*
79 N 05925—Shpg. wt. 8 lbs....... **$7.95**

New 29-pc. Accessory Set

[C] Just what you need to add greater realism to your train set. Includes an assortment of 12 various well-known railroad signs and signals, 12 telegraph poles, plus one each of semaphore, lamp post, crossing gate, grade crossing, railroad crossing sign. Sturdy molded plastic, authentically detailed. Made in a size that's just right for any train set. Shipping weight 1 lb. per set. Track not included.
49 N 6024—Complete 29-pc. set.. **$2.89**

$2.89 29-pc. set

All Electric Train Sets shown operate on 110-120 volts 60-cycle A.C. You pay postage on Marx train items.

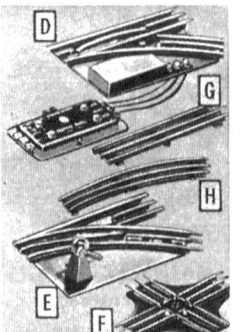

Marx Electric Train Accessories

[D] 49 N 6019—Electric Remote Control Switch Set. One left, one right-hand switch, 4-button control panel, wires. Shpg. wt. 2 lbs. 8 oz. *(Was $7.45).*.......Set **$6.79**

[E] 49 N 6018—Manual Switch Set. One left and one right-hand switch. Shipping weight 2 lbs. **$2.95**

[F] 49 N 6017—7½-inch Cross-over. Wt. 8 oz. **87¢**

[G] 49 N 6010—Extra 8⅞-inch Straight Track. Shipping weight 4 oz.... Each **18¢**

[H] 49 N 6011—Extra 10-inch Curved Track. Shipping weight 4 oz...... Each **18¢**

Accessories for greater realism. Bulbs, connectors included.

[J] 49 N 6023—Revolving Beacon. 12½ in. high. Red reflectors. Shpg. wt. 1 lb. **$1.87**

[K] 49 N 6021—Twin Lamp Post. Metal; 7½ in. high. Double light reflectors. Shipping weight 8 oz...... **$1.45**

[L] 49 N 6034—Automatic Crossing Flasher. Twin lights flash alternately from one side to other. Metal; 7¾ in. high. Shpg. wt. 10 oz.. **$1.87**

[M] 49 N 6027—Automatic Block Signal. Train stops on red light; proceeds on green. Metal; 7 in. Shpg. wt. 1 lb... **$1.87**

Transformers

Variable-speed Transformers for 110-120-volt 60-cycle A.C. U.L. approved. Protected against shorts and overloads by built-in thermal cut-out circuit breaker.
7–13 volts for train speed, 13 volts for accessories. Connectors, cords plugs included. Two sizes:

[N] 49 N 6094—50-watt. Wt. 3 lbs. 4 oz. **$5.79**

[P] 49 N 6083—75-watt. Reverse-control lever. Air-cooled base. Shpg. wt. 4 lbs. 12 oz... **$8.77**

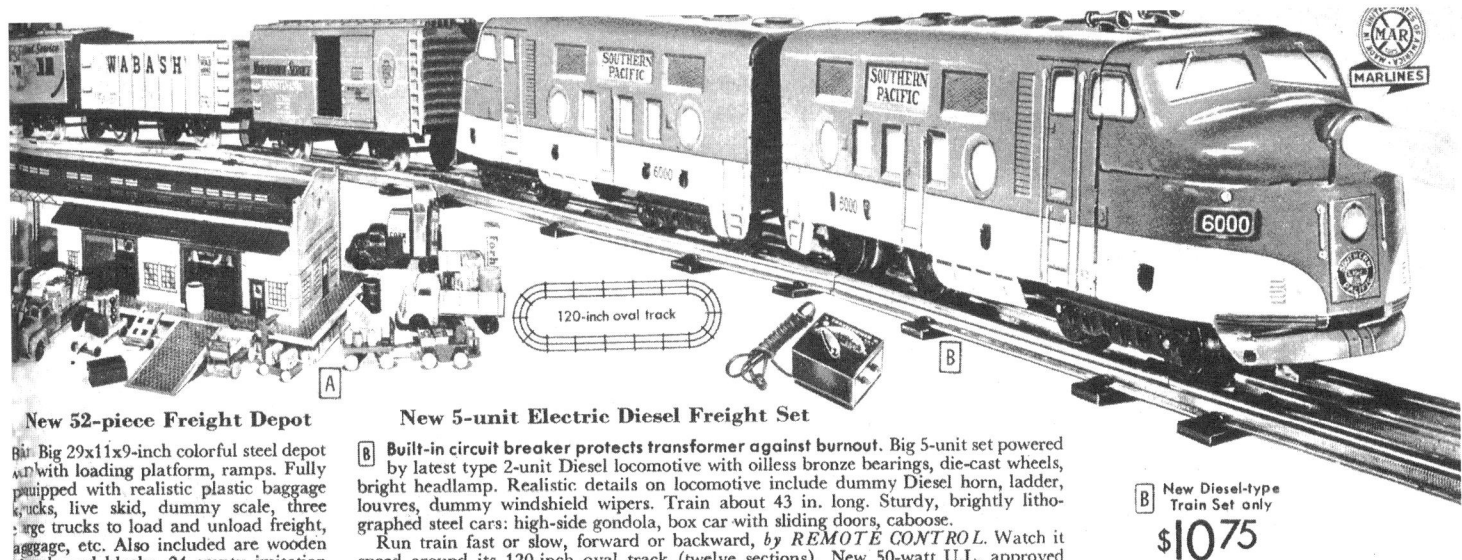

New 52-piece Freight Depot

[A] Big 29x11x9-inch colorful steel depot with loading platform, ramps. Fully equipped with realistic plastic baggage trucks, live skid, dummy scale, three large trucks to load and unload freight, baggage, etc. Also included are wooden barrels and blocks, 24 empty imitation food cartons, etc. . . . 52 pieces in all! Depot easily set up without tools.
49 N 06077—Shpg. wt. 5 lbs. $4.77

New 5-unit Electric Diesel Freight Set

[B] Built-in circuit breaker protects transformer against burnout. Big 5-unit set powered by latest type 2-unit Diesel locomotive with oilless bronze bearings, die-cast wheels, bright headlamp. Realistic details on locomotive include dummy Diesel horn, ladder, louvres, dummy windshield wipers. Train about 43 in. long. Sturdy, brightly lithographed steel cars: high-side gondola, box car with sliding doors, caboose.

Run train fast or slow, forward or backward, *by REMOTE CONTROL*. Watch it speed around its 120-inch oval track (twelve sections). New 50-watt U.L. approved transformer (110-120 volts 60-cycle A.C.) Built-in circuit breaker, reversing lever.

[B] 79 N 05932—Train Set as described above. Shipping weight 9 lbs. $10.75
[AB] 79 N 05991—Train Set [B] plus Freight Depot Set [A]. Shpg. wt. 14 lbs. $14.98

[B] New Diesel-type Train Set only **$10.75**

[AB] Train Set with Freight Station Set **$14.98**

Realistic Marx Electric Train Accessories

Derrick loader, water tower, metal tunnel may be used with mechanical train sets. Light bulbs, wire, track connectors included where needed.

[C] Lighted all-steel Trestle Bridge. Embossed rivets. Light socket and reflector held in position by snap-on slip; adjustable for position.
49 N 6026—Length 24 in.; height 6⅛ in; width 4⅞ in. Shpg. wt. 2 lbs. **$1.89**

[D] Sturdy Steel Derrick Loader. 7¾ in. high. Straddles track. Raises, lowers loads into cars. Swings in circle.
49 N 6020—Shpg. wt. 1 lb. 8 oz. . . **$1.45**

[E] Whistling Station. Press remote control button . . . hear realistic wail of locomotive whistle as train speeds down track! Whistle built into 9-inch lithographed steel station.
49 N 6079—Shipping weight 2 lbs. . . **$3.98**

[F] Automatic grade crossing Shack with Watchman. Shanty 4½-in. high lithographed steel; plastic and steel gate is 8¼ in. long. When train nears, watchman comes out, gate lowers.
49 N 6074—Shpg. wt. 2 lbs. 8 oz. . . **$3.87**

[G] Collapsible Metal Tunnel. Two parts; easily assembled. Lithographed landscape. 10¾ in. long; 9 in. wide; 7 in. high.
49 N 6025—Shpg. wt. 1 lb. **89c**

[H] 13-in. Twin Searchlight Tower. Two powerful lights tilt and revolve on girder-type molded plastic tower. Metal ladder.
49 N 6078—Shpg. wt. 2 lbs. **$2.79**

[J] Big 8¼-inch plastic Water Tower. Adjustable spout; realistic ribs, steel-type understructure. Railroad colors.
49 N 6064—Shpg. wt. 12 oz. **89c**

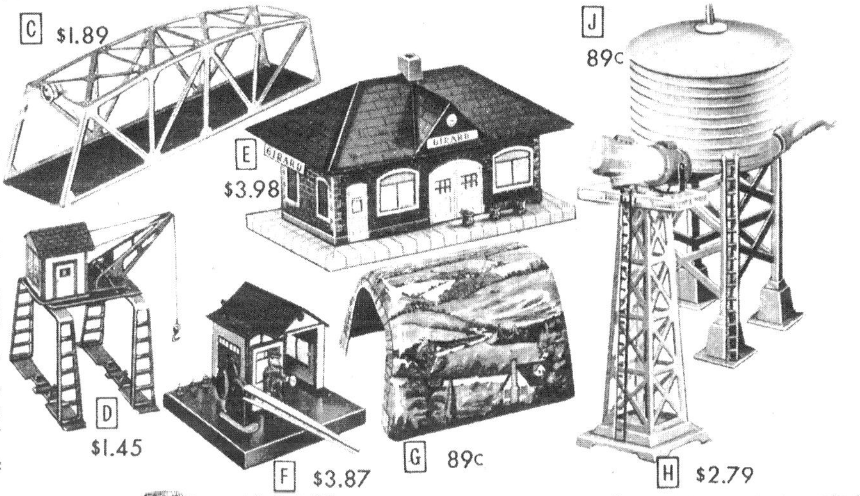

35½-inch Sparkling Freight

[K] 5-unit sturdy steel Mechanical Train. Steam-type locomotive whizzes around its 120-inch oval track, *tiny sparks shooting from smokestack, bell ringing!* Long-running clockspring motor; built-in speed governor and brake. 35½-inch train includes: Locomotive, tender, coal car, box car, caboose. Cars brightly lithographed. Twelve sections of track. A big value at Sears low price!
49 N 5906—Shpg. wt. 3 lbs. 12 oz. **$2.89**

Has Whistle, Crossover Track

[L] Larger Engine—New style cars. *Realistic whistle* blows loudly as train speeds around 176-inch *figure-8 crossover track*. Powerful, long-running clockspring motor; built-in speed governor and brake. Sturdy steel engine. Cars brightly lithographed metal. 5-unit, 43-inch train includes: Locomotive, tender, gondola, box car, caboose. Sixteen sections of track and crossover.
49 N 5918—Shpg. wt. 4 lbs. 8 oz. **$4.98**

37-in. Sparkling Freight with Switches, Accessories

[M] Big 5-unit sparkling mechanical Freight Set includes pair of manually-operated switches and twelve realistic plastic accessories. Sturdy steel steam-type *locomotive shoots sparks from smoke stack, rings bell* as it streaks along. Powerful long-running clockspring motor; built-in speed governor, brake. Colorful lithographed metal cars. Set includes: locomotive, tender, box car, side dump car, caboose; 6 telephone poles, crossing gate, semaphore, lamp post, 3 railroad signs; 14 sections of track plus pair of switches. Accessories in proportion. Youngsters will enjoy hours and hours of play with this big 33-piece Freight Yard Railroad.
49 N 5921—37-inch Train Set as described. Shpg. wt. 6 lbs. 8 oz. **$5.89**

For Easy Terms, see page 283

SEARS CHRISTMAS CATALOG

1951

The marketers at Sears knew a trend when they saw one and electric trains continued to be prominently featured in the 1951 Christmas Wishbook.

"Famous Lionel Electric Trains" were shown ranging from steam to diesels. MagneTraction, which allowed Lionel's engines to pull more cars over steeper grades was featured in a 6-unit "O" gauge Steam Freight set. With track and two operating cars, but no transformer, the set could be yours for just $62.50... $6.50 down... and postpaid too.

O-27 Marx and Sears Happi-Time trains were available too. A lithographed Marx Southern Pacific set with a lavish 43-piece tin freight depot was a reasonable $15.98.

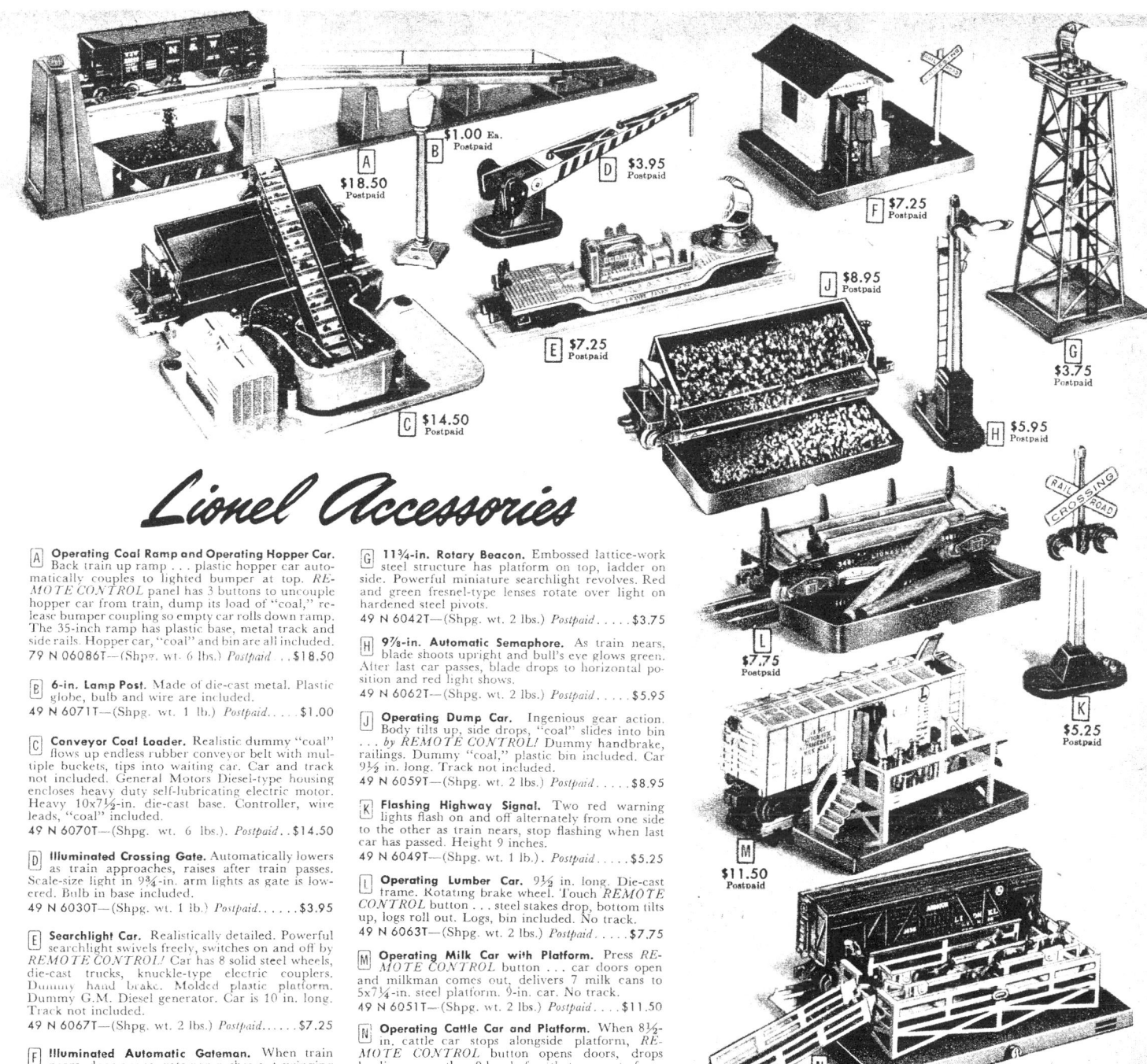

Lionel Accessories

A **Operating Coal Ramp and Operating Hopper Car.** Back train up ramp . . . plastic hopper car automatically couples to lighted bumper at top. *REMOTE CONTROL* panel has 3 buttons to uncouple hopper car from train, dump its load of "coal," release bumper coupling so empty car rolls down ramp. The 35-inch ramp has plastic base, metal track and side rails. Hopper car, "coal" and bin are all included.
79 N 06086T—(Shpg. wt. 6 lbs.) Postpaid ..$18.50

B **6-in. Lamp Post.** Made of die-cast metal. Plastic globe, bulb and wire are included.
49 N 6071T—(Shpg. wt. 1 lb.) Postpaid.....$1.00

C **Conveyor Coal Loader.** Realistic dummy "coal" flows up endless rubber conveyor belt with multiple buckets, tips into waiting car. Car and track not included. General Motors Diesel-type housing encloses heavy duty self-lubricating electric motor. Heavy 10x7½-in. die-cast base. Controller, wire leads, "coal" included.
49 N 6070T—(Shpg. wt. 6 lbs.). Postpaid ..$14.50

D **Illuminated Crossing Gate.** Automatically lowers as train approaches, raises after train passes. Scale-size light in 9¾-in. arm lights as gate is lowered. Bulb in base included.
49 N 6030T—(Shpg. wt. 1 lb.) Postpaid......$3.95

E **Searchlight Car.** Realistically detailed. Powerful searchlight swivels freely, switches on and off by *REMOTE CONTROL!* Car has 8 solid steel wheels, die-cast trucks, knuckle-type electric couplers. Dummy hand brake. Molded plastic platform. Dummy G.M. Diesel generator. Car is 10 in. long. Track not included.
49 N 6067T—(Shpg. wt. 2 lbs.) Postpaid......$7.25

F **Illuminated Automatic Gateman.** When train nears, door opens, gateman rushes out swinging red lantern. After last car has passed, gateman returns to shack, door closes. Metal base; plastic shack and man. Height 5 in.
49 N 6066T—(Shpg. wt. 2 lbs. 8 oz.) Postpaid.$7.25

G **11¾-in. Rotary Beacon.** Embossed lattice-work steel structure has platform on top, ladder on side. Powerful miniature searchlight revolves. Red and green fresnel-type lenses rotate over light on hardened steel pivots.
49 N 6042T—(Shpg. wt. 2 lbs.) Postpaid.....$3.75

H **9⅞-in. Automatic Semaphore.** As train nears, blade shoots upright and bull's eye glows green. After last car passes, blade drops to horizontal position and red light shows.
49 N 6062T—(Shpg. wt. 2 lbs.) Postpaid.....$5.95

J **Operating Dump Car.** Ingenious gear action. Body tilts up, side drops, "coal" slides into bin . . . *by REMOTE CONTROL!* Dummy handbrake, railings. Dummy "coal," plastic bin included. Car 9½ in. long. Track not included.
49 N 6059T—(Shpg. wt. 2 lbs.) Postpaid.....$8.95

K **Flashing Highway Signal.** Two red warning lights flash on and off alternately from one side to the other as train nears, stop flashing when last car has passed. Height 9 inches.
49 N 6049T—(Shpg. wt. 1 lb.) Postpaid.....$5.25

L **Operating Lumber Car.** 9½ in. long. Die-cast frame. Rotating brake wheel. Touch *REMOTE CONTROL* button . . . steel stakes drop, bottom tilts up, logs roll out. Logs, bin included. No track.
49 N 6063T—(Shpg. wt. 2 lbs.) Postpaid.....$7.75

M **Operating Milk Car with Platform.** Press *REMOTE CONTROL* button . . . car doors open and milkman comes out, delivers 7 milk cans to 5x7¼-in. steel platform. 9-in. car. No track.
49 N 6051T—(Shpg. wt. 2 lbs.) Postpaid.....$11.50

N **Operating Cattle Car and Platform.** When 8½-in. cattle car stops alongside platform, *REMOTE CONTROL* button opens doors, drops loading ramp, then 9 head of cattle troop out of car, across platform, back into car. 13¾-in. steel platform and ramp; built-in remote control unit (no remote control track needed). Track not included.
49 N 6069T—(Shpg. wt. 4 lbs.) Postpaid....$15.95

6-unit "O"-gauge Freight with smoke, whistle

$62.50 Cash or Terms
$6.50 Down. Postpaid

• Magnificently scale-detailed 20-wheel die-cast steam turbine locomotive, new Magnetraction. Powerful 8-wheel drive . . 2 six-wheel pony trucks . . piston rod action . . bright headlamp. Just like a real freight thundering down the rails puffing harmless, realistic smoke . . . whistle blowing! Run it fast or slow, forward or backward . . . couple and uncouple cars . . . operate milk or coal dump car . . . sound its deep-toned whistle . . . *all by REMOTE CONTROL without touching track or train!* 6-unit train 55 in. long; includes locomotive, tender with built-in whistle, plastic milk-car, metal oil car and coal dump car, lighted plastic caboose. 16 sections "O"-gauge track, milk platform, 7 milk cans, "coal," bin included.
79 N 05985T—Complete train. Transformer not incl. See facing page. (Wt. 20 lbs.). Postpaid. $62.50

NEW! Happi-Time, Two-trains-in-one, 8 units

$31.75 Cash
$3.50 Down with Remote Control Switches

Biggest Train Value we know of! Big, authentic 8-unit combination passenger and freight is over 7 ft. long. Twin-unit Santa Fe diesel with powerful headlamp alone is over 2 ft. long. Has oilless bronze bearings. **Six scale model cars of latest design** . . . are embossed, lithographed metal . . have double trucks (8 wheels). Box car, high-side gondola, caboose, two passenger cars, observation car. Run train forward, backward . . . fast or slow . . . couple and uncouple cars . . . *all by REMOTE CONTROL* without touching track or cars! **50-watt UL approved transformer** with built-in circuit breaker. 110-120-volt 60-cycle AC. Shpg. wt. 17 lbs.
79 N 05944—With 18 track sections making 195-inch oval **$24.79**

With remote control switches, 4-button control panel opens—closes switches, plus 23 sections of track makes huge layout. 2 uncoupling sections uncouple cars to shuttle freight or passenger cars on inner circle, or have one big train with all cars. Shpg. wt. 18 lbs.
79 N 05945 . . . . **$31.75**

HAPPI-TIME Scale Model Electric Freight Sets

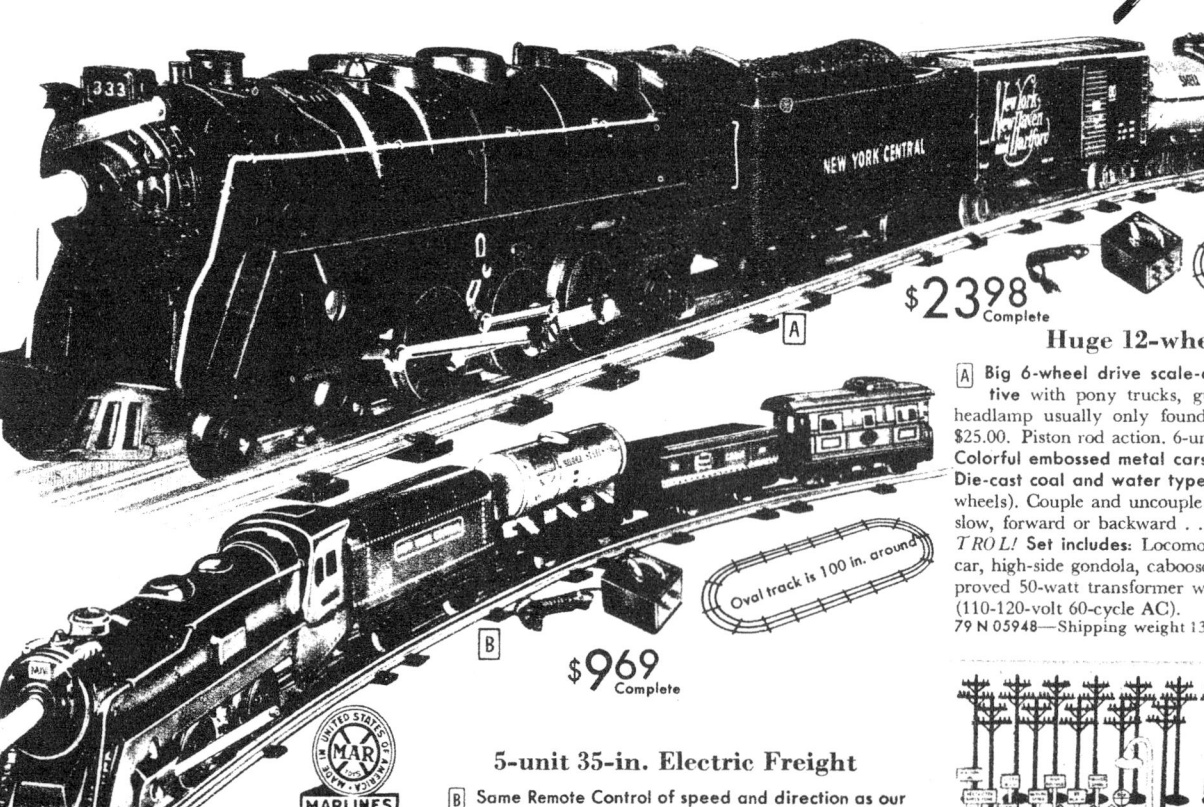

$23.98 Complete
Oval track 175 in. around

Huge 12-wheel Engine

[A] Big 6-wheel drive scale-detailed die-cast locomotive with pony trucks, guide wheels and powerful headlamp usually only found in sets selling at above $25.00. Piston rod action. 6-unit train is over 4 feet long. Colorful embossed metal cars are 3/16-in. scale models. Die-cast coal and water type tender. Double trucks (8 wheels). Couple and uncouple cars . . . run train fast or slow, forward or backward . . . *all by REMOTE CONTROL!* Set includes: Locomotive, tender, tank car, box car, high-side gondola, caboose, 16-section track, UL approved 50-watt transformer with built-in circuit breaker (110-120-volt 60-cycle AC).
79 N 05948—Shipping weight 13 lbs. **$23.98**

$9.69 Complete
Oval track is 100 in. around

5-unit 35-in. Electric Freight

[B] Same Remote Control of speed and direction as our higher priced Electric Train Sets! Run train fast or slow . . . forward or backward *by REMOTE CONTROL* without touching train or track. **Carefully detailed steam-type steel locomotive** equipped with REMOTE CONTROL, oilless bronze bearings, die-cast wheels, realistic piston-rod action and bright headlamp. Metal tender PLUS three brightly lithographed metal freight cars; gondola, tank car and caboose. Train measures 35 in. long overall. **Ten sections of track form oval 100 inches around.** Underwriters' Laboratories, Inc., approved 50-watt transformer for 110 to 120-volt 60-cycle AC only. Durable quality, very low priced for the new young train enthusiast. Wires and track connectors included. Shipping weight 8 pounds.
79 N 05925—Complete Set as described **$9.69**

All Electric Train Sets shown on these two pages operate on 110-120-volts 60-cycle AC only. You pay postage on Marx and Happi-Time train items

29-piece Scale Accessory Set

$2.89 29-pc. set

Just what the young railroader needs to add greater realism to his train set. Made of sturdy molded plastic, authentically detailed. And they're just the right size for any standard electric or mechanical train set. Set includes: 12 telegraph poles (each 7 in. high), 12 Railroad Right-of-way signs, PLUS one each of the following: semaphore, lamp post, crossing gate, grade crossing, railroad crossing sign. Track not included.
49 N 6024—Complete 29-piece Set. Shpg. wt. 2 lbs. . **$2.89**

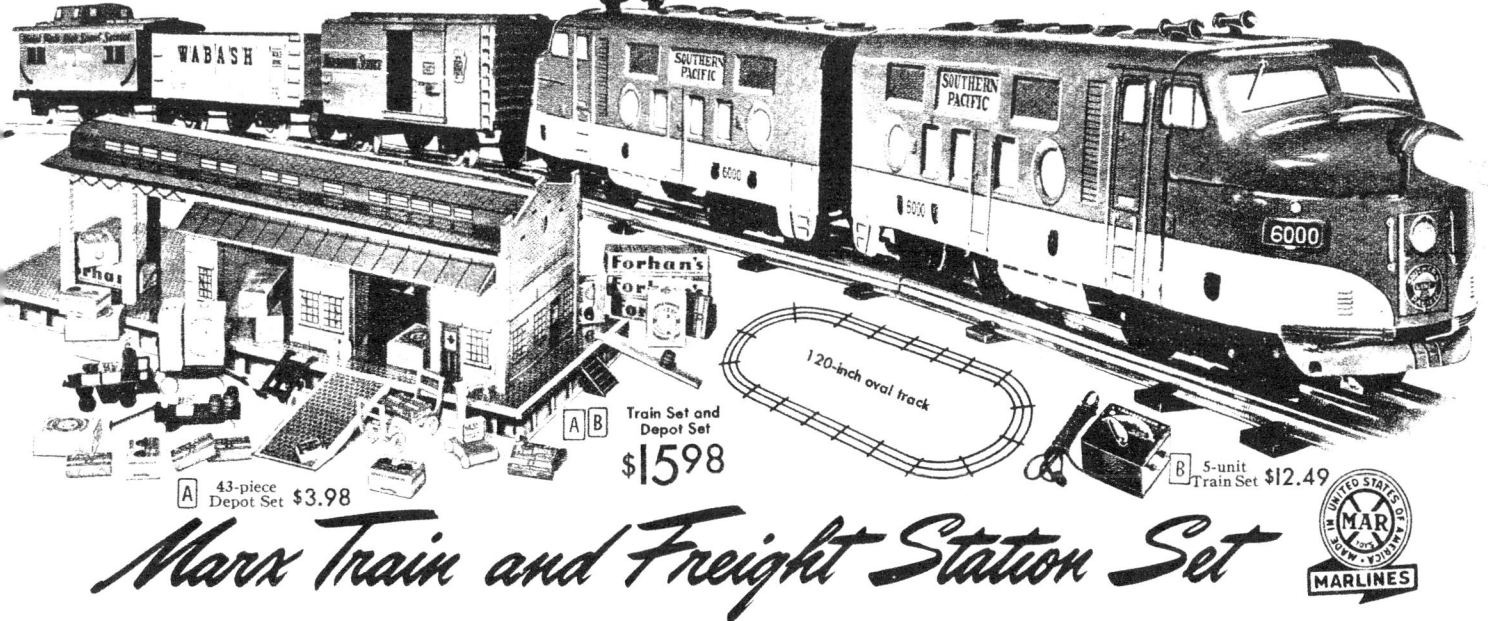

Train Set and Depot Set $15.98

[A] 43-piece Depot Set $3.98
[B] 5-unit Train Set $12.49

Marx Train and Freight Station Set

43-piece Freight Depot

[A] Big 29x11¼x9-in. colorful steel depot with loading platform and ramps. Fully equipped with realistic plastic baggage trucks, live skid, dummy scale, hand truck. Also included are 24 assorted empty imitation food cartons, 6 wooden barrels and 6 wooden blocks. Forty-three pieces in all! Depot shipped unassembled; easily set up without tools!
79 N 06095—Shipping weight 4 lbs....Complete **$3.98**

5-unit Twin-Diesel Remote-Control Electric Freight

[B] Built-in circuit breaker protects transformer against shorts and overload. Big 5-unit set powered by latest type 2-unit Diesel locomotive with oilless bronze bearings, die-cast drive wheels, bright headlamp. Realistic details on locomotive include dummy Diesel horn; lithographed louvers, dummy windshield wipers. Train about 43 in. long. Lithographed steel cars: high-side gondola, box car with sliding doors, caboose.
Run train fast or slow, forward or backward by REMOTE CONTROL. Watch it speed around its 120 inches of oval track (12 sections). 50-watt UL approved transformer (110-120-volt 60-cycle AC) has reversing lever.
79 N 05932—Train Set as described above. Train, transformer, track and cars. Shpg. wt. 9 lbs.....**$12.49**
[A][B] **79 N 05991**—Train Set (B) PLUS 43 pc. Freight Depot Set (A). Shpg. wt. 14 lbs.....**$15.98**

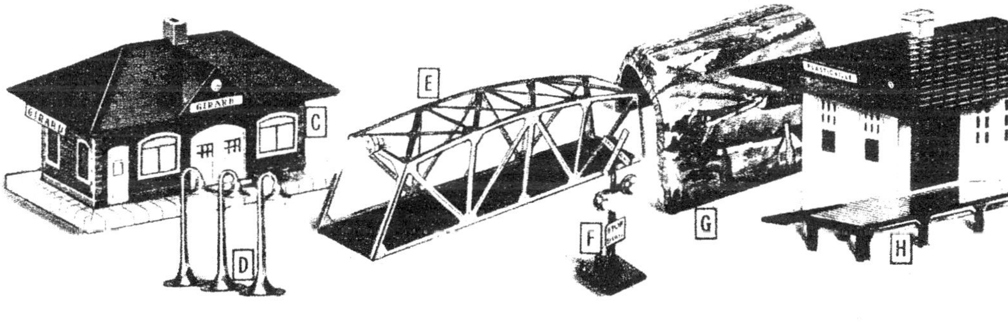

Realistic, low priced Electric Train Accessories

Water tower, metal tunnel, plastic station, foot bridge, church and barn may also be used with mechanical train sets. Asterisk (*) after an item indicates all necessary parts such as wire, track connectors, etc., included with accessories.

[C] **Whistling Metal Station*.** Press remote control button ... hear realistic wail of locomotive whistle as train speeds down track. Whistle is built into 9x5½x5 in. high lithographed steel station.
49 N 6079—Shipping weight 2 lbs.............$4.29

[D] **3 electric Lighted Station Lamps*.** Fluted design.
49 N 6012—6 in. high. Wgt. 6 oz...Set of 3 $1.89

[E] **Lighted all-steel Trestle Bridge*.** Embossed rivets. Light socket and reflector held in position by snap-on slip; adjustable for position.
49 N 6026—24x4⅞x6⅛ in. high. Shpg. wt. 2 lbs...$2.10

[F] **Automatic Crossing Flasher*.** Twin lights flash alternately from one side to other. Metal.
49 N 6034—8 in. high. Shpg. wt. 10 oz.........$1.87

[G] **Collapsible Metal Tunnel.** Comes in two parts; Easily assembled. Lithographed landscape scene.
49 N 6025—10¾x9x7 in. high. Shpg. wt. 1 lb......89c

[H] **Plastic Railroad Station.** Realistically molded detail. Easy to set up, parts snap into place.
49 N 6037—11x6x4½ in. high. Shpg. wt. 10 oz....97c

[J] **Lighted Revolving Beacon*.** Revolves on top of girder-type molded plastic tower. Reflectors green, red.
49 N 6023—12½ in. high. Shipping weight 1 lb...$1.95

[K] **Plastic Barn with Silo.** Realistically molded detail. Easy to set up. Height 6 in. to top of weathervane.
49 N 6057—8 in. long, 4½ in. wide. Shpg. wt. 8 oz.....85c

[L] **Automatic Block Signal*.** Train stops on red light, proceeds on green. Die cast base, 2-track section.
49 N 6027—Metal; 7 in. high. Shpg. wt. 1 lb........$2.15

[M] **Plastic Church.** Detail molded. Roof, trim. 8½ in. high to top of spire. Cross; metal bell. Easy to set up.
49 N 6056—5½ in. long, 4 in. wide. Wt. 8 oz.......85c

[N] **Foot Bridge Crossing.** Five heavy metal sections interlock to form conventional type foot bridge with 2 inclining stairways at each end; crossing bridge in middle.
49 N 6032—13½x15½x7 in. high. Shpg. wt. 1 lb. 12 oz. 95c

[P] **Automatic Grade crossing Shack with Watchman.*** Lithographed steel shanty; 8½ in. plastic gate. When train nears, watchman comes out, gate lowers.
49 N 6074—Base 7x6½ in. House 5 in. high. Very fascinating accessory—low priced. Shipping weight 2 lbs. 8 oz. $3.87

[R] **Twin Searchlight Tower*.** Two powerful lights tilt and revolve on girder-type plastic tower. Metal ladder.
49 N 6078—13 in. high. Shpg. wt. 2 lbs.........$2.79

[S] **New Large Plastic Water Tower.** Like those seen in real freight yards. Realistic ribs and steel-type understructure.
49 N 6081—13¾ in. high. Shpg. wt. 12 oz..........$1.06

Transformers, Track, Switches

[T] **50-watt Transformer.*** For 110-120-volt 60-cycle AC. 2 sets binding posts give variable 7 to 13 volts for controlling train speed plus 13 volts for accessories. UL approved. Built-in circuit breaker. Connectors, cords, plugs.
49 N 6094—Shipping weight 3 lbs. 4 oz..........$5.79

[V] **Electric Remote Control Switch Set.*** One left and one right-hand switch plus 4-button control panel.
49 N 6019—Shipping weight 2 lbs. 8 oz.....Set $6.79
Extra Track for Electric Trains. Shpg. wt. 4 oz. each.
[W] 8⅝-in. Straight Track. [X] 10-inch Curved Track.
49 N 6010.....Each 18c   49 N 6011.....Each 18c

[Y] **Manual Switch Set.** One left, one right-hand switch.
49 N 6018—Shipping weight 2 pounds......Set $2.95
[Z] 49 N 6017—7½-inch Crossover. Shpg. wt. 8 oz....89c

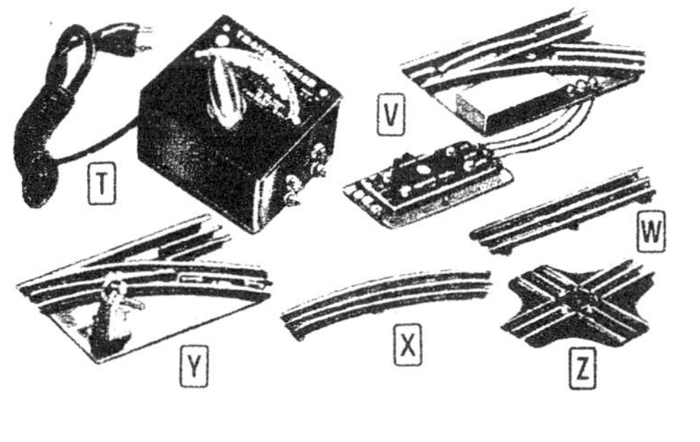

OPB 243..ELECTRIC TRAINS

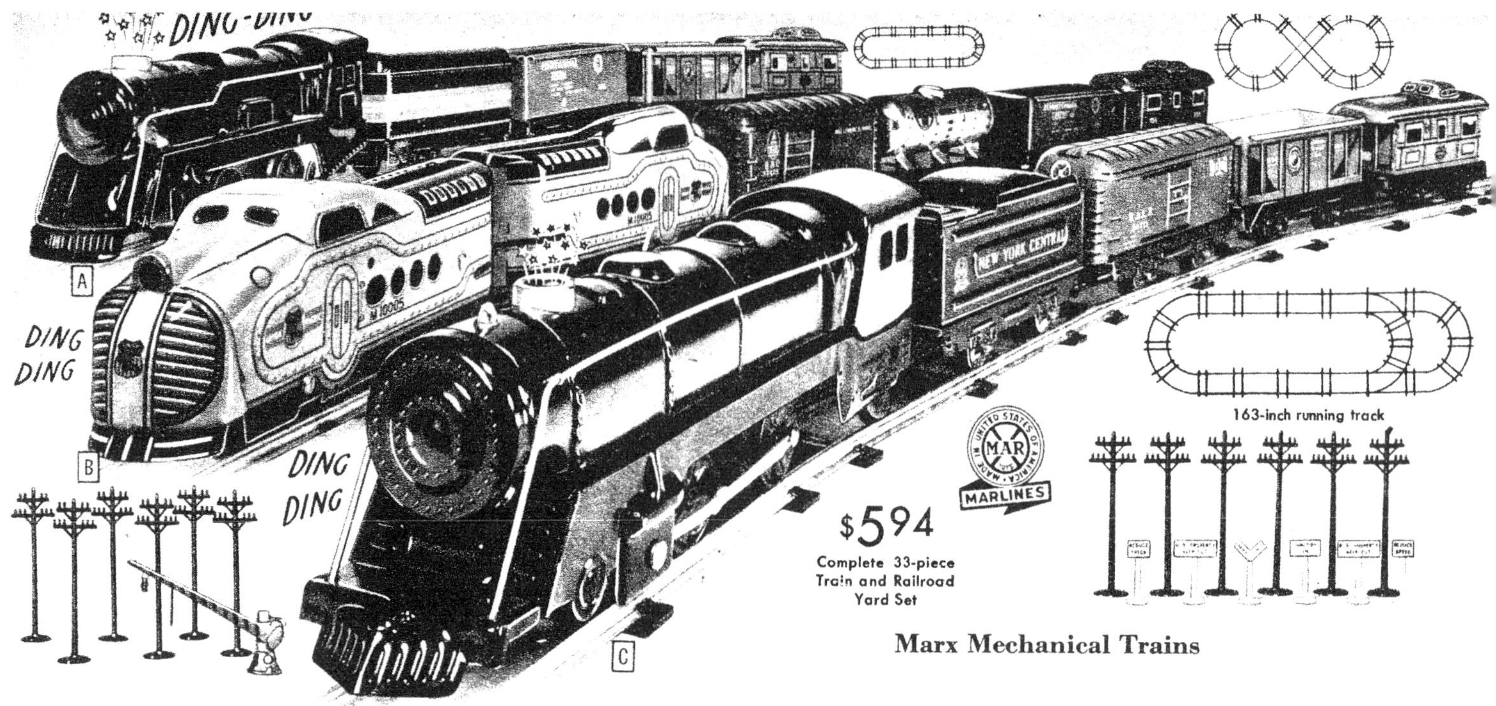

Marx Mechanical Trains

34-inch Sparkling Freight

A **5-unit sturdy steel Mechanical Train.** Steam-type locomotive whizzes around 94-inch oval track, *tiny sparks shooting from smokestack, bell ringing!* Steel engine has long-running clockspring motor; built-in speed governor and brake. Tender, coal car, high-side gondola, caboose lithographed metal. Ten track sections.
49 N 5905—Shpg. wt. 4 lbs. $3.29

New 42-inch Twin Diesel Freight

B **Big 6-unit Mechanical Freight plus seven realistic plastic railroad accessories.** *Bell rings* as train rushes around its 164 inches of figure 8 track. **Complete 30-piece set includes:** Lithographed metal Twin-Diesel locomotive with powerful clockspring motor, gondola, box car with sliding doors, tank car, caboose, six miniature plastic telegraph poles, plastic crossing gate, 16 sections track, crossover.
49 N 5909—Shpg. wt. 5 lbs. $4.98

37-inch Sparkling Freight with Switches and Accessories

C **Big 5-unit sparkling Mechanical Freight Set includes pair of manually-operated switches and twelve realistic plastic accessories.** Sturdy steel steam-type locomotive *shoots sparks from smoke stack, rings bell* as it streaks along! Powerful, long-running clockspring motor; built-in speed governor and brake. Colorful lithographed metal cars. **Set includes** locomotive, tender box car, coal car, caboose, six miniature plastic telephone poles, six miniature railroad signs, 14 sections of track plus pair of plastic switches.
49 N 5913—37-inch Train Set as described. Shpg. wt. 4 lbs. 8 oz. $5.94
Extra Track Sections for Marx mechanical trains. Wt. 6 oz. per 4 sec.
49 N 6001—4 straight sections. . . . . 39c   49 N 6002—4 curved sections. 39c

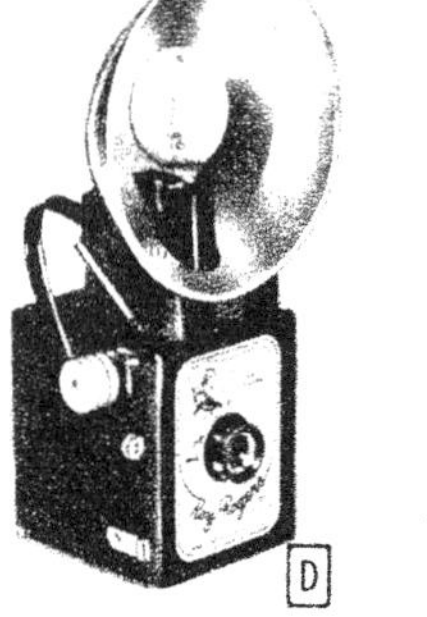

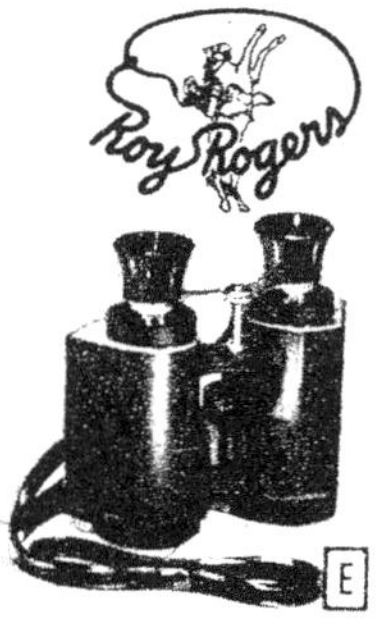

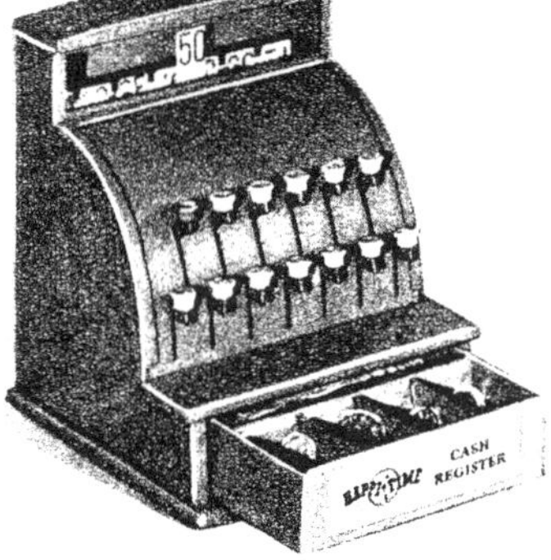

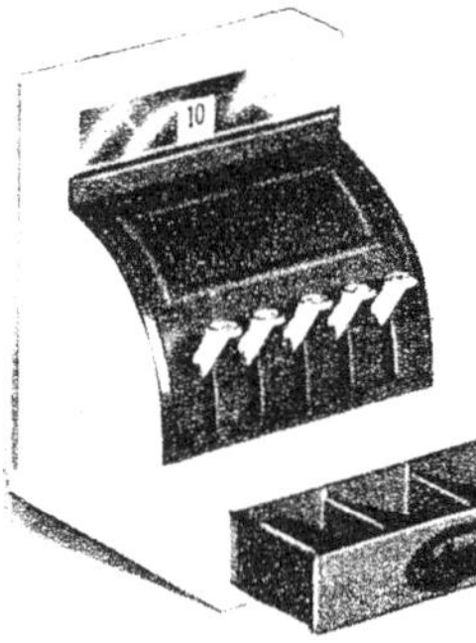

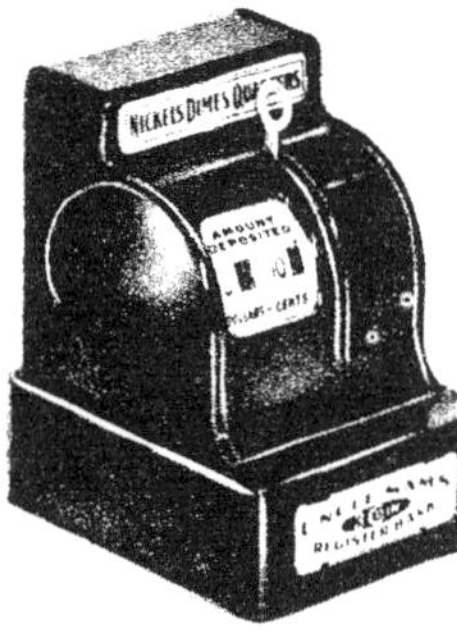

D **Roy Rogers Camera with Flash Attachment.** $3.98 Takes 12 clear 2¼x2¼-in. pictures on roll of 620 film, *indoors or out, day or night!* Film, flash bulbs, 2 penlite batteries not included. Plastic case. 1/50th second shutter. Eye-level sight.
49 N 6240—Shipping weight 1 lb. $3.98
3 N 6918—**Flash Bulbs for above.** (Wt. 12 oz. for 8). *Postpaid*. . . . . . . 8 for $1.17

E **Roy Rogers Binoculars.** $2.79 3-power. Make faraway objects appear close. Adjustable focus and eye separation. Optically ground, polished lenses. Metal and plastic; 4¾x5x2 inches.
49N6330E-20% Federal Tax included. Wt. 1 lb. . . $2.79

Happi-Time metal Cash Register. $2.98 Press key . . . bell rings, partitioned cash drawer pops out, window registers amount. 13 plastic keys; 12 show denominations, one "No Sale." Enameled steel. 7¼x6½x7¼ in. With play "money."
49 N 6380—Wt. 4 lbs. $2.98

Colorful plastic Cash Register. $2.26 Metal back. Five keys: 5c, 10c, 25c, 50c, "No Sale." Press key . . . bell rings, 3-section drawer pops out, amount registers on "flasher." 5x5x6 in. high. It's fun to play store.
49 N 6338—Shipping weight 1 pound 8 ounces. $2.26

3-Coin Register Bank. $3.58 Bell rings once for nickel, twice for dime, 5 times for quarter. Non-registering slot in rear for other coins. Hole for bills. Locks when first quarter is deposited, opens automatically at $10. Holds about $50. Heavy-gauge enameled metal. 6x5¼x4½ in. Computes savings.
49 N 6493—Wt. 2 lbs. 8 oz. . . $3.58

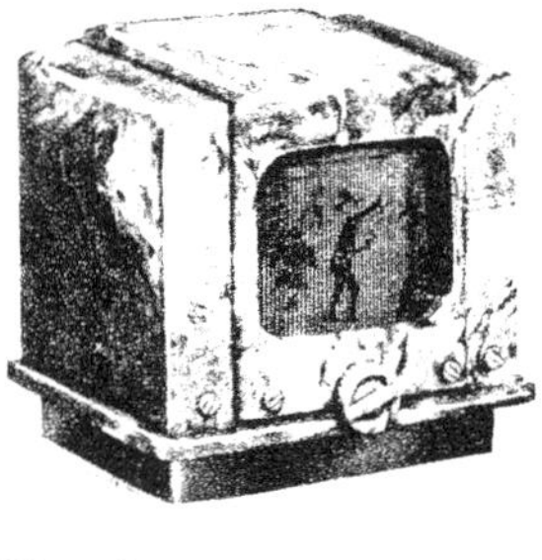

Hopalong Cassidy TV

$1.85 Pull out lever; animated Wild West thriller rolls before you through transparent "screen": "Hoppy," Indians, cowboys, horses, etc. Plastic case, 5¼x5x4½ in. deep. Keywind motor. Includes 4 action strips in color. Shipping weight 1 lb. 8 oz.
49 N 6243. . . . . $1.85

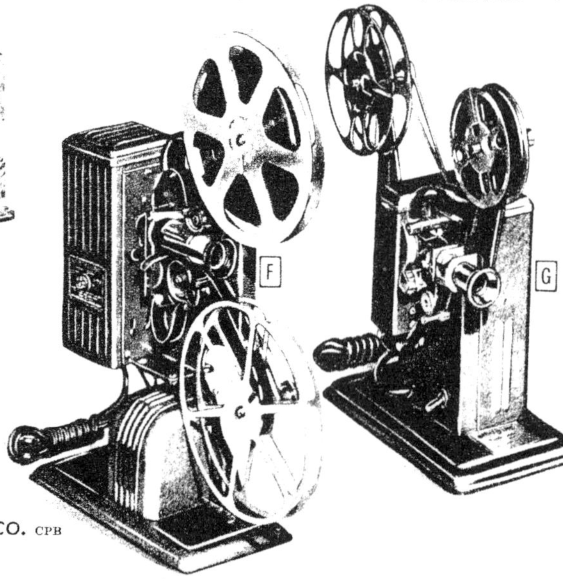

16-mm. Electric Movie Projectors

Ideal for parties, holidays, rainy days. Easy to operate. Show 16x12-inch pictures when about 7 feet from screen. Constant-speed, fan-cooled motors for 110-120-volt 60-cycle AC. UL approved. "On-Off" switch, cord and plug included with each. *Film not included. See page 384 for favorite story and movie film.*

F **Famous Keystone Moviegraph. Uses big 140-watt tubular projection lamp** in vented housing, metal $22.75 reflector and optically ground condenser lens . . . for brighter, clearer pictures! Sliding projection lens. Picture may be raised or lowered. Sturdy steel base; die-cast frame. Bright metallic finish. 9¾x5¼x14 in. high. Carrying handle.
79 N 06272—With empty 400-ft. reel. Shpg. wt. 11 lbs. . . $22.75

G **Happi-Time Projector.** Powerful 50-candlepower auto headlamp projector bulb gives bright, clear $13.98 pictures. Runs COOL AND QUIET. Fiber drive gear. Silent revolving prism. Moving parts enclosed. Sturdy steel frame. 5½x9½x11 in. high; green hammerloid finish.
79 N 06266—With empty 200-ft. reel. Shpg. wt. 7 lbs. . . . $13.98

Easel-type 13x18-inch Movie Screen

(Not shown.) Glass beaded surface for brighter, clearer pictures.
49 N 6219—For above projectors. Shpg. wt. 1 lb. 8 oz. . . . $1.83

You'll want film! See page 384 for popular titles

$16.50
Postpaid

$22.50
Postpaid

"O27"-gauge Track, Switches, Crossover

[A] 49 N 6048T—**Remote Control Switches.** One right-hand, one left-hand switch, control panel, connecting wire. (Shpg. wt. 3 lbs.). *Postpaid*..........Pair $12.95

[B] 49 N 6043T—**Magnetic Track Set.** For remote control uncoupling and unloading. Control panel and wire included. (Shpg. wt. 1 lb.). *Postpaid*..............$3.50

[C] 49 N 6035T—**90-degree Crossover.** 7⅜ in. square. (Shpg. wt. 8 oz.). *Postpaid*..............Each $2.25

[D] 49 N 6004T—**Curved Track Section.** Length 9½ in. (Shipping weight 3 oz.). *Postpaid*..........Each 25c

[E] 49 N 6003T—**Straight Track Section.** Length 8⅞ in. (Shpg. wt. 3 oz.). *Postpaid*..............Each 25c

"O" gauge Track, Switches, Crossover

[F] 49 N 6090T—**Remote Control Switches.** One left, one right-hand switch, control panel, connecting wire. (Shpg. wt. 5 lbs.). *Postpaid*..........Pair $22.50

[G] 49 N 6060T—**90-degree Crossover.** 8¼ in. square. (Shipping weight 8 oz.). *Postpaid*........Each $2.95

[H] 49 N 6061T—**Magnetic Track Set.** For remote control uncoupling and unloading. Control panel and wire included. (Shpg. wt. 1 lb.). *Postpaid*..............$3.75

[J] 49 N 6009T—**Curved Track Section.** Length 10⅞ inches. (Shpg. wt. 4 oz.). *Postpaid*..........Each 30c

[K] 49 N 6008T—**Straight Track Section.** Length 10 inches. (Shpg. wt. 4 oz.). *Postpaid*..............Each 30c

"Trainmaster" Transformers

Built-in self-resetting automatic circuit breakers protect against overloads and shorts. Red light signals short. For 110 to 120-volt 60-cycle AC only.

[L] Type RW . . . 110 watts. Two variable-voltage circuits for running train; 4 fixed voltages for accessories. Two buttons: one blows whistle, one for reversing.
49 N 6088T—**UL approved.** (Wt. 6 lbs.). *Postpaid*...$16.50

[M] Type KW . . . 190 watts. Two independently controlled variable-voltage circuits for running two trains at same time on different layouts. Built-in whistle and separate directional controls for each train. Fixed 14-volt circuit for accessories. Durable molded case.
79 N 06093T—(Shpg. wt. 9 lbs.). *Postpaid*..........$22.50

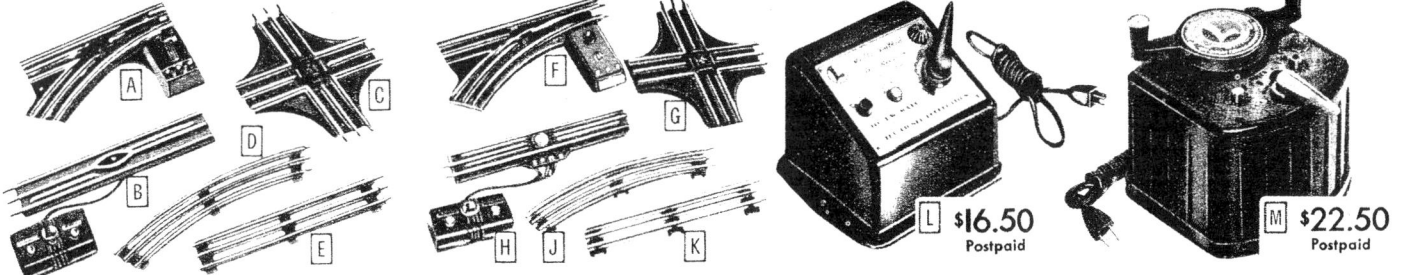

Famous Lionel Electric Trains

$35.75
Postpaid
Only $4.00 Down

Remote Control Types for 110-120-volt 60-cycle AC

All Lionel items shown on these two pages shipped postpaid. Same price Cash or Easy Terms.

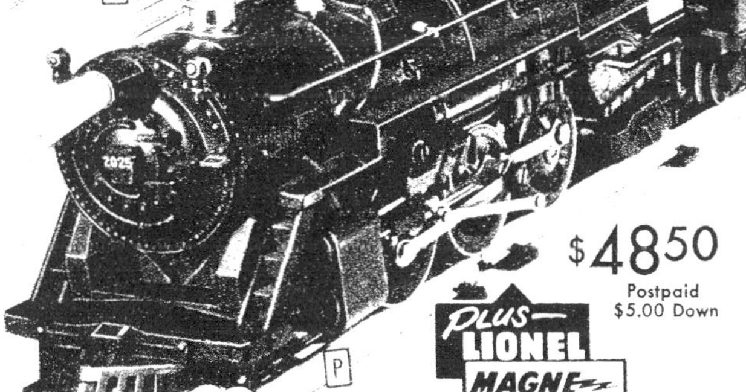

$48.50
Postpaid
$5.00 Down

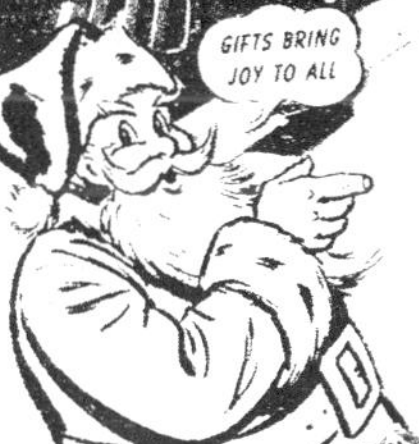

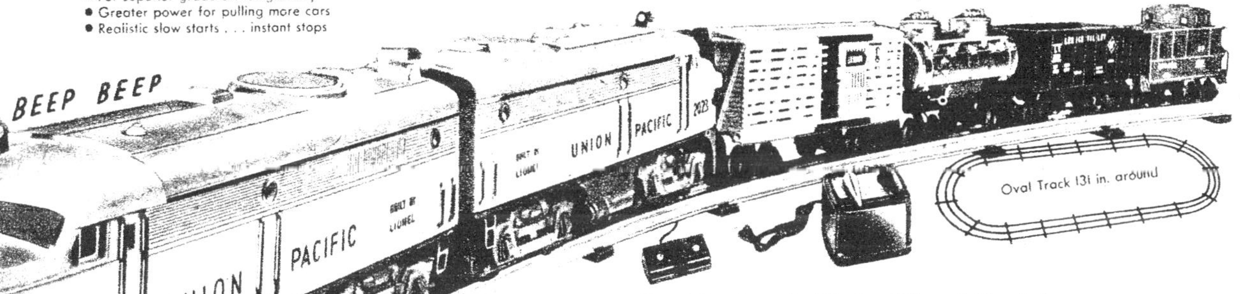

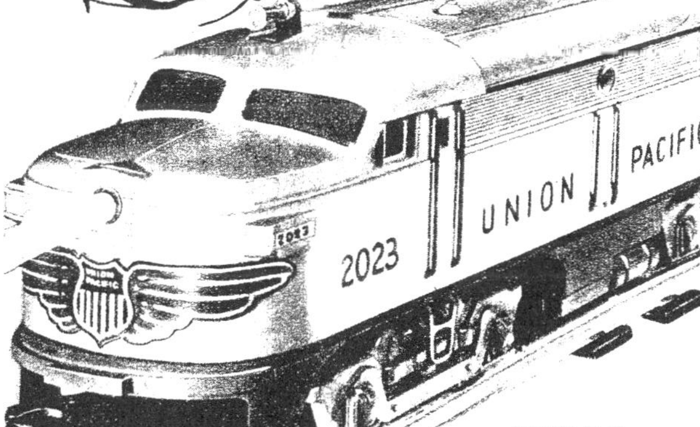

Remote Control "O27" Freights with whistle, smoke

- Start or stop train; run it forward or backward, fast or slow; couple or uncouple cars; blow its realistic built-in whistle . . . *all by REMOTE CONTROL.* Puffs harmless white smoke as it runs!
- Scale-detailed 12-wheel die-cast metal locomotives with 6-wheel drive, piston-rods, headlight.
- Scale-detailed rolling stock. Cars have 8 steel wheels, die-cast trucks, knuckle-type electric couplers.
- UL approved 90-watt transformers with throttle-type speed, whistle and directional controls, built-in circuit breakers. 110-120-volt 60-cycle AC. Each set has 12 sec. "O27"-gauge track.

[N] **44-inch 5-unit Freight.** A set that will thrill any boy Christmas day! Accurately scale-detailed 10-in. steam type locomotive without Magne Traction. Tender, gondola, oil car and caboose. 90-watt transformer included. *Postpaid.* (Shpg. wt. 16 lbs.).
79 N 05951T..............**$35.75**

[P] **Magne Traction 54½-inch 6-unit Freight.** Bigger and better than set at left! More cars PLUS massive 10½-inch steam-type locomotive *with Lionel Magne Traction for greater speed, more pull, more climb, better control.* Set includes: locomotive, tender, hopper car, oil car, gondola, caboose; 90-watt transformer. 12 section track including uncoupling section.
79 N 05955T—(Shipping weight 18 lbs.). *Postpaid*..**$48.50**

PLUS—LIONEL MAGNE-TRACTION

- For greater speeds without derailment
- For superior grade-climbing ability
- Greater power for pulling more cars
- Realistic slow starts . . . instant stops

$57.50
Postpaid
Only $6.00 Down

Union Pacific 6-unit Twin-Diesel Freight

Lionel MagneTraction for greater power!

- Giant 22-inch twin diesel with authentic Union Pacific markings. Super-powered locomotive has wide speed range. Eight steel wheels on each of the 2 units. Gleaming headlamp.
- Even trainmen marvel at its magnificent accuracy of detail, including louvers, ladders, stanchions!
- Remote-controlled deep-toned electric horn.
- Four realistically scale-detailed plastic cars, including new stock car, illuminated caboose.
- Every car equipped with 8 solid steel wheels, die-cast trucks, knuckle-type electric couplers.

Just like being at the controls of a real Diesel! Start and stop train . . . run it forward or backward, fast or slow . . . sound its deep-throated horn . . . couple and uncouple cars . . . *do all this by REMOTE CONTROL!* Locomotive about 22 in., plastic cab; metal frame, trucks. Transparent plastic windshield; simulated wipers. Six-unit train is 56 in. long, includes Twin Diesel units, stock car, oil car, hopper, lighted caboose. 90-watt U.L. approved transformer (110-120-volt 60-cycle A.C.), throttle-type controls and built-in circuit breaker. Fourteen sections "O27" gauge track.
79 N 05958T—(Shpg. wt. 19 lbs.) *Postpaid.* **$57.50**

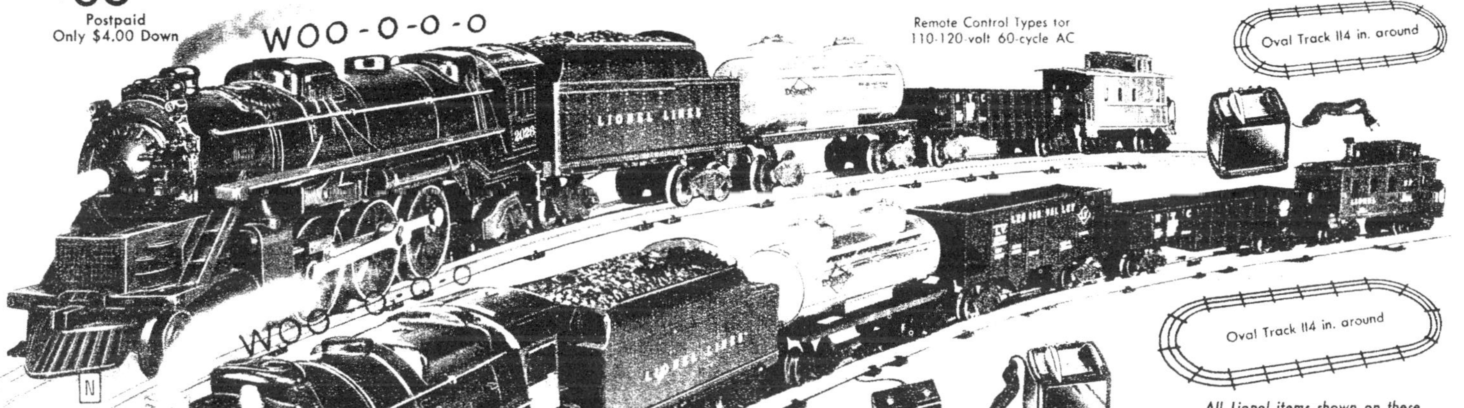

New Plastic Dump Truck
Watch how easily toy truck raises and dumps its load . . . just like a big one. To unload, release wire lever. Overhead cab protector. Dual rear wheels. Colorful sturdy plastic; finely detailed. 11¾ in. long.
49 N 6453—Shpg. wt. 1 lb. $1.44

$1.44

Hauler, Van Trailer Truck
Just like big coast-to-coast freight trucks. Detachable van is raised and lowered by lever. Molded of new, tough, colorful plastic. Doors at rear and side of truck open. Dual wheels on van. Toy 22 in. long.
49 N 6454—Shpg. wt. 3 lbs. 8 oz. $2.98

$2.98

Aluminum Tractor Set
[A] 3-pc. Set. Tractor powered by clockspring motor pulls and pushes 20 times its weight. Climbs 35° grades. Rubber treads for traction. 15½ in. long overall. Trailer and scraper detachable.
49 N 5753—Wt. 1 lb. 8 oz...$1.98

$1.98

Sparking Steel Tank
[B] Crashes toy walls; climbs steep grades; shoots sparks. Clockspring motor rumbles. Metal, camouflage colors. Rubber treads. 9½ in. long.
49 N 5797—Wt. 2 lbs. 6 oz. $2.79

$2.79

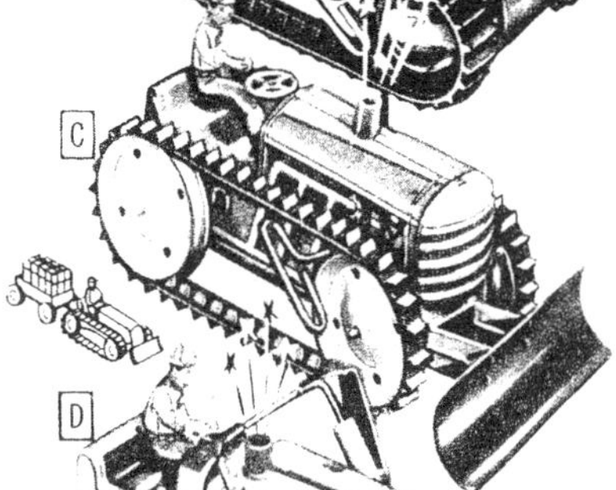

New Sparking Tractor
[C] Climbs steep 35° grades; pulls heavy loads. Shoots sparks from exhaust pipe on hood. Lithographed metal. Rubber treads; clockspring motor. 10 in. long with scraper.
49 N 5733—Wt. 1 lb. 8 oz . . $1.79

$1.79

Bulldozer Tractor
[D] Sparks fly from exhaust pipe. Hydraulic type scraper snaps up or down. Pulls heavy loads, climbs 35° grades. Lithographed metal. Clockspring motor, rubber treads. 10½ in. long.
49 N 5759—Wt. 2 lbs. 10 oz.$3.39

$3.39

New Truck Terminal
Complete with Trucks, Cargo, Baggage

Loaded with play value . . Toy Town Freight Trucking Terminal is a gift to thrill any youngster. Plenty of make-believe jobs for all the kiddies . . . truck driver; freight checker; terminal manager. Fully equipped and ready for business . . 52 pieces in all
Big 29x11x9-inch lithographed metal terminal with loading platform, offices and storage areas. Metal ramp and barrel slide for loading and unloading freight. Equipment includes: 3 large plastic trucks; live skid; dummy scale; 3 plastic baggage wagons; 6 wooden barrels; 24 empty food cartons, etc. Brightly lithographed green tile roof, red brick walls. Lithographed claims office and cashier's window inside. Sturdy colorful metal, reinforced construction. Safe, all turned edges. Terminal shipped flat . . . easy to assemble without tools.
79 N 06440—Shipping weight 5 pounds . . . . 52-piece play set . . $4.79

$4.79 Complete

Sparking Police Riot Car
Loud realistic siren wails, sparks fly from machine gun as "Police Riot Car" speeds along, propelled by strong friction motor. Sturdy plastic. Lots of action—low priced. 9 inches long.
49 N 5752—Shpg. wt. 1 lb. $1.25

$1.25

Pet Shop Truck—6 Dogs
Transparent doors at sides of plastic "Pet Shop" truck actually fold up or down. 6 pet dog breeds of Vinyl plastic 1¾ in. . . . each in its own cubicle. Truck 10 in. long. Play value galore.
49 N 6451—Shpg. wt. 1 lb. $1.45

$1.45

Reversible Tractor Truck
Drive forward or backward . . . or change direction even while in motion with lever control. Powerful clockspring motor with brake. Climbs steep 35° inclines easily; pulls heavy loads. Sure-grip rubber treads. Large stake body 7¼x4½x 2 in. deep. Colorfully lithographed steel body . . removable metal driver. Tractor 13¾ inches long.
49 N 5862—Shpg. wt. 3 lbs. 4 oz. $3.35

$3.35

Siren . . . Flasher Light
Speed to fire in brilliant red plastic fire truck as *siren wails, red light flashes*. Transparent wind shield. 3-section swivel ladder extends from 9 to 21 in. Uses standard flashlight battery (not included). Sturdy steel-reinforced body. Rubber tires; front wheels adjustable. Has long-running clockspring motor. 13 inches long.
49 N 5770—Shpg. wt. 2 lbs. 4 oz. $2.89

$2.89

SEARS CHRISTMAS CATALOG

1952

The Great Train Merchandising Race was on in Sears' 1952 Christmas Wishbook. The number of pages devoted to electric trains had increased to six and a much wider array of trains and accessories were featured.

Lots of new models debuted in 1952 including Lionel's now-classic Santa Fe Twin Diesels. Customers were spending more money on their trains as this engine and its sister New York Central Twin Diesel cost the then amazing sum of $47.50... and that was just for the engines.

Also seen for the first time were three Lionel extruded aluminum streamlined passenger cars. These 15 inch long O-scale Astra-Dome, Pullman and Observation cars had illuminated interiors. Their silhouetted passengers could be seen living the high-life inside. The popular cars were just $9.95 each back then, but sell for hundreds of dollars today.

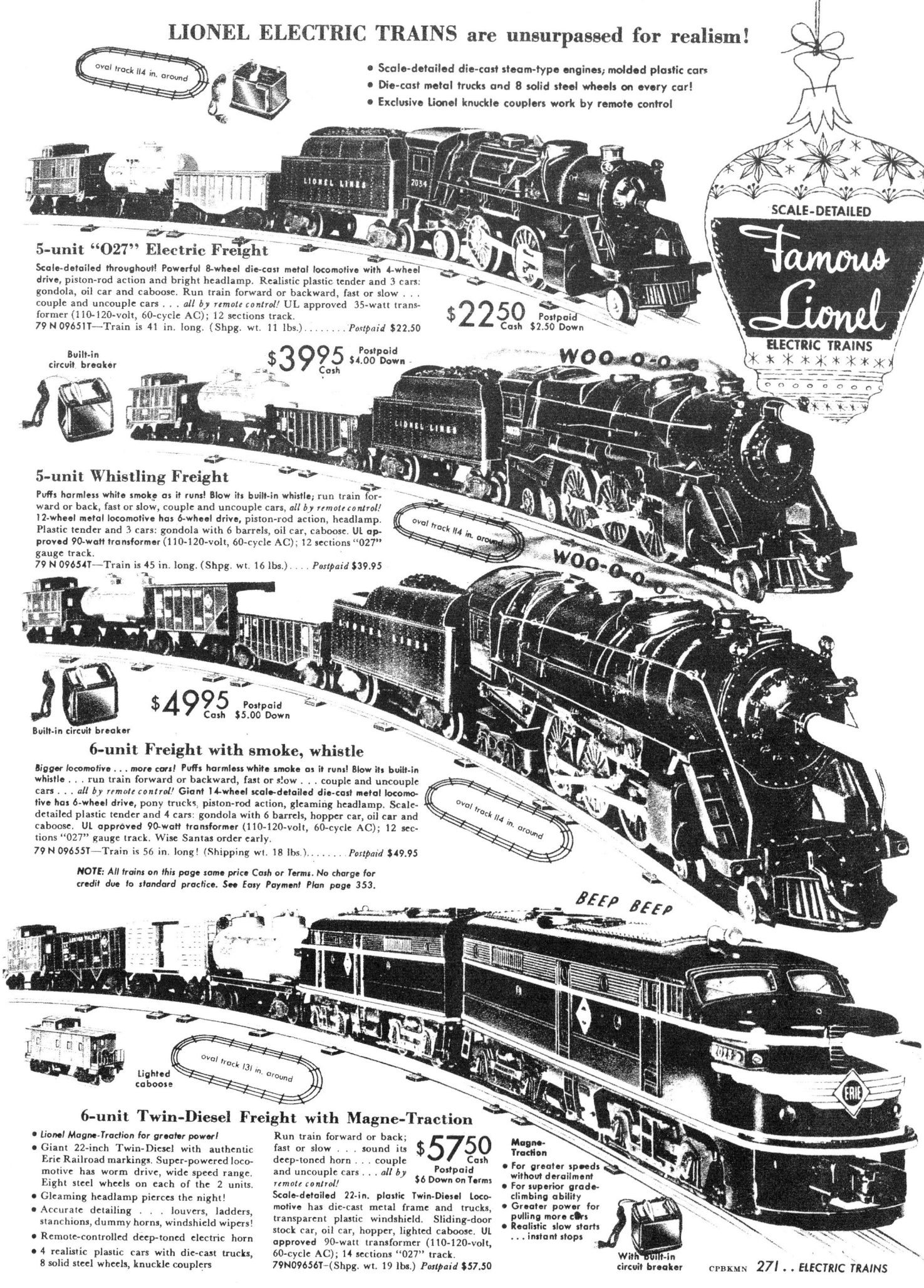

$62.50 Cash or Terms
$6.50 Down. Postpaid

Oval track 149 in. around

Big 7-unit "O"-gauge electric Freight with smoke and whistle

One more car than a year ago . . . at no increase in price! Magnificent scale-detailed 20-wheel die-cast steam turbine type locomotive with powerful 8-wheel drive and 2 six-wheel trucks, side-rod action and bright headlamp. Watch it thunder down the rails, *puffing harmless, realistic smoke . . . whistle blowing.* Run it fast or slow, forward or backward . . . couple and uncouple cars . . . operate milk or coal dump car . . . sound its deep-toned whistle . . .

all by remote control! Big 7-unit train is 64½ in. long . . . includes locomotive, tender with built-in whistle, plastic milk-car, hopper car, coal dump car, gondola with 6 barrels, lighted plastic caboose, 16 sections "O"-gauge track, milk platform, 5 milk cans, "coal" and bin. Transformer not included . . . see facing page.

Unsurpassed fun for youngsters . . . dads too.
79 N 09673T—(Shpg. wt. 20 lbs.) . . . . Postpaid $62.50

[J] $5.95 Postpaid
[L] $3.95 Postpaid
[M] $4.95 Postpaid
[K] 95c Postpaid

[A] $47.50 Cash or Terms Postpaid . . $5 Down
[B] $38.95 Cash or Terms Postpaid . . $4 Down
[C] $25.00 Cash or Terms Postpaid. $2.50 Down

[N] $9.95 Postpaid
[P] $9.95 Postpaid
[R] $9.95 Postpaid

Authentic Lionel Diesel Locomotives with Magne-Traction

- Exclusive Lionel Magne-Traction gives greater power for pulling more cars . . . better grade-climbing ability . . . greater speeds without derailment.
- Magnificently Scale-detailed! So true to life that even seasoned railroad men marvel at their blue-print accuracy. Realistically molded plastic. Authentically marked for greater realism.
- Super-powered Motors with Worm Gear Drive. Wide range of speeds. Powerful 4-wheel drive.
- Bright Headlamp pierces the night. Remote Control Deep-throated horn (except on 49 N 9890T).
- For Any Lionel Train Set. Eight steel wheels per section (2 trucks). Remote Control Couplers.

Twin-Diesel Locomotives with Remote Control Electric Horn and Magne-Traction. Windshields have dummy wipers, lighted number boxes, ladders, stanchions, louvers.

[A] **Santa Fe Twin-Diesel.** Twin motors. 26½ in. long.
79 N 09894T—(Shpg. wt. 10 lbs.). Postpaid $47.50
New York Central Twin-Diesel. Similar to (A) above.
79 N 09895T—Not shown. (Wt. 10 lbs.) . Postpaid $47.50
[B] **Rock Island Twin-Diesel.** Single motor. 22 in. long.
79 N 09892T—(Shpg. wt. 8 lbs.) . . . Postpaid $38.95
[C] **Diesel Yard Switcher with Magne-Traction.** No horn. Single motor; worm drive. Bright headlamp.
49 N 9890T—11½ in. long. (Wt. 8 lbs.) . Postpaid $25.00

Lionel Electric Train Accessories

Breathtaking realism! Ideal gifts for those who already own a Lionel train set. More accessories on facing page.

[J] **Illuminated Automatic Gateman.** As train approaches, shack door opens and tiny gateman rushes out, swinging lantern. After last car of train has passed, gateman returns to his shack and door closes. Metal base; plastic shack and gateman. Height 6¾ inches.
49 N 9835T—(Shpg. wt. 2 lbs. 8 oz.) . . . . . Postpaid $5.95

[K] **6-Inch Lamp Post.** Die-cast metal with fluted column. Plastic globe, bulb, wire all included. Buy several!
49 N 9825T—(Shipping weight 1 lb.) . . . . Postpaid 95c

[L] **Illuminated Crossing Gate.** Automatically lowers as train nears, raises after train has passed. Scale-size imitation jewels in 9¾-in. arm glow as gate is lowered.
49 N 9820T With bulb. (Shpg. wt. 1 lb.) . . . Postpaid $3.95

[M] **Flashing Highway Signal.** Two red warning lights flash on and off alternately from one side to other as train nears, stop flashing when train has passed.
49 N 9832T—9 in. high. (Shpg. wt. 1 lb.) . . . . . Postpaid $4.95

Track, Switches and 90° Crossover

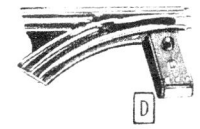
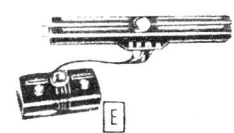

[D] **Remote Control Switches.** One right-hand and one left-hand switch, control panel, wire included.
49 N 9806T—For use with "027"-gauge track layouts. (Shipping weight 3 lbs.) Postpaid . . . . Per pair $12.25
49 N 9815T—For use with "O"-gauge track layouts. (Shipping weight 5 lbs.). Postpaid . . . . Per pair $20.95

[E] **Magnetic Track Section.** For remote control coupling and uncoupling. Control panel and connecting wire included. (Shpg. wt. each 1 lb.)
49 N 9804T—For "027"-gauge. . . . . . Each $3.00
49 N 9813T—For "O"-gauge. Postpaid. . . . . . Each 3.25

[F] **90-degree Crossover.** (Shpg. wt. 8 oz.). Postpaid.
49 N 9803T—For "027"-gauge. 7⅜-in. square $1.95
49 N 9812T—"O"-gauge. 8¼ in. square . Postpaid 2.95

[G] **8⅞-in. Straight Track Section for "027"-gauge.**
49 N 9801T—(Wt. 3 oz.) . . . . Each 25c
10-in. Straight Track Section for "O"-gauge layouts.
49 N 9810T—(Wt. 4 oz.) . . . . . . Each 30c

[H] **9½-in. Curved Track Section for "027"-gauge.**
49 N 9802T—(Wt. 3 oz.) . . . . Each 25c
10⅞-in. Curved Track Section for "O"-gauge.
49 N 9811T—(Wt. 4 oz.) . . . . . . Each 30c

Authentic, Illuminated Pullmans

Magnificently scale-detailed in extruded aluminum. All the sleek grace and gleaming beauty of real-life streamliner Pullman cars! Interiors brightly lighted (Bulbs included). Tiny passengers look out of clear plastic windows. Die-cast metal trucks; 8 solid steel wheels; remote-control knuckle couplers. (Shipping weight 2 pounds 11 ounces.)

[N] 49 N 9854—15-inch Astra-dome Car . . . . . Postpaid $9.95
[P] 49 N 9853—15-inch Pullman Car . . . . . . Postpaid 9.95
[R] 49 N 9855—15-inch Observation Car . . . . Postpaid 9.95

ALL LIONEL TRAINS AND ACCESSORIES ARE POSTPAID!

Sears pays shipping charges on all Lionel trains and accessories. Same price whether you buy for cash or on Easy Terms . . . no extra charge for credit. Only 10% down on Sears Easy Terms. . . see page 353 for details.

Shop early . . then relax and enjoy the Holidays!

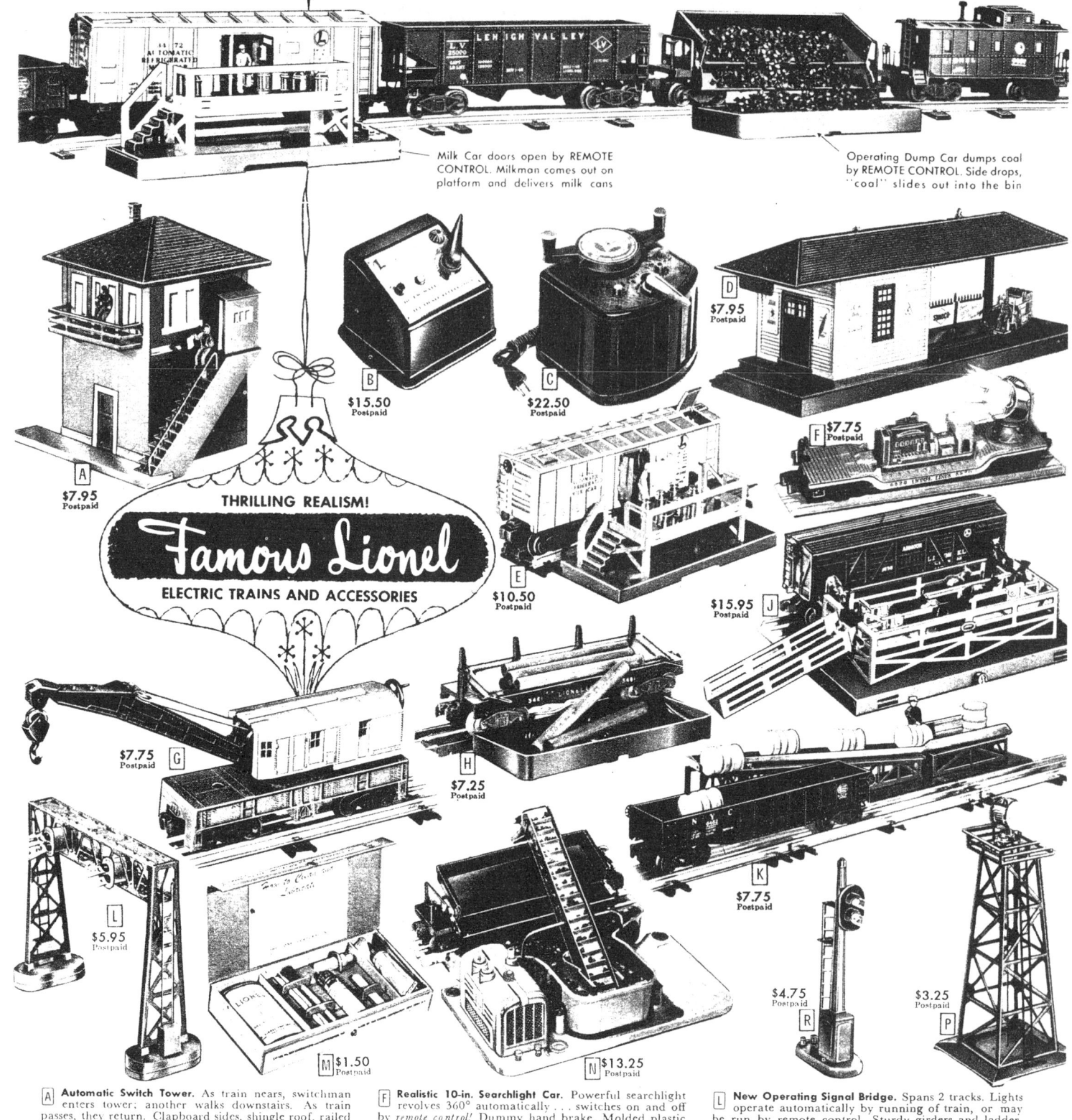

Milk Car doors open by REMOTE CONTROL. Milkman comes out on platform and delivers milk cans

Operating Dump Car dumps coal by REMOTE CONTROL. Side drops, "coal" slides out into the bin

THRILLING REALISM! Famous Lionel ELECTRIC TRAINS AND ACCESSORIES

[A] **Automatic Switch Tower.** As train nears, switchman enters tower; another walks downstairs. As train passes, they return. Clapboard sides, shingle roof, railed platform, 7 in. high. Scale model of plastic and steel.
49 N 9841T—(Shpg. wt. 1 lb. 3 oz.). Postpaid......$7.95

[B][C] **"Trainmaster" Transformers** for 110-120-volt, 60-cycle AC only. Built-in self-resetting automatic circuit breaker protects against shorts and overload. Red light signals shorts. Choice of 2 sizes:

[B] **Type RW—110 watts.** Two variable-voltage circuits for train; 4 fixed voltages for accessories. Two buttons; one for whistle, one for reversing; UL approved.
49 N 9820T—(Shpg. wt. 6 lbs.). Postpaid........$15.50

[C] **Type KW—190 watts.** Two independently controlled variable-voltage circuits for running 2 trains at same time on different layouts. Built-in whistle and separate directional controls for each train. Fixed 14-volt accessory circuit. Molded case.
79 N 09821T—(Shipping weight 9 lbs.) Postpaid..$22.50

[D] **New Operating Freight Station** lighted by 2 bulbs. Press remote control button (included)...two baggage men run their electric cars in and out of station. Clapboard sides; inset bulletin boards. Simulated tile platform, 5x15-in. size. Bulbs, wire included.
49 N 9842T—5½ in. high. (Wt. 2 lbs.) Postpaid....$7.95

[E] **Operating Milk Car** with 5x7¼-in. steel platform. Car doors open and milkman comes out to deliver 5 milk cans to platform. 9-in. car included. Operates by remote control. Track not included.
49 N 9863T—(Shpg. wt. 2 lbs.) Postpaid........$10.50

[F] **Realistic 10-in. Searchlight Car.** Powerful searchlight revolves 360° automatically...switches on and off by *remote control!* Dummy hand brake. Molded plastic dummy generator. Die-cast platform. No track.
49 N 9861T—(Shpg. wt. 2 lbs.) Postpaid........$7.75

[G] **8⅝-in. Operating Crane Car.** Crane swings in circle...boom raises, lowers...pulley block lifts. Hand wheel controls. Die-cast chassis. No track.
49 N 9852T—(Shpg. wt. 2 lbs.) Postpaid........$7.75

[H] **9½-in. Operating Lumber Car.** Die-cast frame. Rotating brake wheel. Steel stakes drop, bottom tilts up, logs roll out. Logs and bin included. Operates by remote control. Track not included.
49 N 9860T—(Shpg. wt. 2 lbs.) Postpaid........$7.25

[J] **8½-in. Operating Cattle Car and Platform.** When cattle car stops alongside platform, remote control button (included) opens doors, drops loading ramp, 9 head of cattle troop out of car, across platform, back into car. 13¾-in. steel platform and ramp. Built-in remote-control unit (no remote-control track needed). Track not included.
49 N 9864T—(Shpg. wt. 4 lbs.) Postpaid........$15.95

NOTE: Cars (E), (F), (G), (H) and (J) all have 8 solid steel wheels, realistic die-cast trucks and knuckle-type remote-control electric couplers.

[K] **New Barrel Loader.** Set barrels upright on lower platform...they move to workman who tips them over onto elevated runway leading to upper platform. Barrels roll off upper platform into car. Six barrels included. Car and track not included.
49 N 9840T—19 in. long. (Wt. 2 lbs. 5 oz.). Postpaid $7.75

[L] **New Operating Signal Bridge.** Spans 2 tracks. Lights operate automatically by running of train, or may be run by remote control. Sturdy girders and ladder. 10½x5x7¾ in. high. 4 bulbs and wire included.
49 N 9836T—(Shpg. wt. 1 lb.) Postpaid..........$5.95

[M] **New Lionel Lubrication Maintenance Kit.** For all Lionel trains. Contains tube of special lubricant, vial of oil, can of special solvent, 2 cleaning sticks, 6 emery boards, wiping cloth, smokestack cleaner, dusting brush and complete instructions.
49 N 9826T—(Shpg. wt. 13 oz.) Postpaid.........$1.50

[N] **Conveyor Coal Loader.** Realistic dummy "coal" flows up endless rubber conveyor belt with multiple buckets, then tips into waiting car. Car and track not included. G.M. Diesel-type housing encloses heavy duty self-lubricating electric motor. Heavy 10x7½-in. die-cast base. Controller, wire, "coal" included.
49 N 9843T—(Shpg. wt. 6 lbs.) Postpaid........$13.25

[P] **11¾-in. Rotary Beacon.** Embossed lattice-work steel structure has platform on top, ladder on side. Powerful miniature searchlight revolves. Red and green fresnel-type lenses rotate over light.
49 N 9828T—(Shpg. wt. 2 lbs.) Postpaid..........$3.25

[R] **Automatic Block Signal.** Lets 2 trains run at same time on same track without colliding. Safety block slows or halts second train. Warning signal glows red or green. Bulbs, wire included.
49 N 9831T—9 in. high. (Shpg. wt. 1 lb.) Postpaid..$4.75

NOTE: Items on this page Cash or Terms. No charge for credit due to standard practice. See Easy Terms page 353

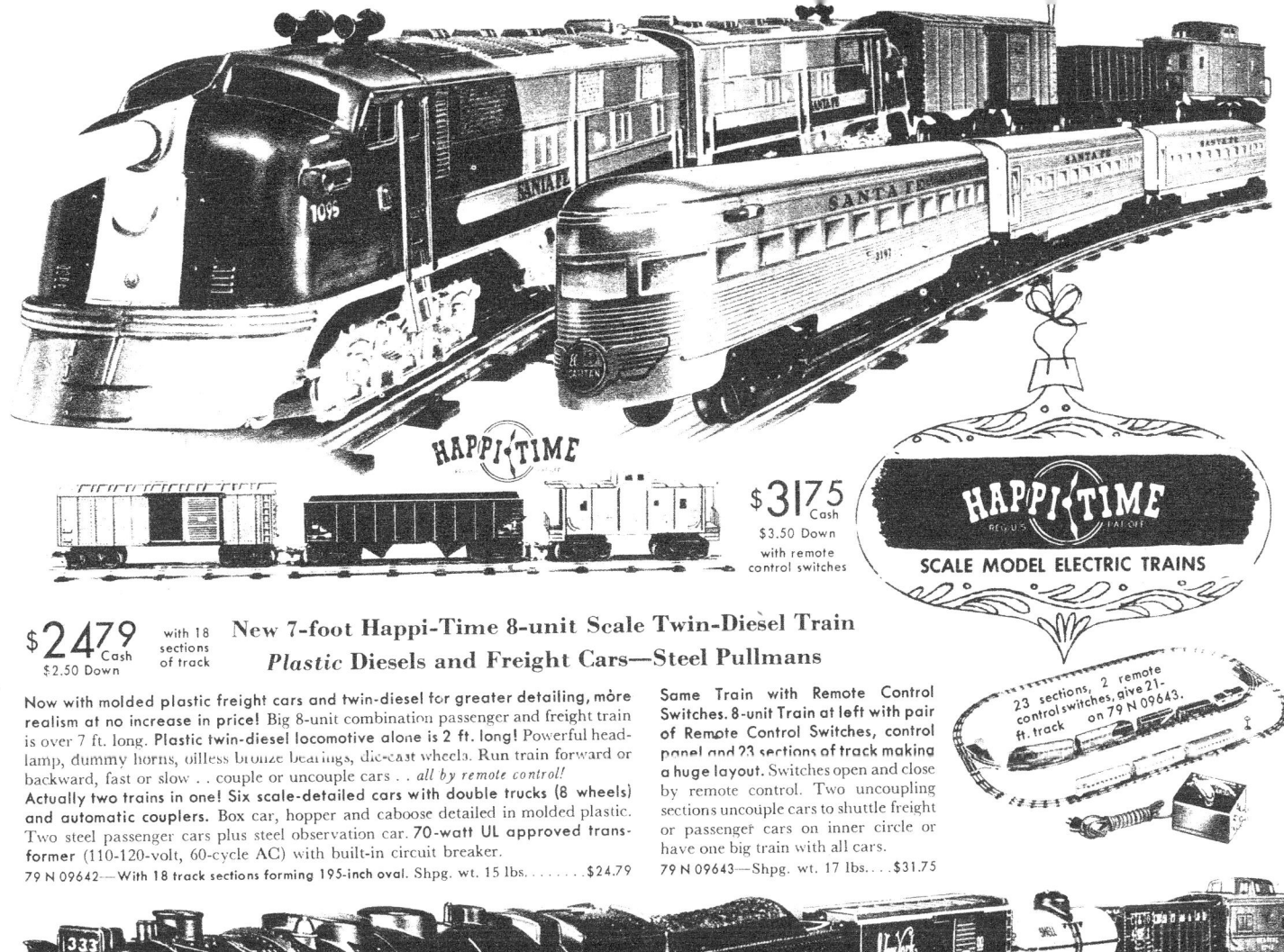

HAPPI-TIME SCALE MODEL ELECTRIC TRAINS

$31.75 Cash
$3.50 Down with remote control switches

$24.79 Cash
$2.50 Down with 18 sections of track

New 7-foot Happi-Time 8-unit Scale Twin-Diesel Train
Plastic Diesels and Freight Cars—Steel Pullmans

Now with molded plastic freight cars and twin-diesel for greater detailing, more realism at no increase in price! Big 8-unit combination passenger and freight train is over 7 ft. long. Plastic twin-diesel locomotive alone is 2 ft. long! Powerful headlamp, dummy horns, oilless bronze bearings, die-cast wheels. Run train forward or backward, fast or slow .. couple or uncouple cars .. *all by remote control!*
Actually two trains in one! Six scale-detailed cars with double trucks (8 wheels) and automatic couplers. Box car, hopper and caboose detailed in molded plastic. Two steel passenger cars plus steel observation car. 70-watt UL approved transformer (110-120-volt, 60-cycle AC) with built-in circuit breaker.
79 N 09642—With 18 track sections forming 195-inch oval. Shpg. wt. 15 lbs........$24.79

Same Train with Remote Control Switches. 8-unit Train at left with pair of Remote Control Switches, control panel and 23 sections of track making a huge layout. Switches open and close by remote control. Two uncoupling sections uncouple cars to shuttle freight or passenger cars on inner circle or have one big train with all cars.
79 N 09643—Shpg. wt. 17 lbs.....$31.75

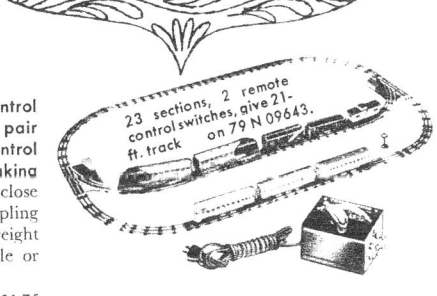

23 sections, 2 remote control switches, give 21-ft. track on 79 N 09643.

$23.98 Cash
Only $2.50 Down

Oval track 175 in. around

Happi-Time 6-unit Electric Freight
3/16-inch Scale Model with 12-wheel Engine

Big 6-wheel drive scale-detailed die-cast steam-type locomotive with pony trucks, guide wheels, piston-rod action, bronze bearings and gleaming headlamp—usually found only in sets selling at more than $25.00. Big 6-unit train is over 4 ft. long! Couple and uncouple cars ... run train fast or slow, forward or backward ... start and stop ... *all by remote control!*

Die-cast coal and water-type tender and 4 embossed steel cars (tank car, box car, high-side gondola, caboose) ... accurate 3/16-in. scale models with double trucks (8 wheels), automatic uncouplers. UL approved 50-watt transformer (110-120-volt, 60-cycle AC) with built-in circuit breaker; 16-section track.
79 N 09635—Shipping weight 13 lbs. Complete $23.98

ONLY 10% DOWN on Sears Easy Terms! See page 353 for full details.

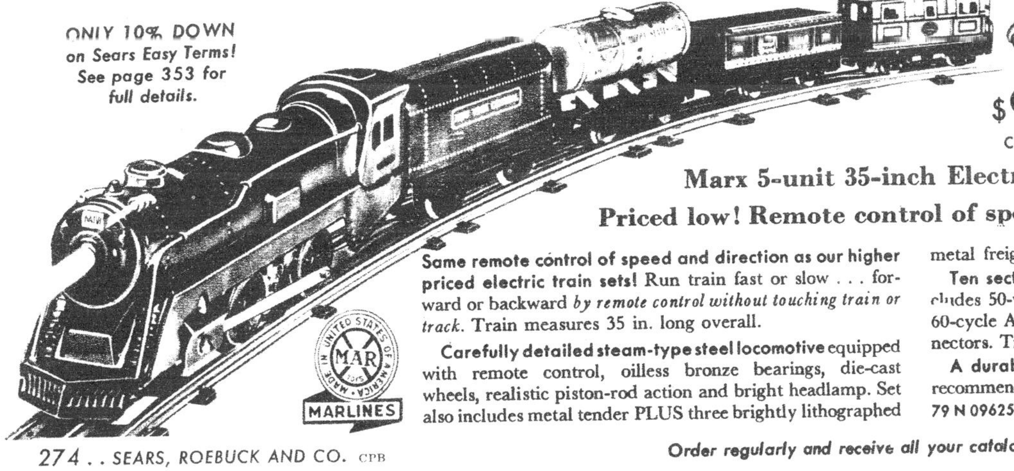

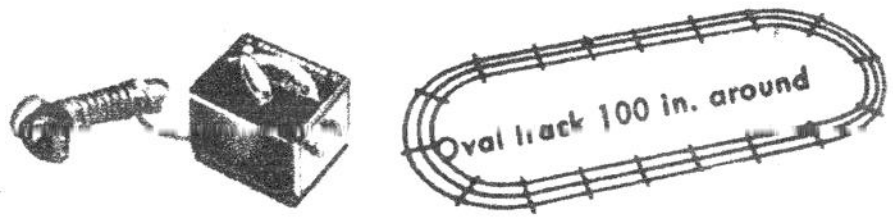

$9.59 Complete

Oval track 100 in. around

Marx 5-unit 35-inch Electric Freight
Priced low! Remote control of speed and direction

Same remote control of speed and direction as our higher priced electric train sets! Run train fast or slow ... forward or backward *by remote control without touching train or track.* Train measures 35 in. long overall.
Carefully detailed steam-type steel locomotive equipped with remote control, oilless bronze bearings, die-cast wheels, realistic piston-rod action and bright headlamp. Set also includes metal tender PLUS three brightly lithographed metal freight cars (gondola, tank car and caboose).
Ten sections of track form oval 100 in. around. Set includes 50-watt UL approved transformer for 110-120-volt, 60-cycle AC only, plus all necessary wires and track connectors. Transformer has lever for varying train speed.
A durable quality, low-priced electric train especially recommended for the new young train enthusiast.
79 N 09625—Shipping weight 8 lbs. .... Complete Set $9.59

274 .. SEARS, ROEBUCK AND CO. CPB   *Order regularly and receive all your catalogs regularly*

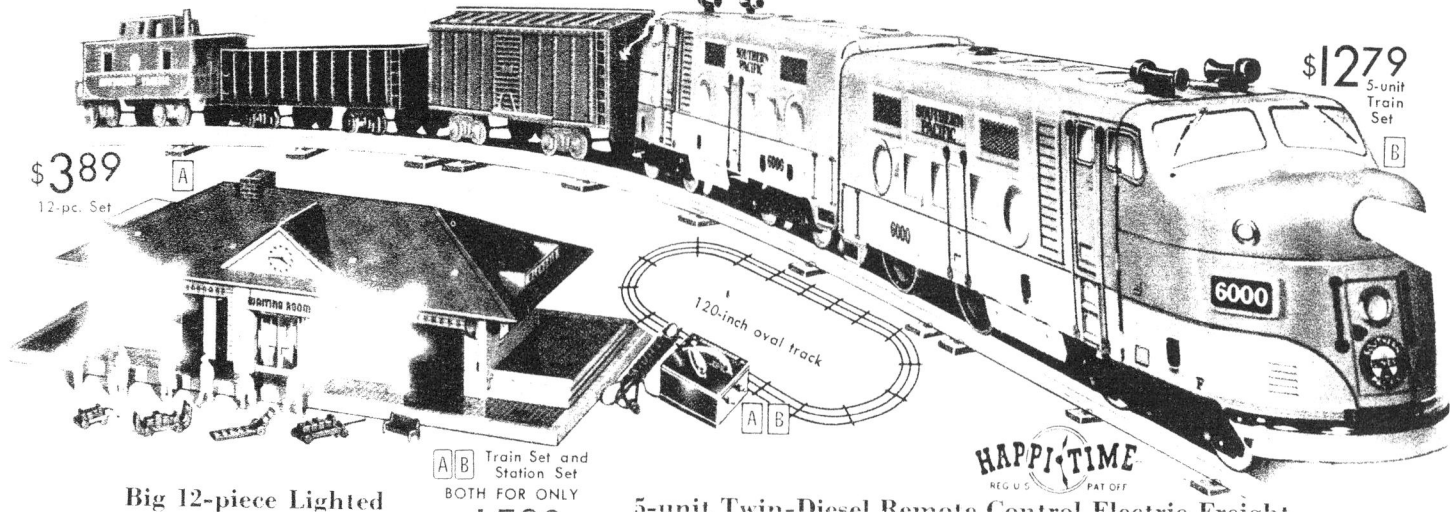

Big 12-piece Lighted Railroad Station Set

$3.89 12-pc. Set

Train Set and Station Set BOTH FOR ONLY $15.98

5-unit Twin-Diesel Remote Control Electric Freight
with new, realistically detailed *plastic* cars!

$12.79 5-unit Train Set

[A] Like a real station! Big 20½x10x5¼-in. colorful steel station, lithographed to show waiting room, express office, baggage room, freight office, etc. Platform and ramp for inbound freight. Six people plus 5 accessories (bench, hand truck, live skid, baggage truck, platform truck) of lifelike molded plastic. Bulb and wire included. Depot shipped unassembled; set up without tools.
49 N 9749 — Shipping weight 2 lbs. 6 oz. ...... 12-pc. Set $3.89

[B] Happi-Time 43-inch 5-unit Freight with new, more realistically detailed molded plastic cars (gondola, box car, caboose). Run train fast or slow, forward or back by REMOTE CONTROL!
Powered by latest type 2-unit lithographed steel diesel with oilless bronze bearings, die-cast drive wheels, bright headlamp. Dummy diesel horn, windshield wipers, louvers add greater realism.

Built-in circuit breaker protects 50-watt UL approved transformer against shorts, overloads. Reversing lever. 110-120-volt, 60-cycle AC. 12 sections of track form oval 120 inches around.
79 N 09632 — Train Set, as above. Train, transformer, track, cars. Shpg. wt. 9 lbs. $12.79
[A B] 79 N 09672 — Train Set (B) PLUS Railroad Station Set (A). Shpg. wt. 12 lbs. 15.98

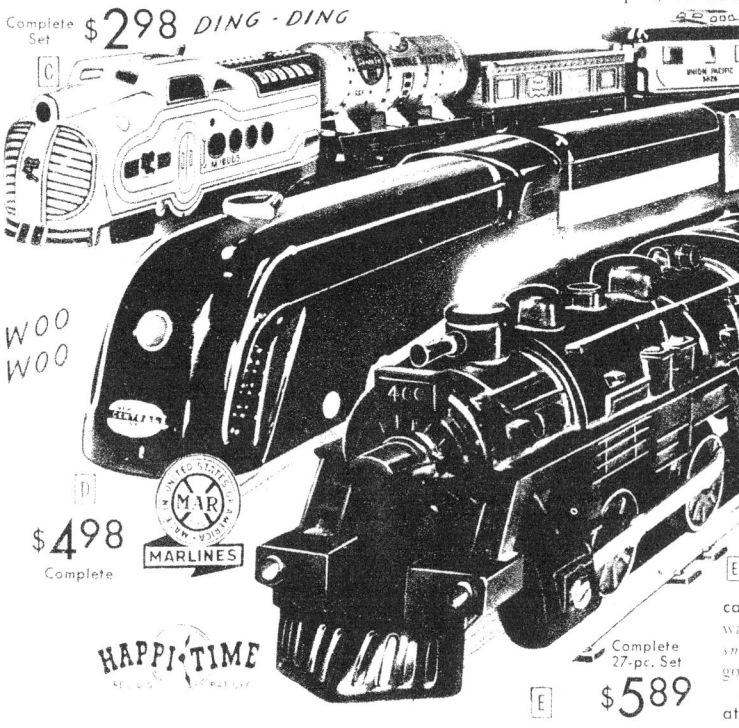

Complete Set $2.98 DING–DING

WOO WOO

$4.98 Complete

HAPPI·TIME

Complete 27-pc. Set $5.89

NEW! Happi-Time 5-unit Freight Set

[E] FIRST TIME EVER AT THIS LOW PRICE! Only $5.89 for this big 39-in. 5-unit smoking mechanical freight with new super-detailed plastic locomotive and cars PLUS switches PLUS 6 miniature railroad signs. You'll thrill as you watch the powerful steam-type locomotive streak around the track with its cars—*smoke puffing* (really powder). Long-running clockspring motor; built-in speed governor and brake.
Most realistic locomotive and cars we've ever seen on any mechanical train at this price! Locomotive, tender, 3 cars (Gondola, box car, caboose)—*all plastic!*
Lots of fun switching the train to the inner track, too! You get two hand-operated switches PLUS 4 sections of straight track and 10 curved sections.
49 N 9513 Train, track, switches and signs. Shpg. wt. 4 lbs. 8 oz. $5.89

Thrifty Marx Mechanical Diesel Freight

[C] Look at this low, low price for a 4-unit mechanical diesel freight with bell! What a thrill to watch this mighty diesel locomotive whiz its cars around the 94-inch oval track ... its merry little bell clearing the track!
Lithographed metal diesel unit modeled after big railroad locomotives. Powerful clockspring motor with built-in speed governor and brake. Lithographed metal tender, gondola and caboose (each with 4 wheels) plus 10 sections of track.
49 N 9502 Train is 28 in. long. Shipping weight 2 lbs. 10 oz. ...... Complete Set $2.98

31½-inch 5-unit Mechanical Freight . . only $4.98

[D] Just imagine ... a 22-piece outfit! Whistling mechanical freight train set with 176-inch crossover track at this sensationally low price! Sturdy steel whistling locomotive has powerful, long-running clockspring motor with built-in speed governor and brake. Lithographed metal tender, high-side gondola, coal car and caboose (each with 4 wheels), 16 sections track PLUS crossover!
Listen to the realistic wail of its whistle as this powerful freight streaks around its 176 inches of track. Truly a gift to gladden the heart of any little railroader!
49 N 9510 Big 5-unit Train, Crossover Track. Shipping weight 5 lbs. ..Complete $4.98

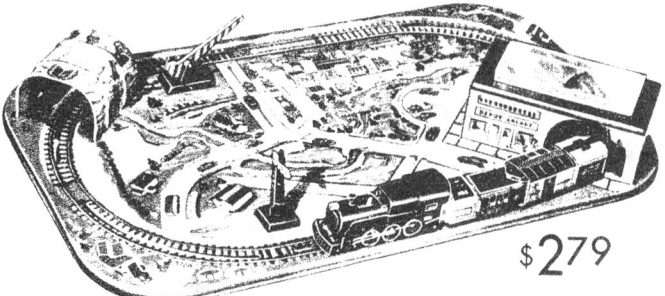

$2.79

Scenic Express Set

Just the set for younger children. All the thrill and fun of a complete railroad system in a minimum of space! Sturdy steel base about 21¾x13 inches, realistically lithographed. Action crossing gate, semaphore for added realism. Long-running clockspring motor whizzes 11-in. train through tunnel and around base in grooved track over 20 times with 1 winding.
49 N 9515 — Shipping weight 2 pounds 8 ounces. Complete set $2.79

Extra Track for Mechanical Trains

Shpg. wt. 6 oz. [F and G].
[F] **Straight Track.** 8⅛ in. 49 N 9701 . Set of 4, 39c
[G] **Curved Track.** 10 in. long. 49 N 9702 . Set of 4, 39c
[H] **90° Crossover.** 7½ in. 49N9703—Wt. 8 oz. 59c
[J] **Manual Switch Set.** One left 1, right-hand switch. 49N9704 Wt. 1 lb. Set $1.79

Easy Terms, page 353   PAGE 275 .. TRAINS, ACCESSORIES

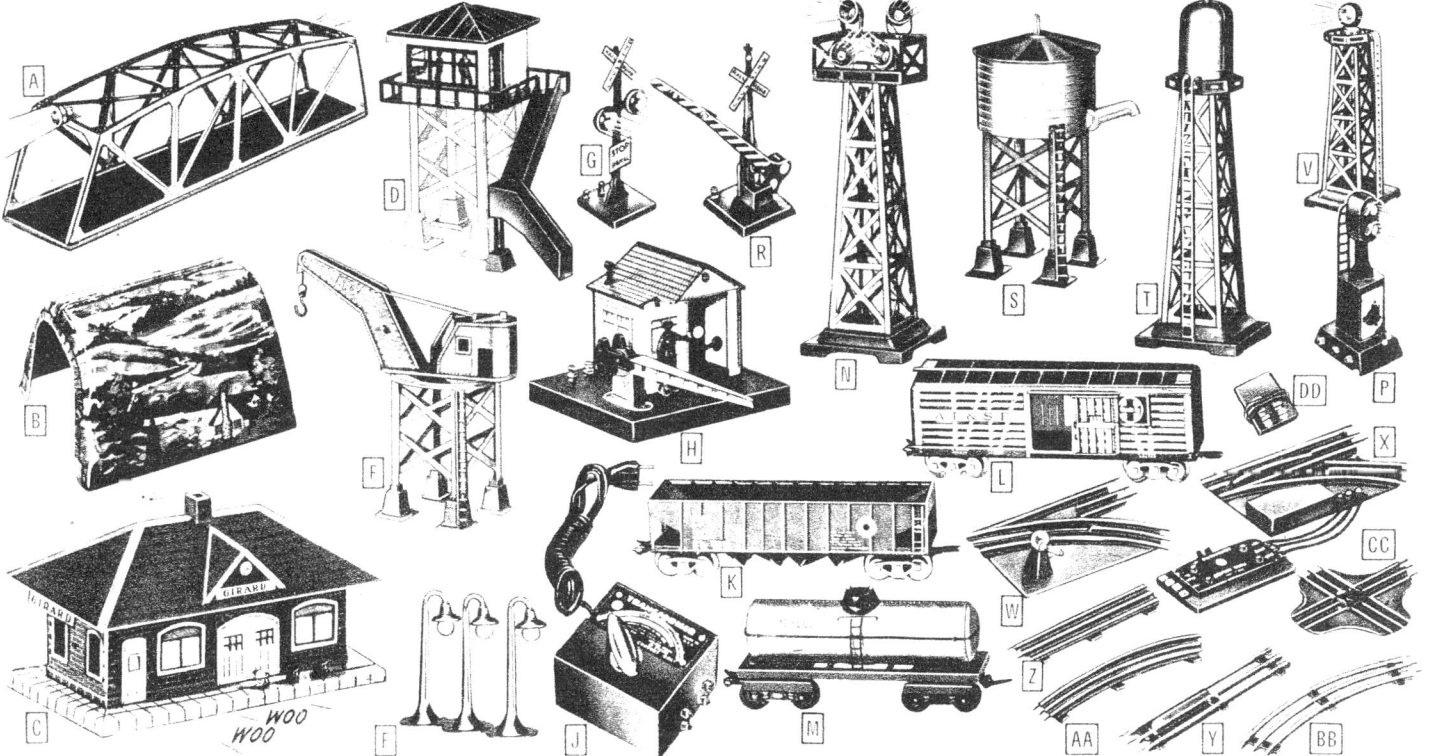

Thrilling, true-to-life accessories for Marx and Happi-Time Electric Trains

NOTE: Metal Tunnel (B), Derrick Loader (E) and Water Tower (S) may also be used with mechanical trains. Asterisk (*) after an item indicates all necessary wire, track connectors, etc. are included.

[A] **Lighted all-steel Trestle Bridge*.** Embossed rivets. Light socket and reflector held in position by snap-on clip; adjustable for position. With bulbs.
49N9739—24x4⅞x6⅛ in. high. Shpg. wt. 2 lbs. **$1.87**

[B] **Collapsible Metal Tunnel.** Comes in 2 parts; easy to assemble. Lithographed landscape scene.
49 N 9729—10¾x9x7 in. high. Shpg. wt. 1 lb. **89c**

[C] **Whistling Metal Station*.** Press remote control button . . . hear the realistic wail of locomotive whistle as train whizzes down the track. Whistle is built into 9x5¼x 5 in. high lithographed steel station.
49 N 9766—With control panel. Shpg. wt. 2 lbs. **$4.29**

[D] **New! Lighted Switchman's Tower*.** As train nears, switchman with green flag appears through door, as second man inside moves to switch controls. Realistic colored plastic. 7½ in. high. Transparent windows.
49 N 9765—With bulb. Shipping weight 1 lb. **$4.77**

[E] **New! Plastic Derrick Loader.** Scale-detailed. Crane housing swings in complete circle. Boom has crank handle; raises, lowers loads.
49 N 9733—8½ in. high. Shpg. wt. 10 oz. **$1.49**

[F] **Three Lighted 6-in. Station Lamps*.** Fluted.
49N9728—With bulbs. Shpg. wt. 6 oz. Set of 3 **1.77**

[G] **Automatic Crossing Flasher*.** Twin lights flash alternately from one side to other as train passes.
49N9742—Metal; 7¾ in. high. Shpg. wt. 10 oz. **$1.87**

[H] **Automatic Grade Crossing Shack with Watchman*.** Lithographed steel shanty; 8½-in. plastic gate. As train nears, watchman comes out with "STOP" sign, gate lowers. Base 7x6½ in.; house 4½ in. high.
49 N 9760— Shipping weight 2 lbs. 8 oz. **$3.87**

[J] **50-watt Transformer*.** 110-120-volt, 60-cycle AC only. Two sets of binding posts give variable 7 to 13 volts for controlling train speed plus 13 volts for accessories. Built-in circuit breaker. Red re-set button. With track connector, wire, cord.
49 N 9725— UL approved. Shpg. wt. 3 lbs. 4 oz. **$5.79**

Extra Freight Cars for Marx or Happi-Time Electric Train Sets. Authentic scale-detailed rolling stock. Each has two trucks (8 wheels in all). Assorted R.R. decorations. PLUS Automatic Coupler for remote control coupling and uncoupling. (You need 49 N 9713, see Y, if your train has manual couplers). Shpg. wt. 10 oz. each.
[K] 49 N 9723— Hopper Car. 9½ inches overall **1.79**
[L] 49 N 9721— Box Car. 9 inches overall **1.79**
[M] 49 N 9722— Tank Car. 8 inches overall **1.79**

[N] **New! 4-light Floodlight Tower*.** Four lights mounted on double platform on girder-type plastic tower. Lights may be revolved, tilted. Metal ladder.
49 N 9751— Height 13½ in. Shpg. wt. 1 lb. **$2.89**

[P] **Automatic Block Signal*.** Train stops on red light, proceeds on green. Die-cast base; 2-track section. Chrome-finish ladder. Switch at rear operates signal. Metal; 7 inches high.
49 N 9745— Shipping weight 1 pound **$2.15**

[R] **Automatic Crossing Gate*.** Striped arm lowers as train passes, then raises. Red jewel at end of gate.
49N9743—Metal; 7½ in. high. Shpg. wt. 10 oz. **$1.89**

[S] **Big 8-in. Plastic Water Tower with Adjustable Spout.** Realistic ribs; metal-type understructure.
49 N 9731— Tank 4¼ in. diam. Shpg. wt. 10 oz. **89c**

[T] **Giant 14¼-in. Plastic Water Tower with Bubbling Light*.** Realistic plates and rivets on tank, girder-type understructure. Light bulb in base lights transparent tube from base to tank, causes bubbles to rise the length of the tube. A clever new accessory.
49 N 9752— Giant Tank. Shpg. wt. 1 lb. **$2.89**

[V] **Lighted Revolving Beacon*.** Revolves on top of girder-type molded plastic tower. Red, green reflector.
49 N 9740— 13½ in. high. Shpg. wt. 1 lb. **$1.87**

[W] **Manual Switch Set.** One left-, one right-hand.
49 N 9715— Shipping weight 2 pounds. Set **2.95**

[X] **Electric Remote Control Switch Set*.** One left- and one right-hand switch plus 4-button control panel.
49 N 9716— Shipping weight 2 lbs. 8 oz. Set **$6.79**

[Y] **Uncoupling Unit for Marx or Happi-Time Trains.** Built into standard length electric straight track. Includes miniature "UNCOUPLE HERE" sign.
49 N 9713— Shipping weight 5 oz. Each **55c**

Extra Track for Electric Trains. Shipping weight 4 oz. each.
[Z] 49 N 9710— 8⅞-in. Straight Track. Each **18c**
[AA] 49 N 9712— 12½-in. Large Radius Curved Track. Ea. **23c**
[BB] 49 N 9711— 10½-in. Standard Curved Track. Ea. **18c**
[CC] 49 N 9714— 7½-in. Crossover. Shpg. wt. 8 oz. Ea. **85c**

[DD] **Bakelite Track Connector.** Metal prongs inserted in track to bring in power from transformer or to take off power for various electric accessories.
49 N 9709— 1¾ x 1⅛ in. Shpg. wt. 2 oz. Each **12c**

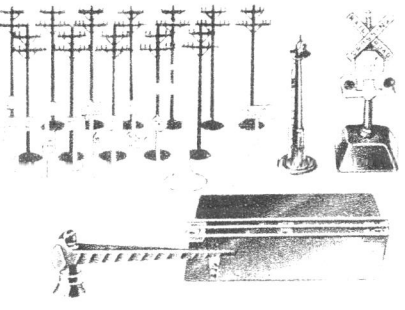

29-piece Accessory Set

Perfect for adding realism to his train set! Authentically scale-detailed in sturdy plastic. Just the right size for any standard electric or mechanical train set. **$2.89**

Set includes: Twelve 7-in. telegraph poles, 12 railroad right-of-way signs, PLUS one each of the following: semaphore, lamp post, crossing gate, grade crossing, railroad crossing sign. Track not included. The low cost way to add realism to your train set.
49 N 9750 Shpg. wt. 2 lbs. Set **$2.89**

Talking Railroad Station

"All aboard! New York . . . Pittsburgh . . . Cleveland . . . Chicago . . . Denver . . . San Francisco!" Just like a real station! Conductor calls off principal station on 3 main line routes . . . then you hear the realistic "choo-choo" sound of train leaving station, fading into distance. **$2.79**

Set needle of plastic loudspeaker on built-in record . . . turn hand crank . . . and it talks! Colorful station made of Masonite and Tekwood. Shipped completely set up. Overall size 17x7½x6½ inches high. A perfect Christmas gift . . . because it's an ideal accessory for any standard electric or mechanical train.
49 N 9775— Shipping weight 3 lbs. 4 oz. **$2.79**

Plastic Buildings . . Accessories

Colorful, realistic Buildings. Carefully detailed in molded plastic. Easily set up; parts snap in place. **As low as 79c**

[EE] **Railroad Station with Platform.** 11x6x4½ in. high.
49 N 9719— Shipping weight 10 oz. **$1.05**

[FF] **Roadside Diner.** The kind you see all along the highways!
49 N 9727— 8¾ inches long. Shipping weight 8 oz. Each **79c**

[GG] **Log Cabin Kit with Rustic Fence and Tree.** Rustic brown color.
49 N 9735— Cabin is 6x4¼x3¾ in. high. Shpg. wt. 10 oz. Kit **79c**

[HH] **3-pc. Plastic Action Accessory Set.** 6-in. semaphore, 4¾-in. crossing sign, and 4½-in. gate. Weight of train passing puts accessory into action. *Can be used with mechanical trains.*
49 N 9732— Appropriate colors. Shpg. wt. 10 oz. 3-piece Set **$1.49**

SEARS CHRISTMAS CATALOG

1953

By 1953 Sears' electric train customers were increasingly sophisticated and demanding more detail and variety in their trains. This year's Wishbook featured a wide array of sets and accessories. Notably, the catalog gave prime coverage to Lionel's full line of train sets in various price ranges from $24.95 to $62.50.

For those looking to buy entry level train sets, Sears offered its own Happi-Time brand, manufactured for Sears by Marx and other firms. There was even a $2.75 wind-up "Scenic Express" toy for younger children.

Accessories abounded in 1953. Lionel released such classics as the Coaling Station which automatically dumped its plastic coal load into a waiting gondola. In the lower price range, Marx displayed its own wide line of accessories, often copying Lionel designs.

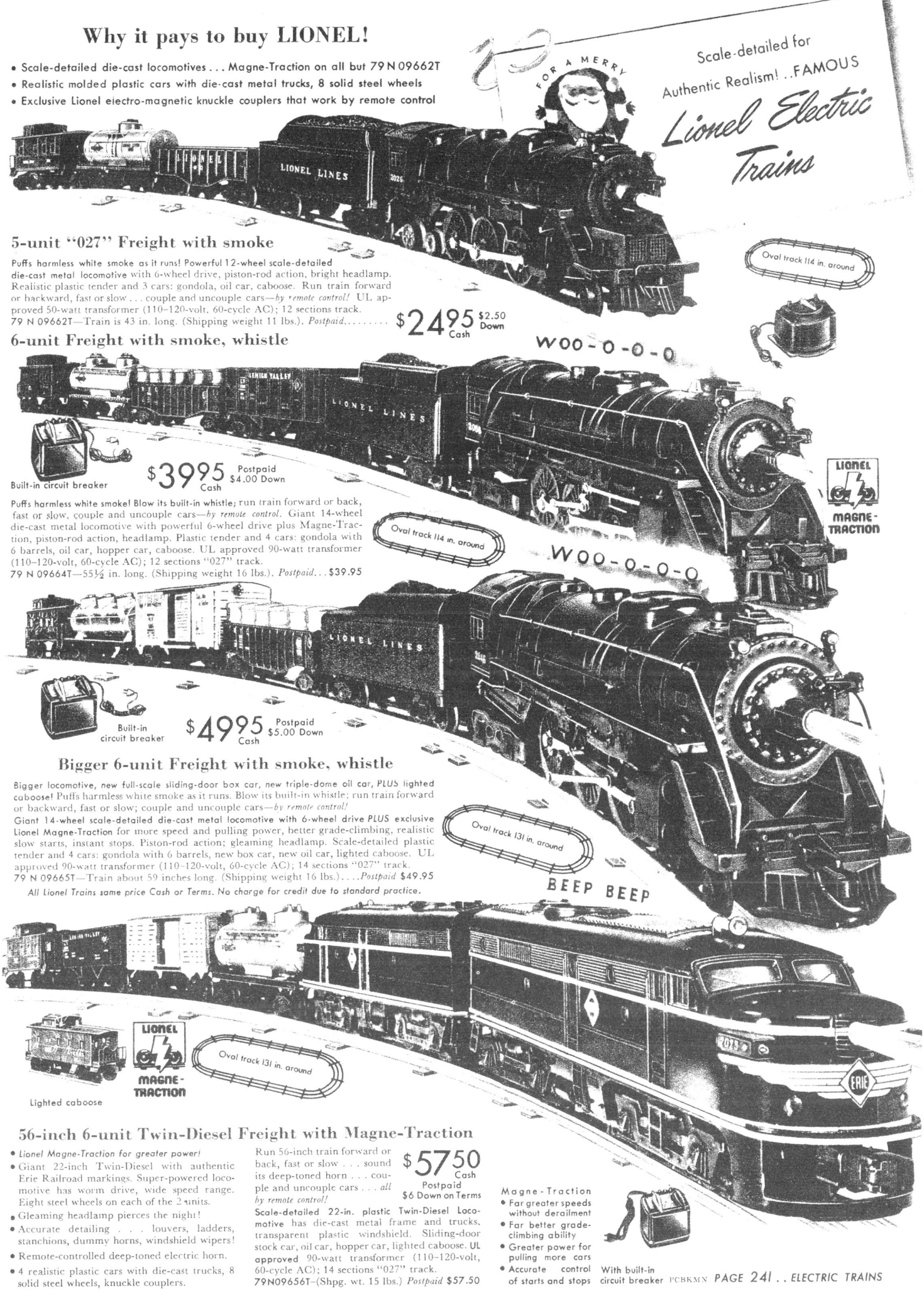

Why it pays to buy LIONEL!

- Scale-detailed die-cast locomotives...Magne-Traction on all but 79 N 09662T
- Realistic molded plastic cars with die-cast metal trucks, 8 solid steel wheels
- Exclusive Lionel electro-magnetic knuckle couplers that work by remote control

Scale-detailed for Authentic Realism!..FAMOUS **Lionel Electric Trains**

5-unit "027" Freight with smoke

Puffs harmless white smoke as it runs! Powerful 12-wheel scale-detailed die-cast metal locomotive with 6-wheel drive, piston-rod action, bright headlamp. Realistic plastic tender and 3 cars: gondola, oil car, caboose. Run train forward or backward, fast or slow...couple and uncouple cars...*by remote control!* UL approved 50-watt transformer (110-120-volt, 60-cycle AC); 12 sections track. 79 N 09662T—Train is 43 in. long. (Shipping weight 11 lbs.). Postpaid........ **$24.95 Cash** $2.50 Down

6-unit Freight with smoke, whistle

Built-in circuit breaker **$39.95 Cash** Postpaid $4.00 Down

Puffs harmless white smoke! Blow its built-in whistle; run train forward or back, fast or slow, couple and uncouple cars—*by remote control.* Giant 14-wheel die-cast metal locomotive with powerful 6-wheel drive plus Magne-Traction, piston-rod action, headlamp. Plastic tender and 4 cars: gondola with 6 barrels, oil car, hopper car, caboose. UL approved 90-watt transformer (110-120-volt, 60-cycle AC); 12 sections "027" track. 79 N 09664T—55½ in. long. (Shipping weight 16 lbs.). Postpaid...$39.95

Built-in circuit breaker **$49.95 Cash** Postpaid $5.00 Down

Bigger 6-unit Freight with smoke, whistle

Bigger locomotive, new full-scale sliding-door box car, new triple-dome oil car, *PLUS* lighted caboose! Puffs harmless white smoke as it runs. Blow its built-in whistle; run train forward or backward, fast or slow; couple and uncouple cars—*by remote control!* Giant 14-wheel scale-detailed die-cast metal locomotive with 6-wheel drive *PLUS* exclusive Lionel Magne-Traction for more speed and pulling power, better grade-climbing, realistic slow starts, instant stops. Piston-rod action; gleaming headlamp. Scale-detailed plastic tender and 4 cars: gondola with 6 barrels, new box car, new oil car, lighted caboose. UL approved 90-watt transformer (110-120-volt, 60-cycle AC); 14 sections "027" track. 79 N 09665T—Train about 59 inches long. (Shipping weight 16 lbs.)....Postpaid $49.95

All Lionel Trains same price Cash or Terms. No charge for credit due to standard practice.

Lighted caboose

56-inch 6-unit Twin-Diesel Freight with Magne-Traction

- *Lionel Magne-Traction for greater power!*
- Giant 22-inch Twin-Diesel with authentic Erie Railroad markings. Super-powered locomotive has worm drive, wide speed range. Eight steel wheels on each of the 2 units.
- Gleaming headlamp pierces the night!
- Accurate detailing...louvers, ladders, stanchions, dummy horns, windshield wipers!
- Remote-controlled deep-toned electric horn.
- 4 realistic plastic cars with die-cast trucks, 8 solid steel wheels, knuckle couplers.

Run 56-inch train forward or back, fast or slow...sound its deep-toned horn...couple and uncouple cars...*all by remote control!* Scale-detailed 22-in. plastic Twin-Diesel Locomotive has die-cast metal frame and trucks, transparent plastic windshield. Sliding-door stock car, oil car, hopper car, lighted caboose. UL approved 90-watt transformer (110-120-volt, 60-cycle AC); 14 sections "027" track. 79N09656T—(Shpg. wt. 15 lbs.) Postpaid $57.50

$57.50 Cash Postpaid $6 Down on Terms

Magne-Traction
- Far greater speeds without derailment
- Far better grade-climbing ability
- Greater power for pulling more cars
- Accurate control of starts and stops

With built-in circuit breaker

PCBKMN PAGE 241..ELECTRIC TRAINS

W-O-O-O-O

$62.50 Cash Postpaid $6.50 Down

Big 6-unit "O"-gauge Electric Freight

Massive, scale-detailed 20-wheel die-cast metal locomotive with Magne-Traction for more pulling power, speed, climb, better control! Powerful 8-wheel drive; two 6-wheel trucks. Side-rod action. Gleaming headlamp.

Watch it thunder down the rails, puffing harmless white smoke . . . whistle blowing. Run fast or slow, forward or back . . . couple, uncouple cars . . . load, unload cattle . . . unload lumber . . . sound its deep-toned whistle—*all by remote control!*

Big 59-inch train includes locomotive, plastic tender with built-in whistle, 4 realistically detailed cars (operating lumber car with railside bin; operating cattle car with platform, *new* scale sliding-door box car, *new* scale lighted caboose), 14 sections "O"-gauge track. No transformer; order below.
79 N 09682T—(Shpg. wt. 21 lbs.) Postpaid $62.50

Authentic Lionel Trains
Exciting, true-to-life realism!

FOR A MERRY CHRISTMAS

BEEP BEEP

[A] [B] [C] $30.00 Postpaid $3.00 Down $25.00 Postpaid $2.50 Down

Realistic Lionel Locomotives with Magne-Traction

- Magnificently scale-detailed! Authentic markings even seasoned railroad men marvel at their blue-print accuracy of detail. Bright headlamps; remote-control electric couplers. For "027" or "O"-gauge trains
- Exclusive Lionel Magne-Traction gives greater power for pulling more cars, better grade-climbing, greater speeds without derailment, better control of starts and stops. Silent, powerful, precision-built motors

[A] **26½-inch Santa Fe Twin-Diesel Locomotive with remote-control electric horn plus Magne-Traction.** Super-powered twin motors; 4-wheel drive. Accurately detailed plastic cab. Dummy windshield wipers, ladders, stanchions, louvers. Lighted number box. Eight steel wheels per section (2 trucks).
79 N 09894T—(Shpg. wt. 12 lbs.). Postpaid $47.50
New York Central Twin-Diesel. Not shown. Like (A).
79 N 09895T—(Shpg. wt. 12 lbs.). Postpaid $47.50

[B] **19-inch "Hudson" type die-cast metal Locomotive with Magne-Traction, realistic smoke, whistle.** Fourteen wheels; powerful 6-wheel drive; two 4-wheel trucks. Piston-rod action. Deep-toned remote-control whistle is built into plastic tender.
79 N 09891T—(Shpg. wt. 7 lbs.) Postpaid $30.00

[C] **11½-in. Diesel Yard Switcher with Magne-Traction.** Bright headlight; powerful worm drive.
49 N 09890T—(Shipping wt. 5 lbs.) Postpaid $25.00

[D] $10.95 Postpaid
[E] $9.95 Postpaid
[F] $10.95 Postpaid

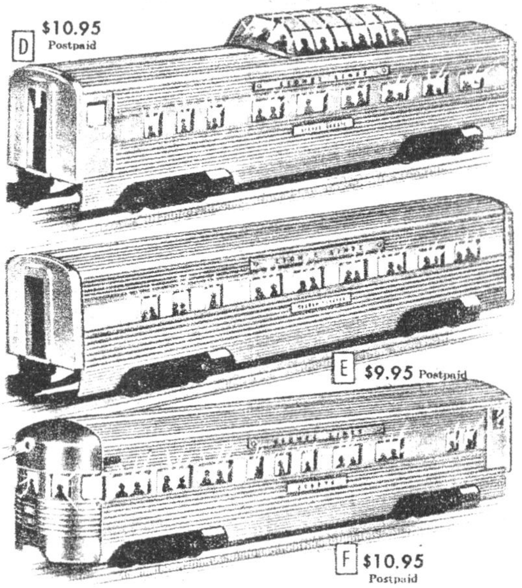

Authentic, Illuminated Pullmans

Magnificently scale-detailed in extruded aluminum. All the sleek grace and gleaming beauty of real-life streamliner. All three cars interiors brightly lighted (bulbs included). Tiny passengers look out of clear plastic windows. Die-cast metal trucks; 8 solid steel wheels; remote control electric knuckle couplers. (Shipping weight 2 lbs. 11 oz.)

[D] 49 N 9854T—15-inch Astra-dome Car............Postpaid $10.95
[E] 49 N 9853T—15-inch Pullman Car................Postpaid 9.95
[F] 49 N 9855T—15-inch Observation Car...........Postpaid 10.95

ALL LIONEL TRAINS AND ACCESSORIES ARE POSTPAID!
Sears pays shipping charges on all Lionel trains and accessories. Same price whether you buy for cash or on Easy Terms . . . no extra charge for credit. Only 10% down . . . see page 369.

Track, Switches and 90° Crossover . . "027" and "O"-gauge

[G] **Remote Control Switches.** One right-hand, one left-hand switch, control panel, wire included.
49 N 9806—For "027"-gauge track layouts. (Shipping weight 3 lbs.) Postpaid........Per pair $13.50
49 N 9815—For "O"-gauge track layouts. (Shipping weight 5 lbs.) Postpaid.........Per pair $22.50

[H] **Magnetic Track Section.** For remote-control coupling and uncoupling. Control panel and connecting wire included. (Shpg. wt. each 1 lb.)
49 N 9804—"027"-gauge. Postpaid..... Each $3.00
49 N 9813—"O"-gauge. Postpaid........ Each 3.25

Shop early . . then relax and enjoy the Holidays

[J] **Illuminated Bumper.** For "027" and "O"-gauge track.
49 N 9859—(Shpg. wt. 1 lb.)...Postpaid $1.95

[K] **90-degree Crossover.** (Wt. 8 oz.) Postpaid.
49 N 9803—"027"-gauge. 7⅜ in. square..$1.95
49 N 9812—"O"-gauge. 8¼ in. square. Ppd. 2.95

[L] **8⅞-in. Straight Track Section, "027"-gauge.**
49 N 9801 (Wt. 3 oz.) Postpaid.......Each 25c
10-in. Straight Track Section for "O"-gauge.
49 N 9810 (Wt. 4 oz.) Postpaid.......Each 30c

[M] **9½-in. Curved Track Section, "027"-gauge.**
49 N 9802—(Wt. 3 oz.) Postpaid......Each 25c
10⅞-in. Curved Track Section for "O"-gauge.
49 N 9811—(Wt. 4 oz.) Postpaid......Each 30c

[N] $13.95 Postpaid
[P] $16.95 Postpaid
[R] $22.50 Postpaid $2.50 Down

"Trainmaster" Transformers

For 110-120-volt 60-cycle AC. Built-in self-resetting automatic circuit breaker guards against overloads. Light signals shorts.

[N] **Type RW—110-watts.** Two variable voltages for train; 4 fixed voltages for accessories. Buttons control whistle and reversing.
49 N 9820T—UL approved. (Shpg. wt. 7 lbs.)...........Postpaid $13.95

[P] **Type TW—175-watts.** One throttle controls train voltage; other for whistle, reversing. Fixed 14 and 16 volts for accessories.
49 N 9824T—(Shpg. wt. 11 lbs.)..................Postpaid $16.95

[R] **Type KW—190-watts.** Two independently controlled variable voltages for running 2 trains on different layouts at same time. Built-in whistle and separate reversing controls for each train. Diesel-type control levers. Fixed 6, 14 and 20-volt accessory circuit.
79 N 09821T—Molded case. (Shpg. wt. 11 lbs.)...Postpaid $22.50

242 . . SEARS, ROEBUCK AND CO. PCBKMN

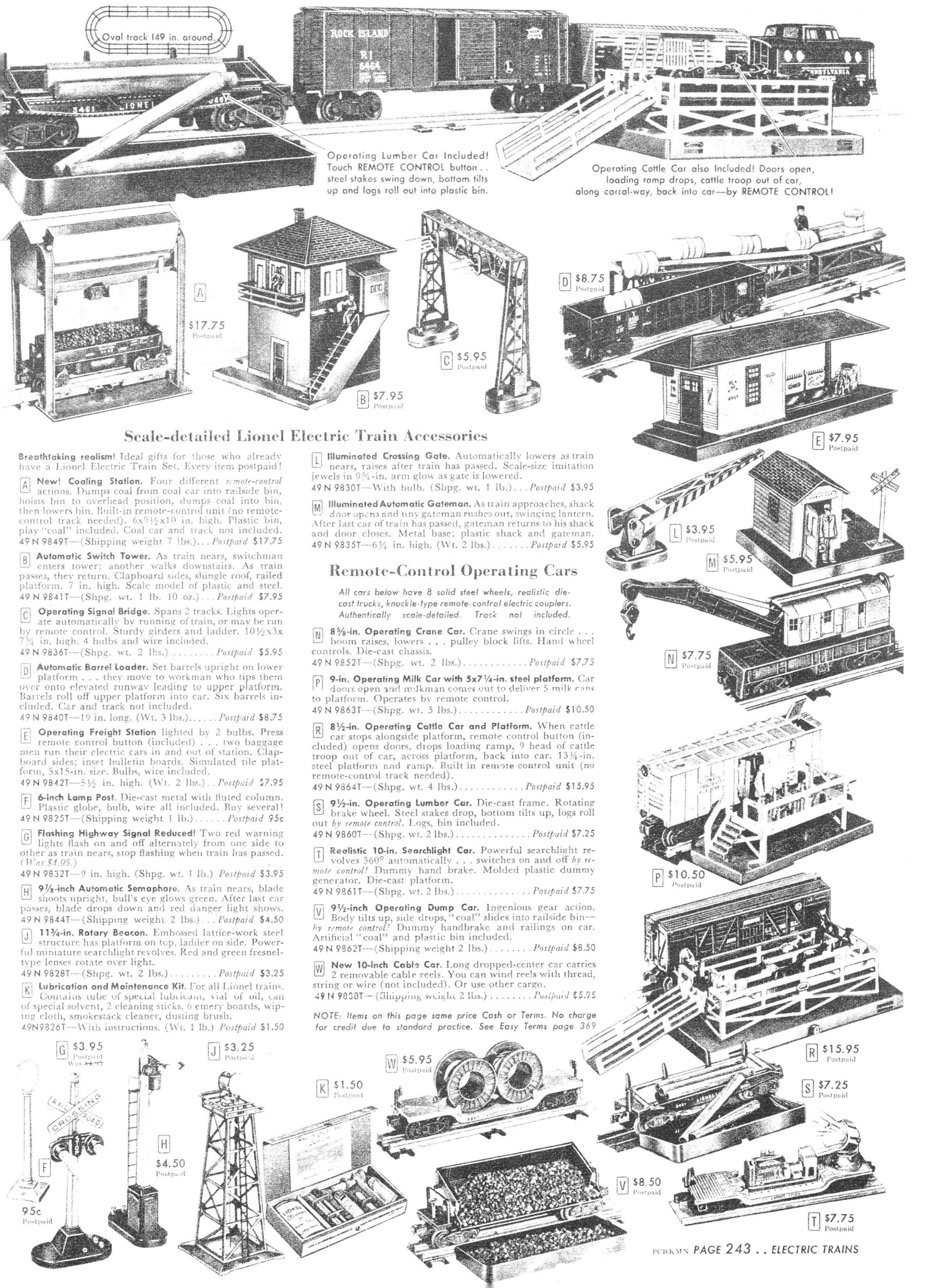

Operating Lumber Car Included!
Touch REMOTE CONTROL button..
steel stakes swing down, bottom tilts
up and logs roll out into plastic bin.

Operating Cattle Car also Included! Doors open,
loading ramp drops, cattle troop out of car,
along corral-way, back into car—by REMOTE CONTROL!

A $17.75 Postpaid
B $7.95 Postpaid
C $5.95 Postpaid
D $8.75 Postpaid
E $7.95 Postpaid

Scale-detailed Lionel Electric Train Accessories

Breathtaking realism! Ideal gifts for those who already have a Lionel Electric Train Set. Every item postpaid!

A New! Coaling Station. Four different *remote-control* actions. Dumps coal from coal car into railside bin, hoists bin to overhead position, dumps coal into bin, then lowers bin. Built-in remote-control unit (no remote-control track needed). 6x9½x10 in. high. Plastic bin, play "coal" included. Coal car and track not included.
49 N 9849T—(Shipping weight 7 lbs.)...Postpaid $17.75

B Automatic Switch Tower. As train nears, switchman enters tower; another walks downstairs. As train passes, they return. Clapboard sides, shingle roof, railed platform. 7 in. high. Scale model of plastic and steel.
49 N 9841T—(Shpg. wt. 1 lb. 10 oz.)...Postpaid $7.95

C Operating Signal Bridge. Spans 2 tracks. Lights operate automatically by running of train, or may be run by remote control. Sturdy girders and ladder. 10½x3x 7¾ in. high. 4 bulbs and wire included.
49 N 9836T—(Shpg. wt. 2 lbs.)........Postpaid $5.95

D Automatic Barrel Loader. Set barrels upright on lower platform . . . they move to workman who tips them over onto elevated runway leading to upper platform. Barrels roll off upper platform into car. Six barrels included. Car and track not included.
49 N 9840T—19 in. long. (Wt. 3 lbs.)......Postpaid $8.75

E Operating Freight Station lighted by 2 bulbs. Press remote control button (included) . . . two baggage men run their electric cars in and out of station. Clapboard sides; inset bulletin boards. Simulated tile platform, 5x15-in. size. Bulbs, wire included.
49 N 9842T—5½ in. high. (Wt. 2 lbs.)......Postpaid $7.95

F 6-inch Lamp Post. Die-cast metal with fluted column. Plastic globe, bulb, wire all included. Buy several!
49 N 9825T—(Shipping weight 1 lb.)......Postpaid 95c

G Flashing Highway Signal Reduced! Two red warning lights flash on and off alternately from one side to other as train nears, stop flashing when train has passed. (*Was $4.95.*)
49 N 9832T—9 in. high. (Shpg. wt. 1 lb.) Postpaid $3.95

H 9⅞-inch Automatic Semaphore. As train nears, blade shoots upright, bull's eye glows green. After last car passes, blade drops down and red danger light shows.
49 N 9844T—(Shipping weight 2 lbs.)...Postpaid $4.50

J 11¾-in. Rotary Beacon. Embossed lattice-work steel structure has platform on top, ladder on side. Powerful miniature searchlight revolves. Red and green fresnel-type lenses rotate over light.
49 N 9828T—(Shpg. wt. 2 lbs.)........Postpaid $3.25

K Lubrication and Maintenance Kit. For all Lionel trains. Contains tube of special lubricant, vial of oil, can of special solvent, 2 cleaning sticks, 6 emery boards, wiping cloth, smokestack cleaner, dusting brush.
49N9826T—With instructions. (Wt. 1 lb.) Postpaid $1.50

L Illuminated Crossing Gate. Automatically lowers as train nears, raises after train has passed. Scale-size imitation jewels in 9¾-in. arm glow as gate is lowered.
49 N 9830T—With bulb. (Shpg. wt. 1 lb.)...Postpaid $3.95

M Illuminated Automatic Gateman. As train approaches, shack door opens and tiny gateman rushes out, swinging lantern. After last car of train has passed, gateman returns to his shack and door closes. Metal base; plastic shack and gateman.
49 N 9835T—6¾ in. high. (Wt. 2 lbs.).......Postpaid $5.95

Remote-Control Operating Cars

All cars below have 8 solid steel wheels, realistic die-cast trucks, knuckle-type remote-control electric couplers. Authentically scale-detailed. Track not included.

N 8⅝-in. Operating Crane Car. Crane swings in circle . . . boom raises, lowers . . . pulley block lifts. Hand wheel controls. Die-cast chassis.
49 N 9852T—(Shpg. wt. 2 lbs.)............Postpaid $7.75

P 9-in. Operating Milk Car with 5x7¼-in. steel platform. Car doors open and milkman comes out to deliver 5 milk cans to platform. Operates by remote control.
49 N 9863T—(Shpg. wt. 3 lbs.)............Postpaid $10.50

R 8½-in. Operating Cattle Car and Platform. When cattle car stops alongside platform, remote control button (included) opens doors, drops loading ramp, 9 head of cattle troop out of car, across platform, back into car. 13¾-in. steel platform and ramp. Built in remote-control unit (no remote-control track needed).
49 N 9864T—(Shpg. wt. 4 lbs.)............Postpaid $15.95

S 9½-in. Operating Lumber Car. Die-cast frame. Rotating brake wheel. Steel stakes drop, bottom tilts up, logs roll out *by remote control.* Logs, bin included.
49 N 9860T—(Shpg. wt. 2 lbs.)............Postpaid $7.25

T Realistic 10-in. Searchlight Car. Powerful searchlight revolves 360° automatically . . . switches on and off *by remote control!* Dummy hand brake. Molded plastic dummy generator. Die-cast platform.
49 N 9861T—(Shpg. wt. 2 lbs.)............Postpaid $7.75

V 9½-inch Operating Dump Car. Ingenious gear action. Body tilts up, side drops, "coal" slides into railside bin—*by remote control!* Dummy handbrake and railings on car. Artificial "coal" and plastic bin included.
49 N 9862T—(Shipping weight 2 lbs.).......Postpaid $8.50

W New 10-inch Cable Car. Long dropped-center car carries 2 removable cable reels. You can wind reels with thread, string or wire (not included). Or use other cargo.
49 N 9830T—(Shipping weight 2 lbs.).......Postpaid $5.95

NOTE: Items on this page same price Cash or Terms. No charge for credit due to standard practice. See Easy Terms page 369

L $3.95 Postpaid
M $5.95 Postpaid
N $7.75 Postpaid
P $10.50 Postpaid
R $15.95 Postpaid
S $7.25 Postpaid
V $8.50 Postpaid
T $7.75 Postpaid
W $5.95 Postpaid
K $1.50 Postpaid
G $3.95 Postpaid *Was $4.95*
J $3.25 Postpaid
H $4.50 Postpaid
F 95c Postpaid

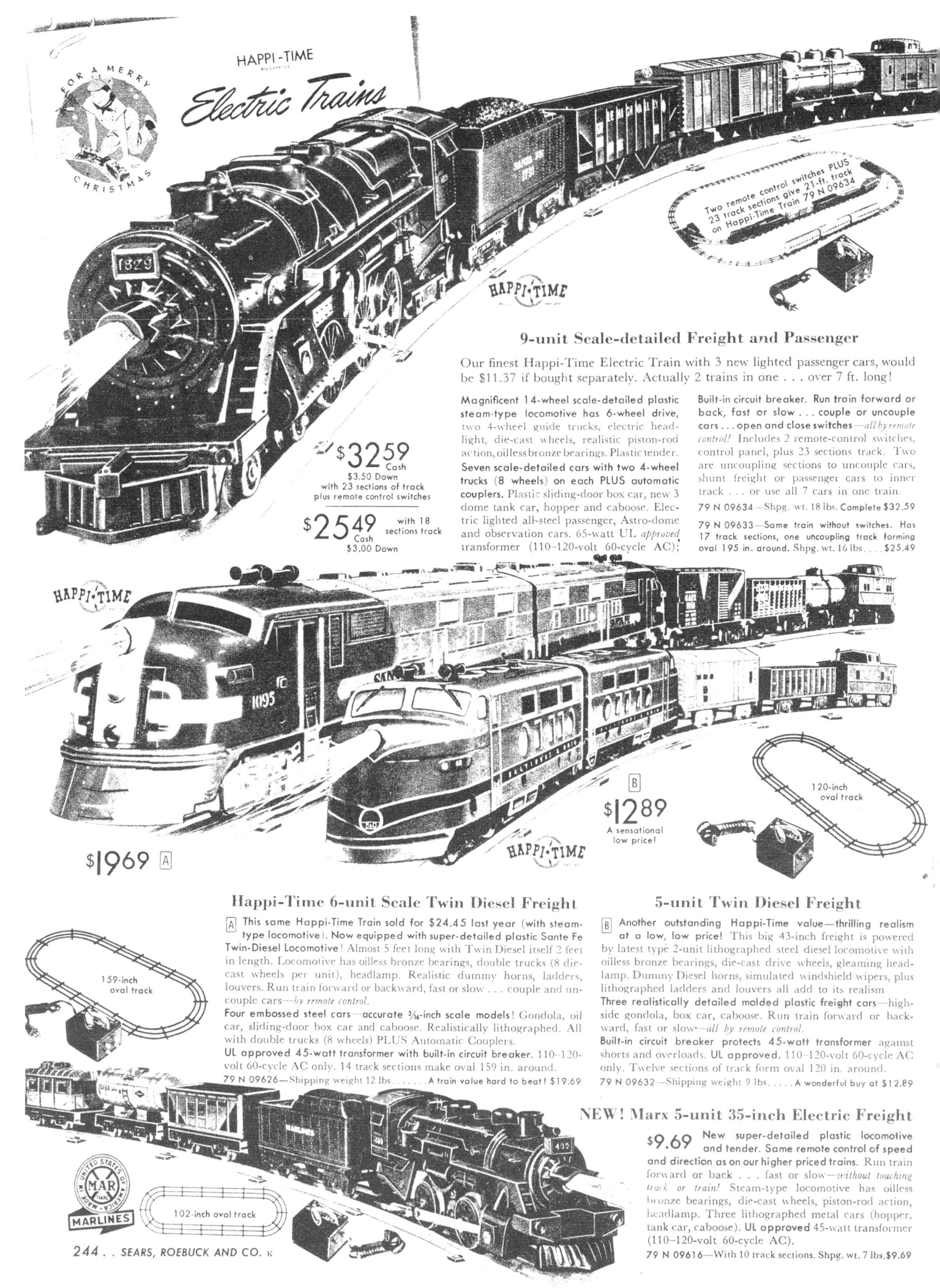

HAPPI-TIME Electric Trains

FOR A MERRY CHRISTMAS

Two remote control switches PLUS 23 track sections give 21-ft. track on Happi-Time Train 79 N 09634

9-unit Scale-detailed Freight and Passenger

Our finest Happi-Time Electric Train with 3 new lighted passenger cars, would be $11.37 if bought separately. Actually 2 trains in one... over 7 ft. long!

$32.59 Cash
$3.50 Down
with 23 sections of track plus remote control switches

$25.49 Cash with 18 sections track
$3.00 Down

Magnificent 14-wheel scale-detailed plastic steam-type locomotive has 6-wheel drive, two 4-wheel guide trucks, electric headlight, die-cast wheels, realistic piston-rod action, oilless bronze bearings. Plastic tender. Seven scale-detailed cars with two 4-wheel trucks (8 wheels) on each PLUS automatic couplers. Plastic sliding-door box car, new 3 dome tank car, hopper and caboose. Electric lighted all-steel passenger, Astro-dome and observation cars. 65-watt UL *approved* transformer (110–120-volt 60-cycle AC);

Built-in circuit breaker. Run train forward or back, fast or slow... couple or uncouple cars... open and close switches—*all by remote control!* Includes 2 remote-control switches, control panel, plus 23 sections track. Two are uncoupling sections to uncouple cars, shunt freight or passenger cars to inner track... or use all 7 cars in one train.

79 N 09634—Shpg. wt. 18 lbs. Complete $32.59
79 N 09633—Same train without switches. Has 17 track sections, one uncoupling track forming oval 195 in. around. Shpg. wt. 16 lbs....$25.49

$19.69 A
$12.89 B — A sensational low price!

120-inch oval track
159-inch oval track

Happi-Time 6-unit Scale Twin Diesel Freight

[A] This same Happi-Time Train sold for $24.45 last year (with steam-type locomotive). Now equipped with super-detailed plastic Sante Fe Twin-Diesel Locomotive! Almost 5 feet long with Twin Diesel itself 2 feet in length. Locomotive has oilless bronze bearings, double trucks (8 die-cast wheels per unit), headlamp. Realistic dummy horns, ladders, louvers. Run train forward or backward, fast or slow... couple and uncouple cars—*by remote control.*

Four embossed steel cars—accurate 3/16-inch scale models! Gondola, oil car, sliding-door box car and caboose. Realistically lithographed. All with double trucks (8 wheels) PLUS Automatic Couplers.

UL approved 45-watt transformer with built-in circuit breaker. 110–120-volt 60-cycle AC only. 14 track sections make oval 159 in. around.
79 N 09626—Shipping weight 12 lbs......A train value hard to beat! $19.69

5-unit Twin Diesel Freight

[B] Another outstanding Happi-Time value—thrilling realism at a low, low price! This big 43-inch freight is powered by latest type 2-unit lithographed steel diesel locomotive with oilless bronze bearings, die-cast drive wheels, gleaming headlamp. Dummy Diesel horns, simulated windshield wipers, plus lithographed ladders and louvers all add to its realism

Three realistically detailed molded plastic freight cars—highside gondola, box car, caboose. Run train forward or backward, fast or slow—*all by remote control.*

Built-in circuit breaker protects 45-watt transformer against shorts and overloads. UL approved. 110–120-volt 60-cycle AC only. Twelve sections of track form oval 120 in. around.
79 N 09632—Shipping weight 9 lbs.....A wonderful buy at $12.89

NEW! Marx 5-unit 35-inch Electric Freight

$9.69 New super-detailed plastic locomotive and tender. Same remote control of speed and direction as on our higher priced trains. Run train forward or back... fast or slow—*without touching track or train!* Steam-type locomotive has oilless bronze bearings, die-cast wheels, piston-rod action, headlamp. Three lithographed metal cars (hopper, tank car, caboose). UL approved 45-watt transformer (110–120-volt 60-cycle AC).
79 N 09616—With 10 track sections. Shpg. wt. 7 lbs. $9.69

102-inch oval track

244 .. SEARS, ROEBUCK AND CO.

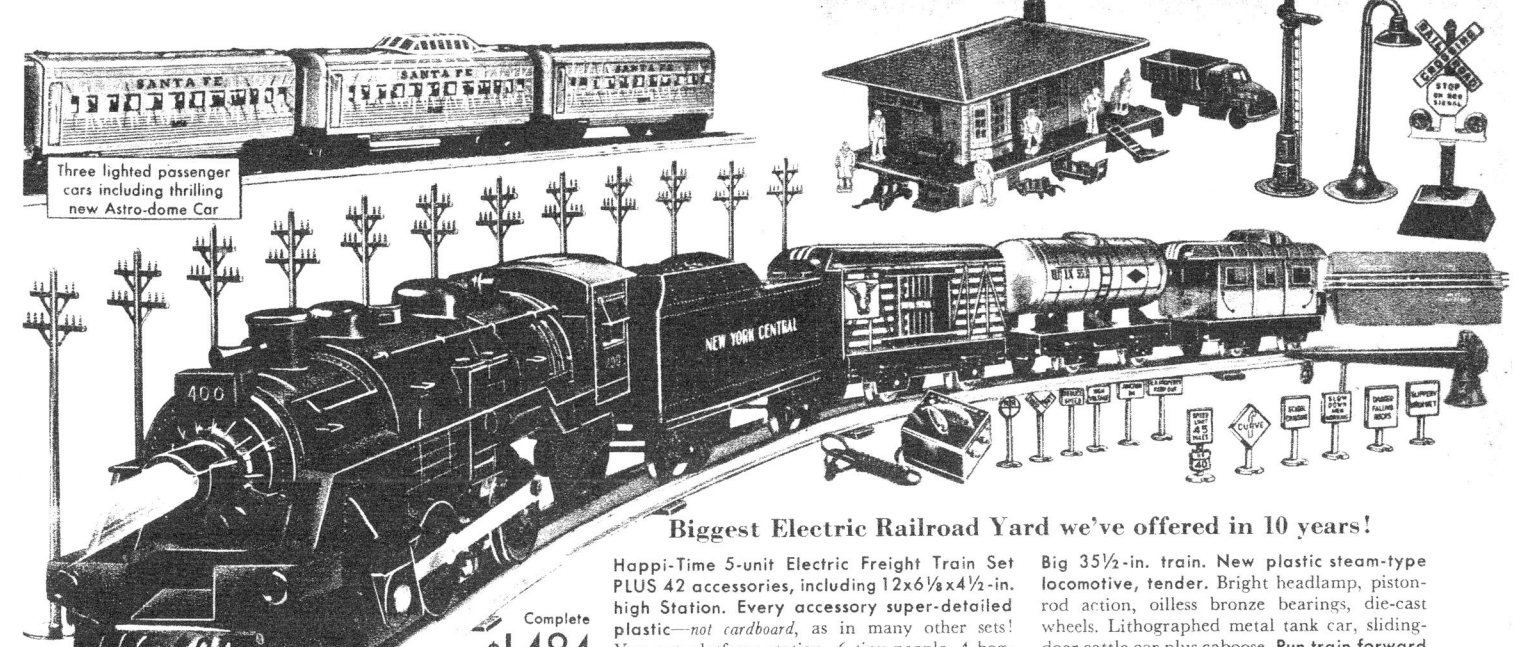

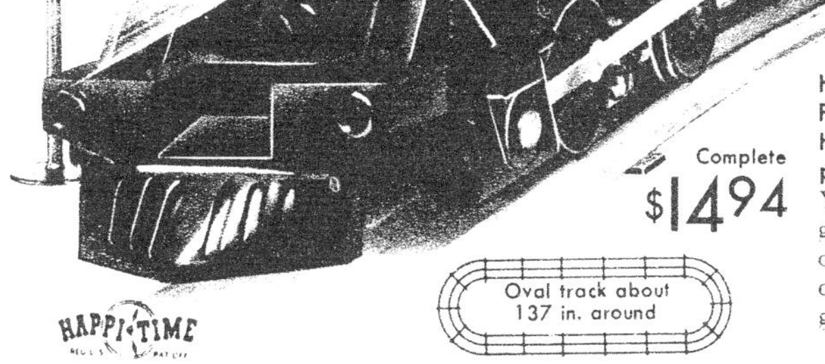

Three lighted passenger cars including thrilling new Astro-dome Car

Biggest Electric Railroad Yard we've offered in 10 years!

Complete $14.94

Happi-Time 5-unit Electric Freight Train Set PLUS 42 accessories, including 12x6⅛x4½-in. high Station. Every accessory super-detailed plastic—*not cardboard*, as in many other sets! You get platform station, 6 tiny people, 4 baggage trucks, bench, 12 telephone poles, 12 right-of-way signs, dummy scenic semaphore, lamp, crossing signal, crossing gate with moving arm, grade crossing and truck all in proportion.

Big 35½-in. train. New plastic steam-type locomotive, tender. Bright headlamp, piston-rod action, oilless bronze bearings, die-cast wheels. Lithographed metal tank car, sliding-door cattle car plus caboose. Run train forward or backward, fast or slow *by remote control*. Has 14 sections of track. 45-watt *UL approved* transformer (110-120-volt 60-cycle AC.).
79 N 09618—Shpg. wt. 9 lbs......Complete $14.94

Oval track about 137 in. around

Mechanical Trains

163-in. running track

176-inch crossover track

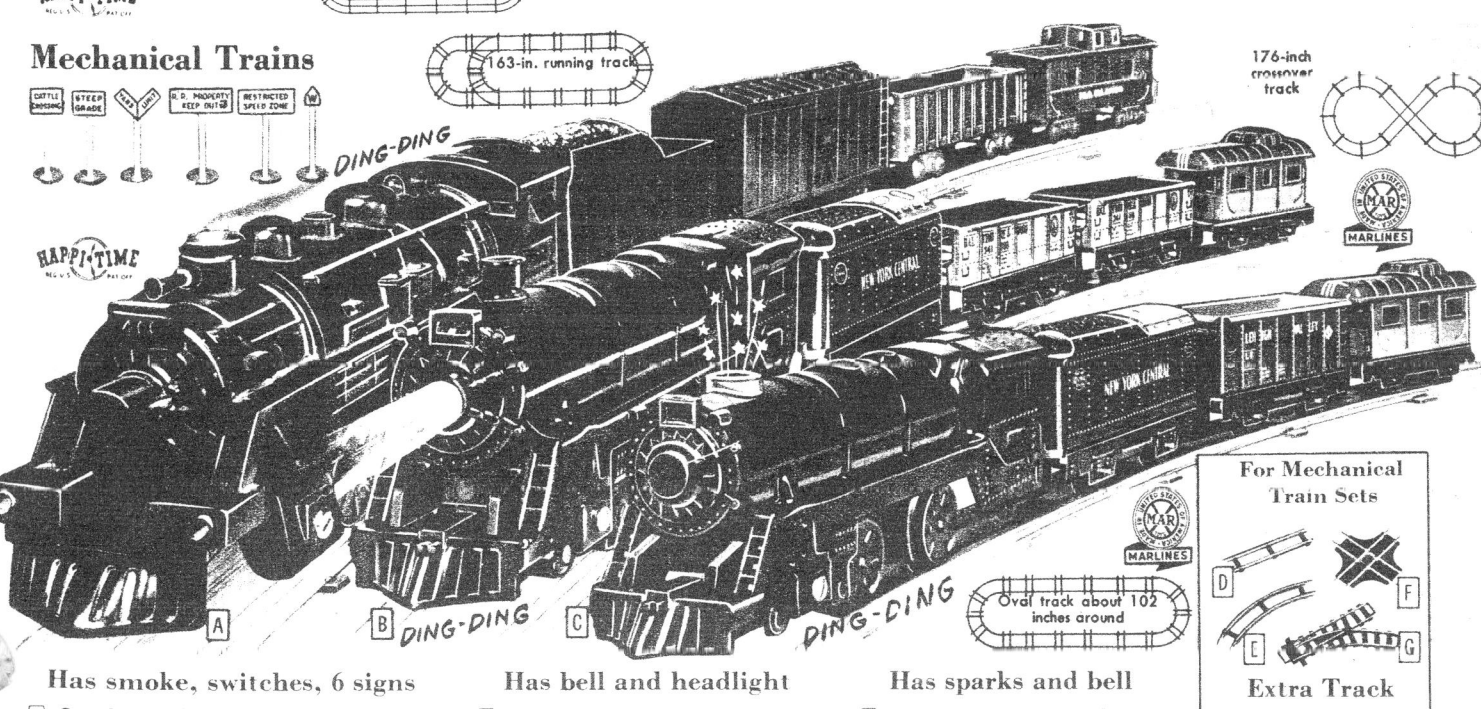

Has smoke, switches, 6 signs

[A] Our finest Happi-Time 5-unit Smoking Mechanical Freight Set. **$5.89** Super-detailed plastic locomotive, tender and cars (gondola, box car, caboose) . . . most realistic we've ever seen on any mechanical train at this price. All this *PLUS* two switches, *PLUS* 6 miniature plastic railroad signs!

Powerful steam-type locomotive with bell puffs smoke (powder) as it pulls cars around track. Run it on outer track, or switch it to inner track. Clockspring motor, speed governor, brake. Two manual switches; 14 track sections.
49 N 9513—Train 40 in. long. Shpg. wt. 4 lbs. $5.89

Has bell and headlight

[B] Marx 5-unit Mechanical Freight with Crossover **$3.94** Track. Steel steam-type locomotive has headlight, bell, realistically detailed plastic front. Powerful, long-running clockspring motor, built-in speed governor and brake.

Lithographed steel tender, 2 gondolas and caboose. Train is 35 in. long. Has 16 sections track PLUS mechanical crossover section. No battery; order below.
49 N 9507—Shpg. wt. 3 lbs. 8 oz.....$3.94
34 N 4659—Batteries. Shpg. wt. 4 oz. 2 for 23c

Has sparks and bell

[C] Marx 4-unit Mechanical Freight, **$2.94** 28¾ inches long. Watch it whiz around its 102-inch oval track, *tiny harmless sparks shooting out, its merry little bell ringing!*

Steel steam-type locomotive with accurately detailed plastic nose-piece. Long-running clockspring motor with built-in speed governor and brake. Lithographed metal tender, gondola, caboose. 10 track sections.
49 N 9503—Shpg. wt. 2 lbs. 8 oz. $2.94

Oval track about 102 inches around

For Mechanical Train Sets

Extra Track

[D] **Straight Track.** 8⅞ in. Shpg. wt. 6 oz.
49N9701—Set of 4, 35c

[E] **Curved Track.** 10 in. Shpg. wt. 6 oz.
49N9702—Set of 4, 35c

[F] **90° Crossover.** 7½ in. Shpg. wt. 8 oz.
49 N 9703....Each 59c

[G] **Manual Switch Set.** One left and one right-hand switch. Shpg. wt. 1 lb.
49 N 9704....Set $1.79

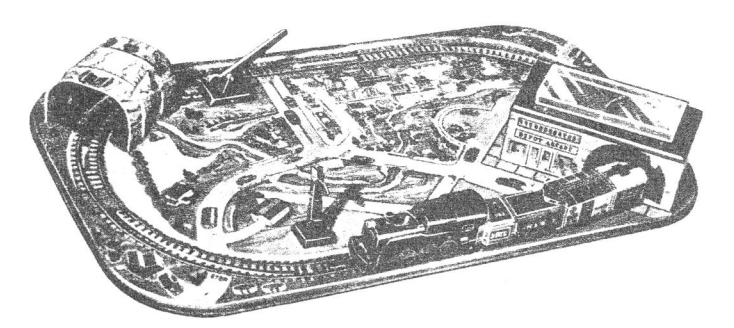

Exciting Scenic Express with Action Signals

$2.75 A complete railroad system, for younger children, with signals that really work! Action crossing gate and semaphore automatically raise and lower as 11-inch train whizzes by. All the thrills and excitement of a big railroad!

Train runs around grooved track in base over 20 times with just one winding. Watch it speed through tunnel and station. Train has long-running clockspring motor. Sturdy steel base, about 21¾x13 inches, realistically lithographed with landscape scene. A wonderful gift at this low price.
49 N 9515—Shipping weight 3 pounds.............$2.75

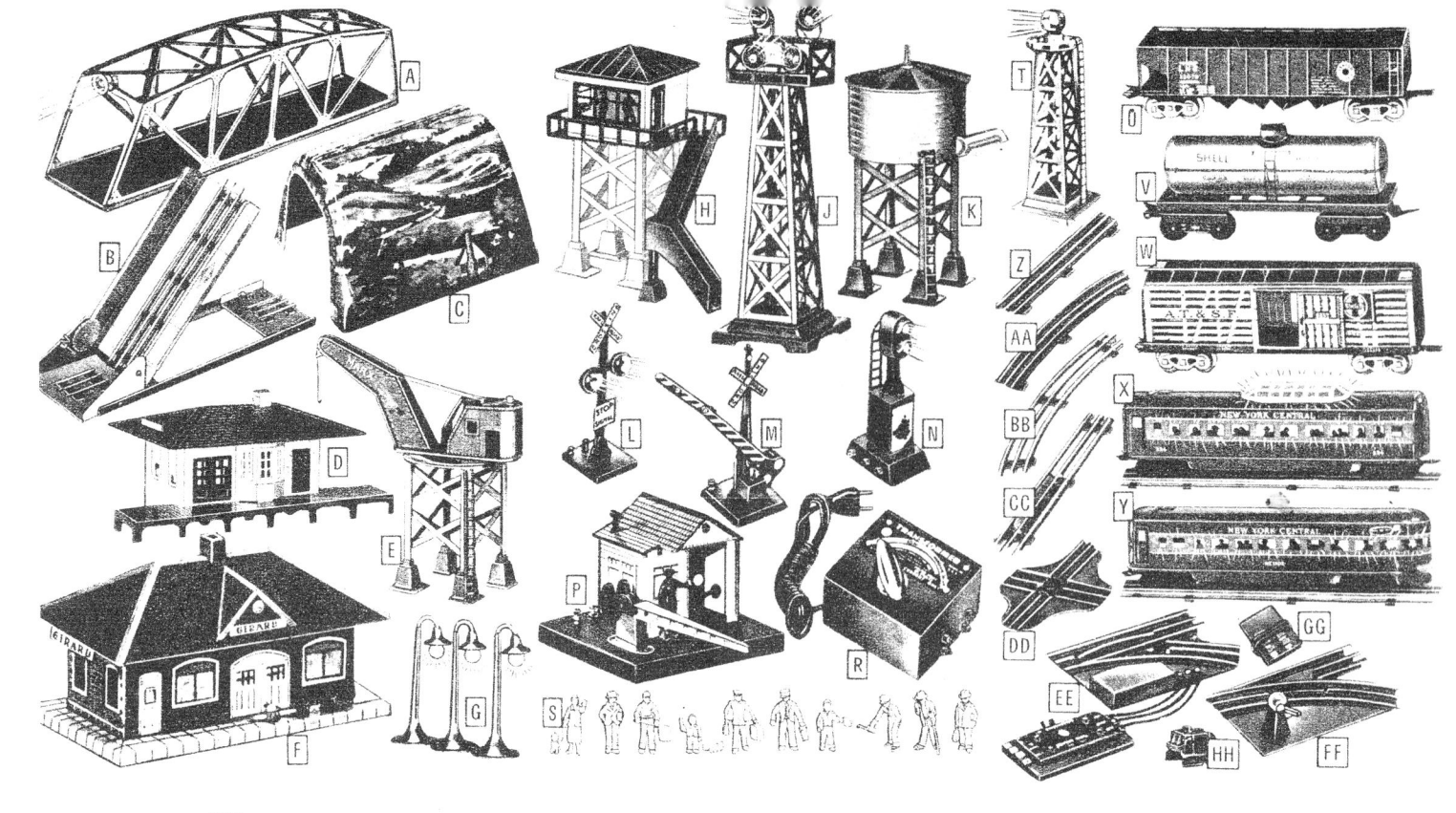

Thrilling, true-to-life Accessories for Marx and Happi-Time Electric Trains

NOTE: Items (C), (D), (E) and (K) may also be used with mechanical trains. Asterisk (*) after item means that all necessary wire, track connectors etc., are included.

[A] **Lighted all-steel Trestle Bridge.*** Aluminum finish. Embossed rivets. Light socket and reflector clip on anywhere; adjusts to any position. With bulb.
49 N 9741—24x4⅞x6⅛ in. high. Wt. 2 lbs.... **$1.98**

[B] **All-steel Railroad Lift Bridge.*** Girder type; rivets embossed. Enameled in authentic colors. Built-in track. Gear and crank raises and lowers bridge.
49 N 9761—18¾x5¼x3 in. high. Wt. 3 lbs.... **$2.98**

[C] **Collapsible Metal Tunnel.** Lithographed landscape.
49 N 9729—10¾x9x7 in. Wt. 1 lb.... **89c**

[D] **Railroad Station with Platform.** Plastic.
49 N 9719—11x6x4½ in. high. Shpg. wt. 10-oz. **89c**

[E] **Plastic Derrick Loader.** Scale-detailed. Crane housing swings in complete circle. Boom has crank handle; raises, lowers loads. Die-cast hook.
49 N 9733—8½ in. high. Shpg. wt. 10 oz..... **$1.49**

[F] **Whistling Metal Station.*** Press remote control button ... hear the realistic wail of locomotive whistle as train whizzes down the track. Whistle is built into 9x5¼x 5-in. high lithographed steel station.
49 N 9766—With control panel. Shpg. wt. 2 lbs. **$4.49**

[G] **Three Lighted 6-in. Station Lamps.*** Fluted plastic.
49N9728—With bulbs. Shpg. wt. 6 oz. Set of 3 **1.79**

[H] **Automatic Switchman's Tower.*** As train nears, switchman with green flag comes through door; second man inside moves to switch controls.
49 N 9757 Plastic; 7½ in. high. Shpg. wt. 1 lb. **$3.79**

[J] **4-light Floodlight Tower.*** Four lights mounted on double platform on girder-type plastic tower. Lights may be revolved, tilted. Metal ladder.
49 N 9751—Height 13½ in. Shpg. wt. 1 lb.... **$2.95**

[K] **Big 8¼-in. Plastic Water Tower with Adjustable Spout.** Realistic ribs; girder-type understructure.
49 N 9731—Tank 4¼ in. diam. Shpg. wt. 10 oz... **89c**

[L] **Automatic Crossing Flasher.*** Twin lights flash alternately from one side to other as train passes.
49 N 9742—Metal; 7¾ in. high. Shpg. wt. 10 oz. **$1.89**

[M] **Automatic Crossing Gate.*** Striped arm lowers as train passes, then raises. Red jewel at end of gate.
49 N 9743—Metal; 7½ in. high. Shpg. wt. 1 lb. **$1.89**

[N] **Automatic Block Signal.*** Train stops on red light, proceeds on green. Die-cast base; 2-track section. Chrome-finish ladder. Switch at rear operates signal.
49 N 9745—Metal; 7 in. high. Shpg. wt. 1 lb. **$2.19**

[P] **Automatic Grade Crossing Shack with Watchman.*** Lithographed steel shanty; 8½-in. plastic gate. As train nears, watchman comes out with "STOP" sign, gate lowers. Base 7x6½ in.; house 4½ in. high.
49 N 9760—Shipping weight 2 lbs. 8 oz...... **$3.79**

[R] **Transformer.*** 50-watt input 110-120-volt, 60-cycle AC only. Two sets of binding posts give variable 7 to 13 volts for controlling train plus 13 volts for accessories. Built-in circuit breaker. Red re-set button. Cord.
49 N 9725—UL approved. Shpg. wt. 3 lbs. 4 oz. **$5.79**

[S] **10 Plastic Figures:** Engineer, porter, conductor, newsboy etc. Soft Vinyl plastic up to 1½ in. high.
49 N 9762—Lifelike poses. Shpg. wt. 10 oz. Set **88c**

[T] **Lighted Revolving Beacon.*** Revolves on top of girder-type molded plastic tower. Red, green reflector.
49 N 9740—12½ in. high. Shpg. wt. 1 lb...... **$1.89**

Scale detailed plastic CARS for Marx or Happi-Time Electric Trains. Automatic Couplers for remote control. If your train has manual couplers, order 49 N 9713, (CC) below.

[U] 49 N 9723—8¾-inch Hopper Car. Shpg. wt. 10 oz. **$1.79**
[V] 49 N 9722—8½-inch Tank Car. Shpg. wt. 10 oz. **1.79**
[W] 49 N 9721—8½-inch Box Car. Shpg. wt. 10 oz. **1.79**

Lighted Pullman Cars. Detailed, lithographed metal.
[X] 49N9770—11-in. Astro-dome Car. Wt. 14 oz. **$3.79**
[Y] 49N9771—10¾-in. Observation Car. Wt. 14 oz. **3.79**

Extra Track for Electric Trains. Shipping weight 4 oz. each.
[Z] 49 N 9710—8⅞-in. Straight Track....... Each **18c**
[AA] 49 N 9711—10-in. Standard Curved Track... Ea. **18c**
[BB] 49N9712—12½-in. Large Radius Curved Track. Ea. **23c**
[CC] **Uncoupling Unit.** Built into standard length electric straight track. "Uncouple Here" sign included.
49 N 9713—Shipping weight 5 oz......... Each **55c**
[DD] 49 N 9714—7½-in. Crossover. Shpg. wt. 8 oz. **75c**
[EE] **Electric Remote Control Switch Set.*** One left- and one right-hand switch plus control panel.
49 N 9716—Shipping weight 2 lbs. 8 oz..... Set **$6.79**
[FF] **Manual Switch Set.** One left-, one right-hand.
49 N 9715—Shipping weight 2 pounds. Set **2.95**
[GG] **Track Connector.*** Brings power from transformer to track, or takes power from track for accessories.
49N9709—Bakelite; 1¾x1⅛ in. Shpg. wt. 2 oz. Each **12c**
[HH] **Lighted Dead-End Bumper.*** Plastic; 3x1⅞x2 in. high. Snaps to track; cars stay on track on spur.
49 N 9707—Bulb included. Shpg. wt. 5 oz... Each **89c**

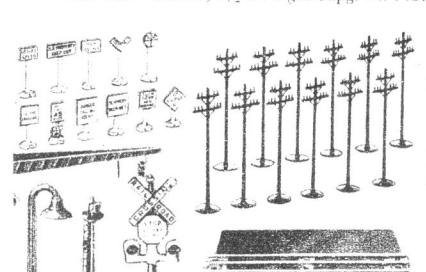

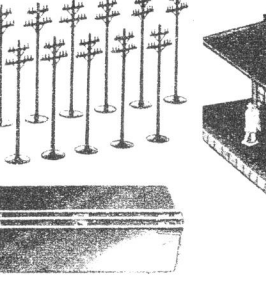

29-piece Accessory Set

Perfect for adding realism to his train set! Authentically scale-detailed in sturdy plastic. Just the right size for any standard electric or mechanical train set.
Set includes: Twelve 7-in. telegraph poles, 12 railroad right-of-way signs, PLUS one each of the following: semaphore, lamp post, crossing gate, grade crossing, railroad crossing sign. Track not included. The low cost way to add realism to your train set!
49 N 9750—Shpg. wt. 2 lbs...... Set **$2.89**

Station with Accessories

What a wonderful way to add greater realism to his mechanical or electric train set! Big 20½x10x6½-in. high station of sturdy steel. Colorfully lithographed to show waiting room, express office, baggage room, freight office, etc. Platform and ramp for inbound freight. Simulated shingled roof, and brick sides. Dummy windows. Easily assembled without tools. Six vinyl plastic figures included! Tiny, scale-size passenger, porter, etc. All this for a low price!
49 N 9756—Shpg. wt. 3 lbs...... Complete **$1.98**

Buy on Sears Easy Terms ... see page 369.

Authentic Marx Electric Locomotives

Realistically detailed molded plastic with authentic markings. Die-cast wheels; oilless bronze bearings. Bright headlamps. Powerful 110-120-volt 60-cycle AC motors. Remote control speed and reversing.

[JJ] **Scale-model Twin-Diesel.** Dummy twin horns, dummy louvers ... and a host of other true-to-life details. Single motor. Two 4-wheel trucks per car (16 wheels in all). Remote control Automatic Couplers.
49 N 9792—Overall length 24½ in. Shipping weight 3 lbs. 14 oz.... Ea. **$12.95**

[KK] **³⁄₁₆-inch Scale-model Heavy Freight Steam-type Locomotive.** Fourteen wheels; powerful 6-wheel drive; two 4-wheel trucks. Compound piston-rod action. Scale-detailed plastic tender has Automatic Couplers, 8 wheels.
49 N 9791—Overall length 18 inches. Shipping weight 3 lbs.... Each **$12.95**

[LL] **Plastic Steam-type Loco., Tender.** 4-wheel drive. Manual couplers.
49 N 9790—Overall length 15½ inches. Shpg. wt. 1 lb.... Each **6.95**

SEARS CHRISTMAS CATALOG

1954

By 1954, electric trains had taken up a large portion of the Wishbook's toy section. Trains for sale ranged from expensive and elaborate sets down to a 27-inch rubber train for toddlers... "washable and sanitary" too! Trains were fast becoming the gift for kids of all ages.

Increasingly, Sears offered its customers individual engines and cars designed to be added to existing home layouts. Such new items for 1954 included Lionel's now-classic "Section Gang" car which could transport its miniature track repairman anywhere they were needed, and a line of new diesel locomotives like the big 16 ½-inch long Fairbanks-Morse "double-ender". Marx offered its own line of locos and diesels for upgrading earlier sets.

Lionel, Marx and Sears' own Happi-Time accessories filled a full page. A beautifully lithographed tin Girard Station, which whistled by remote control, sold for just $4.49.

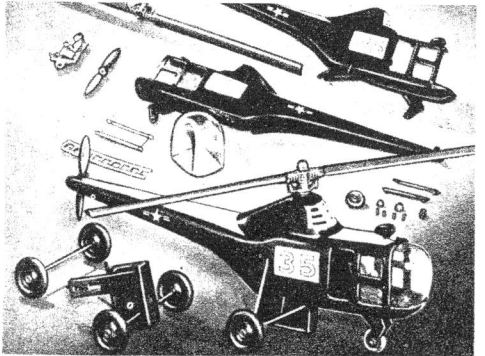

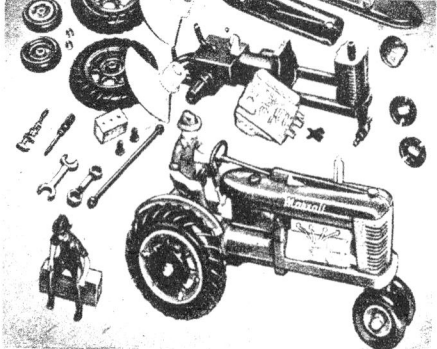

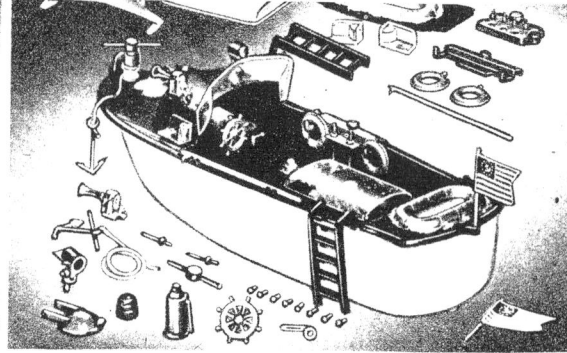

TAKE-APART Toys—the play-filled answer to "What makes it tick"?

Friction-motor Helicopter. Kit is easy to assemble and take apart .. no glue needed. Metal and plastic parts easily assembled with screws. Gyro-friction motor rotates propeller as helicopter taxis along floor. 15x6½ in. high; rotor blade span 17 in. With pilot, ladder, stretcher. **$3.83**
49 N 5390—Instructions included. Wt. 1 lb. 4 oz... $3.83

Fix-All Farm Tractor. Simple for young mechanics to take apart and put together again. Replica of 4-wheel cultivator-type tractor. Four miniature tools in tool box ... use for taking tractor apart. Durable plastic, finely detailed. Makes clicker noise when you push it on floor. **$1.89**
49 N 5313—6 in. high. Shpg. wt. 1 lb.......... $1.89

NEW Harbor Launch. Young ship enthusiasts will have hours of constructive fun taking apart this 36-piece floating model ... putting it ship-shape again. Sturdy plastic, with metal screws. Intriguing parts such as life raft, compass that works, anchor, grappling hooks, etc. 14 in. long. **$2.83**
49 N 5032—Shipping weight 1 lb. 8 oz........ $2.83

Phone Repair Truck with Elevator

A new truck with lots of action. Elevator platform raises so "workmen" can reach telephone lines. Winch on rear. Completely equipped with ladder and repair tools. Little "linemen" will have hours of fun "at work" with this truck. Made of strong plastic with steel frame. 13 in. long. Platform raises to height of 7 inches.
49 N 5252—Wt. 2 lbs. 4 oz. $2.83

NEW Giant Size Aircraft Carrier

Huge 36-inch long "flat-top." All metal with lithographed details. Moves on concealed wheels. Realistic action parts—elevator in ship to raise planes from storage to carrier deck. Movable dummy radar screen. Three 5½-in. planes: Rocket plane shoots 4 rockets individually; Machine-gun plane shoots pellets; Bomber drops bomb. **$3.85**
49 N 5176—Wt. 8 lbs...... $3.85

Elevator to raise and lower planes to and from deck

NEW All Steel Trucking Set

4-piece transportation outfit built of steel. Sized just right for small hands. Each about 8½ in. long. Set includes livestock carrier, refrigerator trailer with cab, fire engine with two removable ladders, and auto transport. Two plastic cars fit onto transport's double decks. All trailers swivel, are detachable. Easy-rolling rubber wheels.
49 N 5120—Shpg. wt. 2 lbs. $1.98

Set **$1.98**

Simple hand controls operate body, mouth to produce comical capers and actions

There's fun for the whole family with these lifelike Marionettes. Hand movements control mouth and body ... give real lifelike motion as you make them "dance," "walk," and "talk." Costumes are authentically designed of cotton. Composition heads and body parts. Just follow the instructions, and you will soon be a skillful marionette operator.
A NEW FAVORITE is added this year... lovable **PINOCCHIO**, with roving eyes, adjustable vinyl nose, moving mouth. He's an authentic replica of Gepetto's boy! Provides hours of playful fun. Order now!

(A) **Howdy Doody**©—16½ in. tall.
49 N 5161—Shipping weight 1 lb.............. $2.99

(B) **Clarabell**—14½ inches tall.
49 N 5160—Shipping weight 1 lb.............. $2.49

(C) **Peter Pan**—16½ in. tall.
49 N 5093—Shipping weight 1 lb.............. $2.49

(D) **Pinocchio**—13½ in. tall.
49 N 5162—Shipping weight 1 lb.............. 2.49

©Kagran

For a truly welcome gift, order now for the small tots on your Christmas list

$1.59

27-inch Rubber Train .. Washable .. Sanitary

Especially fine for the youngest tots. Rubber construction means it's practically unbreakable ... and it's easy on the furniture; won't scratch or mar. Sanitary, too, since it's washable. No tracks needed, pull it along the floor. One-piece engine and tender with 6 wheels; dump car with real dumping action, gondola, and caboose. Four quiet, easy-rolling wheels on each car. Sturdy rubber couplers between all cars. Brightly colored to keep tots quietly amused for many hours. Overall length of train 27 inches. Shipping weight 2 lbs. 4 oz.
49 N 5085.................... $1.59

MNK PAGE 223 .. TOYS

It pays to buy Lionel!
- Scale-detailed die-cast locomotives, all with Magne-Traction!
- Realistic plastic cars with die-cast metal trucks, 8 steel wheels
- Exclusive Lionel remote-control electro-magnetic knuckle couplers
- Built-in circuit breakers and direction controls on transformers

[A] **$29.95**
Cash or Terms
Postpaid—$3.00 Down

Both trains have 114-in. of track

LIONEL
Electric Trains
with magne-traction

Magne-Traction
- Far greater speeds without derailment
- Far better grade-climbing ability
- Greater power for pulling more cars
- Accurate control of starts and stops

[B] **$39.95**
Cash or Terms
Postpaid—$4.00 Down

6-unit "027" Electric Freight with smoke

[A] **Puffs harmless white smoke as it runs!** Powerful 12-wheel scale-detailed die-cast metal locomotive with 6-wheel drive, piston-rod action, bright headlamp, *plus Magne-Traction*. Realistic plastic tender and 4 cars; gondola, oil car, colorful box car, caboose. Run train forward or backward, fast or slow . . . couple and uncouple cars—*all by remote control!* UL approved 50-watt transformer with built-in circuit breaker (110-120-volt, 60-cycle AC); 12 sections "027" track.
79 N 09659T—Train is full 51½ in. long. (Shipping weight 14 lbs.) *Postpaid* $29.95

6-unit "027" Electric Freight with smoke and whistle

[B] **Puffs harmless white smoke!** Blow its built-in whistle; run train forward and backward, fast or slow, couple and uncouple cars—*all by remote control!* Giant 14-wheel die-cast metal locomotive with powerful 6-wheel drive *plus Magne-Traction*, piston-rod action, gleaming headlamp. Realistically-detailed tender and 4 cars: gondola with 6 barrels, oil car, hopper car, caboose. UL approved 90-watt transformer (110-120-volt, 60-cycle AC) with built-in circuit breaker and whistle controller; 12 sections "027" track.
79 N 09664T—Train is 55 in. long. (Shipping weight 16 lbs.) . . . . *Postpaid* $39.95

$49.95
Cash or Terms
Postpaid—$5.00 Down

New 5-unit Diesel Work Train

Powerful, scale-detailed die-cast Switcher Engine has plastic cab, worm-drive motor, *plus Magne-Traction* for pin-point control of yard work. Use it to make or break up trains. Run fast or slow, forward or back, couple and uncouple—*all by remote control!* Couplers at front and rear. Front and rear lights. Four "most-wanted" cars: 8⅜-inch operating crane car with die-cast chassis (Crane swings in circle, boom raises and lowers, pulley block lifts), pipe-carrying car, hopper, caboose. UL approved 75-watt transformer with built-in circuit breaker (110-120-volt, 60-cycle AC); 14 sections "027" track.
79 N 09670T—Train is 49 inches long. (Shpg. wt. 16 lbs.) . . *Postpaid* $49.95

Oval track 131 in. around

Lighted caboose

LIONEL MAGNE-TRACTION

Oval track 131 in. around

BEEP BEEP

$59.95
Cash or Terms
Postpaid—$6.00 Down

65-inch 6-unit Twin-Diesel Electric Freight . . . an accurate scale model of real equipment!

So realistically detailed even seasoned trainmen marvel at its blueprint accuracy. You'll thrill as you watch it thunder down the rails, alive with flashing action—wheels clicking, deep-throated horn wailing mournfully! Run train forward or back, fast or slow . . . sound its horn . . . couple and uncouple cars—*all by remote control*. And, with amazing *Magne-Traction*, it'll match the speed of any mainline train (scale for scale), climb steeper grades, take sharper curves, start and stop more realistically.

- **Super-powered, die-cast, scale-detailed Twin Diesel locomotive** with plastic cab is over 2 feet long! Die-cast metal frame, trucks; 8 solid steel wheels per section. Worm drive with wide range of speeds. Authentic railroad markings. True-to-life details—transparent plastic windshield, dummy windshield wipers, dummy horn on Diesel cab, louvers, ladders, stanchions. Remote-control couplers.
- **Four realistic plastic cars;** die-cast metal trucks, 8 solid steel wheels, knuckle-type couplers. Sliding-door box car, gondola, cable car with 2 reels, lighted caboose. UL approved 90-watt transformer with built-in circuit breaker and control for built-in horn (110-120-volt, 60-cycle AC); 14 sections "027" track.
79 N 09671KT—Train is 65 inches long. (Shipping weight 21 lbs.) *Postpaid* $59.95

New "Section Gang" Car

Built-in motor works on "027" or "O"-gauge track like a locomotive. When buffer plate at either end strikes bumper or similar object, car reverses direction, "gandy dancers" turn to direction of travel. Realistically detailed in plastic. 4¾ in. long. (Shpg. wt. 2 lbs.)
49 N 9846 . . . . *Postpaid* $7.95

$7.95
Postpaid

K PAGE 261 . . LIONEL TRAINS

Lionel Electric Trains and Accessories

WOO-O-O-O
WOO-O O-O
BEEP BEEP

$69.50 Postpaid $7.00 Down — B
Trains [A] and [B] described on opposite page

Operating Lumber Car with logs and bin included!
Touch Remote-Control button. Steel stakes drop, bottom tilts up, logs roll out

C $8.95 Postpaid

Automatic Barrel Loader with 6 barrels. Set barrels upright on lower platform . . they move to workman who tips them over onto elevated runway leading to upper platform. Barrels roll off upper platform into car. Length 19 in. Car and track not included.
49 N 9840—(Shpg. wt. 3 lbs.) *Postpaid*. .$8.95

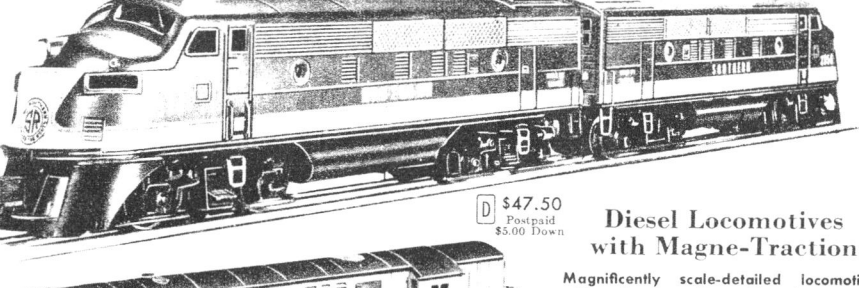

D $47.50 Postpaid $5.00 Down
E $43.50 Postpaid $4.50 Down 
F $25.00 Postpaid $2.50 Down 
G $10.95 Postpaid
H $10.95 Postpaid
J $10.95 Postpaid

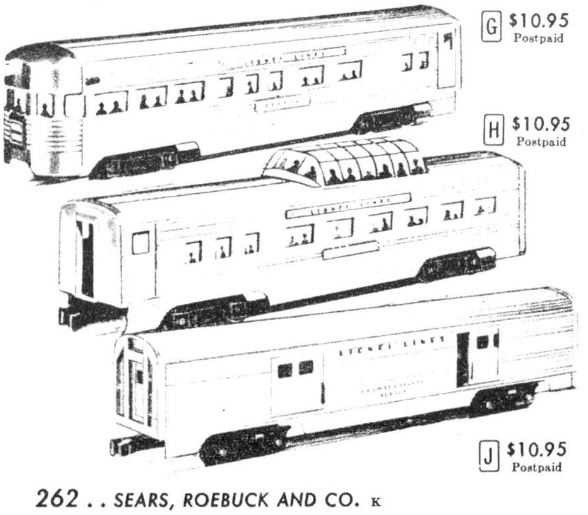

Diesel Locomotives with Magne-Traction

Magnificently scale-detailed locomotives with authentic markings, blueprint accuracy of detail. Lionel Magne-Traction gives greater power for pulling more cars, better grade climbing, greater speeds without derailment, realistic slow starts, pin-point stops. Silent, super-powered worm-drive motors. Bright headlamps. Remote-control electric knuckle couplers

D 26½-in. Southern R.R. Twin-Diesel with remote-control electric horn plus Magne-Traction. Super-powered twin motors; 4-wheel drive. Accurately detailed plastic cabs. Dummy windshield wipers, ladders, stanchions, louvers. Lighted number box. Eight steel wheels (2 trucks) per section. *For "O" gauge track.*
79 N 09897T—(Wt. 11 lbs.). *Postpaid* $47.50

E Brand New . . 16½-inch Fairbanks-Morse "double-ender" Diesel with two motors, built-in horn, bright headlamps at both ends, *plus Magne-Traction* for extra power. Unsurpassed for speed and pulling power. Accurately detailed plastic cab; metal railing. Lighted marker lights and number box. Couplers at both ends. Two 6-wheel trucks, each with own 6-wheel worm-drive motor. *For "O" gauge only.*
49 N 9896T—(Wt. 10 lbs.). *Postpaid* $43.50

F 11⅝-inch Diesel Yard Switcher with Magne-Traction. Authentically detailed in plastic; metal railing. Bright headlamp. Couplers at both ends. Powerful worm-drive motor. Two 4-wheel trucks . . 8 wheels in all. *For "O" or "027" gauge.*
49 N 9890T—(Wt. 5 lbs.). *Postpaid* $25.00

Authentic, scale-detailed 16-inch Lighted Pullmans

Accurately detailed in extruded aluminum . . . sleek, beautiful! Brightly lighted interiors (bulbs included) for Cars (G) and (H) with tiny passengers looking out of clear plastic windows. Die-cast metal trucks; 8 solid steel wheels. Remote-control knuckle-type electric couplers

G Observation Car. (Shpg. wt. 3 lbs.)
49 N 9855—*Postpaid*......Each $10.95

H Astra-Dome Car. (Shpg. wt. 3 lbs.)
49 N 9854—*Postpaid*......Each $10.95

J New Baggage Car with sliding doors but not lighted. (Shpg. wt. 3 lbs.)
49 N 9851—*Postpaid*......Each $10.95

NOTE: All Lionel items postpaid. Sears pays shipping charges. Only 10% Down on Terms. No extra charge for easy payment

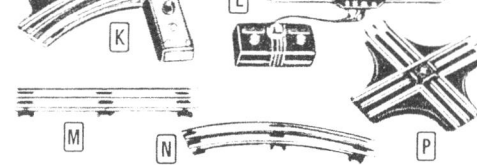

Track, Switches, 90° Crossover

K Remote Control Switches. One right-hand switch, one left-hand switch, control panel, wire included.
49 N 9806—"027" gauge. (Wt. 3 lbs.) *Postpaid*. Pr. $13.95
49 N 9815T—"O" gauge. (Wt. 5 lbs.) *Postpaid*. Pr. 22.50

L Magnetic Track Section. For remote-control coupling and uncoupling. Control panel and connecting wire included. (Shpg. wt. each 1 lb.)
49 N 9804—"027" gauge. *Postpaid*............Each $3.50
49 N 9813—"O" gauge. *Postpaid*............Each 3.95

M 8⅞-in. Straight Track Section, "027" gauge.
49 N 9801—(Shpg. wt. 3 oz.) *Postpaid*........Each 25c
10-in. Straight Track Section for "O" gauge.
49 N 9810—(Shpg. wt. 4 oz.) *Postpaid*..........Each 30c

N 9½-in. Curved Track Section, "027" gauge.
49 N 9802—(Shpg. wt. 3 oz.) *Postpaid*........Each 25c
10⅞-in. Curved Track Section for "O" gauge.
49 N 9811—(Shpg. wt. 4 oz.) *Postpaid*..........Each 30c

P 90-degree Crossover. (Shpg. wt. each 8 oz.) *Postpaid*.
49 N 9803—"027" gauge. 7⅜ in. square.....Each $1.95
49 N 9812—"O" gauge. 8¼ in. square......Each 2.95

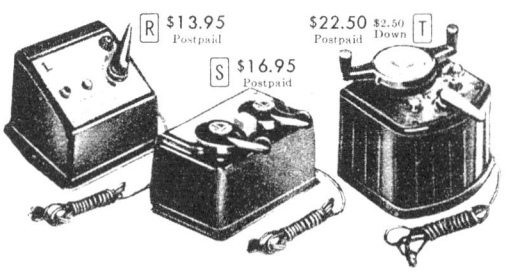

R $13.95 Postpaid
S $16.95 Postpaid
T $22.50 Postpaid $2.50 Down

"Trainmaster" Transformers

For 110-120-volt, 60-cycle AC. Built-in self-resetting automatic circuit breaker guards against overloads. Light shows when there is a short circuit. With cord.

R Type RW—110-watt. Two variable voltages for train; 4 fixed voltages for accessories. Left button blows whistle; right button controls train direction.
49 N 9820—UL approved. (Wt. 7 lbs.) *Postpaid*....$13.95

S Type TW—175-watt. One throttle controls train voltage; other for whistling, reversing. Fixed 14 and 16 volts for accessories separate from train power.
49 N 9824—UL approved. (Wt. 10 lbs.) *Postpaid* $16.95

T Type KW—190-watt. Two independently-controlled variable voltages *for running 2 trains on different layouts at same time*. Whistle and reversing control for each train. Diesel-type control levers. Fixed 6, 14 and 20-volt accessory circuits plus ample power for operating both trains!
79 N 09821T—Molded case. (Wt. 10 lbs.) *Postpaid* $22.50

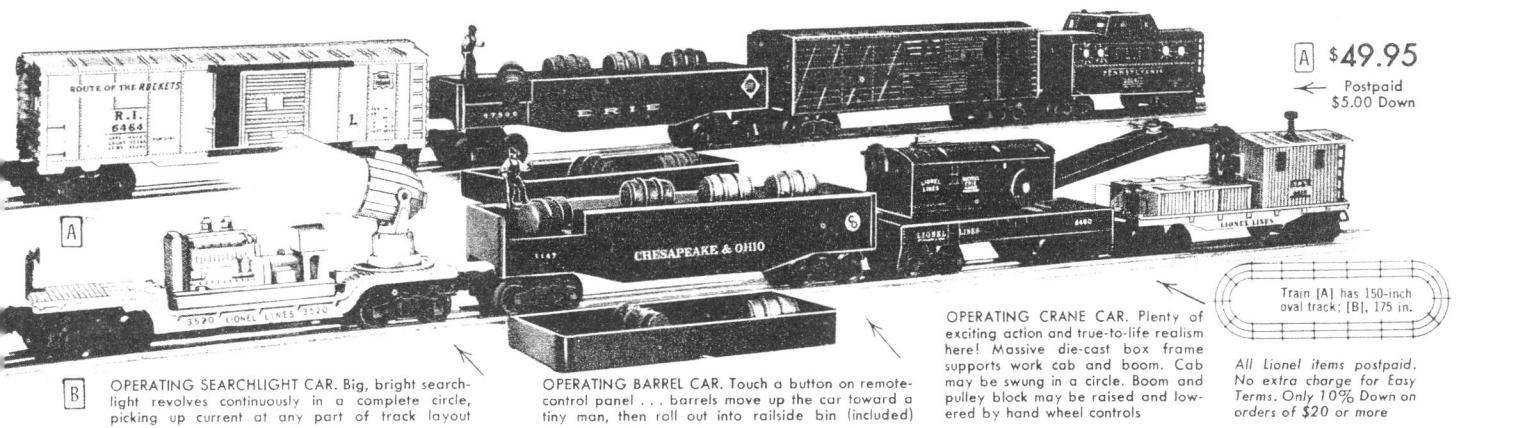

A $49.95
Postpaid
$5.00 Down

OPERATING SEARCHLIGHT CAR. Big, bright searchlight revolves continuously in a complete circle, picking up current at any part of track layout

OPERATING BARREL CAR. Touch a button on remote-control panel . . . barrels move up the car toward a tiny man, then roll out into railside bin (included)

OPERATING CRANE CAR. Plenty of exciting action and true-to-life realism here! Massive die-cast box frame supports work cab and boom. Cab may be swung in a circle. Boom and pulley block may be raised and lowered by hand wheel controls

Train [A] has 150-inch oval track; [B], 175 in.

All Lionel items postpaid. No extra charge for Easy Terms. Only 10% Down on orders of $20 or more

Big, new 6-unit "0"-gauge Electric Freight with smoke, whistle, operating barrel car

[A] New, improved, scale-detailed 20-wheel die-cast metal locomotive with Magne-Traction (shown on opposite page) for greater pulling power, speed, climb, better control. Powerful 8-wheel drive; two 6-wheel trucks; *improved* drive and side-rod action. Watch it thunder down the rails, puffing harmless white smoke . . whistle blowing . . bright headlamp piercing the night! Run it forward or backward, fast or slow . . couple and uncouple cars . . unload barrels . . sound its deep-toned whistle—*all by remote control*.

Train includes locomotive, plastic tender with built-in whistle, plus 4 scale-detailed cars: *remote-control* operating barrel car with barrels and railside bin, sliding-door box car, *new* double-deck stock car with doors, lighted caboose; 14 sections track form oval 150 in. around. No transformer; see facing page.
79 N 09683T—Train is 61 in. long. (Shpg. wt. 19 lbs.) *Postpaid* $49.95

66½-in. 7-unit "0"-ga. Steam-type Electric Work Freight with smoke, whistle, Magne-Traction, 4 operating cars

[B] One of the most amazing model electric trains we've ever offered! Every one of its cars (except caboose) actually operate! Lumber car and barrel car work *by remote control*. Big light on searchlight car operates continuously in a full circle. Hand-operated cranks on crane car raise and lower tackle and boom; cab revolves in any direction. Realistic work caboose. Every car is accurately scale detailed in metal and plastic. Each has two die-cast metal trucks, 8 solid steel wheels, plus exclusive Lionel remote-controlled magnetic couplers.

Powerful scale-detailed 14-wheel locomotive with 8-wheel drive, 2 trucks, realistic side-rod action, plus amazing Magne-Traction for greater pulling power, more speed, more climb, better control. Away it goes to the job—headlamp gleaming, whistle blowing, puffing harmless white smoke! Run train fast or slow, forward or back . . sound its whistle . . couple and uncouple cars . . unload lumber or barrels into 2 railside bins—*all by remote control!* Train 66½ in. long. No transformer; see facing page.
79 N 09687T—16 sections track form oval 175 in. around. (Shpg. wt. 21 lbs.) *Postpaid* $69.50

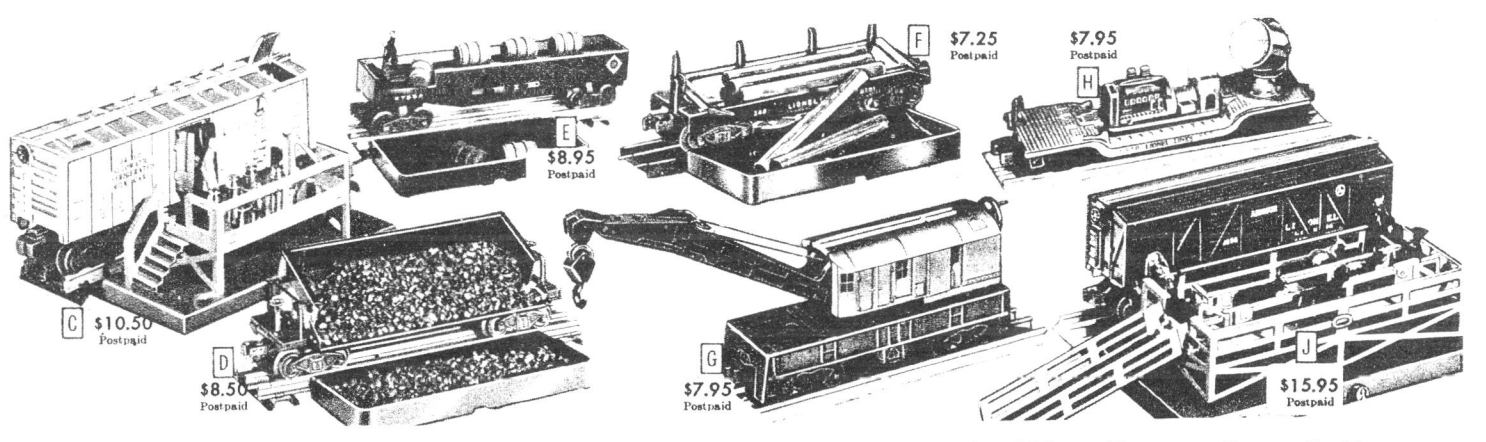

Authentic scale-detailed Lionel Operating Cars. Plenty of exciting action! Many Remote-Controlled!

All cars have 8 solid steel wheels, die-cast trucks, knuckle-type remote-control electric couplers. Track not included

[C] **8¾-in. Operating Milk Car with 5x7¼-in. steel platform.** Car doors open milkman comes out, delivers 5 milk cans to platform.
49 N 9863—Remote-controlled. With cans. (Wt. 3 lbs.). *Postpaid* $10.50

[D] **9½-in. Operating Dump Car.** Body tilts up, side drops, artificial "coal" slides into plastic bin (included). Dummy handbrakes; railing.
49 N 9862—Remote-controlled. (Shipping wt. 2 lbs.) *Postpaid* . . . $8.50

[E] **10½-in. Operating Barrel Car.** Press remote-control button; barrels move up car to little man, roll out into railside bin (included).
49 N 9865—Remote-controlled. (Shipping wt. 2 lbs.). *Postpaid* $8.95

[F] **9½-inch Operating Lumber Car.** Die-cast metal frame. Rotating brake wheel. Press remote-control button . . . steel stakes drop, bottom tilts up, logs roll out into railside bin.
49 N 9860—Logs, bin included. (Wt. 2 lbs.). *Postpaid* $7.25

[G] **7⅞-inch Crane Car.** Hand wheel controls. Crane swings in circle; boom raises and lowers; pulley block lifts.
49 N 9852—Chassis die-cast metal. (Wt. 3 lbs.). *Postpaid.* $7.95

[H] **10-inch Searchlight Car.** Powerful searchlight revolves 360° automatically. Dummy hand brake, generator. Bulb incl.
49 N 9861—Chassis die-cast metal. (Wt. 2 lbs.). *Postpaid.* $7.95

[J] **9¼-inch Operating Cattle Car and Platform.** When car stops at platform, remote-control button (included) opens doors, drops loading ramp, 9 head of cattle troop out of car, across platform, back into car. Lots of action! 13¾-inch platform and ramp. Built-in *remote-control unit* (does not require special remote-control track section). (Shipping weight 4 lbs.)
49 N 9864—*Postpaid* $15.95

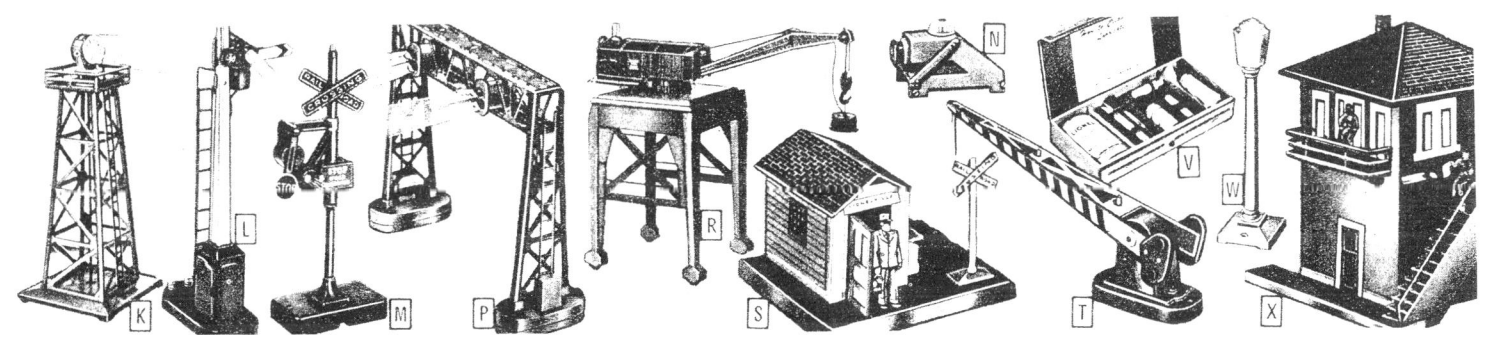

[K] **11¾-in. Rotary Beacon.** Embossed lattice-work steel structure has platform on top, ladder on side. Motorized unit revolves powerful miniature searchlight. Red and green fresnel-type lenses rotate over light. Bulb included. (Shipping weight 2 lbs.)
49 N 9843—*Postpaid* $4.50

[L] **9⅞-in. Automatic Semaphore.** As train nears, blade shoots upright, bull's eye glows green. After last car passes, blade drops down, red light shows. *Postpaid.*
49 N 9844—(Wt. 2 lbs.) $4.50

[M] **8-inch Automatic Banjo Signal.** As train nears, signal lights up, banjo "Stop" sign swings back and forth over light. *Postpaid.*
49 N 9827— (Shpg. wt. 1 lb.) . . . $5.95

[N] **Illuminated Bumper.** For "027" and "0"-gauge track. *Postpaid.*
49 N 9859—(Wt. 1 lb.) $1.95

[P] **Operating Signal Bridge.** Spans 2 tracks. Lights work automatically by running of train, or may be run by remote control. Sturdy girders, ladders. 10½x3x7¾ in. high. With 4 bulbs, wire. *Postpaid.*
49 N 9836—(Shpg. wt. 2 lbs.) $5.95

[R] **New Electro-magnetic Portal Crane.** Scale-detailed plastic. Spans track. Three control levers to turn magnet on or off, raise or lower it, revolve cab. Turn magnet on to lift heavy metal loads, off to dump . . . *by remote control.* Do not order before Nov. 1st.
49N9847—5x5x15 in. high. (Wt. 7 lbs.) *Ppd.* $15.95

[S] **Illuminated Automatic Gateman.** As train nears, shack door opens, gateman rushes out swinging his lantern. After train has passed, gateman returns to shack, door closes. Metal base; plastic shack, man.
49N9835—6¾ in. high. (Wt. 2 lbs.) *Postpaid* $5.95

[T] **Illuminated Crossing Gate.** Automatically lowers as train nears, raises after train has passed. Scale-size imitation jewels in 9¾-in. arm glow.
49 N 9830—With bulb. (Wt. 1 lb.) *Postpaid.* $3.95

[V] **Lubrication and Maintenance Kit.** Tube of lubricant, vial of oil, can of solvent, 2 cleaning sticks, 6 emery boards, wiping cloth, smokestack cleaner, brush, instructions.
49 N 9826—(Wt. 1 lb.). *Postpaid* $1.75

[W] **6-inch Lamp Post.** Die-cast metal. Plastic globe, bulb, wire included.
49 N 9825—(Wt. 1 lb.). *Postpaid* 95c

[X] **Automatic Switch Tower.** Train nears, one man enters tower . . . other walks down stairs. Train passes, they return. Clapboard sides, shingle roof, railed platform. (Wt. 2 lbs.)
49 N 9841—7 in. high. *Postpaid* $7.95

K PAGE 263 . . LIONEL ACCESSORIES

Happi-Time Electric Trains

9-unit Scale-detailed Electric Passenger and Freight

Two remote control switches PLUS 23 track sections give 21-ft. track on Happi-Time Train 79 N 09634

Actually 2 trains in 1—over 7 ft. long! Three lighted passenger cars alone would be $11.37, if sold separately!

$25.49 Cash
$3.00 Down
with 18 sections track

$32.59 Cash
$3.50 Down
with 23 sections of track plus remote control switches

Our finest Happi-Time Electric Train with magnificent 14-wheel scale-detailed plastic steam-type locomotive. Powerful 6-wheel drive, two 4-wheel guide trucks, gleaming headlamp, die-cast wheels, realistic piston-rod action, oilless bronze bearings. Plastic tender. **Seven scale-detailed cars,** each with two 4-wheel trucks (8 wheels) plus automatic couplers. Plastic sliding-door box car, 3-dome tank car, hopper, caboose. 3 electric lighted steel passenger cars. Use freight and passenger cars separately or together. *Run train forward or back, fast or slow . . . couple and uncouple . . . open and close switches—by remote control!* UL approved 65-watt transformer (110-120-volt, 60-cycle AC) has circuit breaker, 4 posts (2 for accessories).

79 N 09634—With 2 remote-control switches, control panel, plus 23 sections of track (2 of them uncoupling sections to uncouple cars, shunt them to inner track). Shipping weight 20 lbs..... Complete Set $32.59

79 N 09633—Without switches. Has 17 track sections, uncoupling section (195-in. oval). Wt. 16 lbs. 25.49

HAPPI-TIME

Trains A and B have remote control uncoupling; couple on contact. No need to touch train

Train A has 159-inch oval track. Trains B and C have 102-inch oval track

6-unit Scale Twin-Diesel Freight

[A] Powered by authentic, scale-detailed plastic Twin-Diesel . . . 2 feet long! Locomotive has oilless bronze bearings, double trucks (8 die-cast wheels per unit), headlamp. Dummy horns, ladders, louvers. Run train forward or back, fast or slow, couple, uncouple cars *by remote control.* **Train is almost 5 feet long. Four embossed steel cars—accurate 3/16-inch scale models!** Realistically lithographed gondola, tank car, sliding-door box car and caboose. All have double trucks (8 wheels) PLUS Automatic Couplers.

UL approved 45-watt transformer; built-in circuit breaker, 4 binding posts (2 for accessories) for 110-120-volt, 60-cycle AC. Fourteen track sections make 159-inch oval.
79 N 09626—Shipping weight 12 lbs. **A grand gift at $19.59**

$19.59

6-unit Scale Electric Freight

[B] Big 47-inch Happi-Time Train with scale-detailed plastic steam-type locomotive. Piston-rod action, oilless bronze bearings, 4 die-cast wheels, bright headlamp. Scale-detailed plastic tender and 4 cars: box car, tank car, flat car with removable stakes and play merchandise, caboose. Two double trucks (8 wheels) PLUS Automatic Couplers. *Run train forward or back, fast or slow . . . couple and uncouple cars—by remote control!* Ten sections of track make 102-inch oval. UL approved 45-watt transformer with 2 posts for 7 to 13 volts; (110-120-volt, 60-cycle AC). Shipping weight 10 lbs.
79 N 09617—Complete $12.95

$12.95

Marx 5-unit Electric Freight

[C] Imagine—a complete 35-inch Electric Train Set with the same remote control of speed and direction as on our higher-priced trains, for less than $10. Powered by super-detailed plastic steam-type locomotive with oilless bronze bearings, realistic piston-rod action, 4 die-cast wheels, gleaming headlamp. **Plastic tender and 3 lithographed metal cars:** coal, tank car and caboose. Run train forward or backward, fast or slow— *by remote control without touching track or train!*

UL approved 45-watt transformer with 2 posts for 7 to 13 volts; (110-120-volt, 60-cycle AC). Ten sections of track.
79N09616—Shipping weight 8 lbs. Complete $9.69

$9.69

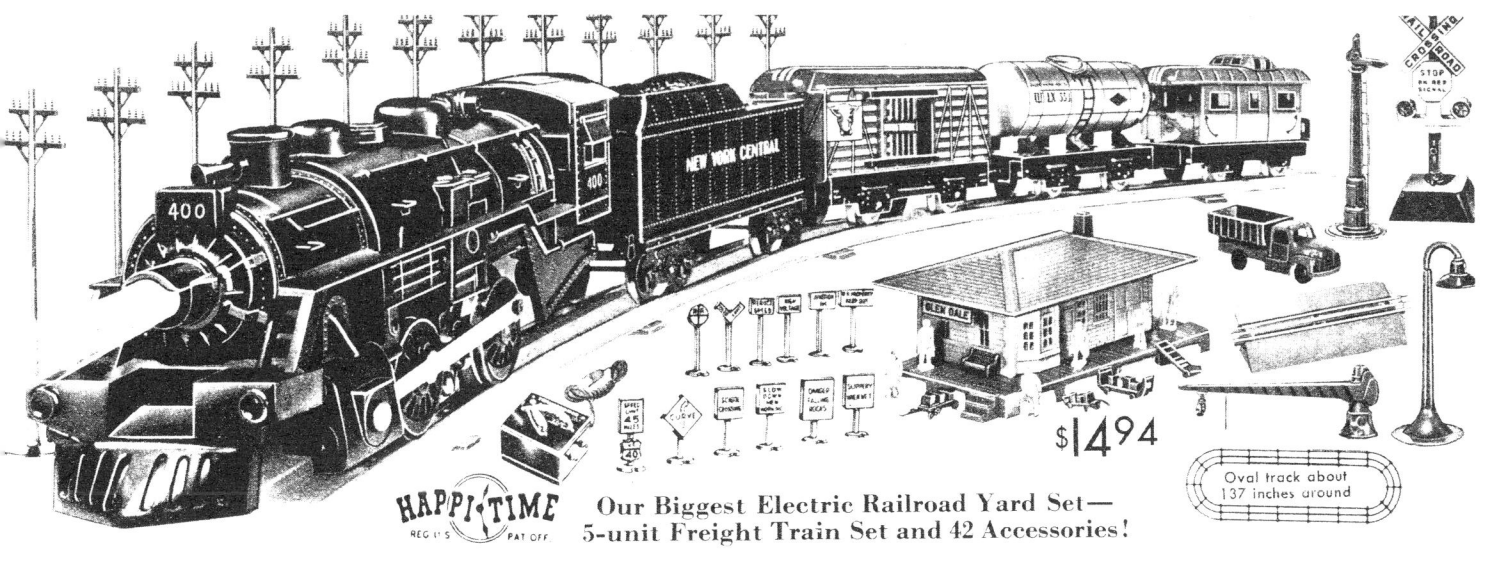

HAPPI-TIME — Our Biggest Electric Railroad Yard Set—
5-unit Freight Train Set and 42 Accessories!

$14.94

Oval track about 137 inches around

Happi-Time 5-unit Electric Freight with transformer, track, PLUS 42 Accessories, including 12x6⅛x4½-inch plastic Station. A complete railroading set that will give him months and months of pleasure. Every accessory is sturdy, super-detailed plastic—*not cardboard* as in many other sets! Accessories include station with platform, 6 tiny people, 4 baggage trucks, bench, 12 telegraph poles, 12 right-of-way signs, dummy scenic semaphore, dummy lamp, dummy crossing signal, crossing gate with movable arm, grade crossing and delivery truck.

Big 35½-inch train with steam-type plastic locomotive and coal-and-water type tender. Realistically detailed locomotive has bright headlamp, piston-rod action, oilless bronze bearings, solid die-cast wheels. Attractively lithographed metal tank car, cattle car with sliding doors, plus caboose make up the rest of train. Run train forward or back, fast or slow—by remote control! Fourteen sections of track. UL approved. 45-watt transformer for 110-120-volt, 60-cycle AC.
79 N 09618—Complete Train and Accessory Outfit. Shipping weight 11 lbs...... **$14.94**

$5.89 — 176-inch crossover track — DING DING

Oval track about 102 inches around

$3.94 — Another exciting, low-priced Happi-Time Mechanical Train... with choice of 2 Speeds!

$2.95 — DING DING

Oval track about 102 inches around — MARX MARLINES

Big 30-pc. Mechanical Set with bell and headlamp, crossover, 7 Accessories

[A] An outstanding value! Big 6-unit Happi-Time Mechanical Freight Train Set PLUS realistic plastic freight depot and 6 plastic telegraph poles. Big 42-inch train has sturdy steel steam-type locomotive with accurately detailed plastic nosepiece, bright headlamp (battery not included... see below) and bell. Long-running clockspring motor has built-in speed governor and brake.
Lithographed metal tender and 4 cars: gondola, tank car, box car, caboose. Sixteen sections of track plus crossover section.
49 N 9509—Shpg. wt. 6 lbs............ **$5.89**
34 N 4659—Batteries. Shpg. wt. 4 oz. 2 for 23c

6-unit Mechanical Train with bell, 2 Speeds

[B] Now—a new Happi-Time Combination Freight and Passenger Train with choice of 2 Speeds! Brake lever has "fast," "slow" and "off" positions. Run train fast or slow, as you wish. You'll thrill as you watch this big 42-inch train thunder by, *its bell ringing!* Realistically detailed steam-type steel locomotive with accurately detailed plastic nosepiece, die-cast wheels, piston-rod action, plus long-running clockspring motor with built-in speed governor. Train set also includes attractively lithographed steel tender, gondola, 2 Pullman passenger cars, caboose, 10 sections of track.
49 N 9508—Shpg. wt. 3 lbs. 10 oz. *Here's a real train buy for Christmas!*.... **$3.94**

Marx 4-unit Mechanical Freight with sparks, bell

[C] An exciting little set for little railroaders, too young for an electric set! Watch this 28¾-inch train whiz around its 102-inch oval track—*tiny, harmless sparks shooting out and its merry little bell ringing gaily!* A really welcome gift at a low price.
Steam-type steel locomotive with accurately detailed plastic nosepiece. Long-running clockspring motor with built-in speed governor and brake. Lithographed metal tender, gondola and caboose. Complete with 10 sections of track.
49 N 9503—Shpg. wt. 2 lbs. 8 oz. **$2.95**

Exciting Scenic Express on metal base with Signals that Really Work!

Crossing gate goes down as train passes

$2.75

A complete railroad system for younger children. Complete with signals that work, just like real railroad signals. Action crossing gate and semaphore automatically raise and lower as 11-inch train whizzes by. All the thrills and excitement of a big railroad!
Train runs around grooved track in base over 20 times with just one winding! Watch it speed through tunnel and station. Train has long-running clockspring motor. Sturdy steel base, about 21¾x13 inches, is realistically lithographed with landscape scene.
49 N 9515—Shpg. wt. 3 lbs. A fine gift! **$2.75**

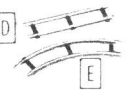

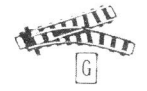

Extra Track
For mechanical train sets

[D] Straight Track. 8⅞ in. long.
49 N 9701—Wt. 6 oz.... Set of 4, 35c
[E] Curved Track. 10 in. long.
49 N 9702—Wt. 6 oz.... Set of 4, 35c
[F] 90° Crossover. 7½ in. square.
49 N 9703—Shpg. wt. 8 oz. Each 59c
[G] Manual Switch Set. One left-hand switch and right-hand switch.
49 N 9704—Shpg. wt. 1 lb.... Set $1.79

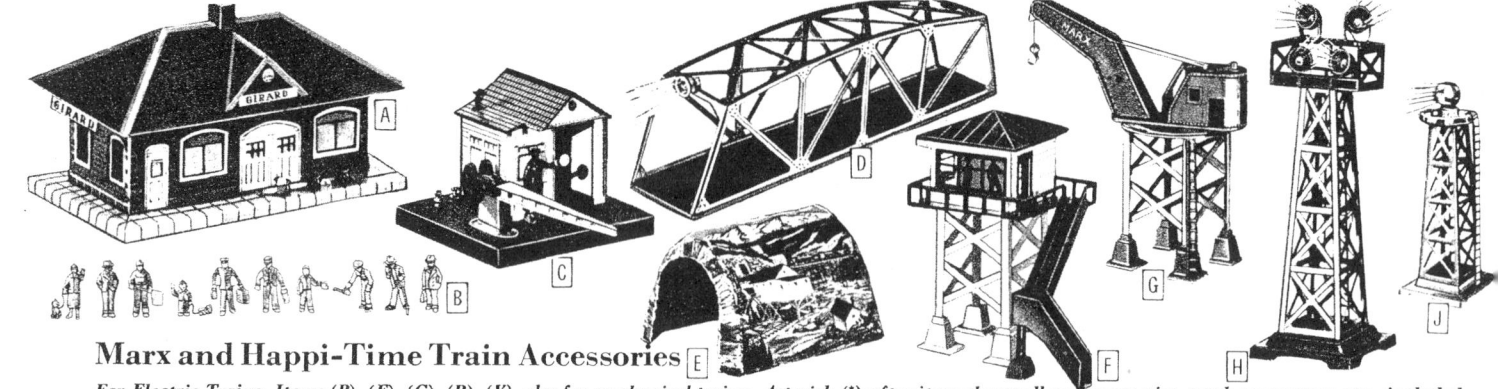

Marx and Happi-Time Train Accessories

For Electric Trains. Items (B), (E), (G), (R), (V), also for mechanical trains. Asterisk (*) after item shows all necessary wire, track connectors, etc., included.

A Whistling Metal Station.* Press remote control button ... hear realistic wail of locomotive whistle, built into 9x5¼x5-in. high lithographed steel station.
49 N 9766—With control panel. Shpg. wt. 2 lbs. **$4.49**

B 10 Plastic Figures: Engineer, porter, conductor, newsboy, etc. Soft Vinyl plastic up to 1½ in. high.
49 N 9762—Lifelike poses. Shpg. wt. 10 oz... Set **88c**

C Automatic Grade Crossing Shack with Watchman.* Lithographed steel shanty; 7-in. plastic gate. As train nears, watchman comes out with "STOP" sign, gate lowers. Base 7x6½ in.; house 4½ in. high.
49 N 9760—Shipping weight 2 lbs. 8 oz. **$3.79**

D Lighted all-steel Trestle Bridge.* Aluminum finish. Embossed rivets. Light socket and reflector clip on anywhere; adjusts to any position. With bulb.
49 N 9741—24x4⅞x6⅛ in. high. Wt. 2 lbs...... **$1.98**

E Collapsible Metal Tunnel. Colorful, realistically lithographed landscape.
49 N 9729—10¾x9x7 in. Wt. 1 lb............. **89c**

F Automatic Switchman's Tower.* As train nears, switchman with green flag comes through door; second man inside moves to switch controls.
49 N 9757—Plastic; 7½ in. high. Shpg. wt. 1 lb. **$3.79**

G Plastic Derrick Loader. Scale-detailed. Crane housing swings in complete circle. Boom has crank handle; raises, lowers loads. Die-cast hook.
49 N 9733—8½ in. high. Shpg. wt. 10 oz....... **$1.45**

H 4-light Floodlight Tower.* Four lights on double platform on girder-type plastic tower. Lights may be revolved, tilted. Chrome-finish metal ladder.
49 N 9751—Height 13½ in. Shpg. wt. 1 lb..... **$2.95**

J Lighted Revolving Beacon.* Revolves on top of girder-type molded plastic tower. Red, green reflector.
49 N 9740—12½ in. high. Shpg. wt. 1 lb....... **$1.89**

Scale-detailed Cars

For Happi-Time Electric Trains only. Remote-control Automatic Couplers. If train has manual couplers, order 49N9713 (EE) below. Wt. 10 oz. each.   **$1.79** Each

[K] 49 N 9724—New 8¼-inch Derrick Car. Plastic cab and boom may be rotated. Hand crank raises and lowers hook........... **$1.79**
[L] 49N9722—7½-inch Metal Tank Car. **1.79**
[M] 49 N 9721—8½-inch Metal Cattle Car with sliding doors. Realistic details....... **$1.79**

Lighted Pullmans. Realistically lithographed metal. Wt. 14 oz. ea.   **$3.79**
[N] 49 N 9770—11-in. Astra-dome Car. **$3.79**
[P] 49 N 9771—10¾-in. Observation Car. **3.79**

Big Station

R Colorfully lithographed to show waiting room, baggage room, express office, freight office, etc. Has platform and ramp for inbound freight. Simulated shingled roof and brick sides. Dummy windows. All-steel construction. Easy to assemble without tools. Adds thrilling realism to any mechanical or electric train set. 20½x10x6½ in. high overall.
49 N 9752—Wt. 3 lbs. **$1.82**

Authentic Marx Electric Locomotives

Realistically detailed plastic; authentic markings. Powerful motors, die-cast wheels, oilless bronze bearings; headlamps. Remote control of speed, reversing. For trains using 110–120-volt 60-cycle AC transformers.   **$12.95**

S Scale-model Twin-Diesel. Dummy twin horns, louvers, other realistic details. Single motor. Two 4-wheel trucks per section (16 wheels in all). Remote Automatic Couplers.
49 N 9792—24½ inches long. Shpg. wt. 3 lbs. 14 oz... **$12.95**

T 3/16-in. Scale-model Heavy Freight Steam-type Locomotive and Tender. Fourteen wheels; 6-wheel drive; two 4-wheel trucks. Compound piston-rod action. Scale-detailed plastic tender with remote-control Automatic Couplers, 8 wheels.
49 N 9791—18 inches long overall. Shpg. wt. 3 lbs. **$12.95**

U Plastic Steam-type Locomotive, Tender. Manual couplers.
49 N 9790—16¼ in. long. 4-wheel drive. Wt. 1 lb. 14 oz. **$6.95**

Accessories

V Big 8¼-in. Plastic Water Tower with adjustable spout. Girder-type understructure; realistic ribs. Water tank is 4¼-in. diameter.   **89c**
49 N 9731—Shpg. wt. 10 oz. **89c**

W Railroad Lift Bridge*. Girder-type; embossed rivets. Enameled steel. 18¾x5¼x3 in. high. Gear and crank raise and lower bridge. Built-in track section.
49 N 9761—Shpg. wt. 3 lbs. **$2.95**

X 3 Lighted Plastic Lamps*. 6¼ in. high. With bulbs.
49 N 9732—Wt. 6 oz. 3 for **$1.79**

29-piece Set

Authentically scale-detailed Railroad Accessories in durable plastic. A perfect, low-cost gift for the young railroader who already has a train set. Just the right size for any standard mechanical or electric train. Will add thrilling realism! Set includes twelve 7-inch telegraph poles, 12 railroad right-of-way signs, PLUS one each of the following: semaphore, lamp post, crossing gate, grade crossing, railroad crossing sign. Track not included. Shipping weight 2 pounds.   **$2.89**
49N9750—Complete Set. **$2.89**

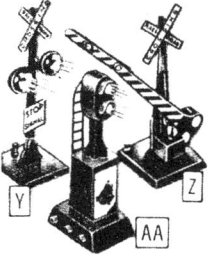

Crossing Needs

Y Automatic Crossing Flasher.* Twin lights flash alternately from one side to other as train passes. Metal; 8 in. high.   **$1.89**
49 N 9742—Shpg. wt. 10 oz. **$1.09**

Z Automatic Crossing Gate*. Striped arm lowers as train passes, then raises. Red simulated jewel at end of gate. Metal; 7¾ in. high. An exciting accessory!
49 N 9743—Wt. 10 oz. **$1.89**

AA Automatic Block Signal*. Train stops on red light, proceeds on green. Switch at rear operates signal. Die-cast base; 2-track section. Chrome-finish ladder. Metal; 7 in. high.
49 N 9745—Wt. 1 lb. **$2.19**

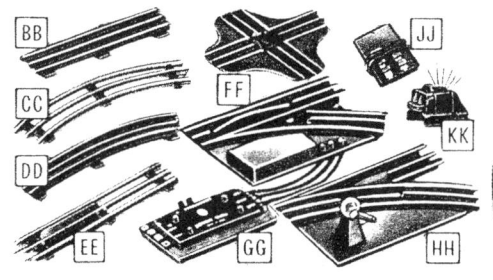

Extra Track for Electric Trains

For Happi-Time or Marx Trains. Shpg. wt. 4 oz. each.
[BB] 49 N 9710—8⅞-in. Straight Track.........Each **18c**
[CC] 49 N 9711—10-in. Standard Curved Track....Ea. **18c**
[DD] 49N9712—12½-in. Wide-Radius Curved Track. Ea. **22c**
[EE] Uncoupling Unit. Built into standard length electric straight track. "Uncouple Here" sign included.
49 N 9713—Shipping weight 5 oz........... Each **55c**
[FF] 49 N 9714—7½-in. Crossover. Shpg. wt. 8 oz. Ea. **87c**
[GG] Electric Remote Control Switch Set.* One left-hand and one right-hand switch plus control panel.
49 N 9716—Shipping weight 2 lbs. 8 oz....... Set **$6.79**
[HH] Manual Switch Set. One left-, one right-hand.
49 N 9715—Shipping weight 2 pounds. Set **2.85**
[JJ] Track Connector.* Brings power from transformer or track, or takes power from track for accessories.
49N9709—Bakelite; 1¾x1⅛ in. Shpg. wt. 2 oz. Each **12c**
[KK] Lighted Dead-End Bumper.* Plastic; 3x1⅞x2 in. high. Snaps to track; cars stay on track on spur.
49 N 9707—Bulb included. Shpg. wt. 5 oz.. Each **89c**

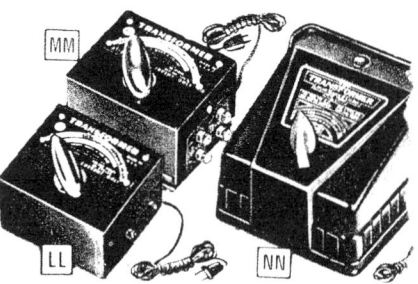

Train Transformers

For Electric Trains. UL approved. 110–120-volt 60-cycle AC. Built-in circuit breaker protects against short circuits and burnout. Attached cord.   **$4.89** 45-watt

LL 45-watt Transformer* Two sets of binding posts: one set gives variable 7 to 13 volts for controlling train speed, other set gives fixed 13 volts for accessories.
49 N 9725—Shipping weight 3 lbs. 4 oz. **$4.89**

MM 70-watt Transformer*. Two sets of binding posts: Variable 5 to 15 volts for running train plus fixed 15 volts for accessories.
49 N 9754—Shipping weight 4 lbs....... **$6.85**

NN Super-powered 150-watt Transformer*. Two sets of voltages: variable 0 to 15 volts for running train plus fixed 15 volts for accessories. Massive plastic case with air-cooled metal base. Throttle-type control.
49 N 9764—Shipping weight 10 lbs..... **$12.95**

SEARS CHRISTMAS CATALOG
1955

With electric trains a big profit center for Sears' toy department, in 1955 the firm made a push to better market its own "improved" Happi-Time house brand train sets, mostly manufactured for Sears by Marx. These trains filled four full pages in that year's catalog.

Of course, Lionel's more expensive trains were included too, though mention is made of "new low prices." Original items for 1955 included the Ice Depot set for $13.75 which unloaded little plastic blocks of ice into a special box car. Another new item was the illuminated Trolley Car which automatically changed direction when it hit a bumper on the track.

In fact, illumination of trains and accessories increased. All the major brands now offered passenger cars that lit up, search light cars which beamed into the night and beacons that scanned the horizon.

Switches light! Large Radius Track!

2 remote control switches (1 right, 1 left with 79 N-09621. Light automatically

6-Unit Freight, 19 tracks; remote control switches above

$29.89 cash $3.00 down

New large radius track... stronger, 5 ties per section...take greater speeds

HAPPI-TIME

6-Unit Freight with 12 track sections
$19.79
[A]

CHUG-CHUG

[B] 7-Unit Work Train; 14 track sections
$24.89 cash
$2.50 down

[C] **$17.89**
6-Unit Switcher; 10 track sections

[D] **$15.89**
6-Unit Freight; 10 track sections

[E] **$9.89**
5-Unit Passenger; 10 track sections

WOO WOO

[F] Whistling Station **$4.39**

[G] Electric Hand Car **$3.69**

236 .. SEARS, ROEBUCK AND CO. PC

NEW IMPROVED HAPPI-TIME ELECTRIC TRAINS

Die-cast wheels, large radius track, longer curves, speedier, less spills .. Circuit breaker transformer protects against shorts

New! 6-Unit Twin-Diesel Freight

[A] Authentic scale-detailed plastic twin-diesel with "B" center unit! Has powerful motor with oilless bronze bearings, double trucks, light.
Entire train over 5 ft. long! Includes power unit above, 3/16-in. scale model hopper car, refrigerator car, caboose; all with double trucks (8 die-cast wheels per unit); plastic and steel.

Run train forward or back . . . fast or slow . . couple or uncouple cars, all by remote control. *UL approved 75-watt transformer* with built-in circuit breaker, 4 binding posts (2 for accessories) for 110-120-volt, 60-cycle AC.

Train with 2 remote control switches that light . . . push button control panel. 7 straight, 10 curved sections large radius track, 2 uncoupling ramps make large 197-in. oval track. With inner track . . over 20 ft. of road bed!
79 N 09621—Set with switches. Shpg. wt. 14 lbs. $29.89

Same Train without switches. 3 sections straight, 8 sections curved large radius track, 1 uncoupling ramp make 152-in. oval. 1 "uncouple" sign. Shipping weight 12 pounds.
49 N U9615 . . $19.79

New 6-Unit Freight, Puffs Smoke

[D] **Lowest-priced electric smoke train we have ever offered.** Big 48-inch freight with steam-type locomotive of die-cast metal. Puffs white non-toxic smoke. Piston rod action, oilless bronze bearings, bright headlight. Scale-detailed plastic tender, flat car with detachable side rails, play cargo, tank car, cattle car and caboose. All have double trucks and automatic couplers.

Runs forward and back, fast or slow, couples and uncouples by remote control. 10 sections of large radius track make 129½-inch oval; 1 section straight, 8 sections curved, 1 uncoupling ramp, and an "Uncouple Here" sign.

UL approved 50-watt transformer with circuit breaker, 2 binding posts for 110-120-volt, 60-cycle AC. 1-oz. bottle smoke liquid.
49 N U9610—Freight set. Shpg. wt. 10 lbs. $15.89

New! 7-Unit Work Train .. Our Best

[B] **Realism plus!** Puffs non-toxic smoke as it moves along with a chug-chug sound. Die-cast metal 3/16-inch scale model of a 4-6-2 wheel drive locomotive. Powerful headlight and illuminated number marker. Oilless bronze bearings, 4-wheel pony trucks, 2 guide wheels. Plastic and steel coal tender, 5 cars all scale detailed. Run train slow or fast, ahead or reverse, couple or uncouple cars, all by remote control.

Entire train almost 5½ feet long. Includes revolving searchlight car, operating milk car with ramp, automobile carrier car with four 4-in. plastic autos, wrecker crane car and wrecker caboose. All amazingly detailed steel and plastic; double trucks; automatic couplers on all cars. Large radius electric track included to make oval 174½ inches in circumference . . . 5 sections straight, 8 sections curved, 1 uncoupling ramp. "Uncouple Here" sign. 1-oz. bottle smoke liquid.
UL approved 100-watt transformer with circuit breaker, 4 binding posts (2 for accessories), for 110-120-volt, 60-cycle AC. Track connector.
79 N 09620—Complete Set. Shpg. wt. 12 lbs. $24.89

New 5-Unit All-Steel Train

[E] **A terrific buy for only $9.98.** Same careful modeling, same remote control, die-cast wheels and large radius track as our higher-priced trains! Steel steam-type locomotive has gleaming headlight, oilless bronze bearings, piston-rod.
Train is 36 in. long overall. Includes tender, 2 passenger coaches and observation coach. Accurately lithographed, manual couplers.

Large radius track (2 sections straight, 8 sections curved) makes oval about 129 in. around. Run train forward or back, fast or slow by remote control without touching track or train. A hard-to-beat value at this amazing low price!
UL approved 50-watt transformer with circuit breaker, 2 posts for 110-120-volt, 60-cycle AC. Track connector.
49 N U9604—Passenger Set. Shpg. wt. 8 lbs. $9.89

New 6-Unit Diesel Switcher

[C] Heavy-duty diesel switcher locomotive with combination die-cast chassis, plastic body. Remote control reversing mechanism. Headlight. Oilless bronze bearings. Double trucks, 8 wheels on each; automatic couplers both front and rear . . . use as switcher engine or line haul locomotive.
Entire train is 58¼ in. long . . . almost 5 feet. Wrecker car, cable car, searchlight car with dummy generator, drop-end gondola, wrecker caboose. High impact plastic and steel, realistically detailed. Large radius track to make 129½-in. oval; 1 section straight, 8 sections curved, 1 uncoupling ramp, "Uncouple Here" sign.
UL approved 50-watt transformer with circuit breaker, 4 binding posts (2 for accessories) for 110-120-volt, 60-cycle AC. Track connector. Run train forward or back, fast or slow, couple and uncouple all by remote control. Shipping weight 10 pounds.
49 N U9612—Complete Diesel Switcher . . . . Set $17.89

[F] **Remote Control Whistling Station** . . . press button, hear wail of locomotive whistle as your train speeds down the track. Mechanism enclosed in lithographed steel station. Control panel, wires incl. Station, 9x5¼x5 in. high.
49 N 9739—Whistling Station. Shpg. wt. 2 lbs. . . . $4.39

[G] **Electric Hand Car** with 2 husky molded railroaders that pump vigorously at cross bars. Authentic style, with electric motor. Interesting addition to a train layout. Car is 6¼ in. long, 2 in. wide, 4½ in. high. Plastic and steel chassis.
49 N 9753—Hand Car. Shpg. wt. 1 lb. $3.69

News! Large Radius Track

Stronger . . . 5 ties per section (only 3 on old type). **Faster speeds possible** . . . gentler curve holds train to track even at full transformer speeds. **Better "track bed"** . . . longer curves make firmer track, about 30% larger . . holds together better. **NOTE:** Do not use new curved sections with old.

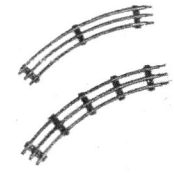

COMPLETE OUTFIT TRAIN PLUS STATION $14.79

Freight Terminal $5.49 5-Unit Train $9.89

Big HAPPI-TIME Electric Freight Train and Terminal With over 60 Play Pieces!

Buy the Freight Terminal or Train Set separately . . . or buy both at one low price! Our biggest freight handling train and outfit.

[H] **Freight Terminal** is lithographed steel with ramp and plastic stairway to loading platform. Has all freight handling equipment the young trainman could want . . . truck, empty cartons, baggage trucks, crates, workers . . . **over 60 plastic pieces in all!** Terminal is 29 in. long, 11 in. wide, 9 in. high. Easily set up without tools.
79 N 09772—Freight Terminal only. Shpg. wt. 7 lbs. $5.49

[J] **Five-unit Steam-type Freight Train.** Steel steam-type electric locomotive, modeled in detail with gleaming headlight, oilless bronze bearings, die-cast wheels. Train overall is 40½ in. Includes coal tender, high-side gondola, box car and caboose, all with die-cast metal wheels. Large radius track (8 sections of curved, 2 sections straight) makes oval about 129½ in. around. Run train forward, back, fast or slow by remote control. *UL approved 50-watt transformer* with circuit breaker to protect against shorts. For 110-120-volt, 60-cycle AC.
49 N U9605—5-unit Freight Train Set only. Shpg. wt. 8 lbs. $9.89

79 N 09607—COMPLETE OUTFIT (H and J) as shown . . . Makes huge, impressive layout for play hours and fun galore . . . Terminal, Train, Track and Transformer. Save on combination! Separately, pieces total $15.38 Shipping weight 15 pounds. **$14.79**

For Marx or Happi-Time Electric Trains .. Scale-detailed Electric Locomotives .. Cars .. Accessories

(A, C and D) Realistically detailed locomotives with authentic markings. Powerful motors, die-cast wheels, oil-less bronze bearings, headlamps. Remote control of speed and reversing. Automatic coupling. For trains using 110-120-volt, 60-cycle AC transformers.

[A] **Twin-Diesel Locomotive.** Steel and plastic with true realism. 2 sections, single motor. Two 4-wheel trucks per section. 24½ in. long overall.
49 N U9792—Shpg. wt. 4 lbs. $12.95

[B] **"Power" B unit** to make 3-unit diesel. Detailed plastic scale model. Two 4-wheel trucks. Manual coupler front and rear. 12 in. long. Has no motor.
49 N 9781—Shpg. wt. 1 lb. $4.79

[C] **Diesel Switcher.** Die-cast chassis, plastic body. Couples front and rear. Two 4-wheel trucks. 10½ in. long.
49 N U9765—Shpg. wt. 3 lbs. $11.45

[D] **Smoking Chug-Chug Locomotive with Tender.** Puffs non-toxic white smoke as it "chug-chugs" along. Die-cast metal scale model of a 4-6-2-wheel drive locomotive. Dull black with nickel-plated trim. Illuminated marker lights. High impact plastic tender with automatic coupler. Liquid for smoke included. Length 17½ inches. Will make a fine gift.
49 N U9767—Shpg. wt. 3 lbs. $17.75

[E, F, G] Cars with Action! Heavy duty plastic and steel, detailed to scale. Die-cast wheels, remote control automatic couplers. 4-wheel trucks. For Marx and Happi-Time electric trains.

[E] **Revolving Searchlight Car.** Light turns as train moves. Dummy motor and generator, picks up current from track shoe. 9¾ inches long.
49 N 9758—Shpg. wt. 1 lb. $3.67

[F] **Operating Milk Car with Platform.** As car is backed to unloading platform, door opens, trainman steps out. At forward speeds, door is closed. Rolling stock, authentic detail. 9 in. long.
49 N 9759—Shpg. wt. 1 lb. $3.67

[G] **Automobile Carrier Car.** 2-deck rack on flat car. 4 autos about 4 inches long . . . detach to unload. 9½ in. long.
49 N 9755—Shpg. wt. 1 lb. $3.67

[H, J] Lighted Passenger Cars. Show silhouettes of passengers. Lithographed metal. Automatic couplers. Sturdy wheels, 4-wheel trucks. Wt. 14 oz.
[H] 49N9770—11-in. Astrodome. $3.67
[J] 49N9771—10¾-in. Observation. . . 3.67

[K] **Lighted Steel Trestle Bridge.*** Aluminum finish. Light socket and reflector clip on, adjust. With bulb, track connector. 24x4⅞x6⅛ in. high.
49NU9741—Shpg. wt. 2 lbs. $1.98

*means all wire, track connectors, etc., necessary are included

[L] **Overhead Double Track Signal Bridge.*** Plastic; 13 in. long, 8 in. high. Light changes from red to green as train approaches. Signal heads removable.
49 N 9738—Shpg. wt. 10 oz. $4.39

[M] **Automatic Grade Crossing Shack and Watchman*** to warn make-believe motorists of approaching train. Lithographed steel shanty and 7-inch plastic gate. As train nears, watchman comes out with a stop sign, gate lowers. Base 7x6½ inches; house 4½ in. high.
49 N 9760—Shpg. wt. 2 lbs. 8 oz. . . $3.49

[N] **Automatic Crossing Gate.*** Arm lowers as train approaches, then raises. Simulated jewel reflector at end of gate. Steel. 7¾ inches high.
49 N 9743—Shpg. wt. 10 oz. $1.87

[P] **Automatic Double Light Block Signal.*** Train stops on red, proceeds on green light. Sturdy plastic. Switch at rear operates signal. 2 track sections included. 7¼ in. high. Asstd. styles.
49N9745—Shpg. wt. 1 lb. $1.87

[R] **Flasher-Wagger Crossing Signal.*** Lights blink, swinging stop sign moves back and forth as train approaches. Sturdy plastic. 7½ in. high.
49 N 9774—Shpg. wt. 1 lb. 4 oz. . . . $3.39

[S] **Lighted Revolving Beacon.*** Light revolves on top of girder-type molded plastic tower. Red, green reflector. 12½ in. high overall. Priced low!
49 N 9740—Shpg. wt. 1 lb. $1.87

[T] **4-light Floodlight Tower*** Reduced! Four lights on double platform at top of plastic tower. Lights can be turned and tilted to focus on any spot you choose in your railroad town. 13½ in. high. Chrome-finish metal ladder.
49 N 9751—Shpg. wt. 1 lb. Was $2.95 $2.75

[V] **Automatic Crossing Flasher.*** Twin lights flash alternately as train passes; stop after train is past. Made of plastic, 7 in. high. Assorted styles.
49 N 9742—Shpg. wt. 10 oz. $1.87

[W] **Set of 3 lighted Lamp Posts*** like you see in your own town. Add realism to your train layout. Bases notched to attach to track. Each post is different . . . one has a mail box, one a police call box, one a fire alarm box on post. Plastic, 6 in. high.
49 N 9737—Shpg. wt. 1 lb. $1.79

NOTE: All these electric accessories are for Marx and Happi-Time electric train layouts using 110-120-volt, 60-cycle AC transformers. Order several, complete your trainman's layout.

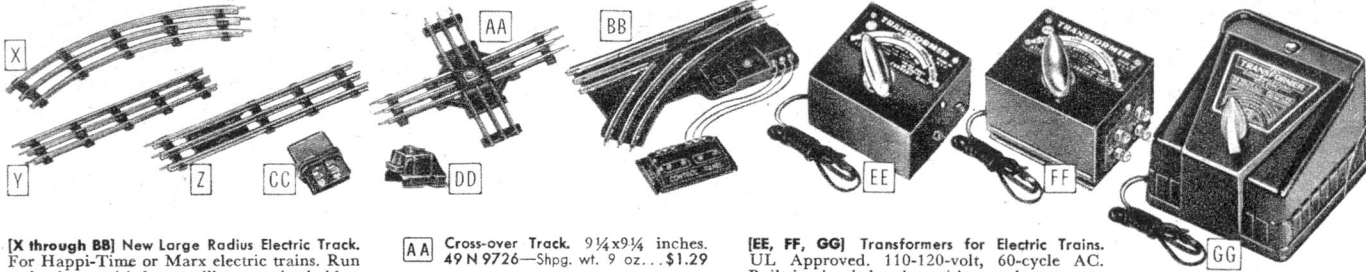

[X through BB] **New Large Radius Electric Track.** For Happi-Time or Marx electric trains. Run trains faster with fewer spills . . . trains hold to track better. Longer sections mean firmer track layout. Better quality than ever before— 5 cross ties per section, not the usual 3 ties. Shipping weight each 4 ounces.

[X] 49 N 9723—12½-in. Curved Track. 22c
[Y] 49 N 9720—11¼-in. Straight Track 22c
[Z] **Uncoupling Unit.** 5 ties to match. "Uncouple Here" sign included.
49 N 9749—Shpg. wt. 5 oz. 75c

[AA] **Cross-over Track.** 9¼x9¼ inches.
49 N 9726—Shpg. wt. 9 oz. . . $1.29

[BB] **New De Luxe Large Radius Remote Control Switch Set** with red, green light. 1 right hand, one left hand switch. 4-button control panel.
49 N 9727—Shpg. wt. 3 lbs. . . . . Set $8.95

[CC] **Track connector** with wires brings power from transformer to track or from track to accessories. 2x1⅛ in.
49 N 9709—Shpg. wt. 2 oz. 12c

[DD] **Lighted Dead-end Bumper.** Plastic; 3x1⅞x2 in. high. Snaps to end of spur track. Bulb included.
49 N 9707—Shpg. wt. 5 oz. 89c

[EE, FF, GG] Transformers for Electric Trains. UL Approved. 110-120-volt, 60-cycle AC. Built-in circuit breaker with reset button protects against short circuits and burnouts. Attached cord, wires, track connector.

[EE] **50-watt Transformer.** Two sets of binding posts; one set gives variable 7 to 13 volts, controls train speed; other set gives fixed 13 volts for accessories. *Last Christmas was $4.89.*
49 N 9725—Shpg. wt. 3 lbs. $4.25

[FF] **75-watt Transformer.** Two sets of binding posts; one set gives variable 5 to 15 volts for controlling train speed; other set gives fixed 15 volts for accessories.
49 N 9754—Shpg. wt. 4 lbs. $6.79

[GG] **Super-Powered 150-watt Transformer.** Two sets of binding posts: one set gives variable 0 to 15 volts for controlling train speed; one set gives fixed 15 volts for accessories. Throttle-type control. Massive plastic case with air-cooled metal base. Shpg. wt. 10 lbs.
49 N U9764 . . . . $12.95

NEW 34-piece Mechanical Set

[A] Big 6-unit Happi-Time Combination Passenger and Freight with switches, PLUS realistic plastic Railway Station, 6 plastic people, 6 telephone poles. Steam-type steel locomotive shoots harmless sparks as it whizzes along with bell ringing.

Long-running clockspring motor has built-in speed governor and brake. Lithographed metal tender, box car, 2 passenger coaches and caboose. Train 41½ in. long. 3 sections straight track, 10 curved, 2 switches (one right, one left) make double oval track layout about 160 in. running track. Priced low for such good quality.
49 N 9510—Shipping weight 6 pounds............$5.94

5-unit Lighted Mechanical Freight

[B] New Happi-Time mechanical Freight Train races around big crossover track, headlight gleaming, bell ringing. Bright headlight operates on battery (not included, see below). Sturdy metal steam-type locomotive has long-running clockspring motor with built-in speed governor and brake. Train 35½ in. long overall with tender, 2 high-side gondolas (1 red, 1 green) and a caboose. 4 sections of straight track, 12 curved, 1 crossover make a 176-inch, figure-8 track layout. Sure to thrill your child, order now.
49 N 9507—Shipping weight 4 pounds............$3.95
34 N 4659—Batteries. Shpg. wt. 4 oz....2 for 28c; 6 for 78c

Marx 4-unit Freight

[C] Watch this 28¾-inch train whizz around its 102-inch oval track ... harmless sparks shooting out and its merry little bell ringing. Steam-type steel locomotive has long-running clockspring motor with built-in speed governor and brake. Realistically lithographed metal tender, gondola, caboose. A wonderful little set for "railroaders" who are too young for an electric set. Complete with 10 sections of track. A real train buy for young trainmasters—order now for Christmas.
49 N 9503—Shpg. wt. 2 lbs. 8 oz..........$2.89

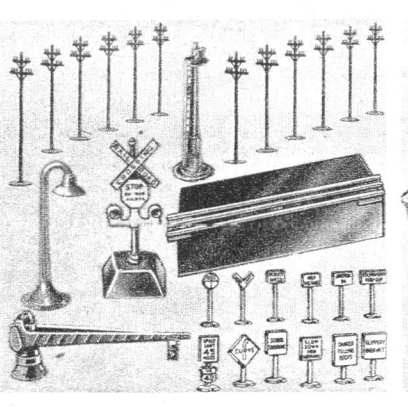

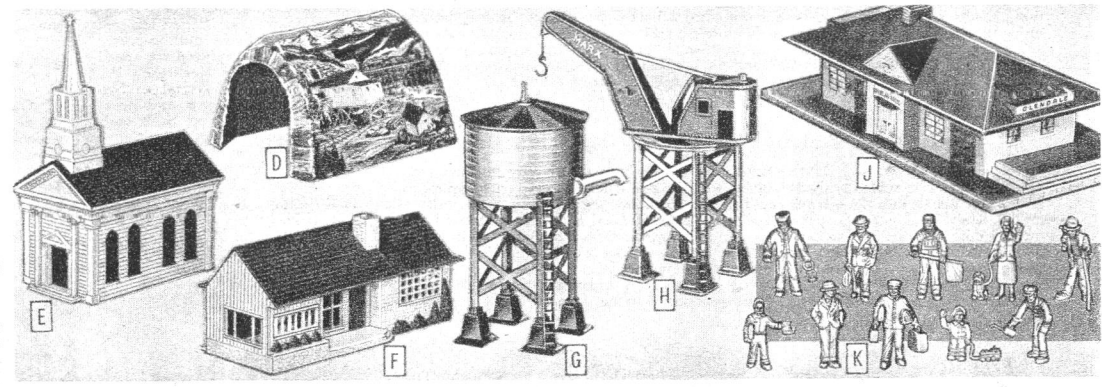

Colorful Detailed Accessories delight young trainmasters .. add realism to their trains

29-piece Set of authentically scale-detailed Railroad Accessories reduced to a new low price. Made of durable plastic. A perfect, low-cost gift for the young railroader who is receiving a new train set ... or already has one. Just the right size for any standard mechanical or electric train. Carefully detailed to please the most particular train lover. Will add thrilling realism, lots of play value. Includes: 12, 7-inch telegraph poles, 12 railroad right-of-way signs, PLUS 1 each of the following: semaphore, lamp post, crossing gate, grade crossing sign and grade crossing (track not included, order at left below).
49 N 9750—Shpg. wt. 2 lbs. Was $2.89........Set $2.69

[D] Metal Tunnel. Watch your train thunder through the tunnel! Colorful lithographed metal. Comes apart for storage. 9x7x10¾ inches long.
49 N 9729—Shipping weight 1 pound............89c

[E][F] Plastic buildings. Strong, interlocking sections make sturdy buildings. Each detailed in true-to-life realism, colorful. Shpg. wt. 8 oz.
[E] 49 N 9768—Church Set. 10¼ x 6¾ x 4½ inches........89c
[F] 49 N 9769—Ranch House. 9x4x4 inches high........89c

[G] Plastic Water Tower with adjustable spout. Tank 4¼ inches in diameter. 8¼ in. high.
49 N 9731—Shipping weight 10 ounces............89c

[H] Plastic Derrick. Crane swings around, boom has crank to raise, lower. Die-cast hook.
49 N 9733—8½ inches high. Shpg. wt. 10 oz.....$1.45

[J] Railroad Station. Colorfully lithographed metal. Platform and ramp, dummy windows. Easy to assemble without tools. Adds thrilling realism to train set. 20½x10x6½ in. high overall.
49 N U9752—Station. Shpg. wt. 3 lbs..........$1.79

[K] 10 Plastic 3-dimensional Figures: Engineer, porter, conductor, etc. Soft vinyl plastic. Up to 1½ in. high. Lots of fun for a low price.
49 N 9762—10 figures. Shpg. wt. 10 oz........Set 87c

Extra Track for Mechanical Trains

[L] Straight Track. 8⅞ inches long.
49 N 9701—Wt. 6 oz. Set of 4 for 35c
[M] Curved Track. 10½ inches long.
49 N 9702—Wt. 6 oz. Set of 4 for 35c
[N] 90° Crossover. 7½ inches square.
49 N 9703—Shpg. wt. 8 oz...Each 59c
[P] Manual Switch Set. One left-hand switch, one right-hand switch.
49 N 9704—Shpg. wt. 1 lb......Set $1.79

Scenic Express with signals that work!

A complete railroad system for younger children. Signals that work just like the real ones do! Action crossing gate and semaphore work automatically as the 11-inch train whizzes by. All the thrills and excitement of a big railroad!

Train runs around grooved track in metal base over 20 times with just one winding. Watch it speed through tunnel and station. Train has long-running clockspring motor. Sturdy steel base, about 21¾ x13 inches, is realistically lithographed with landscape scene. Little tots will love all the action.
49 N U9515—Shipping weight 3 lbs.........$2.75

Avoid Christmas crowds, shop by Sears catalog

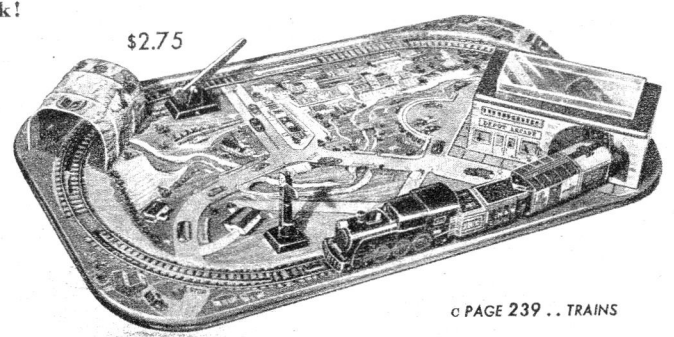

Priced low so you, too, can own Lionel

6-unit "027" Electric Freight with smoke, whistle

[A] Puffs harmless white smoke! Blow its built-in whistle; run train forward and backward, fast or slow, couple and uncouple cars—all by remote control! Giant 14-wheel die-cast metal engine with 6-wheel drive, Magne-Traction, piston-rod action, headlamp. Tender, 4 cars: remote-control barrel car—touch button, barrels move to tiny man, then roll into bin (included); oil car, hopper car, lighted caboose. UL approved 90-watt transformer with built-in circuit breaker and whistle controller (for 110-120-volt, 60-cycle AC). 12 tracks incl., uncoupling section make oval 114 in. around. Train is 58¾ inches long. The most thrilling gift in a boy's life!
79 N 09653—Shipping weight 18 pounds.................$42.95

5-unit Diesel Freight with Horn—Magne-Traction

[B] New GP-7 Diesel with bright headlamp, "beeps" its horn by remote control. Power-packed, scale-detailed switcher with die-cast trucks, has electric couplers at both ends, plastic cab. PLUS Magne-Traction for heavy yard work, greater pull on grades, more staying power at high speeds, pulls more cars. Run fast or slow, couple or uncouple, forward or back—all by remote control. Cars include: operating box car—press button, trainman appears to open door, door closes manually—hopper car, oil car, caboose. UL approved 90-watt transformer with built-in circuit breaker for 110-120-volt, 60-cycle AC. 8 curved, 3 straight, 1 uncoupler section of "027" track form oval 114 inches around. Train is about 50 inches long overall.
79 N 09652—Shipping weight 15 pounds..................$33.45

[C] Powerful 16½-in Fairbanks-Morse "double-ender" Diesel. Two motors, built-in horn, headlamps at both ends. PLUS Magne-Traction for extra pulling-power on grades. Unsurpassed for speed without derailing. Accurately detailed plastic cab; metal railing. Lighted marker lights and number box. Couplers at both ends. Two 6-wheel trucks, each with own 6-wheel worm-drive motor. For "0" gauge track only. Shpg. wt. 7 lbs.
49 N U9896—Was $43.50..$34.95

[D] 19-inch Automatic Barrel Loader with 6 barrels. Set barrels upright on lower platform; they move to workman, who tips them onto elevated runway leading to upper platform, where they roll off into car. Car and track not included.
49 N 9840—Shpg. wt. 4 lbs. Was $8.95......$7.85

[E] Operating Searchlight Car. Well-car carries dummy generator and powerful searchlight which rotates continuously. Car, 10 inches long. Does not require remote control track section. Electro magnetic knuckle couplers, die-cast metal chassis. Price reduced! Was $7.95.
49 N 9861—Shpg. wt. 2 lbs..........Now $6.85

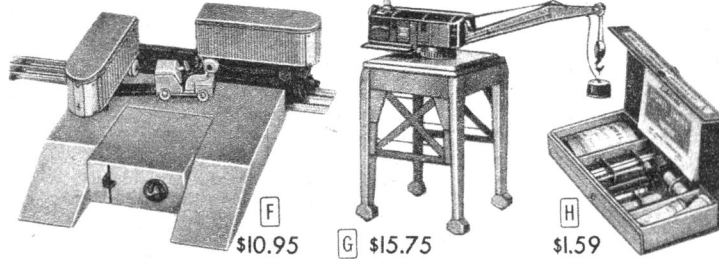

[F] New! Piggy Back Transportation Set. Hand crank on platform moves and lifts trailer trucks onto flat car. When flat car returns, crank loads trailer trucks on platform. 2 trailer trucks, platform and flat car included. About 14x2x5 in. wide. Realistic. Shpg. wt. 4 lbs.
49 N U9853......$10.95

[G] Electro-Magnetic Portal Crane spans track. 3 control levers to turn magnet on or off, raise or lower it, revolve cab. Turn magnet on to lift heavy metal loads, off to dump . . . by remote control. Plastic. 5x5x15 in. high. Shpg. wt. 5 lbs.
49 N U9847......$15.75

[H] Lubrication and Maintenance Kit helps keep your train in top running order. Tube of lubricant, vial of oil, can of solvent, 2 cleaning sticks, 6 emery boards, wiping cloth, smokestack cleaner, brush and instructions. Important for the proper care of every train. Shpg. wt. 1 lb.
49 N 9826—Cut to.....$1.59

[J] Automatic Switch Tower. Operates automatically. Train nears, one man enters tower, the other walks down the stairs. Train passes, they return. Clapboard sides, shingle roof, railed platform. 7 inches high. Scale detailed colorful plastic. Save on new low price, was $7.95. Shipping weight 3 pounds.
49 N 9841......$6.75

[K] 11¾-in. Rotary Beacon. Motorized unit revolves powerful miniature searchlight. Red and green fresnel-type lenses rotate over light. Embossed lattice-work steel structure has platform on top, ladder on side like those in real railroad yards. Bulb incl. Priced for savings. Was $4.50. Shpg. wt. 2 lbs.
49 N 9843......$3.75

[L] New! Ice Depot Set. Press remote control button and a little man on platform pushes simulated ice cakes at the same time opening hatch on "reefer" to receive cubes. Release button and car hatch closes. Ice cakes can be removed manually through side door under hatch. Base of station 11¾x4 in.; 8½ in. high. Refrigerator car is included. No special track needed. Clever realistic action.
49 N U9856—Shpg. wt. 4 lbs. $13.75

11-in. Operating Barrel Car. Press remote control button, barrels move up car to tiny man, roll out into railside bin (incl.). 8 solid steel wheels; die-cast trucks. Knuckle-type remote control electro-magnetic couplers.
49 N 9865—Wt. 2 lbs. Was $8.95....$7.85

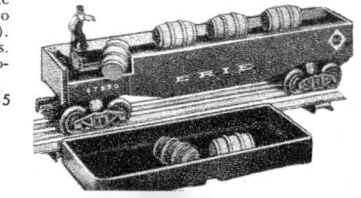

New Illuminated Trolley Car runs on built-in motor. When bumper on either end hits an object, car reverses. Little passengers visible through clear plastic windows. Realistically detailed plastic. About 7 in. long. Die-cast steel wheels. Operates on "027" or "0" gauge track like locomotives. Bulb included.
49 N 9866—Shpg. wt. 3 lbs.....$7.75

LIONEL Electric Trains

A $21.75 cash $2.50 down

B Was $7.95 Now $6.75

C Was $15.95 Now $13.75

D $18.95

E $25.95 cash $3.00 down

LIONEL—NEW LOW PRICES!

New 5-Unit Diesel Switcher Electric Freight

D Scale-detailed black and yellow diesel Switcher Engine has plastic cab plus a powerful motor for pin-point control of yard work. Use it to make or break up trains. Run fast or slow, forward or back, couple or uncouple cars all by remote control. Has couplers at front and rear. Four big cars: box car, oil car, gondola and caboose. Die-cast steel wheels on double trucks make 8 wheels to each car and engine. 8 sections curved, 1 section straight plus uncoupling "027" track form oval 102 in. around. *UL approved.* 40-watt transformer for 110–120-volt, 60 cycle, AC. Train about 44⅞ inches long overall.

The top gift on your youngster's Christmas list. Priced low for such high quality.
49 N U9601—Shipping weight 12 pounds $18.95

5-Unit Steam-type Switcher with Operating Crane

E The powerful "0-4-0," the work horse of the railroad yard! Use it to make or break up trains, run it fast or slow, couple or uncouple—all by remote control. Scale-detailed, rugged die-cast metal steam-type switcher has long-beamed headlamp, electro-magnetic couplers at front and rear. 8-in. manually-operated crane car; crane swings in circle, boom raises and lowers, pulley block lifts. Steam-type switcher tender, red gondola with barrels, red and black work caboose—all cars couple and uncouple. 8 sections of curved, 1 section of straight, 1 uncoupling "027" track make oval 102 in. around. *UL approved.* 40-watt transformer for 110–120 volt, 60 cycle AC. Train is 42¼ in. long overall.

One of the most exciting gifts you can find for your boy!
79 N 09651—Shipping weight 14 pounds $25.95

A New GP-7 Milwaukee Road Diesel in black and orange with horn. All-purpose switcher with Magne-Traction to give it greater power, higher speeds without spills. Authentically detailed in plastic and die-cast metal. Electric coupler at both ends. Powerful worm-drive motor. Two four-wheel trucks, 8 wheels in all. 14 in. long. Use it for switching or your main line. For "027" or "0" gauge track. An ideal gift for your trainman.
49 N 9895—Wt. 5 lbs..... $21.75

B 4¾-in. Section Gang Car. When buffer plate at either end strikes bumper, car reverses direction, "gandy dancer" turns around. Plastic and steel built-in motor works on "027" or "0" gauge track like a locomotive. Reduced—order now!
49 N 9846—Shpg. wt. 2 lbs. Was $7.95....... $6.75

C 9¼-in. Operating Cattle Car with 13¾-in. Platform and Ramp. When car stops at platform, remote-control button (incl.) opens doors, drops ramp, 9 cattle troop out of car, across platform, back into car. Built-in remote control, no special track needed. Lots of clever action.
49 N 9864—Shpg. wt. 4 lbs. Was $15.95..... $13.75

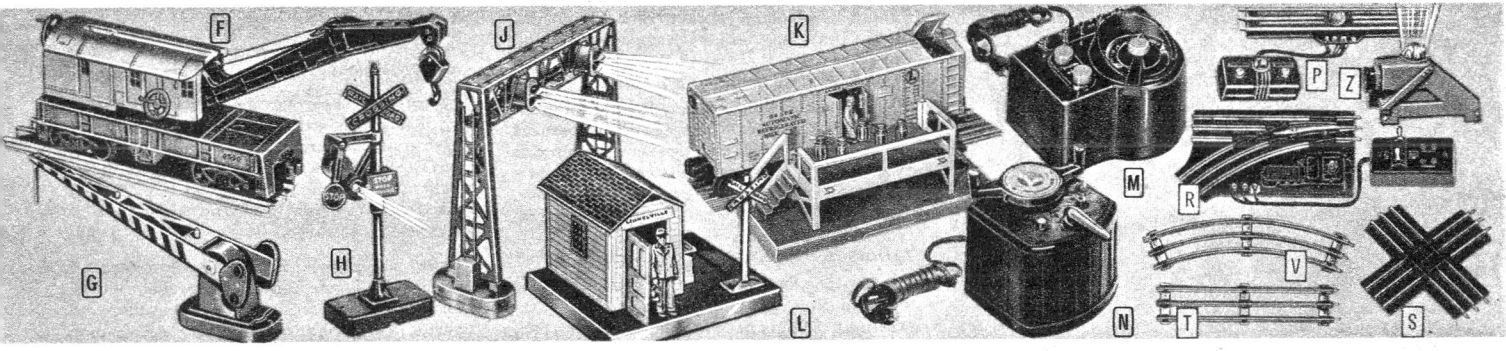

Make your trainyard more fun with realistic, action-packed Lionel accessories!

F 7⅞-in. Crane Car. Hand wheel controls. Crane swings in circle; boom raises and lowers; pulley block lifts. Die-cast metal trucks, 8 solid steel wheels, knuckle-type remote control electric couplers. Price cut, order now!
49 N 9852—Wt. 3 lbs. Was $7.95.... $6.85

G Illuminated Crossing Gate automatically lowers as train nears, raises after train has passed. Scale-size imitation jewels glow in 9¾-in. arm. With bulb.
49 N 9830—Wt. 1 lb. Was $3.95.... $3.29

10⅞-in. Operating Lumber Car. Press remote control button, section of platform tilts, logs roll off into bin. Rotating brake wheel. Die-cast metal trucks. 8 steel wheels, knuckle-type remote control electric couplers. Logs, bin incl.
49N9870—Wt. 1 lb. Was $7.25.... $6.85

H 7½-in. Automatic Banjo Signal. As train nears, signal lights up, banjo "Stop" sign swings back and forth over light.
49 N 9827—Wt. 1 lb. Was $5.95.... $4.45

J Operating Signal Bridge. Spans 2 tracks. Lights work automatically. Girders, ladders. 10½x3x7¾ in. high.
49 N 9836—4 bulbs incl. Wt. 2 lbs... $5.89

K New 10⅛-in. scale Operating Milk Car 5x7¼-in. steel platform. Doors open, man comes out, delivers cans to platform. 8 steel wheels, die-cast truck, knuckle-type remote control electric couplers. *Same quality but smaller size was $10.50.*
49 N 9869—With 5 cans. Wt. 3 lbs... $9.75

L Illuminated Automatic Gateman rushes out swinging lantern as train nears. After train has passed, man returns to shack, door closes. Metal and plastic. 6¾ in. high.
49 N 9835—Shpg. wt. 2 lbs. Was $5.95..... $4.95

Trainmaster Transformers. For 110-120 volt, 60-cycle AC. Self-setting automatic circuit breaker guards against overloads. Light shows when there is a short. Cord, plug.

M New! Type LW-125-watt. Full speed range for any train. Fixed 14 and 18 volts have common ground with track. Useful when there are accessories connected to track which require different voltages. Illuminated dial. *UL approved.*
49 N U9819—Shpg. wt. 10 lbs........... $12.75

N Type KW—190-watt. 2 independently-controlled variable voltages for running 2 trains on different layouts at same time. Whistle, reversing control for each train. Fixed 6, 14, 20 volt accessory circuits plus ample power to run both trains. Molded case.
49 N U9821—Wt. 11 lbs. Was $22.50.... $21.75

P "027" Magnetic Track Section for remote control coupling and uncoupling. Controller and connecting wire incl.
49 N 9804—Shpg. wt. 1 lb..... Each $3.45

R "027" Remote Control Switches. New device throws swivel rails automatically, lets train run through. Red, green lights on switch and controller also change. 1 right, 1 left switch. Wt. 3 lbs.
49 N 9806—Were $13.95. Pair.... $11.85

S "027" 90-degree Crossover 7⅜ in. sq.
49N9803—Wt. 8 oz. Was $1.95.. $1.65

T "027" 8⅞-in. Straight Track Section.
49N9801—Wt. 3 oz. Was 25c. Each .22c

V "027" 9½-in. Curved Track Section.
49N9802—Wt. 3 oz. Was 25c. Each .22c

Z Illuminated Bumper. For "027" or "0" Ga.
49N9859—Wt. 1 lb. Was $1.95. Ea. $1.65

SEARS CHRISTMAS CATALOG
1956

Cowboys were kings in 1956. Roy Rogers, Hoppy and Gene Autry were television heroes and Sears' Christmas catalog was jam-packed with rootin' tootin' cowboy accessories for kids. Still, electric trains continued to be best sellers.

Sears dropped its Happi-Time brand name in 1956 in favor of the more serious-sounding Allstate. Virtually every loco, car and accessory manufactured by Lionel, the industry leader, was now copied in a slightly cheaper version by Marx and Allstate. Sears even sold a "battery powered" train set for $5.79.

More electronic devices began to appear in the catalog's train pages, including two different P.A. systems which allowed young engineers to announce their train's arrivals and departures, as well as a new "Talking Railroad Station" which did the work automatically.

COWBOY SHOOTIN' IRONS
Big and flashy for fast-drawing frontiersmen

[A] **New Daisy Cowboy Outfit.** A smoking carbine with telescopic sight, a 50-shot pistol, a holster and a snap-off canteen—everything a young ranger needs on the trail. The 32-inch carbine has a detachable 2-power sight with 4 lenses for long-range magnification. Pull trigger, carbine smokes at muzzle, bangs and recoils realistically. Cocks like a real carbine. Rust-resistant blue metal barrel, brown plastic stock. Fast-firing, break-barrel pistol is made of die-cast metal for true-to-life detailing. 9½ inches long with ivory color plastic grip. Two-tone holster is made of lustrous genuine leather with jaunty fringe trim. Pint canteen fastens to belt that fits sizes 21 to 27¼ inches.
79 N 02689—Shipping weight 6 pounds $8.95

[B] **Wild Bill Hickok 2-Gun Hipsling Holster Set** with badge and identification card. Hipsling style puts guns at hand level, ready for a fast draw! Wear either single holster or both. Top grain leather holsters and belts backed with comfortable felt. Metal conchas with make-believe jewel centers on each holster front. Twelve silver-color bullets in each belt. Silver color metal nailhead decorations complete he-man western styling. Two side-loader cap pistols, 11½ inches long. Simulated ivory horsehead grips.
49 N 2688—Fits waist sizes 24 to 31. Shipping weight 4 pounds $8.95

[C] **New! Young Buffalo Bill 2-Gun Hipsling Holster Set.** Guns at hand level draw in a flash! Wear singly or "two-gun" style. Top grain russet leather holsters and belts in fine hand-tooled effect with black inlay; plated bullets. Two 10½-inch 50-shot metal cap pistols, bronze metal grips.
49 N 2661—Fits waist sizes 22 to 30. Shipping weight 3 pounds.......... $4.79

[D] **New! Texas Ranger Sheriff's 1-Gun Holster Set.** Jailer's keys to the cells of playland badmen dangle from the smart two-tone leather holster belt. Mahogany color belt and back, black holster front. Nickel-plated nailhead decorations. 8¼-inch 50-shot metal cap pistol.
49 N 2655—Belt fits waist sizes 22 to 30. Shipping weight 1 pound 7 ounces $1.89

[E] **New! Gold color 2-gun Holster Set.** Gold color die-cast metal holster fronts gleam with bright highlights. Belt decorated with silver color steerhead metal conchas and bullets. Belt and holster backs of top grain blue-black leather with soft, comfortable felt backing. Leather leg ties. Two bright gold color 50-shot magazine-loading cap pistols, 10½ inches long, black pistol grips.
49 N 2681—Belt fits waist sizes 22 to 30. Shipping weight 3 pounds 4 ounces $7.69

[F] **New! 2-Gun Double Holster Set.** Genuine leather in handsome simulated alligator design. Duded up with engraved metal medallions that have just-pretend jewelled centers. Silver color bullets, nickel-plated studs. Two 10½-inch 50-shot break barrel cap pistols of die-cast metal; bronze metal grips.
49 N 2659—Belt fits waist sizes 22 to 30. Shipping weight 2 pounds 8 ounces $3.79

[G] **Big Special Purchase! Texas Ranger 2-Gun Holster Set.** Top grain genuine leather in western-look natural color with red holster fronts. Felt backing. Nickel-plated studs, pretend-jewel centers; plated bullets. Leg ties. Two big "44" die-cast metal cap pistols, 11½ in. long, with revolving cylinder. Simulated ivory grips.
49 N 2708—Belt fits waist sizes 22 to 30. Shipping weight 3 pounds 4 ounces $6.69

[H] **Big Special Purchase! Texas Ranger 2-Gun Holster Set.** A beautifully decorated set straight out of an Old West tale! Top grain russet cowhide leather belt and holsters have fine embossed cowboy hand-tooled effect. Silver color bullets on belt. Two gleaming nickel-plated 50-shot cap pistols with break barrel action, 8½ inches long. Simulated ivory horsehead grips.
49 N 2702—Belt fits waist sizes 23 to 30. Shipping weight 1 pound 12 ounces $2.89

[J] **New! Gene Autry Complete Cowboy Outfit.** Western-styled from vest to spurs! *Leather holster set* has hand-tooled effect; make-believe jewels decorate metal medallions. Silver color bullets. Tough leg ties. *Two 9¾-inch 50-shot break barrel cap pistols* of die cast metal. Embossed leather *cuffs*. *Metal spurs*, adjustable *spur straps*. Suede-front *vest* has simulated fur trim.
49 N 2744—Belt fits waist sizes 22 to 30. Shipping weight 3 pounds 12 ounces ... $5.95

NOTE: Ohio prohibits sale of cap firing guns to minors under 16 years of age

[K] **Roy Rogers 2-Gun Holster Set.** Genuine leather belt and holsters with hand-tooled effect on holster fronts. Roy's name on adjustable belt; diamond-shaped decorations and silver color plastic bullets. Leather leg ties hold holsters steady while you draw. Two 10¾-inch 50-shot break barrel pistols of die cast metal. Engraved pistol grips.
49 N 2657—Belt fits waist sizes 23 to 30. Shipping weight 2 pounds 7 ounces........ $3.79

[L] **Roy Rogers Battery Lantern.** Metal frame. Clear plastic chimney. On-off switch. 7½ inches high. Uses 1 battery, not incl.
49 N 4922—1½-volt bulb included. Shipping weight 14 ounces................... 89¢
34 N 4659—Two baby size flashlight batteries. Shpg. wt. 4 oz. .... 2 for 28¢

Roy Rogers 2-Gun Holster Set. Trim belt and buckle decoration, silver color nailheads on fine top grain russet leather holster fronts. Russet top grain leather belt has fine tooled effect, with Roy's name, silver color bullets. Fancy engraved floral design grips on two 50-shot 10¾-in. break barrel cap pistols.
49 N 2677—Belt fits waist sizes 23 to 28. Shipping weight 2 pounds 9 ounces........ $5.79

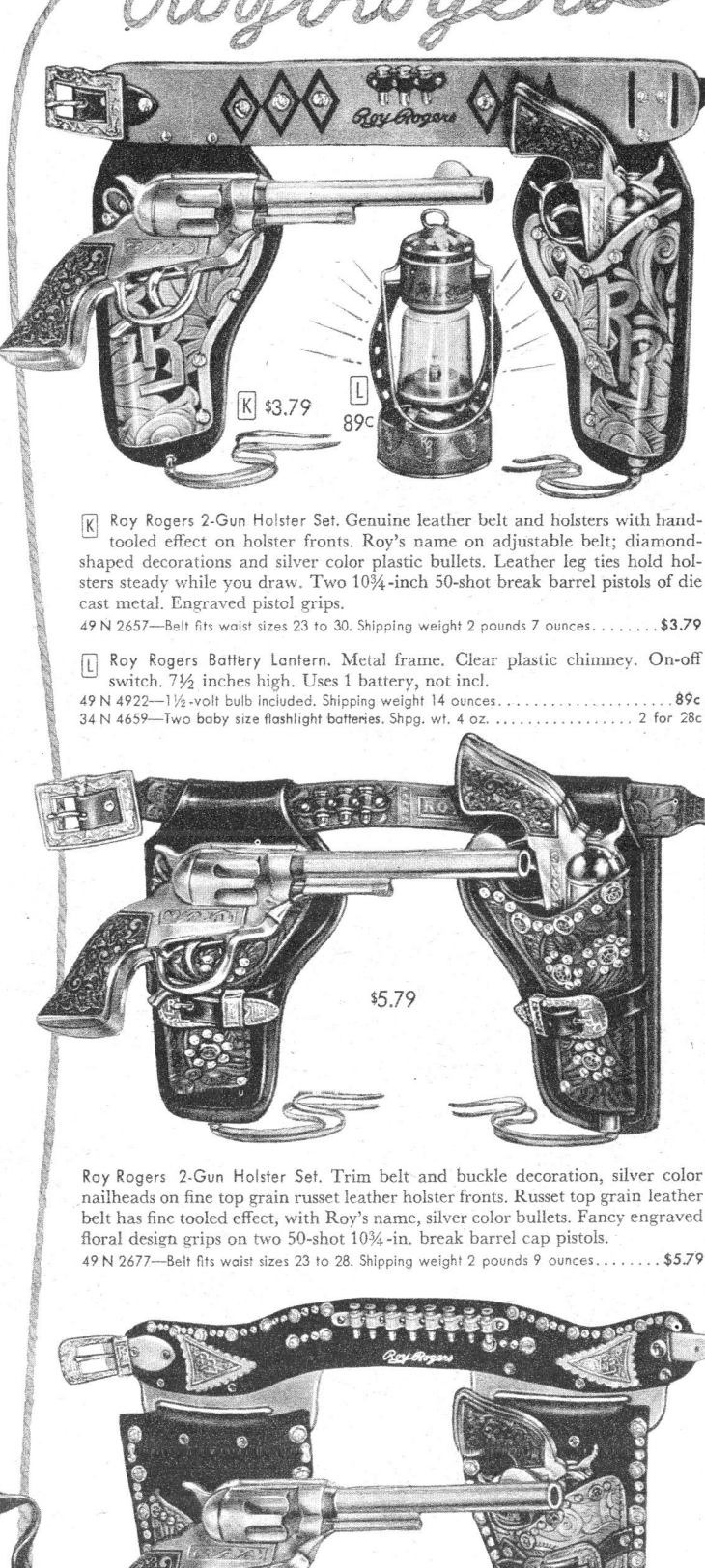

Finely Decorated Roy Rogers 2-Gun Holster Set. Make-believe jewels, nickel-plated nailheads highlight top grain leather holsters and belt. Fancy cross strap decoration on holster fronts. Silver color bullets. Two 10¾-in. 50-shot break barrel cap pistols of die-cast metal, metal grips.
49 N 2682—Belt fits waist sizes 23 to 30. Shipping weight 2 pounds 5 ounces..... $7.69

New Improved ALLSTATE features add realism!

2 remote control switches (1 right and 1 left). Lights change red to green automatically

New large radius track... stronger, 5 ties per section take greater speeds, make firmer layouts

NEW! Electric 6-unit Diesel Freight... Remote Control Switch Track

Listen to the diesel "roar" hum from the heavy-duty switcher. Action galore... and the stock-loading ramp adds hours of fun. Entire train almost 5 ft. long. Includes plastic diesel switcher with gleaming headlamp, powerful motor and oilless bronze bearings, rear unit, tractor car with 2 tractors, stock car, gondola, bay window caboose. All with double trucks (8 die-cast wheels per unit) plastic and steel.

19 track sections and pair of switches form 197-inch outer oval (with inner oval, over 20 ft. of roadbed). Loading ramp with stock, 14 pcs. of fence. Run train forward or back, couple or uncouple cars, all by remote control. *UL approved* 75-watt transformer with circuit breaker. 110-120-volt, 60-cycle AC. 4 binding posts, 2 for accessories. Electric train 55 inches long.
79 N 09630—Complete 43-pc. set. Wt. 18 lbs. $28.98

$28.98 cash
$3.00 down with Switches

Make this the best Christmas ever, with an ALLSTATE Electric Train

Crane Car Has Electric Light. Boom, Tackle operate with 2-Wheel Control

ALLSTATE

[A] $24.95 cash $2.50 down
7-unit Work Train, 14 track sections

[B] $17.95
6-unit Freight, 10 track sections

[C] $9.69
5-unit Passenger, 10 track sections

[D] Electric Hand Car $3.69

[E] Whistling Station $4.39

[F] Automatic Barrel Loader $5.49

272 .. SEARS, ROEBUCK AND CO. c

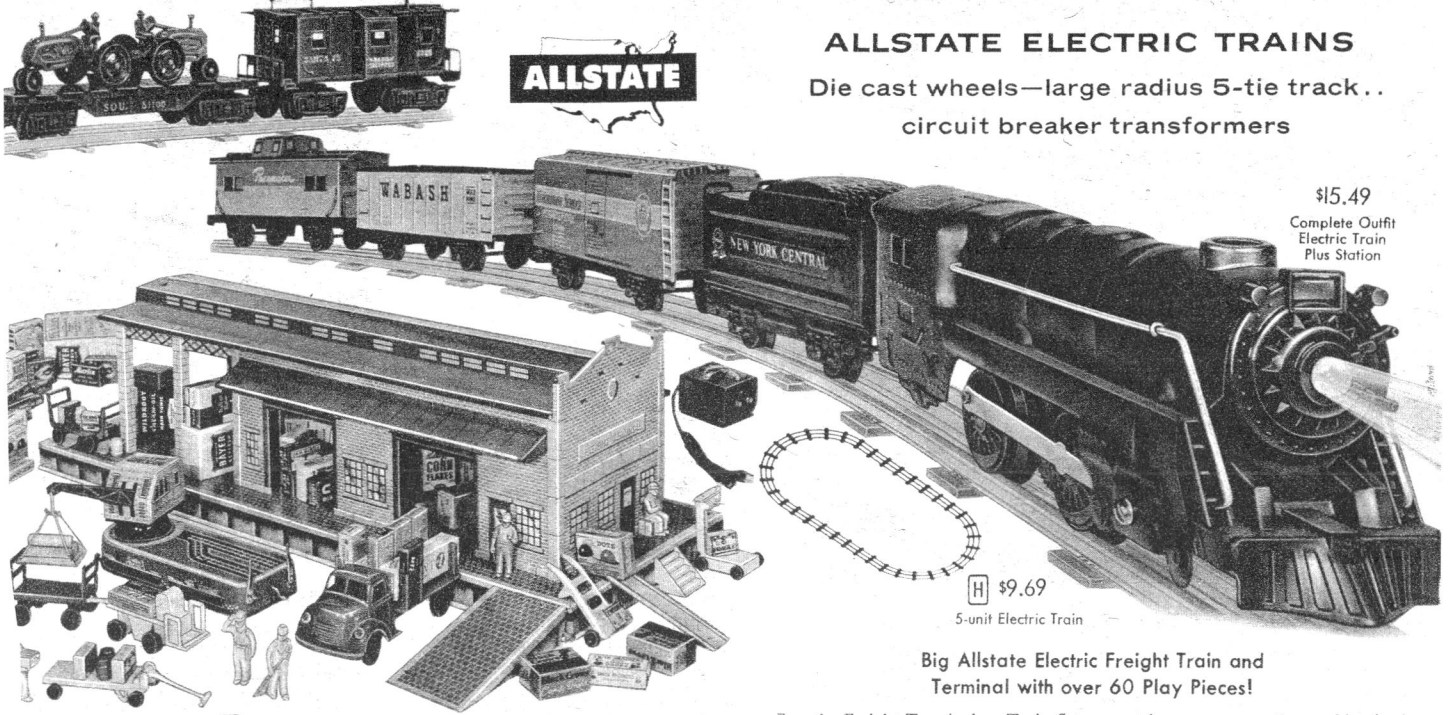

ALLSTATE ELECTRIC TRAINS
Die cast wheels—large radius 5-tie track..
circuit breaker transformers

$15.49
Complete Outfit
Electric Train
Plus Station

[H] **$9.69**
5-unit Electric Train

[G] **$6.79** Freight Terminal

◀ ELECTRIC TRAINS DESCRIBED BELOW SHOWN ON OPPOSITE PAGE

All Allstate Trains have large radius track. Stronger . . . 5 ties per section (only 3 on old type). Faster speeds possible . . . gentler curve holds train to track even at full transformer speeds. Better "track bed" . . . longer curves make firmer track, about 30% larger . . . holds together better.

[A] **New! 7-unit Train . . . Our Best.** Puffs non-toxic smoke as it rolls along with a chug-chug sound. Die-cast metal 3/16-in. scale model of a 4-6-2-wheel drive locomotive. Powerful headlight and illuminated number marker. Oilless bronze bearings, 4-wheel pony trucks, 2 guide wheels. Plastic and steel coal tender, 6 cars are scale detailed. (Notice the authentic features on the new crane car!) Run train slow or fast, ahead or reverse, couple or uncouple cars, all by remote control.

Train almost 5½ feet long. Searchlight car, operating milk car with ramp . . man comes out; automobile car with four plastic autos, new wrecker crane car and wrecker caboose. All 3/16 inch scale, steel and plastic; double trucks; automatic couplers. Large radius track makes oval 174½ inches around with 5 sections straight, and 8 curved. 1 uncoupling ramp, "Uncouple Here" sign. 1-oz. bottle of harmless smoke liquid. UL approved 100-watt transformer with circuit breaker and 4 binding posts (2 for accessories). For 110-120-volt, 60-cycle AC. Electric train 63 inches long.
79 N 09629—Shipping weight 14 pounds........................**$24.95**

[B] **New! 6-unit Work Train** with heavy-duty, steam-type locomotive. Puffs non-toxic smoke. Scale detailed die cast metal. Remote control reversing mechanism. Run train forward, backwards, fast or slow. Uncouple cars . . recouple cars by contact all by remote control. Headlight casts a sharp beam down the mainline. Oilless bronze bearings. 4-wheel drive, pony trucks, 2 guide wheels, coal and water type tender.

Entire train is 52½ inches long . . . over 4 feet of fast-rolling fun. Wrecker car, searchlight car with powerful light, drop-end gondola with 35 plastic construction tools, caboose. All cars have die cast wheels, double trucks (8 wheels on each car). Automatic couplers. Scale detailed plastic and steel. Large radius track makes 129½-in. oval with 1 section straight, 8 sections curved, 1 uncoupling ramp, "Uncouple Here" sign, 1-oz. bottle harmless smoke liquid.

UL approved 50-watt transformer with circuit breaker, 2 posts. For 110-120-volt, 60-cycle AC. A powerful electric train with a lot of play value.
49 N 9628—Shipping weight 11 pounds.........................**$17.95**

[C] **New! 5-unit Diesel Passenger Train . . .** a terrific buy at this low price. This set has the same careful modeling, remote control speed, reversing, die-cast wheels and superior large radius track as our higher-priced trains! Streamlined, scale-detailed twin-diesel locomotive has gleaming headlight, powerful motor, oilless bronze bearings.

Train is 37½ inches long. Includes diesel locomotive with rear unit, 2 passenger coaches and 1 observation coach all with manual couplers. Accurately and colorfully lithographed to the finest detail . . . makes a "real-life" appearance!

Large radius track (2 sections straight, 8 sections curved) makes oval about 129½ in. around. Run train forward or back, fast or slow by remote control without touching track or train. UL approved 50-watt transformer with circuit breaker, 2 posts. For 110-120-volt, 60-cycle AC.
49 N 9624—Shipping weight 7 pounds 12 ounces...................**$9.69**

Exciting Accessories for Electric Trains

[D] **Electric Hand Car** with 2 husky railroaders that pump at crossbars. Plastic and steel chassis. Powerful electric motor. 6¼x2x4½ inches high.
49 N 9753—Shipping weight 12 ounces..........................**$3.69**

[E] **Remote Control Whistling Station.** Press button, hear the realistic wail of locomotive whistle as your train speeds down the track. Mechanism enclosed in lithographed steel station. 9x5¼x5 inches high. Control panel and wires included.
49 N 9739—Shipping weight 2 pounds..........................**$4.39**

[F] **New! Remote Control Barrel Loader.** Press button, lift truck takes barrel from loading chute to car. Realistically detailed molded plastic. Easily installed on any track layout. All wires and controls included. 8¾x7⅞x5 in. high.
49 N 9779—Car and track not included. Shipping weight 1 pound 6 ounces........**$5.49**

Big Allstate Electric Freight Train and Terminal with over 60 Play Pieces!

Buy the Freight Terminal or Train Set separately . . or save on the combination!

[G] **New! Freight Terminal** with dual lever control mechanical crane . . . lifts, swivels, turns in all directions. Made of lithographed steel with ramp and plastic stairway to loading platform. Has all freight handling equipment the young trainman could want . . . truck, empty cartons, baggage trucks, crates, workers . . . *over 40 play pieces in all!* Terminal is 29 inches long, 11 inches wide, 9 inches high. Easily set up without tools.
79 N 09789—Freight Terminal only. Shipping weight 7 pounds.............**$6.79**

[H] **Five-unit Steam-type Freight Train.** Steel steam-type electric locomotive, modeled in detail with gleaming headlight, oilless bronze bearings, die-cast wheels. Train overall is 40½ in. Includes coal tender, high-side gondola, box car and caboose, all with die-cast metal wheels. Large radius track (8 sections of curved, 2 sections straight) makes oval about 129½ in. around. Run train forward, back, fast or slow by remote control. UL approved 50-watt transformer with circuit breaker to protect against shorts.
49 N 9605—For 110-120-volt, 60-cycle AC. Shipping weight 8 pounds..........**$9.69**

Complete Outfit (G and H) as shown . . . Makes huge, impressive layout for play hours and fun galore . . . Terminal, Train, Track and Transformer. Save on combination.
79 N 09627—Separately, pieces total $16.48. Shipping weight 15 pounds......**$15.49**

New Rugged Gantry Crane for high overhead action!

$6.49
Gantry Crane

Brawny looking in every detail . . . add this important railroading operation to your train layout! Crane is mounted on wheels, straddles track or operates alongside.

Massive boom lowers and raises with a crank, lifting hook operates with separate crank, loads and unloads cargo. Crane cab revolves, swivels and turns in all directions.

Durable die-cast base, authentically detailed. Body and boom of crane in high-impact plastic to withstand hard use in the railroad yard. Die-cast hook. Base is 6x6 inches square, length with boom up is 14½ inches. Priced low for so much fun. Order early, in time for Christmas giving!
49 N 9782—Shipping weight 3 lbs..... **$6.49**

$2.89 Talking Railroad Station

New Railroad Station with a talking "voice"!

Turn the crank, hear: "All aboard for Detroit, Chicago, etc.," then the realistic "choo-choo" of the train rolling off to far-away places. Colorful lithographed metal. Includes 6 plastic figures and accessories. 20⅝x10x6¼ in. high.
49 N 9787—Shipping weight 3 pounds 8 ounces...................**$2.89**

C PAGE 273 .. ALLSTATE TRAINS

Scale-detailed Electric Diesels .. Interurban Car

(A through C) Realistically designed with authentic markings. Powerful motor, die-cast wheels, oilless bronze bearings. Remote control of speed and reversing. (A) and (B) have automatic coupler. For ALLSTATE, Happi-Time or Marx Electric Train layouts using 110-120-volt, 60-cycle AC. Order early!

A Twin-Diesel Locomotive. Steel and plastic with true realism. 2 sections, single motor. Two 4-wheel trucks per section. 24 in. long over all. Headlamp.
49 N 9792—Shpg. wt. 4 lbs..... **$12.95**

"Power" B unit (not illustrated). Make above twin-diesel unit into a 3-section diesel .. perfect match. Detailed plastic scale model. Two 4-wheel trucks. Manual coupler front, rear. 12 in. long. No motor.
49 N 9781—Shpg. wt. 1 lb...... $4.79

B New Diesel Switcher with automatic coupling front and rear. Hums like a real diesel. Die-cast metal chassis, plastic body. Measures 10½ in. long.
49 N 9783—Shpg. wt. 2 lbs. 4 oz.. $11.45

C New Electric-lighted Interurban Car. 11⅞ inches long. Boston and Maine design and color, with dummy air horns on top. Red and green marker lights. Manual coupler can be incorporated in any standard track layout. Will make a fine gift—order now.
49 N 9784—Shpg. wt. 2 lbs. 12 oz.. $9.45

Action-packed Cars for ALLSTATE, Happi-Time or Marx Electric Trains

(D thru H) Cars with Action! Heavy duty plastic and steel. Detailed to scale. Die-cast wheels, remote control automatic couplers. 4-wheel trucks. Bring your railroad stock up to date.

D New Operating Crane and Wrecker Car. 12¼ in. long, 4¾ in. high. Plastic control cab and boom revolve on die-cast metal flat car chassis. 7-inch boom is raised and lowered by crank-type wheel on side of cab .. another wheel for operating the hook. Lighted searchlight swivels, tilts, turns in all directions.
49 N 9786—Shpg. wt. 1 lb. 10 oz........ $4.79

E Operating Milk Car with Platform. As car is backed to unloading platform, door opens; trainman steps out. At forward speeds, door is closed. Rolling stock, authentic detail. 9 inches long. Sure to delight the young trainmaster.
49 N 9759—Shpg. wt. 1 lb............. $3.67

F Revolving Searchlight Car. Light turns as train moves. Dummy motor and generator picks up current from track shoe. 9¾ inches long.
49 N 9758—Shipping weight 1 lb........ $3.67

G Automobile Carrier Car. 2-deck rack on flat car. 4 autos about 4 inches long .. detach to unload. 9½ in. long.
49 N 9755—Shipping weight 1 lb........ $3.67

H Lighted Passenger Cars (astrodome shown). Show silhouettes of passengers. Lithographed metal. Automatic couplers. Sturdy wheels, 4-wheel trucks. Shipping weight each 14 ounces.
49 N 9770—11-in. Astrodome.......... $3.67
49 N 9771—10¾-in. Observation....... 3.67

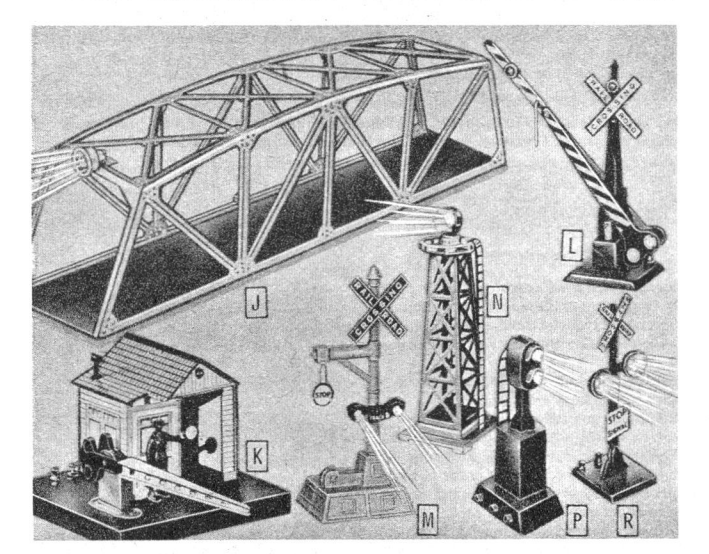

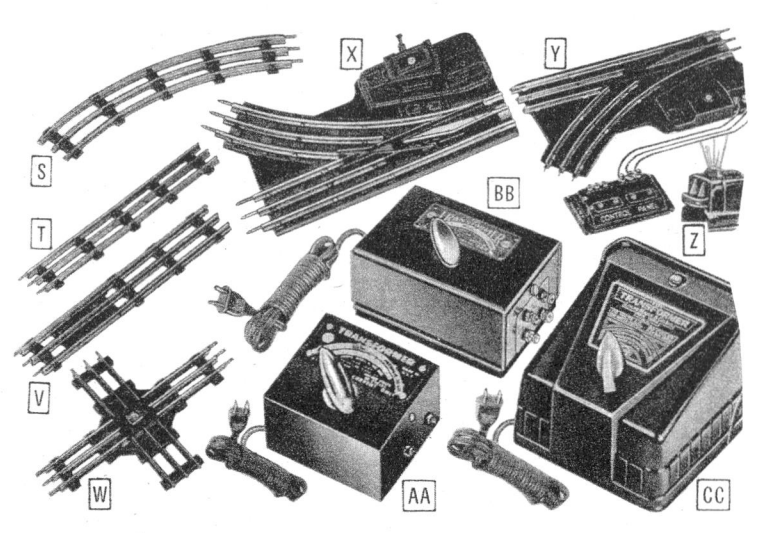

Scale-detailed Accessories, Transformers and Extra Track for ALLSTATE, Happi-Time or Marx Electric Trains

means all wire, track connectors, etc., necessary are included

J Lighted Steel Trestle Bridge.* Aluminum finish. Light socket and reflector clip on, adjust. With bulb, track connector. 24x4⅞x6⅛ in. high.
49 N 9741—Shpg. wt. 2 lbs. 4 oz..... $1.98

K Automatic Grade Crossing Shack and Watchman* warns of approaching train. Lithographed steel shanty and 7-inch plastic gate. As train nears, watchman comes out with a stop sign, gate lowers. Base 7x6½ inches; house 4½ in. high.
49 N 9760—Shpg. wt. 2 lbs......... $3.49

L Automatic Crossing Gate.* Arm lowers as train approaches, then raises. Simulated jewel reflector at end of gate. Steel. 7¾ inches high.
49 N 9743—Shpg. wt. 10 oz........ $1.87

M Flasher-Wagger Crossing Signal.* Lights blink, swinging stop sign moves back and forth as train approaches. Sturdy plastic. 7½ in. high.
49 N 9774—Shpg. wt. 10 oz........ $3.39

N Lighted Revolving Beacon.* Light revolves on top of girder-type molded plastic tower. Revolves constantly, beams a bright red light in one direction, green in the other. 12½ in. high.
49 N 9740—Shpg. wt. 10 oz..... $1.87

P Automatic Double Light Block Signal.* Train stops on red, proceeds on green light. Sturdy plastic. Switch at rear operates signal. 2 track sections included. 7¼ inches high.
49 N 9745—Shpg. wt. 10 oz..... $1.89

R Automatic Crossing Flasher.* Twin red lights flash alternately as train approaches; stop after train is past. Made of plastic, 7 in. high. Fully automatic.
49 N 9742—Shpg. wt. 10 oz..... $1.89

NOTE: All these electric accessories are for Allstate, Happi-Time or Marx electric train layouts using 110-120-volt, 60-cycle AC transformers. Order several, complete your trainman's layout.

(S through Y) Large Radius Electric Track. For ALLSTATE, Happi-Time. or Marx electric trains. Run trains faster .. trains hold to track better. Longer sections mean firmer track layout. 5 cross ties per section, not the usual 3 ties. Shpg. wt. ea. 4 oz.
(S) 49 N 9723—12½-in. Curved Track...... 22c
(T) 49 N 9720—11¼-in. Straight Track...... 22c

V Uncoupling Unit. 5 ties to match. "Uncouple Here" sign included.
49 N 9749—Shpg. wt. 5 oz............... 75c

W Cross-over Track. 9¼x9¼ in. square.
49 N 9726—Shpg. wt. 9 oz............$1.29

X New Electric Switch Set. Operates manually. For wide radius track layout. One right and one left hand switch.
49 N 9776—Shpg. wt. 2 lbs......... Set $4.79

Y Large Radius Remote Control Switch Set; red, green light. 1 right hand, one left hand switch. 4-button control panel.
49 N 9727—Shpg. wt. 2 lbs. 8 oz..... Set $8.95

Z Lighted Dead-end Bumper. Plastic; 3x1⅞x 2 in. high. Snaps to end of spur track. Bulb included.
49 N 9707—Shpg. wt. 5 oz............. 89c

(AA, BB, CC) Transformers for Electric Trains. UL Approved. 110-120-volt, 60-cycle AC. Built-in circuit breaker with reset button protects against short circuits and burnouts. Attached cord, wires, track connector.

AA 50-watt Transformer. Two sets of binding posts; one set gives variable 7 to 13 volts, controls train speed; other set gives fixed 13 volts for accessories. Steel case, air-cooled base.
49 N 9725—Shpg. wt. 3 lbs............$4.?

BB New 100-watt Transformer. Two sets of binding posts; one set gives variable 5 to 15 volts for controlling train speed; other set fixed 15 volts for accessories. Steel, air-cooled base.
49 N 9777—Shpg. wt. 4 lbs. 8 oz........ $8.49

CC Super-Powered 150-watt Transformer. Two sets of binding posts; one set gives variable 0 to 15 volts for controlling train speed; one set gives fixed 15 volts for accessories. Throttle-type control. Massive plastic case with air-cooled metal base.
49 N 9764—Shpg. wt. 10 lbs...........$12.95

Sears guarantees satisfaction or your money refunded

ALLSTATE

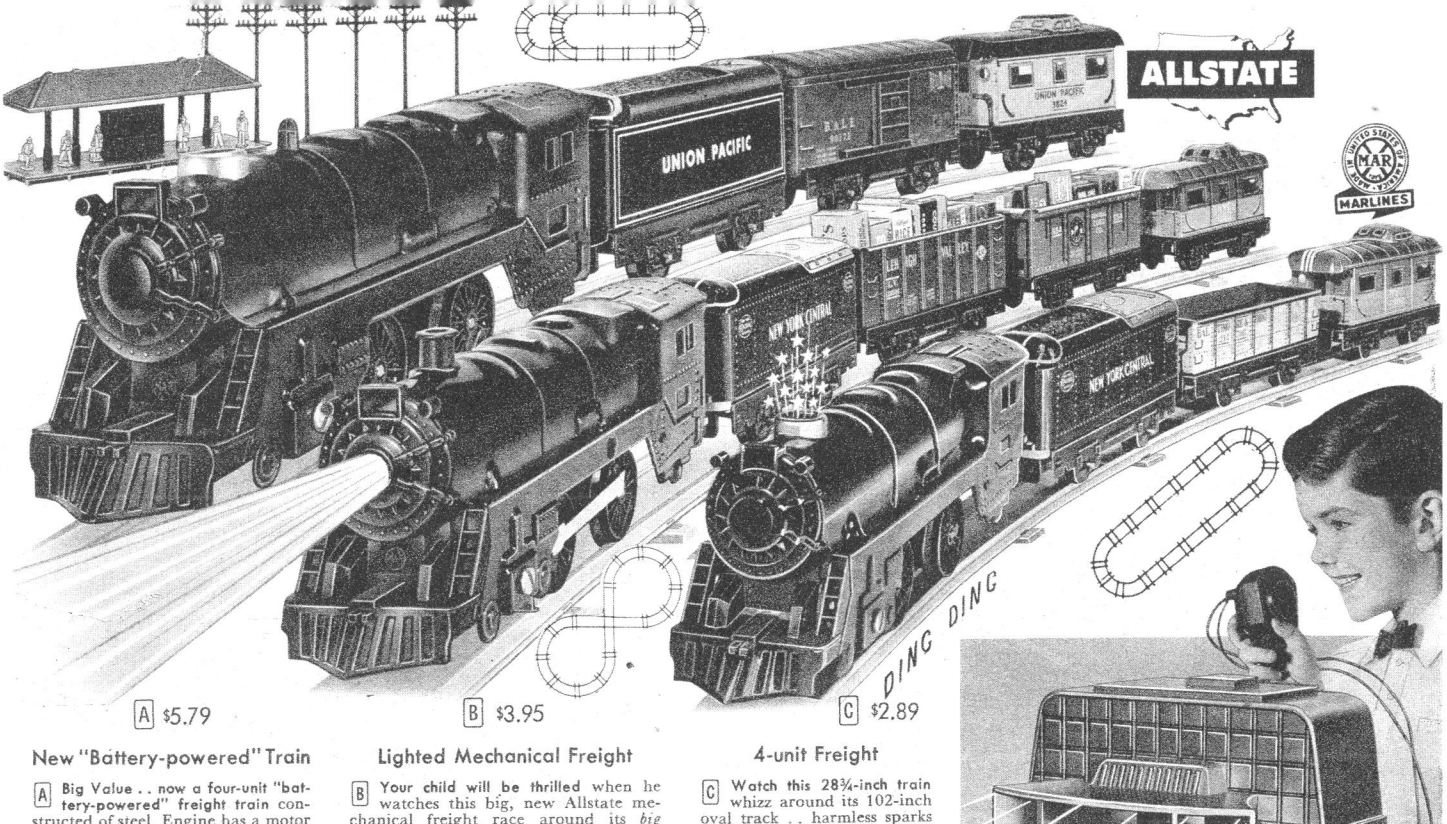

[A] $5.79 [B] $3.95 [C] $2.89

New "Battery-powered" Train

A Big Value .. now a four-unit "battery-powered" freight train constructed of steel. Engine has a motor which operates on two standard flashlight batteries (not included, order batteries below). Train runs forward or backward. Stop-and-go switch is on top of locomotive. Includes: detailed 13-inch plastic railroad station with people, 6 telegraph poles. Train 28¾ in. long. Lithographed metal tender, box car and caboose. 6 sections of straight track, 10 curved sections; 1 left-hand and 1 right-hand manually-operated switch. Makes a double oval track layout .. 138-in. outer oval; 90-in. inner oval. 5½-inch two-tone metal mouth whistle to blow Woo-o-o-o. An outstanding value, order now.
49 N 9512—Wt. 4 lbs. 12 oz. . . $5.79
34 N 4650—Standard batteries.
Shpg. wt. 8 oz. for 2. . . . . . . 2 for 27c

Lighted Mechanical Freight

B Your child will be thrilled when he watches this big, new Allstate mechanical freight race around its *big crossover track*. Bell rings, electric headlight gleams brightly down the track. Steel locomotive has long-running clockspring motor with built-in speed governor and brake. Train 34½ inches long with tender, 2 highside gondolas (1 red, 1 green) and a caboose. 4 sections of straight track, 12 curved and crossover make an 176-inch, figure-8 track layout .. or you can make a double oval track layout by ordering manual switch set from extra track listings below. Headlight operates on baby-size 1-inch battery (not included, order battery below). A real train buy for young "train-masters". For extra fun and realism, order several of our thrifty accessories shown below.
49 N 9511—Shpg. wt. 3 lbs. 8 oz. . . . $3.95
34 N 4659—Batteries. Shpg. wt. 4 oz. for 2
2 for 28c . . . . 6 for 78c

4-unit Freight

C Watch this 28¾-inch train whizz around its 102-inch oval track .. harmless sparks shooting out and its merry little bell ringing as it rolls along. Steam-type steel locomotive has long-running clock-spring motor with built-in speed governor and brake. Realistically lithographed metal tender, gondola and caboose. A wonderful little set for "railroaders" who are too young for an electric set. Complete with 10 sections of track .. a thrifty train. Just the right size for the young train enthusiast.
49 N 9503—Shipping weight 2 pounds 8 ounces. $2.89

Sears liberal Add-on Plan makes it easier than ever to buy on Easy Terms. See page 373

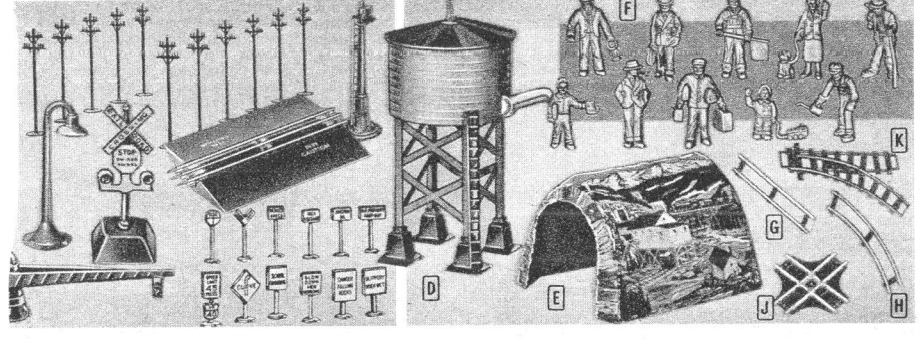

$5.39

Announce trains, page passengers on New Loudspeaker-Microphone Set

All aboard for fun! Here's the most sensational train accessory you've ever seen—it's just like the public address systems used in real train stations. Now you can call out stations, track numbers, announce arrivals and departures and page passengers over a real loudspeaker system. Speak into the microphone, the powerful 4-inch Alnico speaker in the tower sends your voice loud and clear all over the "station." Realistically detailed; made of high impact molded plastic in true-to-life railroad colors. Railroad-type microphone has control button, communication wire cable. Operates on 4 flashlight batteries included. Size overall 5x6x8 in. high.
49 N 9878—Shipping weight 1 pound 4 ounces. $5.39

Colorful Accessories for young trainmasters .. add realism to trains

29-piece Set of authentically scale-detailed railroad accessories. Made of durable plastic. A perfect, low cost gift for the young railroader who is receiving a new train set or already has one. Just the right size for any standard mechanical or electric train. Carefully designed to please the most particular train lover. Set includes 12, 7-inch telegraph poles, 12 railroad right-of-way signs, plus 1 each: semaphore, lamp post, crossing gate, grade crossing and grade crossing plate (track not in order below). A large set for such a low price. Order now for Christmas.
49 N 9750—Shpg. wt. 2 lbs. . . . . Set $2.59

D Plastic Water Tower with adjustable spout. 4¼ in. diameter, 8¼ inches high.
49 N 9701—Shipping weight 10 ounces. 89c

E Metal Tunnel. Watch your train thunder through the tunnel. Lithographed metal. Comes apart for storage. 9x7x10¾ in. long.
49 N 9729—Shipping weight 1 pound. 89c

F 10 Plastic 3-dimensional Figures. Includes engineer, porter, conductor, etc. Soft vinyl plastic. Up to 1½ inches high. Lots of fun for a low price, adds realism to train sets.
49 N 9762—Shipping weight 10 ounces. 89c

Set of 3 Lighted Lamp Posts

Add realism to any train layout. Bases notched to attach to electric track. One post has mail box; others police call box, fire alarm box. Wire and track connectors included. A thrifty, realistic set. Order now for Christmas.
49 N 9737—Shipping weight 1 pound. $1.89

Extra Track for Mechanical Trains

G Straight Track. Each 8⅞ inches long.
49 N 9701—Shpg. wt. 6 oz. . . . . Set of 4, 35c

H Curved Track. Each piece 10½ in. long.
49 N 9702—Shpg. wt. 6 oz. . . . . Set of 4, 35c

J 90° Crossover. Each piece 7½ in. square.
49 N 9703—Shpg. wt. 8 oz. . . . . Each 59c

K Manual Operating Switch Set. One left-hand switch, one right-hand switch.
49 N 9704—Shipping weight 1 lb. . . . . Set $1.79

$2.79

Fast-moving Scenic Express with signals that work

Here's a complete railroad system for younger children. Signals that work just like the real ones do! Action crossing gate and semaphore work automatically as the 11-inch train whizzes by. All the thrills and excitement of a big railroad! Train runs around grooved track in metal base over 20 times with just one easy winding. Watch it speed through tunnel and station. Train has long-running clockspring motor. Sturdy steel base, about 21¾ x 13 inches, is realistically lithographed with landscape scene. Order early! Priced low, an ideal first train for your toddler.
49 N 9515—Shipping weight 3 pounds. $2.79

A $39.25 cash
$4.00 down

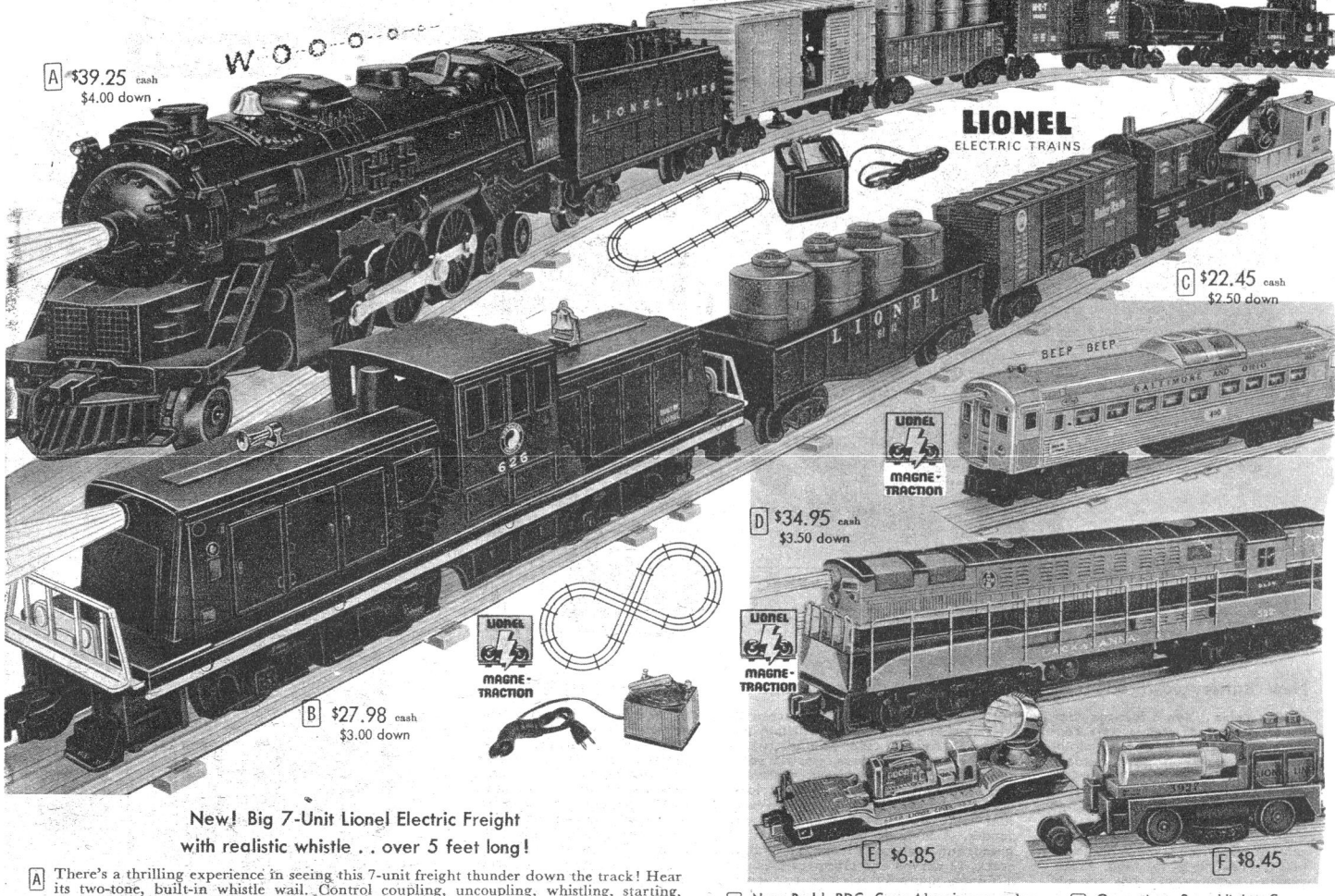

C $22.45 cash
$2.50 down

B $27.98 cash
$3.00 down

D $34.95 cash
$3.50 down

E $6.85

F $8.45

New! Big 7-Unit Lionel Electric Freight with realistic whistle .. over 5 feet long!

A There's a thrilling experience in seeing this 7-unit freight thunder down the track! Hear its two-tone, built-in whistle wail. Control coupling, uncoupling, whistling, starting, stopping, reversing and speed, all by remote control. Big 12-wheel die-cast metal engine with headlights, 6-wheel drive, piston rod action. Tender, 5 cars: box car, gondola with canisters, 1 remote box car—touch button, man pops out of door—oil car, caboose. All with double trucks, 8 wheels on each car, remote control, knuckle couplers. UL approved 90-watt transformer with built-in circuit breaker, whistle controller. 110-120-volt, 60-cycle AC. 8 curved, 3 straight, 1 uncoupler section of "027" track form oval 118-inches around. Train 66 in. long.
79 N 09606—Shipping weight 16 pounds $39.25

5-unit Electric Diesel Freight .. Magne-Traction .. Working Crane Car

B Here's one of the greatest values in the toy train field! Freight is pulled by powerful GE-44 B&O diesel with headlight .. knuckle couplers on front, rear .. Magne-Traction for high speeds without spills, even on curves and grades. Remote control of speed, forward or reverse, coupling and uncoupling with knuckle couplers. The set has a gondola with canisters, box car, operating crane car and work caboose. It's great fun to lift, lower and shift cargo with this crane car. Figure eight "027" track; 12 sections curved, 3 straight; 1 coupler section and a crossover form a 27x62-in. layout. 45-watt UL approved transformer for 110-120-volt, 60-cycle AC. Train is about 46 inches long. Sturdy steel and plastic. Order early for Christmas.
79 N 09602—Shipping weight 10 pounds $27.98

C New Budd RDC Car. Aluminum color, self-propelled car is a reproduction of the diesel car that is taking over short runs for the big railroads. Runs fast or slow, forward or back. Equipped with rail-gripping Magne-Traction. Has horn, headlight, marker lights and operating couplers on both ends. Interior lights show passengers in the window. 16½ in. long.
49 N 9834—Shpg. wt. 6 lbs $22.45

D Powerful 16½-inch Fairbanks-Morse "Double-Ender" Diesel. Two powerful motors built-in horn, couplers and headlamp at both ends. PLUS Magne-Traction for extra pulling power. Accurately detailed plastic cab; metal railing. Lighted marker lights and number box. Two 6-wheel trucks, each with own 6-wheel worm-drive motor. For "0" gauge track only.
49 N 9896—Shpg. wt. 7 lbs $34.95

E Operating Searchlight Car. Well car carries dummy generator and powerful searchlight which rotates continuously. Does not require remote control track. Magnetic knuckle couplers, die-cast metal chassis. 10 inches long. Realistically detailed.
49 N 9861—Shpg. wt. 2 lbs. $6.85

F New Track Cleaning Car. Actually cleans the track! Couples to locomotive. Built-in motor rotates brush .. move lever to start or stop rotation. Reservoir holds liquid track cleaner. Liquid solvent included. Track is wiped dry by pad fitted on rear of car. One remote control coupler. 6½ in. long.
49 N 9877—Shpg. wt. 2 lbs. $8.45

G $8.95

H $7.75

J $6.75

K $13.75

$11.75

New Sound Dispatching Station

Train fans can now call out stations—start and stop trains. Station contains loudspeaker connected to a microphone from which operator can announce arrival of train, call passengers, etc. Control in the handle of the mike can stop or start the train. Simulated microwave antenna is mounted on the roof. Building shows dispatchers working at a huge dispatching and control board. Batteries for loudspeaker included. Size: 8x11 in.
49 N 9880—Shpg. wt. 2 lbs. $11.75

G Brand New! Operating Lumber Mill. Gives a complete illusion of a buzzing saw-mill. Logs can be placed in entry bin either manually or by your own Lionel Operating Lumber Car. Remote control then causes logs to be slowly conveyed into mill and they appear to come out the other side as dressed lumber. True-to-life buzzing sound accompanies action. Imitation sawdust collector is mounted on roof. Logs, dressed lumber and controller are included. Dimensions: 16½x 6x6 inches high. A real value .. order now! An ideal gift for your young trainman.
49 N 9823—Shpg. wt. 3 lbs $8.95

H Illuminated Trolley Car runs on its built-in motor. When bumper on either end hits an object, car and trolley pole reverse. Little passengers visible through clear plastic windows. Realistically detailed plastic. About 7 inches long. Die-cast steel wheels. Operates on "027" or "0" gauge track like locomotive. Bulb included.
49 N 9866—Shpg. wt. 2 lbs $7.75

J 4¾-inch Section Gang Car. When buffer plate at either end strikes bumper and car reverses direction, "gandy dancer" turns around. Plastic and steel. Built-in motor works on "027" or "0" gauge track like a locomotive. Order now!
49 N 9846—Shpg. wt. 2 lbs $6.75

Operating Electric Accessories

K Brand New Operating Culvert Loader! This set loads culvert pipes into a special gondola by remote control. Several sections of large culvert pipe are placed on loader platform manually. Pressure of remote control button causes traveling crane to pick up one section of pipe at a time and drop it in the car where it rolls to the end to provide room for more. Platform is on a heavy beamed structure. Workmen's shack houses the mechanism. Set includes the station, gondola, pipes and controller. Station 11½x10x6 in. high. Car length 10½ inches.
49 N 9874—Shpg. wt. 4 lbs . . . $13.75

LIONEL ELECTRIC TRAINS

A Self-propelling Burro Crane $13.79

B $9.75

C $7.95

D $19.98 — LIONEL MAGNE-TRACTION

E $44.75 cash, $4.50 down — LIONEL MAGNE-TRACTION

A **New Operating Burro Crane.** Pulls its own work cars. Three levers on cab: one has 2 positions, one for propelling the car, the other rotates the cab. Second lever controls the hook; third, reverses the direction of any of the three motions at any point. Hand wheel operates 7¼-in. boom. Railside bumper provides automatic reversing. Die-cast frame, one operating coupler. Cab 4 in. long.
49 N 9875—Shipping weight 2 lbs............$13.79

B **New! Navy Yard Switcher.** Powered by electric motor. Lionel 3-position remote control reversing unit. With 2-4-2 wheel set, knuckle-type remote control couplers front and rear. 110-120-volt, 60-cycle AC.
49 N 9879—7½ in. long. Shpg. wt. 3 lbs......$9.75

C **New! Operating Freight Car with 2 Tell-Tale Poles** to warn trainman atop car of low tunnels, bridges and other overhead obstructions. First tell-tale pole causes man on top of car to fall prone to avoid being struck. Second tell-tale pole brings him upright again. Power is taken from track. Car is 10½ inches long. Tell-tale poles 7½ inches high. Car is ruggedly built of high-impact plastic with die-cast metal wheels. Order now for Christmas.
49 N 9876—Shpg. wt. 1 lb... $7.95

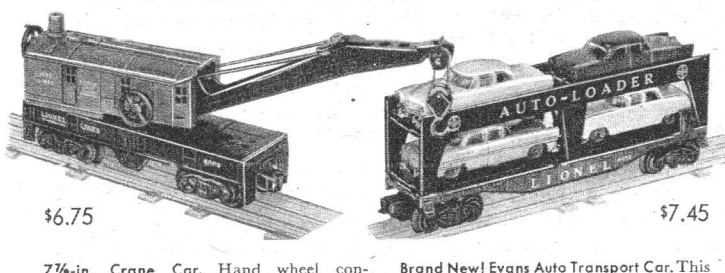

Lionel "Lehigh Valley" 4-Unit Diesel .. Magne-Traction

D Here's an ideal beginner's set. 3-car freight pulled by a GE-44 Lehigh Valley Diesel. Red with white striping. Run fast or slow, forward or back, couple or uncouple at front and rear, all by remote control. Three big cars: flat car with pipes, gondola with industrial canisters and a caboose. Die-cast steel wheels on double trucks make 8 wheels to each car and engine. 8 sections curved track, 1 section straight, plus 1 section of "027" uncoupling track form oval 101 in. around. UL approved 45-watt transformer for 110-120-volt, 60-cycle AC. Train set 37 inches long. Lock-on, lubricant and instructions included. A real value .. order early! A top gift on your youngster's list.
49 N 9668—Shipping weight 9 pounds.............$19.98

Lionel! "Milwaukee Road" 6-Unit Diesel with horn .. Magne-Traction

E Everything about this GP-7 Diesel is NEW! Twin sealed-beam headlights, classification light, running lights .. all illuminated at both ends of diesel. Warning horn is an exact replica of the original, operates by remote control. Power-packed with die-cast trucks, electric couplers at both ends, plus Magne-Traction for greater pull on grades, more staying power at high speeds .. pulls more cars! Run fast or slow, couple or uncouple, forward or back—all by remote control. Includes "New Haven" box car, flat car with 2 vans, gondola with barrels, ALCOA cement car and caboose. UL approved 60-watt transformer for 110-120-volt, 60 cycle AC. 8 curved, 3 straight, 1 uncoupler section of "027" track form oval 119 inches.
79 N 09613—Train set about 65 inches in length. Shpg. wt. 15 lbs........$44.75

$6.75

$7.45

7⅞-in. Crane Car. Hand wheel controls. Crane swings in circle; boom raises and lowers; pulley block lifts. Die-cast metal trucks, 8 solid steel wheels, knuckle-type remote control electric couplers. Order with your train set.
49 N 9852—Shpg. wt. 2 lbs.............$6.75

Brand New! Evans Auto Transport Car. This Lionel auto transport car comes with four removable precision-scale-model Ford autos right on board. Car is bright red, with black and white color insignia. Car measures 11 inches.
49 N 9868—Shipping weight 1 lb.....$7.45

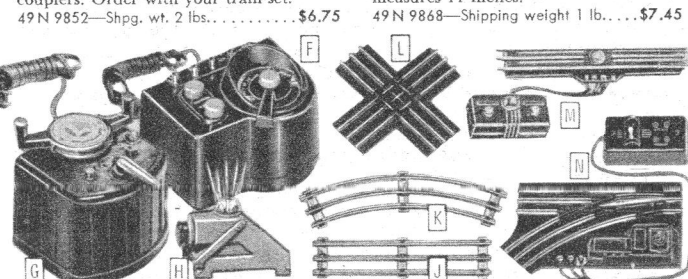

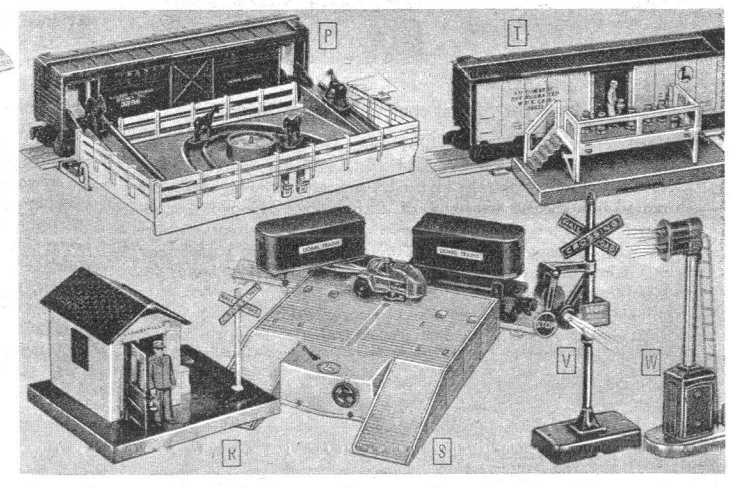

Trainmaster Transformers. For 110-120-volt, 60-cycle AC. Circuit breaker guards against overloads. Light shows short.

F Type LW-125-watt. Full speed range for any train. Fixed 14 and 18 volts have common ground with track. Useful when there are accessories connected to track which require different voltages. Illuminated dial. UL approved.
49 N 9819—Shpg. wt. 5 lbs..........$12.75

G Type KW-190-watt. 2 independently-controlled variable voltages for running 2 trains on different layouts at same time. Whistle, reversing control for each train. Fixed 6, 14, 20-volt accessory circuits.
49 N 9821—Shpg. wt. 11 lbs........$23.95

H Illuminated Bumper. For "027" or "0"
49 N 9859—Shpg. wt. 1 lb....Each $1.65

J "027" 8⅞-in. Straight Track Section.
49 N 9801—Shpg. wt. 3 oz....Each 22c

K "027" 9½-in. Curved Track Section.
49 N 9802—Shpg. wt. 3 oz....Each 22c

L "027" 90-degree Crossover 7⅜ in. sq.
49 N 9803—Shpg. wt. 8 oz......$1.65

M "027" Magnetic Track Section for remote control coupling and uncoupling. Controller and connecting wire incl.
49 N 9804—Shpg. wt. 1 lb......$3.45

N "027" Remote Control Switches. New device throws swivel rails automatically, lets train run through. Red, green lights on switch and controller also change. 1 right, 1 left switch.
49 N 9806—Shpg. wt. 3 lbs......$12.85

Lionel Accessories for Electric Trains

P New 11-in. Operating Horse Car. Push button and horses move out and into car by remote control. Horses can also be maneuvered by the use of gates into the center of corral to simulated drinking pool. Includes car, horses and controls. Does not require a remote control track. Corral 12x5¾ inches.
49 N 9873—Shpg. wt. 3 lbs.......$13.79

R Illuminated Automatic Gateman rushes out swinging lantern as train nears. After train passes man returns and door closes. Metal and plastic. 4½ in. high.
49 N 9835—Shpg. wt. 1 lb. 10 oz....$4.98

S "Operation Piggy Back" Set. Turn crank to load truck trailers on flat car or platform. 2 trucks, platform, flat car. 14x2x5 in.
49 N 9853—Shpg. wt. 4 lbs........$10.95

T 10⅛-in. scale Operating Milk Car, 5x 7¼-in. steel platform. Doors open, man comes out, delivers cans to platform. 8 steel wheels, die-cast trucks, knuckle-type remote control electric couplers. 5 cans.
49 N 9869—Shpg. wt. 3 lbs...........$9.75

V 7½-in. Automatic Banjo Signal.* As train nears, signal lights up, banjo "Stop" sign swings back and forth over light.
49 N 9827—Shpg. wt. 1 lb............$4.49

W Automatic Block Signal.* Stops train automatically for a period of time, set with lever on base. Lights change red to green, then train proceeds. 7 in. high.
49 N 9808—Shpg. wt. 1 lb............$4.59

*Means wire, track connectors, etc. included

C PAGE 277 .. LIONEL TRAINS

SEARS CHRISTMAS CATALOG 1957

The arrival of 1957's Sears Christmas Wishbook brought big news... the debut of H-O Scale electric trains. Exactly half the size of O-guage trains (H-O stood for "half-O") they were designed to fit more model train excitement into a smaller layout space.

H-O scale would eventually dominate the train marketplace. Although more delicate than the larger scales, H-O trains were cheaper to manufacture and cheaper to buy. But Sears was reluctant to go full steam into the H-O business so the majority of the 1957 catalog's train space was still devoted to O and O-27 scale trains and accessories.

The start of the Cold War and its media attention brought another new trend to model train design: in 1957 Sears' Allstate brand released its Military Train with Rocket Launcher, priced at $19.95 for the set. Now every kid could guard his home railroad system from the Communist Invasion.

Complete Set
$28.97
cash
$3.00 down
[A]

[B] $24.57 $2.50 down cash

All 3 sets include track and Powerpack

[C] $19.47 $2.00 down cash

NEW HOBBY-SIZE TRAINS
New HO Gauge Electric Trains are detailed miniatures of real trains with high-impact plastic cars, remote-control action

Run trains forward or back, fast or slow, couple or uncouple cars—by remote control. Rerailer uncoupler acts as grade crossing. Weighted cars have nylon trucks, wheels, N.M.R.A. couplers. Includes UL approved Powerpack with 2 circuit breakers . . 45-volt amps. output (110-120-volt, 60-cycle AC.); track as listed.

[A] **6-unit Steam-type Smoking Freight.** Hudson 14-wheel die-cast metal locomotive has 6-wheel drive, piston-rod action; puffs harmless smoke. Tender, box car, tank car, hopper, caboose. 12 curved, 3 straight track sections and rerailer uncoupler make 126-in. oval. 28 plastic accessories. Smoke refill, track connector.
49 N 9972—36 in. long. Shpg. wt. 9 lbs. **$28.97**

[B] **6-unit Santa Fe Twin Diesel.** Locomotive, rear unit, hopper, box car, gondola, caboose. Connector, 12 curved, 3 straight tracks, uncoupler make 126-in. oval.
49 N 9971—Train is 36 in. long. Shpg. wt. 9 lbs. **$24.57**

[C] **4-unit Santa Fe Diesel Set.** Diesel locomotive, box car, gondola car and caboose. 12 curved and 1 straight track section plus uncoupler unit make 112-in. oval track.
49 N 9970—Train is 24¾ in. long. Shpg. wt. 9 lbs. **$19.47**

Extra HO Gauge Track Sections. Shpg. wt. 4 oz. each

[D] 7 ½-in. Straight Track.
49 N 9904 . . . . . Each 13c

[E] 8-in. Curved Track.
49 N 9905 . . Each 13c

[F] 49 N 9908—Uncoupler Rerailer Track. Wt. 4 oz. **77c**

[G] **45-Amps. Output Powerpack.** 2 built-in circuit breakers, throttle control. Variable 0-14 volts for train, fixed 15 volts for accessories. UL approved.
49 N 9909—110-120-volt, 60-cycle AC. Shpg. wt. 6 lbs. **$9.97**

[H] **Steel Trestle Bridge.** 9x2½x3 inches high.
49 N 9907—Rails built in. Shpg. wt. 1 lb. **1.17**

New! Low-priced Trains for Little Tots

[J] **4-unit Battery-operated Freight Train Set** at record new low price. Made of steel, appropriately colored. Steam-type locomotive has electric motor operated with 2 standard flashlight batteries (not included). Run it forward or back; switch is located on top of boiler. Train is 28½ inches long and includes steel locomotive, lithographed metal tender, tank car and caboose. Two sections of straight, 8 sections of curved, 2-rail track make a 102-inch oval.
49 N 9521—Batteries not included. Shpg. wt. 3 lbs. **$3.77**
34 N 4650—2 Standard Batteries. Shpg. wt., two, 8 oz. . . . **2 for 35c**

[K] **New Battery-operated Table Train.** A real old-fashioned Iron Horse choo-choo with big smoke stack and cow catcher. Molded in durable plastic with amazing details. Powered by single standard flashlight battery (not included, order above). Engine pulls 3 coupled and attached brightly-colored metal coaches. Train 14 inches long, set includes 4 sections of curved 2-rail track forming 63-inch circle. Truly a big value and for the first time, an inexpensive battery-operated train set for even the littlest tot.
49 N 9502—Shipping weight 1 pound 10 ounces **$1.97**

[J] $3.77   [K] $1.97

New! Huge 48-piece Train Layout

[L] **Our Finest ALLSTATE Mechanical Freight Set** with 28 scale-detailed, molded, durable, plastic accessories and 5 vinyl plastic people, all in 3 dimensions. Realistic steam-type steel locomotive has long-running keywind clock-spring motor, built-in on-off switch, and speed governor. Bell rings and harmless sparks shoot from stack as it whizzes around its 102-in. oval track. The 28½-in. train includes locomotive, lithographed-metal tender, gondola and caboose. Eight curved and 2 straight sections of 2-rail track. 12 telegraph poles, 12 right-of-way signs, semaphore, lamp post, crossing signal, crossing gate with movable arm, billboard and five people.
49 N 9522—Train, track, accessories. Shpg. wt. 4 lbs. **$5.74**

Extra Track for 49N9521 and 49N9502 or Standard Marx Mechanical and Battery-operated Trains

[M] 8 ½-in. Straight Track.
Wt. 6 oz. for set of 4.
49 N 9701—Set of 4 for 34c

[N] 10 ½-in. Curved Track.
Wt. 6 oz. for set of 4.
49 N 9702—Set of 4 for 34c

[P] 7 ½-in. 90° Crossover.
49 N 9703—Wt. 8 oz. Ea. 57c

[R] Manually-operated Switch Set. Two switches: 1 right, 1 left hand. Wt. 1 lb.
49 N 9704—Set of 2 for $1.77

[L] $5.74 Complete Set

c SEARS 257

New Allstate Military Train with Rocket Launcher

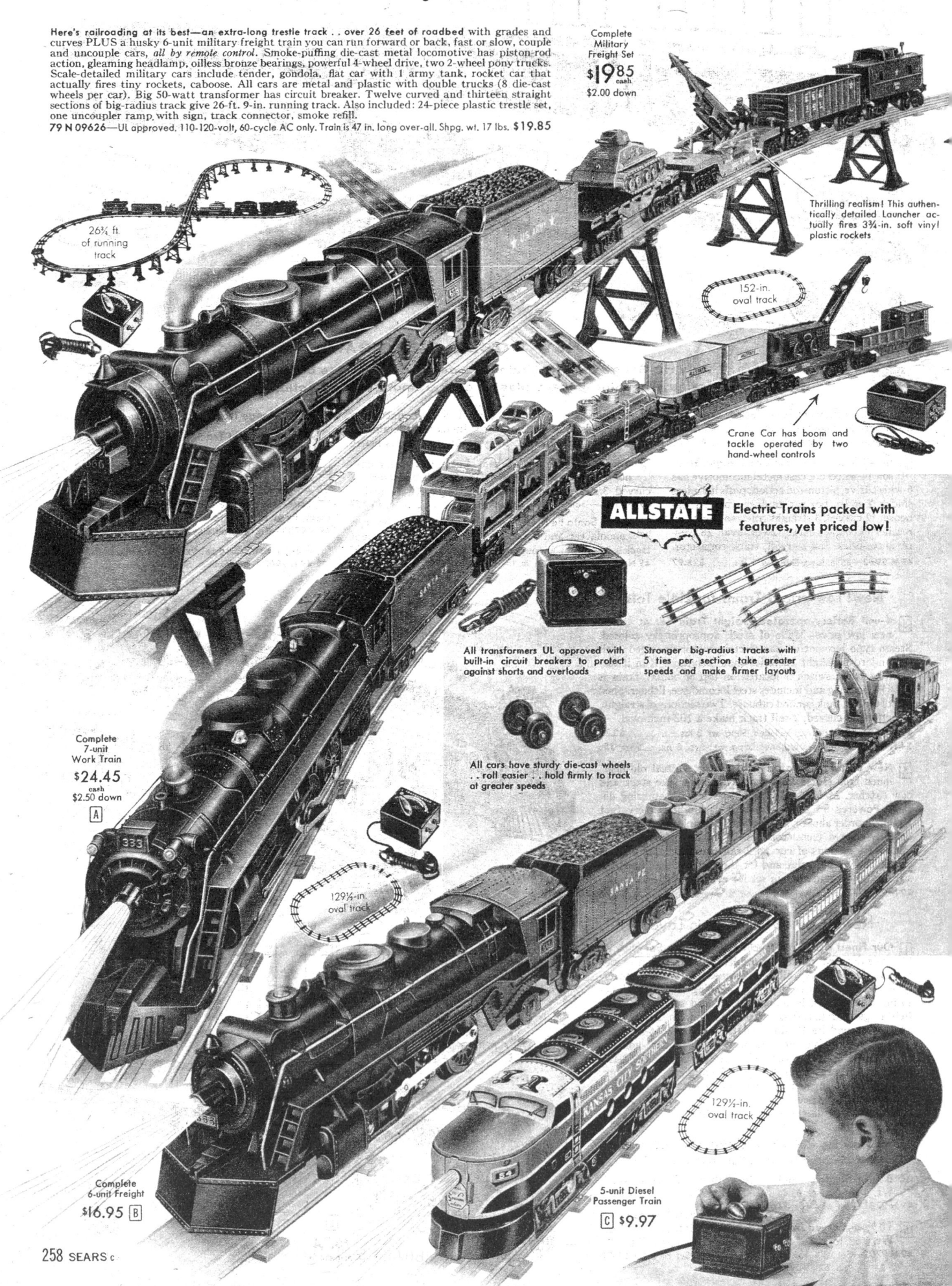

Here's railroading at its best—an extra-long trestle track.. over 26 feet of roadbed with grades and curves PLUS a husky 6-unit military freight train you can run forward or back, fast or slow, couple and uncouple cars, *all by remote control.* Smoke-puffing die-cast metal locomotive has piston-rod action, gleaming headlamp, oilless bronze bearings, powerful 4-wheel drive, two 2-wheel pony trucks. Scale-detailed military cars include tender, gondola, flat car with 1 army tank, rocket car that actually fires tiny rockets, caboose. All cars are metal and plastic with double trucks (8 die-cast wheels per car). Big 50-watt transformer has circuit breaker. Twelve curved and thirteen straight sections of big-radius track give 26-ft. 9-in. running track. Also included: 24-piece plastic trestle set, one uncoupler ramp with sign, track connector, smoke refill.
79 N 09626—UL approved. 110-120-volt, 60-cycle AC only. Train is 47 in. long over-all. Shpg. wt. 17 lbs. $19.85

Complete Military Freight Set
$19.85 cash
$2.00 down

26¾ ft. of running track

Thrilling realism! This authentically detailed Launcher actually fires 3¾-in. soft vinyl plastic rockets

152-in. oval track

Crane Car has boom and tackle operated by two hand-wheel controls

ALLSTATE Electric Trains packed with features, yet priced low!

All transformers UL approved with built-in circuit breakers to protect against shorts and overloads

Stronger big-radius tracks with 5 ties per section take greater speeds and make firmer layouts

All cars have sturdy die-cast wheels .. roll easier .. hold firmly to track at greater speeds

Complete 7-unit Work Train
$24.45 cash
$2.50 down
[A]

129½-in. oval track

Complete 6-unit Freight
$16.95 [B]

5-unit Diesel Passenger Train
[C] $9.97

129½-in. oval track

258 SEARS

From Santa's Roundhouse

thunders this powerful 6-unit Twin Diesel Freight!
Remote-control Switches have Electric-lighted Signals

ALLSTATE — Loaded with features at a low, low price!

Stock pen and loading ramp add lots of fun!

6-unit Diesel Freight complete
$28.95 cash
$3.00 down

Listen to the "roar" of the powerful Twin Diesel locomotive, realistically detailed in plastic with bright headlamp, 4-wheel drive and oilless bronze bearings. Train is almost 5 ft. long and includes Power Diesel and rear unit, tractor car with 2 tractors, sliding-door stock car, flat car and bay-window caboose. All cars realistically detailed in plastic and steel with double trucks (8 wheels per car). Run train forward or back, fast or slow, couple and uncouple cars, operate switches—all by electric remote control. The pair of switches and 17 sections of big-radius track give a huge 197-in. outer oval and 146-in. inner oval—a total of 20 ft. of running track. Lights on switches change automatically from red to green.

Plastic loading ramp and 14 plastic fence sections enclose 11 realistic plastic animals that can be loaded into and unloaded from stock car. Big 75-watt transformer has built-in circuit breaker and 4 binding posts (2 of them provide variable voltage for operating train, other 2 provide fixed voltage for accessories). UL approved for 110-120-volt, 60-cycle AC.
79 N 09633—Train is 59¾ in. long. Shpg. wt. 19 lbs. $3.00 down, $5.00 a month on Easy Terms..Cash **$28.95**

ELECTRIC TRAINS BELOW SHOWN ON OPPOSITE PAGE

All 3 sets below use stronger big-radius track with gentler curves for faster train speeds. 5 ties per section, not just 3. Scale-detailed locomotives have powerful motor, bright headlamp, oilless bronze bearings, remote control of speed and direction. (A) and (B) have scale-detailed plastic and steel cars with double trucks (8 die-cast wheels per car). Diesel train (C) has steel cars; 4 die-cast wheels per car. Circuit-breaker transformers. UL approved. 110-120-volt, 60-cycle AC.

[A] New 7-unit ALLSTATE Train—our best! Accurate 3/16-in. scale model. Die-cast 6-wheel-drive locomotive puffs harmless smoke as it runs; has 4-wheel pony truck, 2 guide wheels. Plastic and steel coal tender and 5 cars including new piggy-back car, ALLSTATE tank car, automobile car with 4 plastic autos, wrecker crane car and wrecker caboose. Run train forward or back, fast or slow, couple and uncouple cars—all by remote control! Three straight and 8 curved sections of big-radius track plus uncoupling ramp (with "Uncouple Here" sign) make 152-in. oval track. 100-watt transformer; 4 binding posts (2 for accessories). Track connector, 1-oz. bottle harmless smoke liquid also included.
79 N 09631—Train is 64½ inches long over-all, almost 5½ feet. Shipping weight 15 pounds........**$24.45**

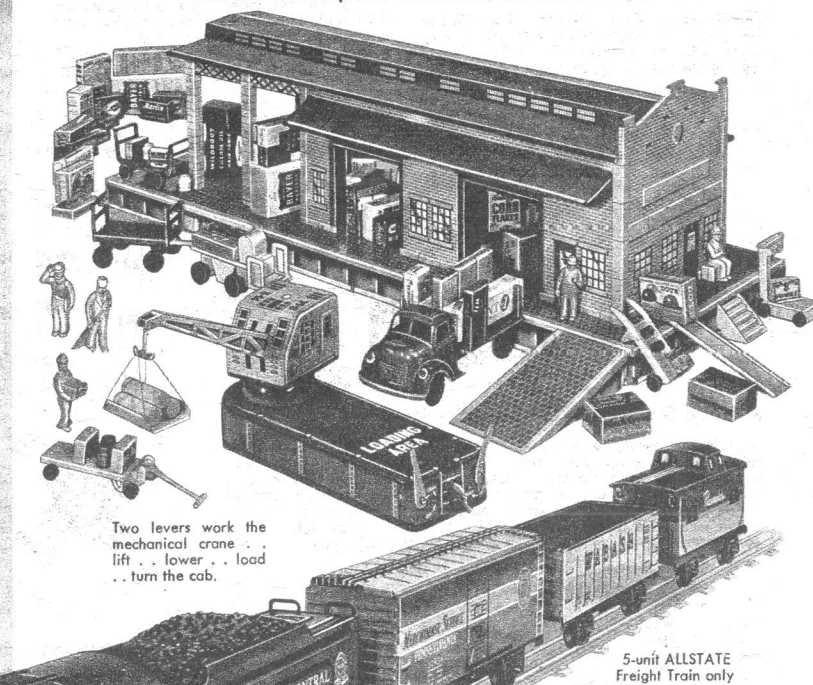

[B] Big 6-unit Work Train with steam-type die-cast metal locomotive that puffs harmless smoke. 4-wheel drive, pony truck and 2 guide wheels. Tender, 3 cars and caboose, all scale-detailed in plastic and steel. Cars include wrecker car, searchlight car with powerful light and drop-end gondola with 35 plastic construction tools. Run train forward or back, fast or slow, couple and uncouple cars—by remote control. One straight and 8 curved sections of big-radius track plus uncoupling ramp (with "Uncouple Here" sign) make 129½-in. oval. 50-watt transformer; 2 binding posts. Also included 1-oz. bottle of harmless smoke liquid.
49 N 9628—Train is 52½ inches long over-all. Shipping weight 11 pounds. **$16.95**

[C] Imagine—only $9.97 for a 5-unit Diesel Passenger Train Set! Same accurate scale detailing, remote control of speed and direction, die-cast wheels and superior big-radius track as on our higher-priced trains. Diesel locomotive, rear unit, 2 passenger coaches and 1 observation coach—all with manual couplers. All-metal, realistically lithographed. Two straight sections and 8 curved sections of big-radius track make 129½-in. oval. 50-watt transformer; 2 binding posts.
49 N 9604—Train is 37 inches long over-all. Shipping weight 8 pounds..... **$9.97**

OVER 60 PLAY PIECES IN ALL!
Here's a complete outfit for hours of fun!

Two levers work the mechanical crane.. lift.. lower.. load.. turn the cab.

5-unit ALLSTATE Freight Train only
$9.97

Complete Outfit 5-unit Train plus Terminal Set
$15.45

ALLSTATE 5-unit Freight Train PLUS big 45-pc. Terminal Set

Big 40½-in. long train has scale-detailed steel steam-type locomotive with bright headlamp, oilless bronze bearings, 4 die-cast wheels. Lithographed metal tender, high-side gondola, box car and caboose have 4 die-cast wheels, manual couplers. Run train forward or back, fast or slow—by remote control. Two straight and 8 curved sections of big-radius track make 129½-in. oval. UL approved 50-watt circuit-breaker transformer. 110-120-volt, 60-cycle AC.

Lithographed steel Freight Terminal, 29x11x9 in. high, has ramp and stairway to loading platform. Mechanical crane with 2 control levers. Included is a truck, empty cartons, baggage trucks, crates and workers—45 pieces. Terminal easy to assemble.
79 N 09627—Train, Track, Transformer, Terminal, accessories. Shpg. wt. 15 lbs....... **$15.45**

5-unit ALLSTATE Freight Train only. Metal locomotive, tender and 3 cars. Die-cast wheels. Ten sections of 5-tie big-radius track make 129½-in. oval. 50-watt circuit-breaker transformer.
49 N 9605—Shipping weight 8 lbs... **$9.97**

Low-priced 5-unit Marx Freight. Not shown. Like set at left, but plastic engine, tender, 3 metal cars (wheels not die-cast). 10 sections of 3-tie track.. 102-in. oval. 30-watt transformer; no circuit breaker.
49 N 9601—Shipping weight 7 lbs.... **$7.97**

c SEARS 259

Exciting Realistic Accessories for ALLSTATE, Happi-Time and Marx Electric Trains .. ideal low-cost gifts!

(A) through (F). Action-packed Extra Cars. Scale-detailed in heavy duty plastic and steel. Remote control automatic couplers. Two 4-wheel trucks, die-cast wheels. Track not incl. (except A).

[A] **Operating Lumber Car.** Press a button.. logs unload into plastic bin. Bin, five logs, track section, control panel, all necessary wiring and connectors included.
49 N 9761—8¾ in. long. Shpg. wt. 1 lb. .**$4.27**

[B] **Track Sweeper Car.** Two felt sweepers can be lowered to clean track as car rolls. Chassis and cab red; silver-color tank.
49 N 9766—9½ in. long. Shpg. wt. 1 lb. .**$3.27**

[C] **Operating Crane, Wrecker Car.** Plastic cab and boom revolve on die-cast metal chassis. Crank wheels work boom.
49 N 9786—12 in. long. Wt. 1 lb. 10 oz. ..**$4.27**

[D] **Operating Cattle Car** with ramp, platform. Car stops, door opens. Cow comes out, draws back when train starts.
49 N 9763—Car 9½ in. long. Wt. 1 lb. .**$3.27**

[E] **Automobile Carrier Car.** Two-deck rack on flat car carries 4 little autos that detach to unload (each about 4 in. long).
49 N 9755—Car 9½ in. long. Wt. 1 lb. .**$3.27**

[F] **Lighted Passenger Cars.** Lithographed metal. Silhouettes of passengers show in windows. Shpg. wt. each 14 oz.
49N9770—11-in. Astrodome (shown) **$3.27**
49N9771—10¾-in. Observation (not shown). 3.27

(G) to (K). Locomotives, Interurban and Hand Cars. Built-in electric motor, die-cast wheels, oilless bronze bearings. Track not included.

[G] **Twin-Diesel**, scale-detailed in plastic, steel. Two coupled sections. Front unit has motor. Rear of second has automatic coupler. Headlamp. Dummy horns.
49N9792—24 in. long. Wt. 4 lbs.**$12.67**
49 N 9781— Power "B" Unit (not shown). No motor. Manual couplers. Plastic. 12 in. long. Shpg. wt. 1 lb. **$3.97**

[H] **Diesel Switcher** with automatic couplers at both ends. Realistic hum. Die-cast metal chassis; plastic body. Headlamp. 10½ in. long.
49N9783—Shpg. wt. 2 lbs. 4 oz. **$10.97**

[J] **Electric Hand Car.** Plastic and steel. 2 railroaders pump crossbars. Built-in motor. Operates on track layout like an electric train.
49N9753—6¼ in. long. Wt. 12 oz.**$3.27**

[K] **Electric-lighted Interurban Car.** Remote-control speed, reversing. Dummy air horns. Red and green marker lights. Manual coupler. Use with any standard ALLSTATE, Marx or Happi-Time track layout. 11 in. long.
49 N 9784—Shpg. wt. 2 lbs. 12 oz.**$8.67**

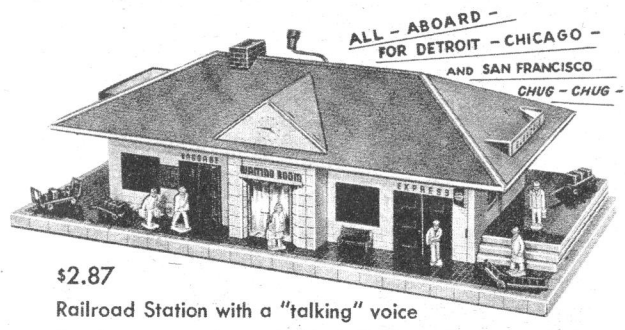

$2.87
Railroad Station with a "talking" voice

A perfect accessory for any standard-size electric or mechanical train set. Hand crank operates voice box. You'll hear the stationmaster announce train's destination: "All aboard for Detroit, Chicago and San Francisco." Then, in the background, you'll hear the realistic "chug-chug" sound of the train starting up and rolling out of the station. Colorful lithographed metal, 20½x10x6 inches high.
49 N 9787—With plastic figures and accessories. Wt. 3 lbs. 8 oz. **$2.87**

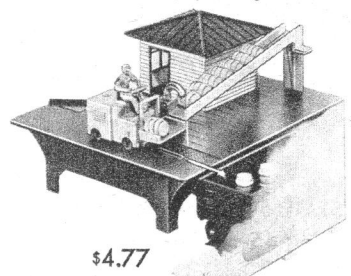

$4.77
Remote Control Automatic Barrel Loader

This exciting accessory works by remote control. Press a button.. lift truck takes a barrel from loading chute to the car. Entire unit realistically molded plastic, 8¾x8x5 in. high. Easily installed on any electric train layout. Plastic "barrels," control panel, all necessary wires included. Car and track not included. A wonderful gift if he has a train set!
49N9779—Shpg. wt. 1 lb. 6 oz.**$4.77**

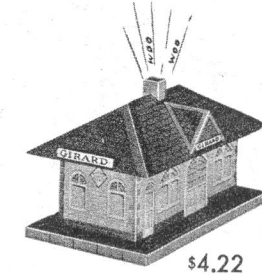

$4.22
Remote Control Whistling Station

Another realistic remote control accessory! Press a button.. hear the realistic wail of a locomotive as your train thunders down the track. Whistle mechanism fully enclosed within the lithographed steel station for protection. 9x5¼x5 in. high. Control panel and all necessary wires included. Easily installed on any electric train layout.
49N9739—Shipping wt. 2 lbs.**$4.22**

NOTE: Use with ALLSTATE, Happi-Time or Marx train layouts using 110-120-volt, 60-cycle AC.

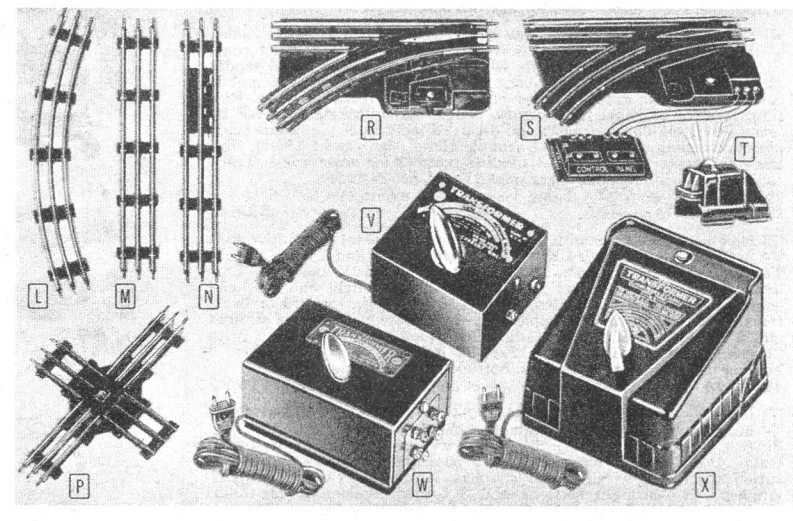

Extra Track and Switches for ALLSTATE, Happi-Time or Marx Electric Trains

Big-radius type with gentler curves for faster speeds. Five cross ties per section—not just the 3 on most electric train tracks!

[L] 12½-in. Curved Track. Big-radius type.
49 N 9723—Shipping weight 4 oz. Each **21c**

[M] 11¼-in. Straight Track. Big-radius type.
49 N 9720—Shipping weight 4 oz. Each **21c**

[N] Uncoupling Section with "Uncouple Here" sign. Big-radius type track.
49 N 9749—11¼ in. long. Shpg. wt. 5 oz. ...**76c**

[P] Crossover Track. 9¼x9¼ in. square.
49N9726—Big-radius type. Wt. 9 oz. Ea. **$1.22**

[R] Manually operated Switch Set for electric trains. One right and one left-hand switch.
49 N 9776—Big-radius type. Wt. 2 lbs. Set **$4.27**

[S] Remote-control Switch Set for electric trains. Red and green light. One right and one left-hand switch. Control panel included.
49 N 9727—Shpg. wt. 2 lbs. 8 oz. Set **$8.27**

[T] Lighted Dead-end Bumper. Plastic; 3x1⅞x2 inches high. Snaps to end of spur track.
49 N 9707—Bulb included. Wt. 5 oz. ...**81c**

Track Connector (not shown). Carries electric power from the transformer to the track.
49 N 9709—Shipping weight 2 ounces. Each **12c**

UL Approved Transformers for Electric Train Sets, all with circuit breakers

For 110-120-volt, 60-cycle AC. Reduces household power voltage to a safe low voltage for operating electric trains and accessories. Built-in circuit breaker with reset button protects against short circuits and burnouts. With cord, wires, track connectors.

[V] 50-watt Transformer. Has two separate sets of binding posts: one set gives variable 7 to 13 volts to control train speed; other set gives fixed 13 volts for operating accessories. Housed in steel case with air-cooled base. Ideal for average electric train set.
49 N 9725—Shipping weight 3 lbs. **$5.27**

[W] Bigger 100-watt Transformer for train sets with bigger trains and more accessories. Steel case with 2 sets of binding posts; one set gives variable 5 to 15 volts for train speed; other set, fixed 15 volts for accessories.
49 N 9777—Shipping weight 4 lbs. 8 oz. **$8.32**

[X] Our biggest. Super-powered 150-watt Transformer. Two sets of binding posts: one set gives variable 0 to 15 volts for controlling train speed; other set gives fixed 15 volts for accessories. Throttle-type control. Housed in a massive plastic case with air-cooled base.
49 N 9764—Shipping weight 10 lbs. **$12.57**

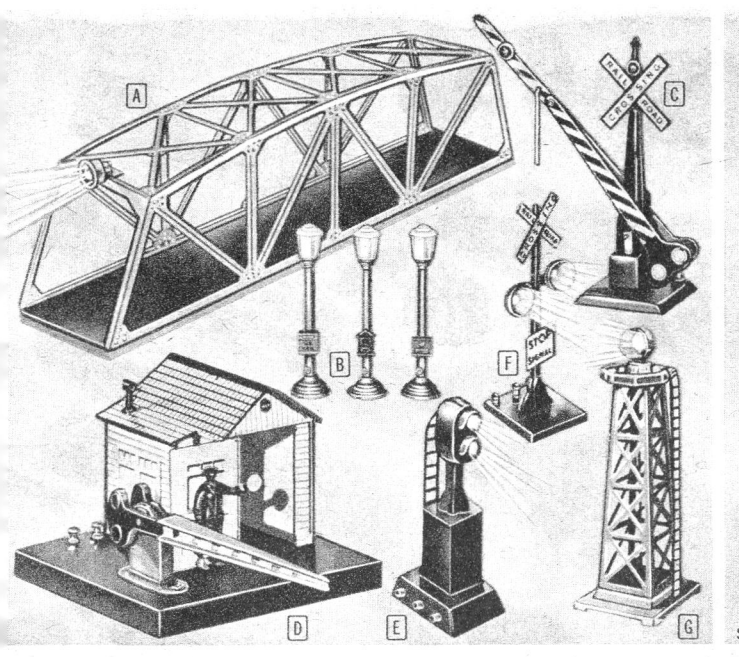

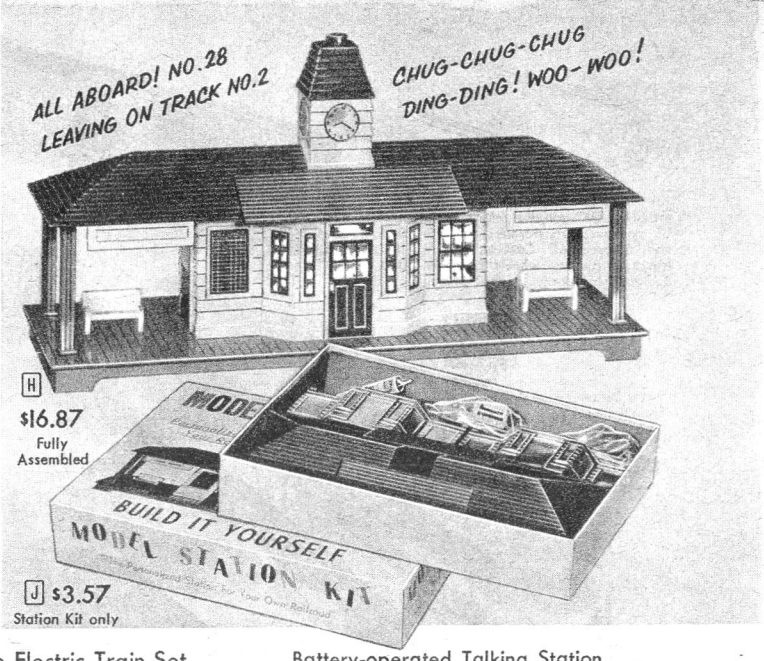

Accessories add realism to any Marx, ALLSTATE or Happi-Time Electric Train Set

(A) through (G) include light bulbs where needed, PLUS all necessary track connectors and wires .. ready to install!

A Lighted Steel Trestle Bridge. Aluminum finish. Light socket and reflector clip-on are adjustable. 24x5x6 inches high. Shipping weight 2 lbs. 4 oz.
49 N 9741..........$2.37

B 3 Lighted Lamp Posts. Plastic. Bases notched to attach to electric train track. One post has mail box; others, fire alarm box and police call box. 6 in. high.
49N9737—Shpg. wt.1 lb.$1.87

C Automatic Crossing Gate made of realistically-lithographed steel. 7¾ in. high. Arm lowers as train approaches, raises when train has passed. Simulated jewel reflector at end of gate.
49 N 9743—Shpg. wt.10 oz.$1.67

D Automatic Grade Crossing Shack and Watchman. As train nears, watchman comes out with stop sign, gate lowers. Shack is lithographed steel 4½ inches high. Base 7x6½ inches.
49 N 9760—Shpg. wt. 2 lbs. $3.22

E Automatic 2-light Block Signal. Train stops on red, goes on green signal. Switch at rear operates signal. Made of plastic, 7¼ in. high. Two track sections included.
49 N 9745—Shipping weight 10 oz.......$1.67

F Automatic Crossing Flasher. Twin red lights flash alternately as train goes by.
49 N 9742—Plastic, 7 in. high. Wt. 10 oz..$1.67

G Lighted Revolving Beacon. Light on girder-type tower revolves constantly, beams a bright red light in one direction and green in the other. Made of plastic, 12½ in. high.
49 N 9740—Shipping weight 10 oz.......$1.67

Battery-operated Talking Station

H It's fascinating and fully automatic! Touch a button in the chimney .. hear the stationmaster announce train departure and the realistic sound of a chugging engine with its bell ringing and whistle wailing. Self-contained .. no connections to track. Works on 2 flashlight batteries (included). Station building, 16x6x8 in. high, made of high-impact polystyrene plastic with red roof, silvery-color windows, colorful walls and benches on pillar platform. Voice and sound effects last 55 seconds, shut off automatically. Instructions, 2 batteries, 3 records.
49 N 9757—Fully assembled. Shpg. wt. 5 lbs......$16.87

J Station Kit only. Station as above, 16x6x8 in. without batteries, voice and sound mechanism or records. Brightly colored. Easy to assemble.
49 N 9734—With instructions, cement. Wt. 3 lbs....$3.57

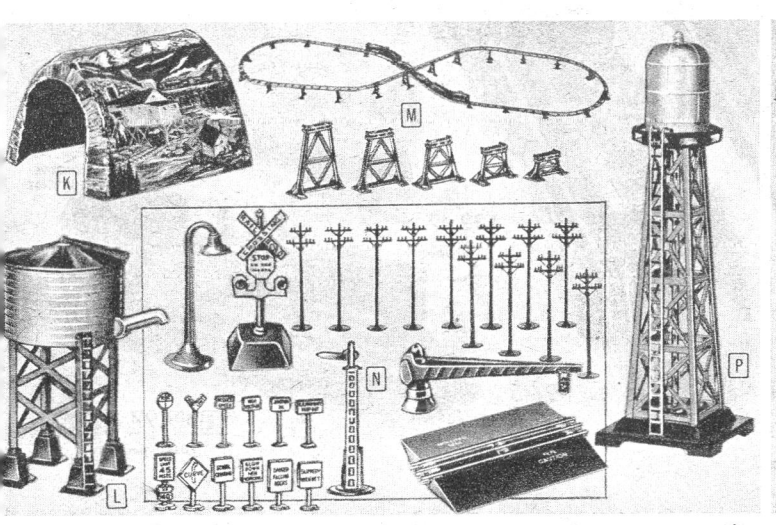

K Metal Tunnel colorfully lithographed with landscape scene. Watch the train thunder through it! Comes apart for storage. Measures 9x7x10¾ in. long.
49 N 9729—Shipping weight 1 pound......81c

L Plastic Water Tower with adjustable spout. Diameter 4¼ in.; 8½ inches high.
49 N 9731—Shipping weight 10 ounces....81c

M 24-pc. Plastic Trestle Set. A series of 24 graduated plastic trestles for up to 24 feet of track layout. Numbered in proper sequence to set up figure "8" track set-up with exciting overhead and underpass arrangements. Track not included.
49 N 9738—Shipping weight 2 lbs........$4.52

N Big 29-pc. set of authentically scale-detailed Railroad Accessories. Made of durable plastic in just the right size for any standard mechanical or electric train set. Carefully detailed to please the most particular young "Casey Jones." Set includes 12 seven-inch telegraph poles, 12 railroad right-of-way signs, and one each of the following: semaphore, lamp post, crossing gate, grade crossing sign and grade crossing plate (track not included). A really big set for such a low, low price. A grand low-cost gift for the young railroad enthusiast!
49 N 9750—Shipping weight 2 lbs........$2.57

P Plastic Water Tower with bubbling light. The 2¼-in. diameter tank has realistic plates and rivets, girder-type understructure. Heat from light bulb in 4½x4½-in. base creates water bubbles which rise in the transparent plastic tube that runs from the base to tank. Light also shows through tube.
49 N 9751—14 in. high. Shpg. wt. 1 lb....$2.64

R 30-pc. Railroad People and Accessory Set. Realistically molded plastic. Set includes 15 railroad people in various poses, 5 railroad accessories (hand truck, bench, freight wagon, etc.), 10 other accessories (mail box, trash can, parking meter, etc.).
49 N 9772—Shipping weight 10 oz......Set 97c

S Newest type 5-light Block Signal. Here's another exciting new accessory for his electric train set—an authentic miniature replica of the very latest type 5-light block signal that is now being used on so many railroad rights-of-way! As the train approaches the block signal, amber light pattern changes from vertical to horizontal. After train has passed, light pattern returns to vertical position. Signal is realistically detailed in high-impact plastic and metal. 8¾ in. high, 3 in. wide. Base is 3x2½-in. size. Signal includes all necessary bulbs, track connectors and rail clip assembly.
49 N 9746—Shipping weight 1 pound.....$2.37

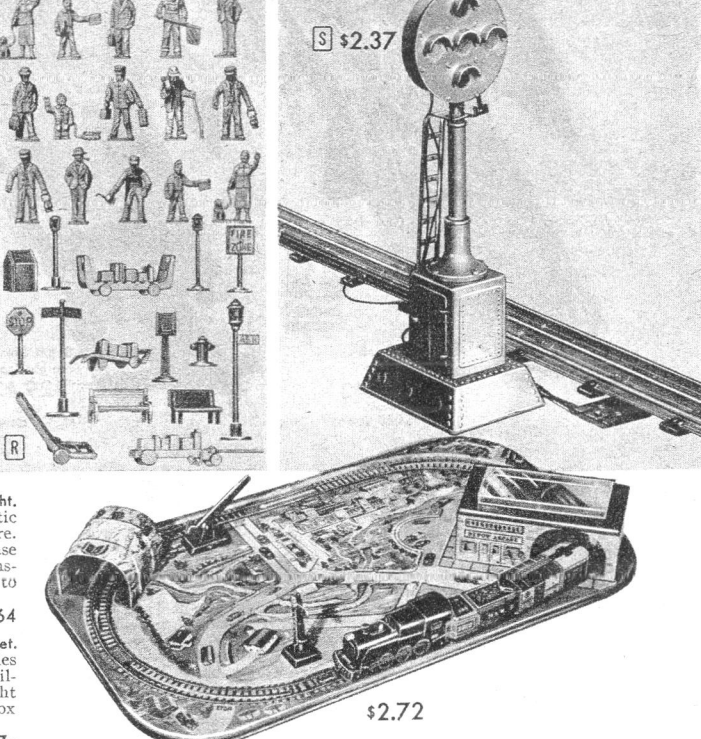

Scenic Express with Signals that really work!

Here's a complete railroad system for younger children .. an ideal first train for your toddler. Youngsters will love its exciting action .. it's equipped with a tunnel, station and signals that work just like the real ones do. Action crossing gate and semaphore operate automatically as 11-in. train whizzes by. All the thrills and excitement of a big railroad! Train runs around a grooved track in metal base .. circles track over 20 times on a single winding of its long-running clockspring motor. Sturdy steel base, about 21¾x13 inches, realistically lithographed with a landscape scene.
49 N 9515—Priced low .. makes an ideal gift. Shpg. wt. 3 lbs..........$2.72

All sets below realistically detailed. All include "027"-gauge track as listed and UL approved transformers for 110-120-volt, 60-cycle AC. Cars have 2 double trucks (8 die-cast wheels per car). All equipped for remote-control uncoupling.

[A] 9-unit Diesel Freight Train **$49.33** cash $5.00 down

[B] 8-unit Freight **$39.43** cash $4.00 down

[C] 8-unit Diesel Freight Train **$29.43** cash $3.00 down

[D] **$19.95** cash $2.00 down 6-unit Steam-type Train

[E] **$10.27**

[F] **$22.47** cash $2.50 down

[G] **$19.97** cash $2.00 down

4 Lionel "027" Electric Trains Sold Only at Sears

[A] **Huge 9-unit Diesel Freight** with remote-control horn. Powerful GP-7 switcher locomotive has twin sealed-beam headlights, running lights and classification lights illuminated at both ends. Magne-Traction gives it tremendous pulling power, greater speeds on curves without derailment. Cars include operating searchlight car with removable searchlight, flat car with 2 removable autos, flat car with lumber, refrigerator car, hopper, miscellaneous car, stock car and work caboose. Run train forward or back, fast or slow, couple and uncouple cars, sound its deep-toned horn—all by remote control.
Eight curved, 7 straight, and 1 uncoupling sections make up 147-in. oval track. 90-watt transformer with built-in circuit breaker has plenty of power for accessories. Train is 96 inches long.
79 N 09643—With lock-on, lubricant, instructions. Shpg. wt. 18 lbs..... **$49.33**

[B] **Big 8-unit Steam-type Freight** with powerful 12-wheel locomotive that puffs harmless smoke, sounds its whistle by remote control. Locomotive has bright headlight, realistic piston-rod action, 6-wheel drive PLUS Magne-Traction for greater pulling power and speeds—without derailment! Run train forward or back, fast or slow, couple and uncouple cars, sound whistle—all by remote control. Long 71-in. train includes locomotive, tender, operating crane car, gondola with 4 canisters, box car, flat car with logs, oil car, work caboose. Eight curved, 5 straight and 1 uncoupling sections, make up 129-in. oval track. 50-watt transformer has built-in circuit breaker. Instructions included.
79N09642—Has lock-on, lubricant, smoke pellets. Shpg. wt. 15 lbs...... **$39.43**

[C] **Big 8-unit Diesel Freight** has high-impact plastic GE-type "N2" switcher locomotive with headlamp PLUS Magne-Traction for bigger loads, faster speeds. Two box cars, wheel car, stock car, gondola with 4 canisters, flat car with 3 pipes, caboose.
Run train forward or back, fast or slow, couple and uncouple cars at front or rear of locomotive—by remote control. Eight curved, 3 straight and 1 uncoupling sections make 117-inch oval track. 45-watt transformer. Lock-on, lubricant and instructions are included.
79 N 09641—78 in. long. Shpg. wt. 11 lbs...**$29.43**

[D] **6-unit Steam-type Freight Train.** 8-wheel locomotive has 4-wheel drive, realistic piston-rod action, headlamp. Tender, flat car with lumber, gondola with 4 canisters, flat car with 3 pipes, caboose. Run train forward, backward, fast, slow by remote control; couple, uncouple cars with uncoupling control. 8 curved, 2 straight tracks make 103-in. oval. 45-watt transformer, uncoupler, lock-on and lubricant. 52 inches long.
79 N 09640—Shpg. wt. 11 lbs............**$19.95**

[E] **New Denver and Rio Grande Locomotive** with snow plow at front. Designed after unusual Vulcan 30-ton gear-drive Diesel. Yellow and black markings. Simulated headlights front and rear; dummy bell. 8 die-cast wheels; 4-wheel drive.
49N9870—7½ in. long. Shpg. wt. 2 lbs....**$10.27**

[F] **Budd RDC Car** with remote-control horn and rail-gripping Magne-Traction. Self-propelled aluminum car is replica of the Diesel car used for short runs by big railroads. Runs forward or back, fast or slow, sounds its horn by remote control! Bright headlights, marker lights and operating knuckle couplers at both ends. Silhouettes of passengers in windows. 8 die-cast wheels.
49N9834—16½ in. long. Shpg. wt. 5 lbs..**$22.47**

[G] **New Seaboard Diesel Switcher** with rail-gripping Magne-Traction, remote-control built-in horn. Bright headlight. Authentic black and red markings. Self-centering knuckle couplers at both ends. 8 wheels.
49N9883—12¼ in. long. Shpg. wt. 7 lbs..**$19.97**

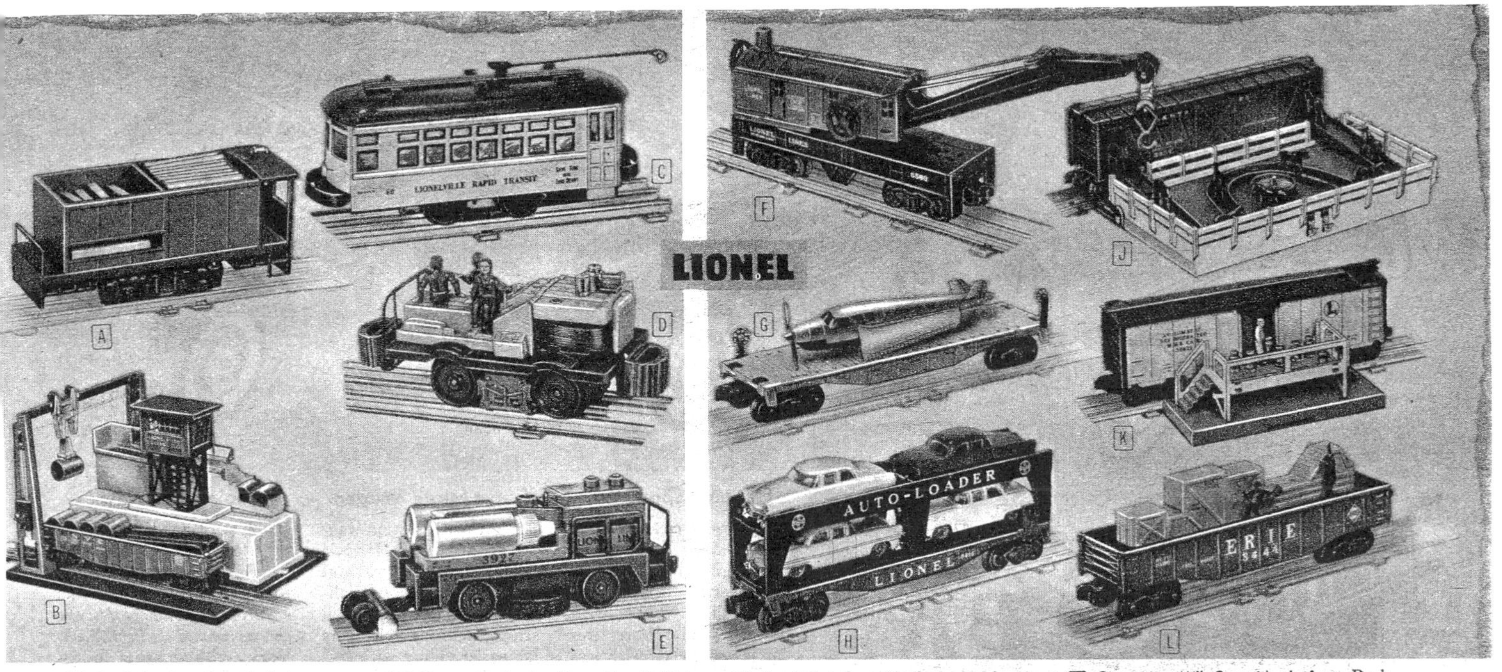

A Tie Unloading Car. Built-in motor. Distributes railroad ties along railside while in motion. Action started by railside bumper, stopped by second bumper. Coupler. 6½ in. long.
49 N 9840—Shipping weight 3 lbs. $8.57

B Culvert Unloading Station with gondola car. Travelling crane lowers magnetic boom and transports culvert section onto station. Station 11½x10 inches wide. Controller, necessary wires, car included.
49 N 9829—Shipping wt. 6 lbs. . $14.27

C Illuminated Trolley Car. Built-in motor. Car and trolley reverse automatically. Plastic, 7 in. long. Bulb incl. Fits "027" or "0" gauge.
49N9866–Shipping weight 3 lbs. . .$7.27

D Operating Section Gang Car. Built-in motor. Car and workers reverse automatically when buffer plate at either end strikes bumper. Plastic and steel. For "027" or "0" gauge.
49 N 9846—4¾ in. long. Wt. 2 lbs. . . $6.16

E Track Cleaning Car. Couples to locomotive. Built-in motor turns brush. "On-off" lever. Reservoir holds cleaning fluid (included). Pad wipes track. 6⅛ in long. One remote-control coupler.
49 N 9877—Shipping weight 3 lbs. . . $9.27

F Operating Wrecking Crane. Two separate hand wheels: one raises, lowers boom; other raises, lowers hook. Cab rotates. Die-cast metal trucks; steel wheels. 7⅞ in. long. Remote control couplers.
49 N 9852—Shipping weight 2 lbs. . . $6.16

G New! Flat Car with demountable Airplane. Plane wings retract for transport, extend for "flying" position. 10⅞-in. car; remote-control couplers.
49 N 9838—Shipping weight 2 lbs. $4.71

H Evans Auto Transport Car with 4 removable scale model automobiles on board. 11-in. long car is red; black and white trim. Remote-control couplers.
49 N 9868—Shipping weight 2 lbs. . $6.16

J Operating Horse Car. Touch a remote-control button . . horses move in and out of car and around the 12x5¾-in. corral. Set includes 11¼-in. car with remote-control couplers, horses, corral, control, all necessary wires. Does not require remote-control track section.
49 N 9873—Shipping weight 4 lbs. . $14.27

K Operating Milk Car with platform. Push a button . . car door opens, man comes out to deliver cans to 5x7¼-in. steel platform. Car is made of plastic, 10⅞ in. long; 8 die-cast wheels and remote-control couplers. Requires special uncoupling track (R) below, left, (not included).
49 N 9869—Shipping weight 3 lbs. . . . $8.61

L New! Animated Gondola. Really funny! The old "hobo-railroad" feud recreated realistically. Railroad policeman chases hobo around top of car. "On-off" switch shuts off action. Car is standard gondola type with fixed cargo. 10⅜ in. long. 8 die-cast metal wheels. Remote-control couplers. Works from track current . . remote-control track section not needed. Order early in time for Christmas.
49 N 9839—Shipping weight 2 lbs. . . . $7.67

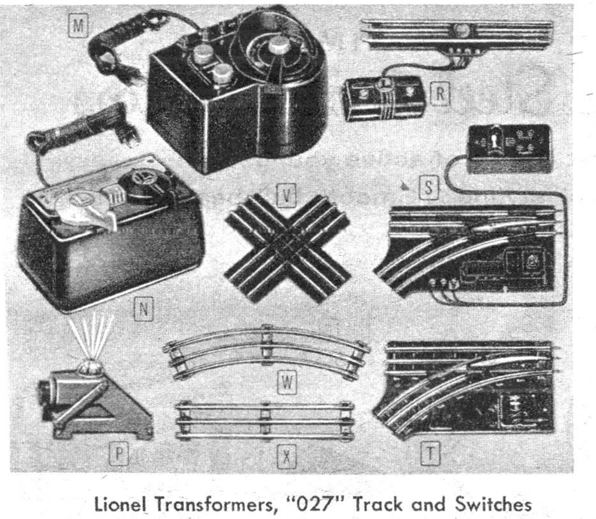

Lionel Transformers, "027" Track and Switches

M N Trainmaster Transformers for Electric Trains. Famous Lionel quality throughout! Built-in circuit breaker guards against overloads and short circuits. Light signals shorts. 110-120-volt, 60-cycle AC. UL approved.

M Type LW—125-watt. Full range of train speeds PLUS fixed 14 and 18-volt circuits with common ground to track. Ideal for track-connected accessories that need different operating voltages. Built-in whistle and direction controls.
49N9819–Shpg. wt. 6 lbs. . $12.57

N Type TW—175-watt. Left-hand throttle controls variable voltage for train. Right-hand throttle controls starting, stopping and reversing, sounds train whistle or horn. Three fixed accessory voltages—14, 18 and 25 volts. Two separate built-in circuit breakers.
49N9842–Shpg. wt. 10 lbs. $19.75

P Lighted bumper for '027,' '0.'
49N9859–Wt. 1 lb. . . . $1.84

R "027" Magnetic Track Section for remote control uncoupling and unloading. Control panel and connecting wires included.
49N9804–Shpg. wt. 1 lb. Ea. $3.77

S "027" Remote Control Switch Set. Non-derailing device throws switch rails automatically, lets train run through. Green and red lights on switch and controller also change. One right and one left-hand switch, control panel and wires included.
49N9806–Wt. 3 lbs. . . Set $12.87

T "027" Manually Operated Switch Set. One right and one left-hand switch. Non-derailing type.
49N9805–Wt. 2 lbs. . . . Set $5.14

V "027" 7⅜-in. 90° Crossover.
49N9803–Wt. 8 oz. . . $1.51

W "027" Curved Track. 9½ in. long.
49N9802–Wt. 3 oz. . . . . Ea. 20c

X "027" Straight Track. 8⅞ in.
49N9801–Wt. 3 oz. . . Ea. 20c

Realistic Lionel Electric Train Accessories add fun to any train set!

Y New! 24-pc. Trestle Set for making a figure "8" over-and-under track layout and other interesting overpass arrangements. Trestles may be used with any type track; 24 graduated piers! Use with Magne-Traction locomotives.
49 N 9845—Shpg. wt. 3 lbs. . . . . . 24-pc. Set $4.62

Z New! Rotating Radar Antenna. Like those used at airports for traffic control. Built-in "Vibrotor" mechanism rotates antenna continuously; works off track current. Connecting wire included. Realistic 12-inch tower.
49 N 9814—Shipping weight 1 lb. $4.27

AA Illuminated Automatic Banjo Signal. As the train approaches, signal lights up and a banjo-shaped "STOP" sign swings back and forth over the light. Action stops automatically after train has passed. Necessary connectors, wire and bulb included.
49 N 9827—7½ in. high. Shpg. wt. 1 lb. $3.72

BB Illuminated Automatic Block Signal stops train automatically for time set with lever in base. Then light changes from red to green and train proceeds on its way. Realistic details include ladder at rear. Two bulbs, track connectors and wire included. A fine gift for railroad hobbyists . . order today.
49 N 9808—7 in. high. Shpg. wt. 1 lb. $4.67

CC Illuminated Automatic Gateman. As train approaches, shack door opens and gateman hurries out swinging lantern. After train has passed, gateman returns to shack and door closes. Metal and plastic. 7x5⅛x4½ in. high. Bulb, connectors, wires included. An entertaining addition for your train layout.
49 N 9835—Shipping weight 2 lbs. $5.17

DD Operating Fork-lift Platform. Miniature fork-lift truck runs up to loaded lumber car, grips and lifts miniature board, backs up, turns around to drop the board to the platform, and returns for more boards . . all by remote control. Steel framed, platform has simulated concrete base. 8½x10 in. long. Includes lumber car and boards.
49 N 9826—Shipping weight 4 lbs. $13.67

EE New! Illuminated Remote-control Dispatching Board. Push the remote-control button . . attendant hurries across catwalk in front of the big 4x10x8-in. high board, illuminated schedule automatically changes. Train names and times can be chalked in. Illuminated clock has movable hands; dummy loudspeakers are mounted on top of the board. Realistically detailed. Bulb, control button and necessary wire included.
49 N 9841—Shipping weight 3 lbs. $9.27

Do your Christmas shopping the easy Sears way . . lots of low-priced gift suggestions on these pages

SEARS CHRISTMAS CATALOG 1958

1958 brought a new high point to Sears' electric train marketing. This year the catalog contained eight pages devoted to model trains and accessories. More than ever before.

Interestingly, a special offer was made on an American Flyer two-train set. Marked down to $38.98 from $59.98, Sears was unusually anxious to move these trains. Perhaps Lionel's crack marketing team was putting the pressure on. The unique set included a Baldwin Diesel locomotive and another steam engine, each pulling separate freight trains over a figure-eight track layout. A Styrofoam mountain pulled the trains over and under each other. Of course, the American Flyer trains rolled over their patented two-rail track as opposed to Lionel's competing three-rail track system.

"Sears' Best" Lionel Train was the Wabash GP-7 Diesel Locomotive set with MagneTraction. For $49.95 (a very steep price for 1958) the set was intended for serious model railroaders only.

HOLIDAY SPECIALS START HERE

Index starts on page 257

Exclusive American Flyer Two-Train Set
Save $21.00

Normally our price would be $59.98

$38.98 cash

Only $4 down

Two freights thunder over same track .. never collide

Giant track system has 3-dimensional mountain with tunnel and overpass for fascinating, simultaneous over-and-under train operation

THIS SET SOLD ONLY AT SEARS!

Train speeds are controlled automatically so that as the lead train goes through the tunnel the rear train thunders above it on the overpass. There is no other train set in America we know of that provides this type of railroading action!

All the excitement, all the thrilling action of a regular railroad, with train movements so realistic youngsters will be amazed. As the two trains race over the rails an automatic control slows down the rear train momentarily until lead train gains safe distance; then as one speeds through the tunnel, the other crosses the overpass above. Railroad system includes Baldwin Diesel locomotive heading up hopper car, box car, tank-car and caboose. Second freight train features 10-wheel steam locomotive and tender hauling a box car, gondola car and caboose.

Both locomotives are metal and plastic, have worm drive motors, Pull-Mor® power. Both trains are 40 in. long over-all. Styrofoam® mountain is 18½x10 in. 24-pc. plastic trestle set rises from ⅞ in. to 4¼ in. Track includes 8 sections of 2-rail "T" straight track and 18 sections curved; forms figure "8" approximately 92x42 in. Outfit totals 65 pieces .. includes 50-watt transformer below.
79 FN 09994—Shipping weight 15 pounds...........$38.98

50-watt circuit-breaker transformer, UL approved for 110-120 volt, 60-cycle AC.

For a more complete listing of trains and train accessories please see pages 370 through 376 in this catalog. For Easy Terms information see page 264.

SCPB KMNL SEARS 249

Huge 8½-foot long ten-unit Freight Train

$29.79 cash $3 down

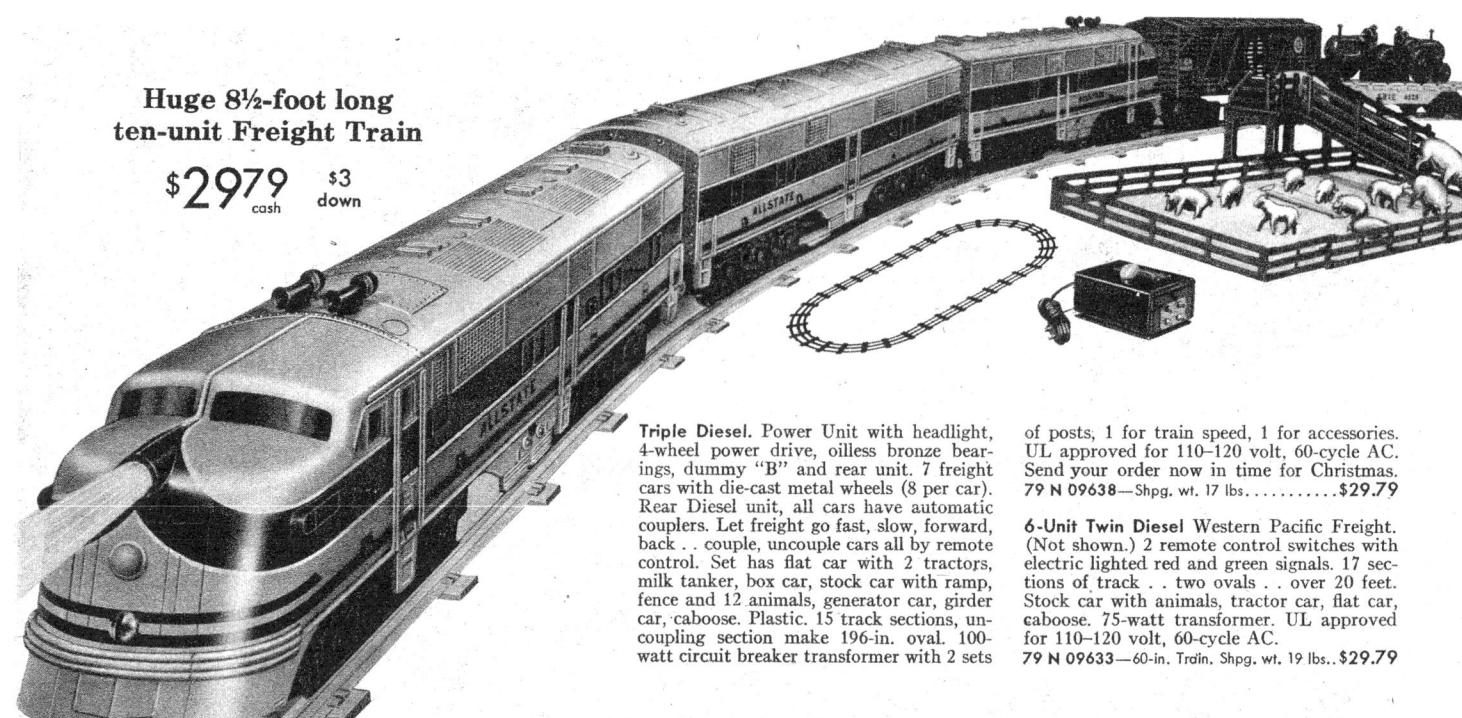

Triple Diesel. Power Unit with headlight, 4-wheel power drive, oilless bronze bearings, dummy "B" and rear unit. 7 freight cars with die-cast metal wheels (8 per car). Rear Diesel unit, all cars have automatic couplers. Let freight go fast, slow, forward, back .. couple, uncouple cars all by remote control. Set has flat car with 2 tractors, milk tanker, box car, stock car with ramp, fence and 12 animals, generator car, girder car, caboose. Plastic. 15 track sections, uncoupling section make 196-in. oval. 100-watt circuit breaker transformer with 2 sets of posts, 1 for train speed, 1 for accessories. UL approved for 110–120 volt, 60-cycle AC. Send your order now in time for Christmas.
79 N 09638—Shpg. wt. 17 lbs...........**$29.79**

6-Unit Twin Diesel Western Pacific Freight. (Not shown.) 2 remote control switches with electric lighted red and green signals. 17 sections of track .. two ovals .. over 20 feet. Stock car with animals, tractor car, flat car, caboose. 75-watt transformer. UL approved for 110–120 volt, 60-cycle AC.
79 N 09633—60-in. Train. Shpg. wt. 19 lbs..**$29.79**

Allstate® Electric Trains with Circuit
Every Train has die-cast wheels .. strong track .. scale detailing

Santa Special!
Your choice of these 5-unit trains for only **$9.98** each

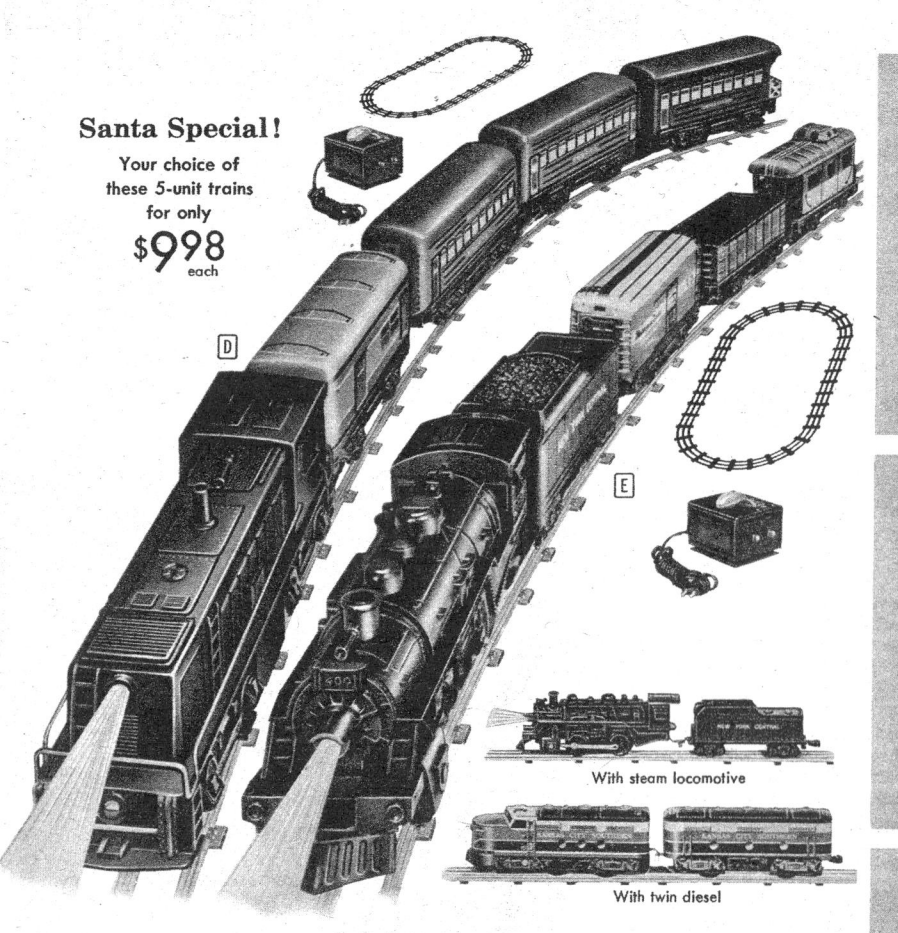

With steam locomotive

With twin diesel

Low-priced 5-unit passenger and freight trains

[D] **5-Unit Diesel Passenger Train Set.** Plastic Diesel switcher locomotive, with headlight, pulls four lithographed steel cars .. baggage car, 2 passenger cars, observation car, all with manual couplers. 8 curved sections, 2 straight sections of big radius track make 129½-in. oval. Train is 34 in. long. Track connector. 50-watt transformer with circuit breaker. UL approved, 110–120 volt, 60-cycle AC.
49 N 9639—Shipping weight 8 lbs.......**$9.98**

[E] **5-Unit 36-in. Freight** .. your choice of twin Diesel or steam locomotive .. both have headlight, oilless bronze bearings, manual couplers. Rest of train consists of lithographed steel box car, steel gondola and caboose. 10 sections big radius track form 129½-in. oval. 50-watt circuit breaker transformer, UL approved for 110–120 volt, 60-cycle AC.
49 N 9620—(With plastic steam-type locomotive and tender.) Shipping weight 7 lbs........**$9.98**
49 N 9644—(Same train with lithographed steel twin diesel engine.) Shipping weight 7 lbs........**$9.98**

Reduced! Allstate® Trestle Train

[A] Smoke-puffing 6-unit train runs up, down and around on more than 26 feet of roadbed, filled with grades and curves. Die-cast metal locomotive has piston rod action, bright headlight and oilless bronze bearings. Scale-detailed tender, box car, tank car, stake car with cartons, and caboose .. all made of metal and plastic with double trucks (8 die-cast wheels on each car). Run train forward or in reverse, fast or slow, even couple and uncouple cars by remote control. 12 sections of curved, 13 sections of straight large-radius track make a 26-foot 9-inch running track layout. 24-piece plastic trestle set. Uncoupler track with ramp and "Uncouple Here" sign, track connector, smoke refill incl. Train is 47¾ in. long. 50-watt transformer with circuit breaker. UL appr. 110–120 volt 60-cycle AC.
79 N 09625—Shipping weight 16 lbs. Was $18.97.......**$17.88**

5-Unit Smoking Locomotive Freight Train Set

[B] Young railroaders will be delighted with this steam-type locomotive that puffs harmless smoke as it chugs along. Die-cast metal, with four-wheel drive, pony trucks and two guide wheels. Cars include new slant-back tender, refrigerator car, ALLSTATE® tank car and caboose .. all scale detailed in plastic and metal. You can control the operation of the train .. move it forward or back, speed it up or slow it down, couple or uncouple cars .. by remote control. One straight and eight curved sections of big-radius 5-tie track, plus uncoupling ramp with sign, make a huge 129-inch oval. 50-watt transformer with circuit breaker for protection from shorts. UL approved for 110–120 volt, 60-cycle AC. Track connector and bottle of smoke liquid also included in set.
79 N 09619—40½ in. long. Shipping weight 10 lbs.......**$15.79**

Big 9-Unit Allstate® Electric Freight Train

[C] Accurate detailing .. over 7 feet long. Die-cast steam-type metal locomotive puffs harmless smoke, has four-wheel drive, pony trucks and two guide wheels. Also new power pull feature for pulling heavy loads. Plastic and steel coal tender and 7 cars, including tank car, automobile car with 4 cars, piggyback car, crane car, Boston & Maine box car, flat car with girder, and wrecker caboose. Run train forward or back, fast or slow, couple or uncouple cars, all by remote control. 3 straight and 8 curved sections of big radius track, plus uncoupler section make 129½-inch oval. 100-watt transformer with circuit breaker, 4 binding posts (2 for accessories). UL approved for 110–120 volt, 60-cycle AC. Track connector, bottle of smoke liquid.
79 N 09634—Train 89 in. long. Shpg. wt. 16 lbs...........**$26.39**

®ALLSTATE .. Sears registered trademark

Our Best Allstate® 6-unit Passenger Train has triple Diesels!

$29.79 cash — $3 down

Guaranteed to thrill young railroaders. Big triple Diesel locomotive, realistically detailed in plastic. Power unit has bright headlight, four wheel drive, oilless bronze bearings and new power pull feature (friction-grip driving wheels). Set also includes diesel "B" unit, diesel rear unit, two fully lighted Astro-Dome coaches and one lighted observation coach. Five sections of straight, eight sections of curved large-radius track, and one uncoupler section with sign form 174½-inch oval. Train measures 69 inches overall. Run it forward and back, speed it up or slow it down, couple and uncouple cars, all by remote control. 100-watt transformer with circuit breaker and 2 sets of binding posts .. one to operate train .. other for accessories. UL Approved for 110–120 volt, 60-cycle AC. Track connector. *Use Sears Easy Terms on orders of $20 or more.*
79 N 09632—Shipping weight 15 lbs............$29.79

Breaker Transformers..5-tie Track
.. with more play value than most trains we've ever seen

Lowest Price Ever! WAS $18.97
[A] $17.88

[B] $15.79

[C] $26.39 cash — $3.00 down

[B] Scale-detailed Twin Diesel $12.79 [C] Unloads lumber! $4.37 [D] Moving Cattle! $3.37

[E] $10.98 [F] $3.37 [G] Astrodome $3.37 [H] $3.37

[J] $2.67 [K] $4.89 [L] $3.37 [M] $3.37

Accessories for Electric Trains

[A] $4.39

(A, C, D, G, H, J, L and M) Action-packed extra cars. Heavy-duty plastic and steel. Remote control automatic couplers. Two 4-wheel trucks, die-cast wheels. B, E, F. Locomotives and Hand Car. Built-in electric motor, die-cast wheels, oilless bronze bearings. Track not incl. (except C).

[A] **Operating Crane. Wrecker Car.** Plastic cab, boom revolve.
49 N 9786—12 in. Long. Wt. 1 lb. 10 oz. $4.39

[B] **Twin Diesel** in plastic and steel. Two units. Front unit has motor. Rear unit has automatic coupler. Head lamp. Dummy horns. 24 inches long.
49 N 9792—Shpg. wt. 4 lbs........ $12.79

[C] **Operating Lumber Car.** Press remote control button .. logs unload into plastic bin. Includes bin, 5 logs, track section, control panel, all wiring and connectors. 8¾ in. long.
49 N 9761—Shpg. wt. 1 lb......... $4.37

[D] **Operating Cattle Car** with ramp, platform. Car stops, door opens. Cow comes out, draws back when train starts. 9½ inches long.
49 N 9763—Shipping weight 1 lb..... $3.37

Build your train accessories order to $20 or more and pay only 10% down!

[E] **Diesel Switcher.** Automatic couplers at both ends. Realistic hum. Die-cast metal chassis; plastic body. Headlamp. 10½ inches long.
49 N 9783—Shpg. wt. 2 lbs. 4 oz.... $10.98

[F] **Electric Hand Car.** Plastic and steel. 2 railroaders pump crossbars. Built-in motor. Operates like an electric train. 6¼ inches long.
49 N 9753—Shpg. wt. 12 oz........ $3.37

[G] **Lighted Passenger Cars.** Colored metal. Riders silhouetted in windows. Shipping weight each 14 oz.
49 N 9770—11-in. Astrodome (shown) $3.37
49 N 9771—10¾-in. Observation.... 3.37

Interurban Car. (Not shown). Electric motor .. remote controlled. 11 inches.
49 N 9784—Wt. 3 lbs. Was $8.67.... $6.97

[H] **Automobile Carrier Car.** Two-deck rack on flat car carries 4 little autos that detach to unload (each about 4 in. long). Car 9½ inches long.
49 N 9755—Shipping weight 1 lb..... $3.37

[J] **Plastic Tractor Car.** Two detachable tractors. Car 9½ inches long.
49 N 9773—Shipping weight 14 oz... $2.67

[K] **Remote Control Automatic Barrel Loader.** Press a button .. truck takes barrel from loading chute to car (not included). Unit of plastic 8¾x8x5 in. high. Includes plastic "barrels," control panel, wires.
49 N 9779—Shipping weight 1 lb. 6 oz. $4.89

[L] **Track Sweeper Car.** 2 felt sweepers clean as car rolls. 9½ in. long.
49 N 9766—Shpg. wt. 1 lb......... $3.37

[M] **Allstate Piggy-Back Car.** 11½ in. long. Carries 2 semi-trailers.
49 N 9775—Shpg. wt. 14 oz........ $3.37

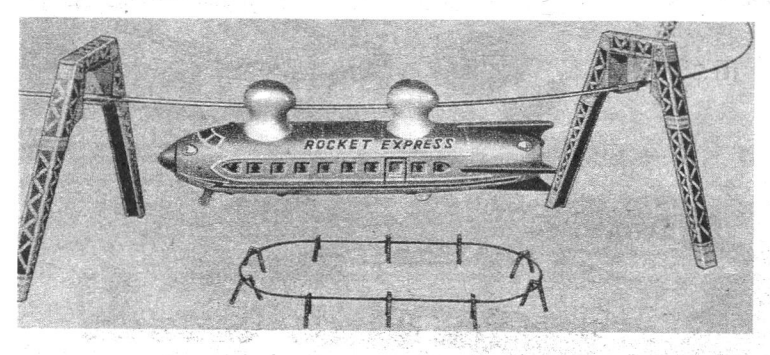

New! Rocket Ship Monorail Set $3.39

Give your youngster a realistic peep into his transportation future! Brightly colored metal rocket ship is suspended from a sturdy steel monorail supported by 10 steel trestles. In operation, the rocket ship travels on monorail continuously. Uses one standard battery (not included). Ship 10 in. long, has forward, reverse lever. Monorail has 6 curved, 4 straight rails, easily assembled. 12-ft. circumference. Trestles 5½ in. high. Imported from Japan.
49 N 9516—Shpg. wt. 3 lbs.. Set $3.39   34 N 4650—Batteries, shpg. wt. 8 oz.. 2 for 35c

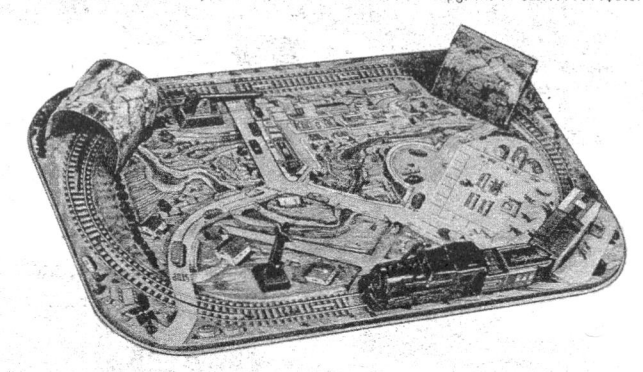

New Mechanical Scenic Fast Freight Train on Base $2.79

Plastic locomotive powered by long running motor—speeds at high rate around grooved track. Has brightly colored metal cars. Key attached. Grooved track portion around outside depicts tracks and acts as guide. Train passes through 2 tunnels; crossing gate and semaphore move up and down as it passes. Metal base attractively decorated in all-over full scenic design. Base 21¾ in. long, 13⅛ in. wide. Train 11½ inches long overall. Train travels around track about 20 times on one winding. Inexpensive fun for young railroaders; a long time favorite in play value.
49 N 9513—Shipping weight 3 pounds................................ $2.79

Add Realism to Your Electric Train Set

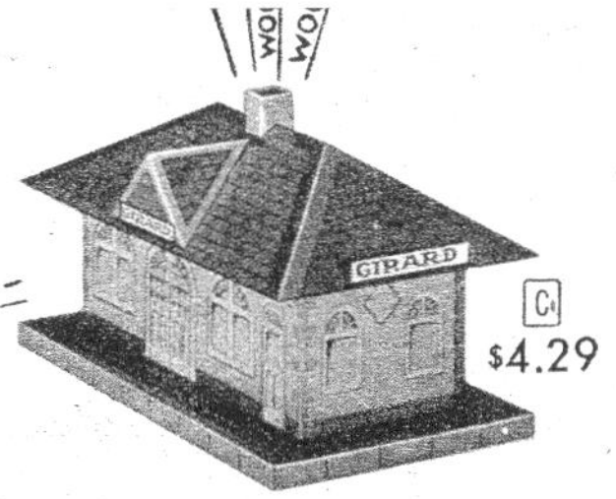

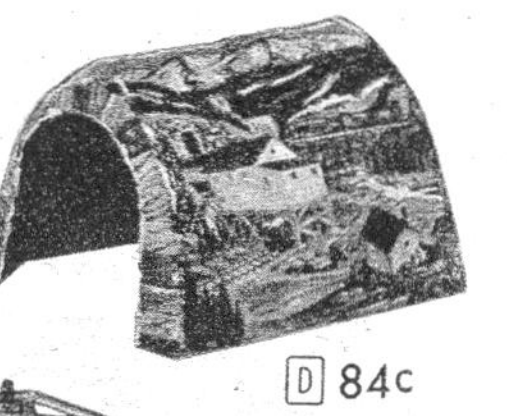

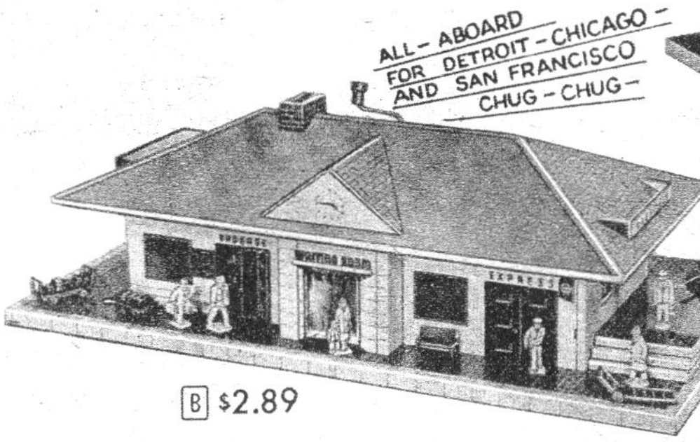

Life-Like Scene-O-Rama Kit — Makes 4x8-foot Scenic Landscape
[A] $7.89

[B] $2.89

[C] $4.29

[D] 84c

[E] $2.39

[F] $1.89

[G] $4.49

[A] **Natural setting.** 15 trees, all kinds, sizes. True color lichen in 3 shades for shrubbery. It's fun to cut grass, road mats any shape for contrasts. Snow capped tunnel; 3 lamps wired to attach to any electric track.
79 N 09713—Shpg. wt. 5 lbs. Complete Kit...$7.89

[B] **"Talking Voice" Station** announces trains. Hand crank operated. Plastic people, etc. Metal, 20½x10x6 in. high.
49 N 9787—Shipping weight 3 lbs. 8 oz....$2.89

[C] **Remote Control Whistling Station.** Whistle mechanism protected within steel station. Includes control panel, all wires. Easy to install on any electric train layout. 9x5½x5 in. high. Gives real life sound effect.
49 N 9739—Shipping weight 2 pounds......$4.29

[D] **Metal Tunnel.** Colorfully decorated. Take apart easily for storage. 9x7x10¼ in. long.
49 N 9729—Shipping weight 1 pound........84c

[E] **Lighted Steel Trestle Bridge.** Aluminum finish. Socket, reflector clip-on is adjustable. Shipping weight 2 lbs. 4 oz.
49 N 9741—24x5x6 in. high...........$2.39

[F] **3 Lighted Plastic Lamp Posts.** Easy to attach to your electric train track.
49 N 9737—6 in. high. Shpg. wt. 1 lb.......$1.89

[G] **Plastic Trestle Set.** 24 graduated trestles for up to 24 ft. of track for figure 8 set-up with overpass or hilly road. Track not incl.
49 N 9738—Shipping weight 2 lbs..........$4.49

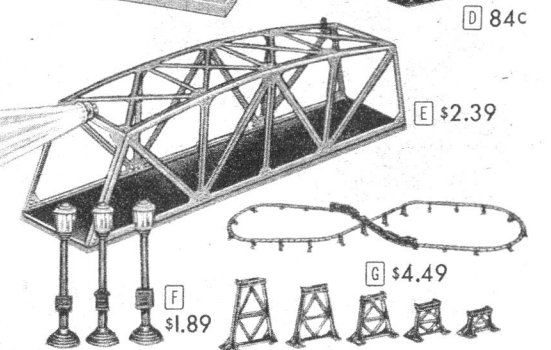

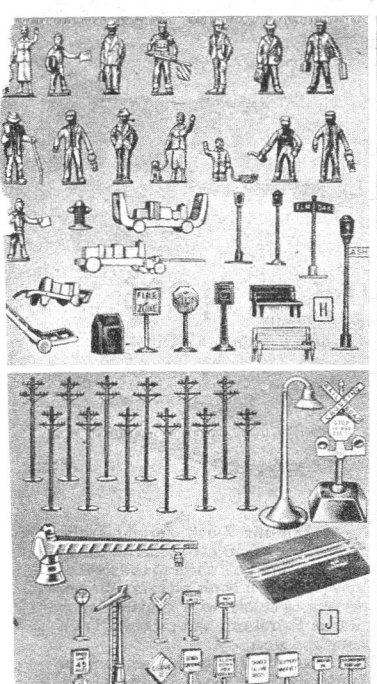

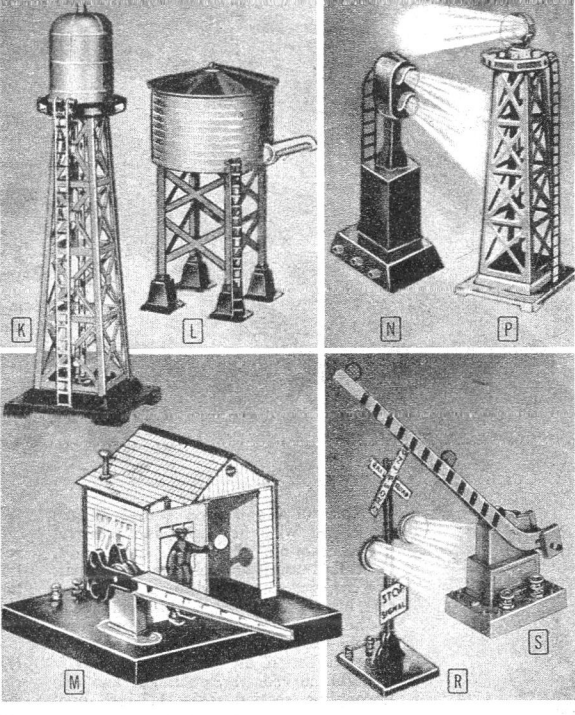

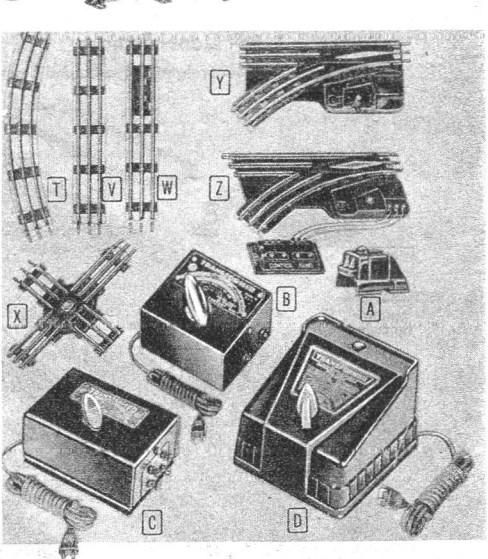

[H] **30-pc. Railroad People and Accessory Set.** Realistically molded plastic set. Includes 15 railroad people in various poses, 5 railroad accessories (hand truck, bench, freight wagon, etc.), 10 other accessories (mail box, trash can, parking meter, etc.).
49 N 9772—Shpg. wt. 10 oz......98c

[J] **29-pc. Railroad Accessories Set.** Made of durable plastic in just the right size for any standard mechanical or electric train set. Carefully scale detailed to please the most particular young "Casey Jones." Set includes 12 seven-inch telegraph poles, 12 railroad right-of-way signs, and one each of the following: semaphore, lamp post, crossing gate, grade crossing sign and grade crossing plate. (Track not included.) A really big set for a low price! Build your order to $20.00... use Easy Terms.
49 N 9750—Shpg. wt. 2 lbs....$2.59

[K] **Plastic Water Tower with bubbling light.** 2¼-inch diam. tank has realistic plates and rivets, girder-type understructure. Heat from light bulb in 4½x4½-inch base creates rising water bubbles in the transparent plastic tube that runs from the base to the tank. Light also shows through the tube. 14 inches high. Shipping weight 1 pound.
49 N 9751................$2.69

[L] **Plastic Water Tower with adjustable spout.** Diameter 4¼ inches; 8¼ inches high. Shipping weight 10 ounces.
49 N 9731..............84c

[M] **Automatic Grade Crossing Shack and Watchman.** As train passes, watchman comes out with stop sign, gate lowers. Shack is brightly colored steel 4½ inches high. Base is 7x6½ inches. Shipping weight 2 pounds.
49 N 9760..............$3.29

[N] **Automatic 2-light Block Signal.** Train stops on red, goes on green signal. Switch operated. Made of plastic, 7¼ inches high. Includes two track sections.
49 N 9745—Shpg. wt. 10 oz...$1.69

[P] **Lighted Revolving Beacon.** Light on girder-type tower revolves constantly; beams red in one direction and green in the other. Plastic. 12½ in. high.
49 N 9740—Shpg. wt. 10 oz...$1.69

[R] **Automatic Crossing Flasher.** Twin red lights flash alternately as train goes by. Made of plastic. 7 inches high.
49 N 9742—Shpg. wt. 10 oz...$1.69

[S] **Automatic Crossing Gate.** Made of plastic. Regulation railroad design. 7½ in. high, base 2¼ in., gate arm 8 in. long. Gate arm rises and lowers automatically. Includes wires and track clips.
49 N 9743—Shpg. wt. 10 oz...$1.69

Extra Track, Switches for Allstate, Happi-Time or Marx Electric Trains. With wider curves for faster speeds. 5 cross ties per section—not usual 3!

[T] 12½-in. Curved Track. Big-radius type.
49 N 9723—Shipping weight 4 oz.....each 21c

[V] 11¼-in. Straight Track. Big-radius type.
49 N 9720—Shipping weight 4 oz......each 21c

[W] Uncoupling Section. With "Uncouple" sign.
49 N 9749—11¼ in. Big-radius type. Wt. 5 oz..79c

Track Connector (not shown). Carries electric power from transformer to track.
49 N 9709—Shipping weight 2 ounces....Each 12c

[X] Crossover Track. 9¾x9¾ inches square.
49 N 9726—Big-radius type. Wt. 9 oz...Ea. $1.27

[Y] Manually Operated Switch Set. 1 right, 1 left-hand switch. Big-radius type.
49 N 9776—Shipping weight 2 lbs......Set $4.29

[Z] Remote Control Switch Set. Red and green light. Right and left-hand switch. Control panel.
49 N 9727—Big-radius type. Wt. 2 lbs. 8 oz..$8.29

[A] Lighted Dead-end Bumper. Plastic. 3x1⅞x2 in. high. Snaps to end of spur track.
49 N 9707—Shipping weight 5 ounces..........84c

UL Approved Transformers. 110–120 volts, 60 cycle AC. Safe, low voltage for trains, accessories. Built-in circuit breaker, reset button, protects from shorting. Cord, wires, track connectors.

[B] 50-watt Transformer. 2 separate sets binding posts. (1) Variable 7-13 volts controls train speed; (2) 13 volts for accessories. Steel case.
49 N 9725—Shipping weight 3 lbs............$5.47

[C] Bigger 100-watt Transformer for larger sets with more accessories. Steel case with 2 sets of binding posts. (1) 5-15 volts for train speed; (2) fixed 15 volts for accessories.
49 N 9777—Shipping weight 4 lbs. 8 oz......$8.39

[D] Our Biggest, Super-powered 150-watt Transformer. 2 sets binding posts: (1) variable 0-15 volts for train speed; (2) 15 volts for accessories. Throttle-type control. In plastic case.
49 N 9764—Shipping weight 10 pounds......$12.69

PCBKMN SEARS 373

Our Best Lionel Train has 9 Units
New .. features Magne-traction drive
$49.75 cash · $5 down

Big new 9-unit Work Train powered by huge "Wabash GP-7" Diesel-type locomotive. How he'll thrill to its power .. running train forward or back, fast or slow .. coupling or uncoupling cars by remote control .. the built-in "live" sounding wail of a real Diesel horn .. bright headlight .. rail-gripping Magne-traction .. the crane car with its realistic rotating cab and separate hand wheel controls for boom and hook .. the New Haven box car with its sliding doors .. loading and unloading the plane, autos and lumber on de luxe flat cars .. the remote control lumber car with logs, unloading bin, new transformer car and unique work caboose. Plastic and steel.

8 curved pieces, 7 straight and 1 uncoupling section form 147-in. oval track. 90-watt circuit breaker transformer has two controls: one for horn, the other for speed. Two fixed voltage ranges for accessories. Track lock-on and lubricant. Shipping weight 18 pounds.
79 N 09658—97 in. long.....................$49.75

Exciting, Powerful New Lionel "O27" Gauge Trains

8-unit Lionel Train
Powerful Twin Diesel Freight .. Plastic and Steel
$29.79 cash Only $3 down

[A]

7-unit Freight
Steam-type with real piston-rod action!
$19.95 cash Only $2.00 down

[B]

All sets have UL approved transformers for 110-120-volt, 60-cycle AC. Cars have 2 double trucks, 8 die-cast wheels with remote-control uncoupling.

[A] Colorful 8-unit Twin Diesel 79-inch freight with headlight and powerful magne-traction. M.K.T. power unit, M.K.T. dummy unit, flat car with boat, box car, girder car, gondola car with canisters, hopper and caboose. Load and unload the boat, canisters and girder .. couple, uncouple the cars, travel fast or slow in either direction, all by remote control.

Eight curved, three straight and one uncoupling section make 117-inch oval track. 45-watt transformer, lock-on and instructions are included.
79 N 09656—Shipping weight 11 lbs...$29.79

[B] New! Realistic 7-unit Freight Train. Steam-type locomotive with real piston rod action .. how he'll thrill to the sight of its lively power as it hauls six cars—tender, hopper car, gondola with canisters, box car, Range Patrol car, and caboose. Train is plastic and steel.

Eight curved, 2 straight sections of track form 94-inch oval. Automatic uncoupler unit for uncoupling the cars fits any straight track section. 45-watt transformer, lock-on, instructions included. Train is 61 in. long.
79 N 09655—Shipping wt. 9 lbs........$19.95

Denver and Rio Grande locomotive with Snow Plow. Modeled after the Vulcan, gear-driven "workhorse" of the mountains. Simulated lights front and rear; dummy bell. 8 die-cast wheels; 4 wheel drive, operating coupler. 8 in. long.
49 N 9870—Shpg. wt. 3 lbs. **$11.95**

New! Union Pacific Diesel Switcher. Two-tone yellow and gray combination—a versatile "workhorse" with headlight and self-centering couplers front and rear, 8 wheels. Magne-traction gives it tremendous pulling power, greater speeds on curves without derailment. 12¼ in. long.
49 N 9867—Shpg. wt. 4 lbs. **$18.97**

New! Executive Inspection Car. Actual model of station wagon used by railroad executives for inspection of their right-of-way. 4 extra flanged wheels for rail travel. Illuminated interior. 2-position reverse gives direction by remote control. Car 7½ in. long.
49 N 9857—Wt. 2 lbs. **$10.98**

Operating Section Gang Car. Built-in motor. Car and workers reverse automatically when buffer plate at either end strikes object. Plastic and steel. For "027" or "O" gauge. 6 inches long over-all.
49 N 9846—Wt. 2 lbs. **$6.29**

Buy the trains of your choice on Sears Easy Terms .. only 10% down on $20 or more!

New! Firefighting Car. Self-propelled, reverses direction when contacting another object and helmeted fireman swivels automatically. Car equipped with outrigger type dummy sprinklers, red light flashes when in motion, carries reel of fire hose which actually unrolls! 7 in. long.
49N9860—Wt. 2 lbs. **$10.98**

Train set has UL approved transformer, 110-120-volt, 60-cycle AC. Cars have 2 double trucks, 8 die-cast wheels, remote-control uncoupling

New! Big 8-unit Freight by Lionel has whistle, smoke . . 6-wheel drive

$39.79 cash **$4** down

New huge Steam-type Locomotive with headlamp . . puffs smoke and sounds its whistle by remote control! Magne-Traction and 6-wheel drive give it tremendous pulling power. Long work train includes 2-6-4 locomotive with piston-rod action, whistling tender, box car, hopper, flat car with transformer, gondola car with 3 canisters, car carrying airplane, and the caboose. Youngsters enjoy loading and unloading the canister and airplane cars . . running train forward or back, fast or slow, coupling and uncoupling cars . . sounding its realistic whistle—all by remote control! Train over 6 feet long. Scale detailed of strong steel and plastic.

8 curved, 5 straight and 1 uncoupling section make up 129-in. oval track. 60-watt transformer has built-in circuit breaker and whistle control; lock-on and lubricant. Smoke pellets included.

79 N 09657—Shipping weight 14 lbs. $39.79

Realistic, up-to-the-minute Train Accessories

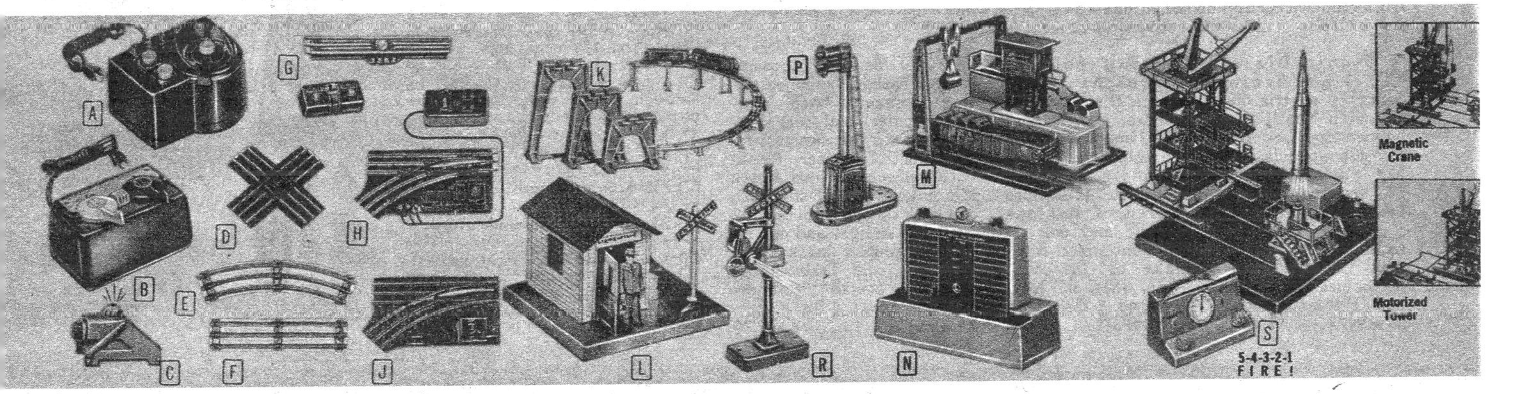

(A) (B) Transformers. Built-in circuit breakers. 110 120 volt, 60-cycle AC. UL approved.

A Type LW—125-watt. Full range of train speeds PLUS fixed 14 and 18-volt circuits for accessories. Built-in whistle, direction controls.
49 N 9819—Shpg. wt. 6 lbs. $13.98

B Type TW—175-watt. Two throttles: 1 controls train speed; 2nd controls direction, sounds whistle or horn on your train. 3 fixed accessory voltages: 14, 18, 25. Two circuit breakers.
49 N 9842—Shpg. wt. 9 lbs. $21.95

C Lighted Bumper. For '027,' '0.'
49 N 9859—Shpg. wt. 1 lb. $1.97

D "027" 7⅜-in. 90° Crossover.
49 N 9803—Shpg. wt. 8 oz. $1.59

"027" Track Sections. Wt. each 3 oz.
(E) 49 N 9802—9½ in. Curved. . . . Ea. 21c
(F) 49 N 9801—8⅞ in. Straight. . . . Ea. 21c

G "027" Magnetic Track Section. For remote uncoupling and unloading. Control panel, wires included.
49 N 9804—Shpg. wt. 1 lb. . . . . Each $3.97

H "027" Remote Control Switch Set. Non-derailing device throws switch rails automatically, lets train run through. Green and red lights on switch and controller also change. One right and one left-hand switch, control panel and wires included.
49 N 9806—Shpg. wt. 3 lbs. . . . . Set $14.97

J "027" Manual Switch Set. 1 right, 1 left hand. Non-derailing type.
49 N 9805—Shpg. wt. 2 lbs. . . . . . Set $6.45

K Trestle Set. 24 piers. Use with Magne-Traction locomotives. Make over and under layouts.
49 N 9845—Plastic. Wt. 3 lbs. . . . Set $4.79

L Automatic Gateman. Shuttles in and out of shack, lantern lights as train passes. 7x5½x4½ inches high.
49 N 9835—Shpg. wt. 2 lbs. $5.79

M Culvert Unloading Station with gondola car. Station 11½x10 in.
49 N 9829—Shpg. wt. 6 lbs. $16.95

N Illuminated Remote-control Dispatching Board. Schedule automatically changes. 4x10x8 in. high.
49 N 9841—Shpg. wt. 3 lbs. $9.95

P Illuminated Automatic Block Signal. Stops train for time set.
49 N 9808—7 in. high. Wt. 1 lb. $5.98

R Illuminated Automatic Banjo Signal. Signal lights as train approaches, 'STOP' sign swings back and forth. 7½ inches high. Action stops automatically after the train has passed. Bulb, wires, connector included.
49 N 9827—Shpg. wt. 1 lb. $4.69

S New! Lionel's Rocket Launcher! Minute detailing of firing procedure used for earth satellite. Includes motorized launching tower moving on its own track; a remote control illuminated console with realistic count-down mechanism; tower control button, firing button; launching platform, rocket with polyurethane nose cone. Base 11x11 in., tower and crane are 17 inches high.
49 N 9854—Shpg. wt. 9 lbs. $14.95

Operating Horse Car. Touch a remote-control button . . horses move in and out of car and around the 12x5¾-inch corral. Set includes 11¼-in. car, with remote control couplers, horses, corral, control, all necessary wires. Does not require remote-control track section.
49 N 9873—Wt. 4 lbs. $14.95

New Lionel Twin Auto Carrying Car. Boys' love for trains and automobiles all wrapped up in one fun-happy combination! Specially built flat car carries two perfectly detailed model automobiles. He'll spend happy hours loading and unloading autos from their flat car cradle. Car is 11 inches long.
49 N 9844—Shpg. wt. 2 lbs. $3.98

Airplane-Carrying Flat Car. Plane is mounted on flat car with wings retracted. Plane can be removed from car and wings extended . . ready for "take off." 10⅞-in. flat car; remote control couplers; 8 die-cast metal wheels.
49 N 9838—Wt. 2 lbs. $3.98

Tie Ejector Car. Built-in motor. Moves under its own power and throws railroad ties along railside while in motion. Action started by railside bumper, stopped by second bumper. Coupler. 8⅞ in. long.
49 N 9840—Wt. 3 lbs. . . . $8.97

Operating Wrecking Crane. 2 separate hand wheels: 1 raises and lowers the boom; other wheel raises, lowers hook. Cab rotates. Die-cast metal trucks; steel wheels. Remote control couplers. 7⅞ in. long.
49 N 9852—Wt. 2 lbs. . . . $6.49

All trains, cars on these 2 pages are plastic and steel

Hobby Size
ALLSTATE® HO Electric Trains

[A] $10.59
[B] $15.59
[C] $19.79

HO Gauge Engines and Cars are detailed miniatures of regular trains

Run trains forward or back, fast or slow, couple or uncouple cars, all by remote control. Rerailer uncoupler acts as grade crossing. Weighted plastic cars have nylon trucks and wheels. Sets do not include Powerpacks, which are necessary for operation of trains .. order these separately at right (49 N 9909)

[A] **5-unit Diesel Freight Train.** Santa Fe electric diesel with headlight, hopper car, box car, low-side gondola and bay window caboose. 12 sections curved, 1 section straight track, 1 rerailer uncoupler section form 112-in. oval. One track connector incl. Train 30 in. long. Wt. 2 lbs. 10 oz.
49 N 9974......$10.59

[B] **6-unit Switcher Freight Train.** Electric Diesel switcher locomotive, flatcar with 2 bulldozers, hook car, cable car, remote control log car, wrecker caboose. 12 sections curved, 3 sections straight and one rerailer-uncoupler track make 127-in. oval. Train 38¼ in. long. Shpg. wt. 2 lbs. 12 oz.
49 N 9975......$15.59

[C] **7-unit Smoking Locomotive Freight Train.** Steam-type locomotive with headlight, tender, coal car, ALLSTATE® tank car, box car, remote control log car, (push-button on control panel; watch logs unload into plastic bin), and work caboose with tank. 12 curved, 3 straight and one rerailer uncoupler track make big 127-in. oval. Train is 42¼ inches long overall .. scale detailed. Shpg. wt. 4 lbs. 8 oz.
49 N 9981............$19.79

[D] **Powerpack.** O-14 volts DC for varying train speed. 45 volt amps. output. 15 volts AC for accessories. 2 separate circuit breakers. UL approved for 110-120-volt 60-cycle AC. Cord included.
49 N 9909—Shpg. wt. 6 lbs....$9.39

[E] **12 Plastic Phone Poles.** Wt. 10 oz.
49 N 9985—3½ in. high......$1.29

[F] **Diesel Switcher Loco:** 4½x2x1½ in. Nylon geared, 4-wheel drive. Brass wheels, knuckle couplers.
49 N 9997—Shpg. wt. 1 lb......$4.79

[G] **Plastic Water Tower.** Has light on the top. 7½ inches high.
49 N 9986—Shpg. wt. 10 oz.....$1.98

[H] **Trestle Bridge.** 8¾x3¼x2¾ in. high. Plastic girder type. Makes nice addition to any HO set.
49 N 9907—Shpg. wt. 10 oz.....$1.19

[J] **8-in. Curved Track .. HO gauge.**
49 N 9905—Wt. 4 oz.....Each 13c

[K] **7½-in. Straight Track .. HO gauge.**
49 N 9904—Wt. 4 oz.....Each 13c

[L] **7½-in. Uncoupler Rerailer Track.**
49 N 9908—Shpg. wt. 4 oz.....46c

[M] **Manual Switches .. right and left.**
49 N 9982—Wt. 14 oz.....Set $4.49

[N] **Remote Control Switch Set.** Incl. right, left-hand switches.
49 N 9983—Shpg. wt. 1 lb.....Set $7.49

[P] $3.89
[R] $2.98
[S] $5.89

New Mechanical Train Sets .. low priced, yet loads of fun

[P] **Bigger 5-unit 34½-in. Freight Train Set.** Realistic steam-type plastic locomotive has long-running keywind clockspring motor, bell, piston-rod action .. governor and brake. One steel tender, steel tank car, steel hopper car, and steel caboose. 8 sections of curved track, 2 sections of straight track form 102-inch oval. One winder key included. Build your order to $20.00 and use Sears Easy Terms, you pay only 10% down.
49 N 9519—Shpg. wt. 3 lbs......$3.89

[R] **4-unit 28-inch long Sparking Freight Set.** Steam-type locomotive of sturdy plastic and steel has keywinding clockspring motor .. emits harmless sparks through the smokestack as the train moves along .. its bell ringing. Set also includes a tender, a low-side gondola, and a caboose. Cars are made of colorfully lithographed steel. 8 sections of curved track form 84-inch circle. An inexpensive stocking stuffer youngsters will enjoy all year long.
49 N 9504—Shpg. wt. 2 lbs. 8 oz. $2.98

All Allstate trains are ® Reg. T.M. Sears, Roebuck and Co.

Our Best Battery-Operated Freight

[S] **4-unit 28½-inch Allstate Freight Train Set with Accessories.** Realistic plastic and steel steam-type locomotive has powerful battery-operated motor, built-in switch for on-or-off, also directs train forward or backward. Uses 2 batteries (not incl.), order below. Set also includes one steel tender, one steel low-side gondola and one steel caboose. 2 sections straight, 8 sections curved track make 102-in. oval. 6 plastic phone poles, semaphore, crossing gate, crossing sign, billboard, 12 Rite-O-Way signs and 10 vinyl-plastic people .. all in 3 dimensions.
49 N 9520—Shipping weight 4 pounds......$5.89
34 N 4650—Batteries. Shpg. wt. 8 oz....2 for 35c

Extra Track and Switch Set

Items below are for trains at left, or standard Marx mechanical and battery-operated trains.

[T] **8½-in. Straight Track.** Shpg. wt. 6 oz. for set of 4.
49 N 9701.........Set of 4 for 37c

[V] **10½-in. Curved Track.** Shpg. wt. 6 oz. for set of 4.
49 N 9702.........Set of 4 for 37c

[W] **Manually-operated Switch Set.** Two switches: 1 right hand and 1 left hand. Shpg. wt. 1 lb.
49 N 9704.........Set of 2 for $1.79

[X] **7½-in. 90 degree Crossover.**
49 N 9703—Wt. 8 oz.......Ea. 59c

SEARS CHRISTMAS CATALOG
1959

The eight big train pages featured in the 1959 Sears Wishbook had a larger variety of models trains for sale, in both O-27, Super-O and H-O scales.

Allstate (manufactured for Sears by Marx) advertised several unique items, including the Two-Train "Over and Under" Trestle Outfit for $29.67. This set came with two complete freight trains which were kept from colliding by an automatic flashing block signal. Also available for the first time, from both Marx and Lionel, were 1880's-era wood-burner steam trains, probably capitalizing on the Fifties' continuing interest in Western lore.

One of the most unique trains ever offered was the now-rare Lionel Atomic Age Train Set with Rocket Launcher. In Super-O gauge, this amazing set came with a sleek locomotive with a visible control center inside. The rocket launcher was an astounding toy in its own right, with a motorized gantry and launch pad for firing satellites into outer space.

Big 9-unit Allstate® Electric Freight Train

All this for **$25.97**

A real railroading beauty .. scale detailed .. over 6½ feet long from engine to caboose. Die-cast steam-type metal locomotive puffs harmless smoke for greater realism. Locomotive has four-wheel drive, pony trucks and two guide wheels. All wheels die-cast. Also features Power Pull to pull heavy loads or extra cars.

Plastic and steel coal tender and 7 cars, including tank car, automobile car with 4 autos, piggy-back car, crane car, Boston & Maine box car, flat car with girder, and wrecker caboose. You can run train forward or back, fast or slow, couple or uncouple cars, all by remote control.

Three straight and eight curved sections of big radius, 5-tie track, plus an uncoupler section make a big 152-inch oval. 100-watt transformer with circuit breaker, 4 binding posts (2 for accessories). UL approved for 110–120-volt, 60-cycle AC. Track connector and bottle of smoke liquid included.

79 N 09634—Train 81 inches long overall. Shipping weight 16 pounds. $3 down......Cash **$25.97**

Trains on both pages feature Power Pull, circuit-breaker transformers, die-cast wheels, 5-tie large-radius track with wide curves for faster speeds.

Rocket really fires

8-unit Diesel [1] **$19.79**

[2] **$17.69**

8-Unit Electric Diesel Switcher Freight

[1] Diesel locomotive has Power Pull for extra traction .. also headlight, oilless bronze bearings. Scale detailed hopper car, rocket car that really fires, refrigerator car, ALLSTATE tank car, wrecker car, gondola and ALLSTATE caboose .. all plastic and steel. Run train forward or back, fast or slow, couple or uncouple cars, all by remote control. 3 sections of straight, 8 sections of curved large-radius 5-tie track, plus uncoupler unit, make 152-in. oval. 50-watt circuit-breaker transformer UL approved 110–120-volt, 60-cycle AC. Order now and give your little Engineer a real Christmas surprise.

79 N 09630—75½ inches long overall. Shipping weight 12 pounds............**$19.79**

6-unit Twin Diesel. (Not shown.) 2 remote control switches with signal lights. 17 sections of track .. 2 ovals .. over 20 feet. Stock car, tractor car, flat car, caboose. 75-watt transformer. UL approved for 110–120-volt, 60-cycle AC.

79 N 09633—60-inch Western Pacific TWIN Diesel Freight. Shpg. wt. 19 lbs......**$29.95**

5-unit Smoking Freight Train with Trestles

[2] Railroading at its exciting best .. brawny freight runs up, down, around grades and curves, thunders over 24-piece trestle span. Smoke-puffing locomotive has realistic piston rod action, bright headlight and oilless bronze bearings. Also features Power Pull for greater traction.

Detail-scaled ALLSTATE tender, Santa Fe box car, low-side gondola and a caboose .. eight die-cast wheels on each car. Run train forward or reverse, fast or slow, couple or uncouple cars .. all by remote control. 13 sections of straight and 12 sections of curved large-radius 5-tie track make a giant 26-foot 9-inch track layout. 24-piece plastic trestle set, one uncoupler ramp with "Uncouple Here" sign, a track connector and a bottle of smoke refill included. 50-watt transformer with circuit breaker. Underwriter's Laboratories approved for 110–120-volt, 60-cycle AC. Order now .. avoid the Christmas rush!

79 N 09629—40 inches long overall. Shipping weight 16 pounds....................**$17.69**

USE EASY TERMS .. only 10% down on orders of $20 or more .. See page 294

ALLSTATE® Electric Trains
Die-cast wheels .. 5-tie track .. scale detailing

Two-Train Trestle Set

Trains run on same track, yet never collide .. action is controlled by automatic block signal

$29.67 cash **$3.00 down**

Automatic block signal flashes green for train to proceed through underpass .. red for it to stop

Allstate® Two-Train "Over and Under" Trestle Outfit .. over 26 feet of track

One of the most exciting train sets we've seen. Giant trestle track system has automatically controlled electric block signal which flashes green for one train to go through the underpass, red to hold the other train back until pass is clear.

Set includes two complete freight trains. Diesel switcher set has diesel locomotive with headlight, one gondola, a box car and a caboose .. 34 inches long. Steam freight set has engine that puffs smoke, a coal and water-type tender, a flat car with racks, tank car and caboose .. 40½ in. long. Both locomotives have Power Pull for better traction. Engines and cars are plastic and metal. Die-cast wheels, manual couplers. Trains run fast or slow by remote control but do not reverse or uncouple. 50 watt circuit-breaker transformer Underwriters' Laboratories approved for 110–120-volt, 60-cycle AC. 11 sections of curved, 10 sections of straight large-radius, 5-tie track .. 26 feet 1 inch long overall. 2 special sections of straight track, special pin-end track, special no-pin straight track, automatic block signal, 24-piece set of plastic trestles, one railroad bridge and one track connector. Buy on Sears Easy Terms .. see page 294.

79 N 09637—Shipping weight 18 pounds..................$29.67

From the days of early America
An Old-Style Wood-Burner $18.77

Patterned after the trains that helped settle our last frontier

Here it comes 'round the bend, chugging and puffing right out of one of the most exciting pages in the history of America .. the taming of the West.

Old fashioned steam-type locomotive puffs smoke as it moves along .. has drive pistons, oilless bronze bearings for smooth running. Tender shows molded imitation logs. Locomotive and tender measure 14½ inches long. Combination baggage and mail car .. 8½ in. long. Regular passenger car .. 8½ in. long. Move train fast or slow, forward or back, couple or uncouple cars .. all by remote control.

Heavy-duty 50-watt transformer has built-in circuit breaker for long life. Underwriters' Laboratories approved for 110–120-volt, 60-cycle AC. 10 sections of large radius track: 8 curved sections, one straight section and one uncoupler track section with an "Uncouple Here" sign. Bottle of smoke refill and a lock-on connector included.

79 N 09622—Track circumference measures 129½ in. Train is 31 in. long overall. Shpg. wt. 8 lbs. .. **$18.77**

PCBKMN SEARS 435

Thrifty ALLSTATE® Trains

[1] **5-Unit Electric Smoking Locomotive Train Set.** Die-cast metal locomotive has 4-wheel drive. Plastic, metal tender, refrigerator car, tank car, caboose. Run train forward or back, fast or slow, couple or uncouple cars by remote control. 9 sections of big-radius 5-tie track, uncoupler ramp make 129-inch oval. 50-watt circuit-breaker transformer UL approved 110–120-volt, 60-cycle AC.
79 N 09619—40½ in. long. Wt. 10 lbs. Was $15.79..**$14.98**

[2] **5-Unit Electric Passenger Train Set.** Electric switcher locomotive with metal mail car, two passenger coaches, and observation coach. Plastic and metal engine. Manual couplers. 2 straight, 8 curved sections large-radius 5-tie track make 129½-inch oval. 30-watt transformer UL approved for 110–120-volt, 60-cycle AC. Track connector. 35½-inch long train travels fast or slow by remote control.
49 N 9608—Shipping weight 6 lbs. 10 oz...... **$8.98**

[3] **5-Unit Electric Freight** .. choose plastic steam type engine with tender or steel diesel engine with rear unit .. both engines have oilless bronze bearings. Manual couplers, run fast or slow by remote control. Steel box car, low-side gondola, caboose. 10 sections of 5-tie large-radius track for fast speeds on curves, make 129½-in. oval. 30-watt transformer UL approved for 110–120-volt, 60-cycle AC.
49 N 9603—Steam Engine Train. 36¾ in. long. Shpg. wt. 7 lbs...... **$8.98**
49 N 9606—Diesel Engine and rear unit set ... pulls same cars as above. 37 in. long overall. Shpg. wt. 7 lbs........................**$8.98**

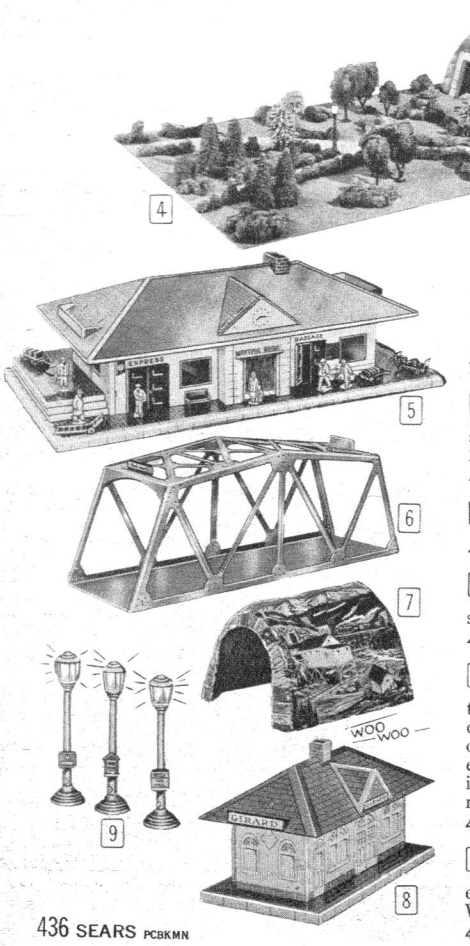

True-to-life Accessories

[4] **Scene-O-Rama Kit** makes big 4x8-foot natural scenic landscape. 15 trees, true color lichen in 3 shades for shrubbery. Cut road and grass mats any shape. Snow capped tunnel; 3 lamps wired to attach to any electric track. Instructions.
79 N 09713—Shpg. wt. 5 lbs...... **$7.89**

[5] **Big Passenger Station.** With plastic people, baggage carts, other station accessories. Metal station 20½x10x6 in. high.
49 N 9787—Shpg. wt. 3 lbs. 6 oz. .. **$2.89**

[6] **Railroad Trestle Bridge.** Steel. Accurately embossed. 18 in. long.
49 N 9732—Shpg. wt. 2 lbs....... **$1.87**

[7] **Metal Tunnel.** Colorfully decorated. Takes apart easily for storage. 9x7x10¼ inches long.
49 N 9729—Shpg. wt. 1 lb......... **84c**

[8] **Remote Control Whistling Station.** Whistle mechanism protected within steel station. Includes control panel, all wires necessary to operation. Easy to install on any electric train layout. Metal station is 9x5½x5 inches high. Gives very realistic engine whistling sound.
49 N 9739—Shpg. wt. 2 lbs....... **$3.97**

[9] **Three Lighted Plastic Lamp Posts.** Easy to attach to your electric train set .. light up like real. Wires included. Posts are 6 in. high.
49 N 9737—Shpg. wt. 10 oz...... **$1.89**

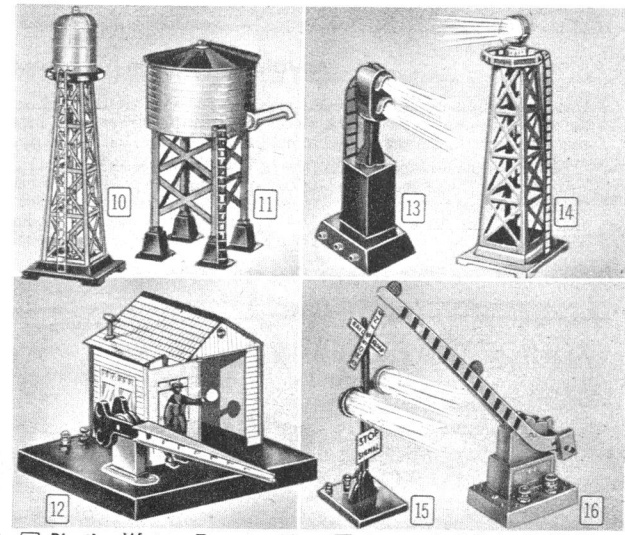

[10] **Plastic Water Tower with Bubbling Light.** 2¼-in. diameter tank shows realistic plates and rivets .. girder-type understructure. Heat from light bulb in base creates rising water bubbles in transparent plastic tube that runs from base to tank. 14 in. high.
49 N 9751—Shpg. wt. 1 lb...... **$2.69**

[11] **Plastic Water Tower with Adjustable Spout.** 4¼-in. diameter, 8¼ inches high.
49 N 9731—Shpg. wt. 10 oz...... **84c**

[12] **Automatic Grade Crossing Shack and Watchman.** As train nears, watchman comes out with a stop sign, gate lowers. Shack is brightly colored steel .. 4½ in. high. Base is 7x6½ inches.
49 N 9760—Shpg. wt. 2 lbs..... **$3.29**

[13] **Automatic 2-light Block Signal.** Train stops on red, goes on green. Switch operated. Plastic, 7½ in. high. 2 track sections.
49 N 9745—Shpg. wt. 10 oz..... **$1.77**

[14] **Lighted Revolving Beacon.** Light on tower revolves .. beams red one direction, green the other. Plastic. 12½ in. high.
49 N 9740—Shpg. wt. 10 oz..... **$1.67**

[15] **Automatic 7-in. Crossing Flasher.** 2 red lights flash alternately as train goes by. Plastic.
49 N 9742—Shpg. wt. 10 oz..... **$1.77**

[16] **Crossing Gate.** Gate arm rises, lowers automatically. Plastic. 7½ in. high .. arm 8 in. long. Wires, track clips included.
49 N 9743—Shpg. wt. 10 oz..... **$1.67**

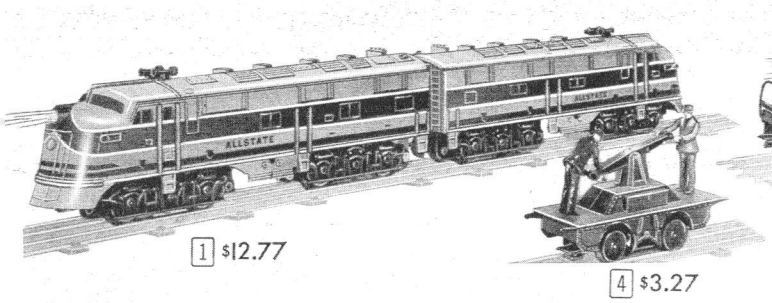

[1] $12.77
[4] $3.27
[7] $10.97
[10] $4.97
[11] $3.37
[2] $3.97
[5] $2.77
[8] $3.27
[12] $4.39
[3] $4.47
[6] $3.37
[9] $2.77

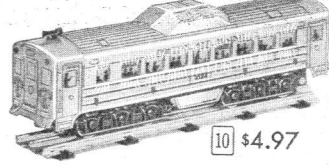

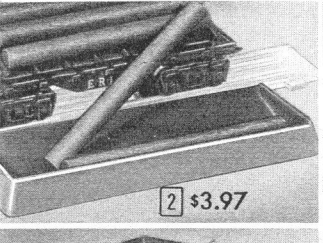

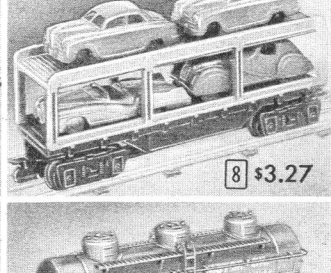

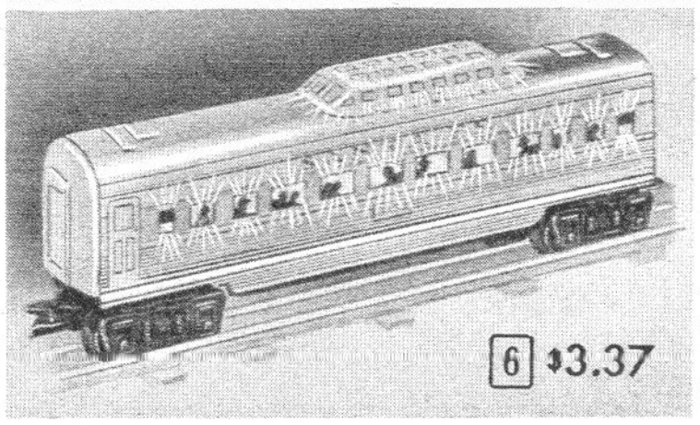

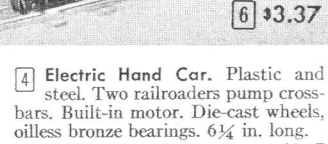

Fun-packed Extras for little engineers

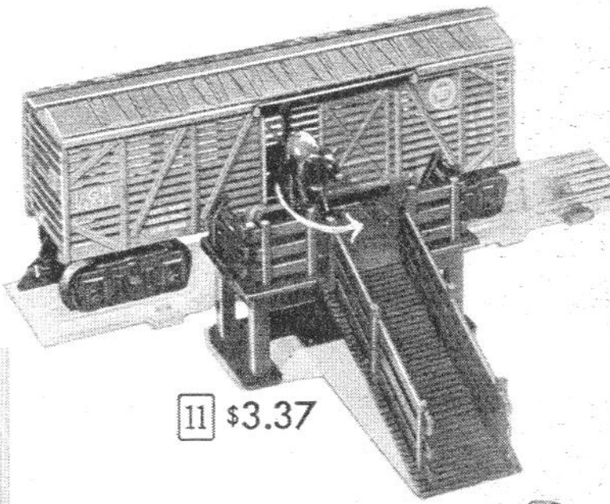

[1] **Twin Diesel.** Plastic, steel. Electric motor, automatic coupler. Headlight. Dummy horns. Die-cast wheels, oilless bronze bearings. 24 in. long.
49 N 9790—Shpg. wt. 3 lbs. 8 oz....$12.77

[2] **Operating Lumber Car.** Press remote control button .. logs unload into plastic bin. Bin, 5 logs, track section, control panel, wiring, connectors. Car plastic, steel. 8¼ in. long.
49 N 9761—Shpg. wt. 1 lb.........$3.97

[3] **Remote Control Barrel Loader.** Press a button .. truck takes barrel from loading chute to car (not incl.). Plastic, 8¾x8x5 inches high. Plastic barrels, control panel, wires.
49 N 9779—Shpg. wt. 1 lb. 6 oz.....$4.47

[4] **Electric Hand Car.** Plastic and steel. Two railroaders pump crossbars. Built-in motor. Die-cast wheels, oilless bronze bearings. 6¼ in. long.
49 N 9753—Shpg. wt. 12 oz.......$3.27

[5] **Plastic Tractor Car.** Two detachable tractors. Car 9½ in. long.
49 N 9773—Shpg. wt. 14 oz.......$2.77

[6] **Lighted Passenger Cars.** Colored metal. Riders silhouetted in windows. Shipping weight each 12 oz.
49 N 9770—Astrodome Car (shown). 11 inches long.....................$3.37
49 N 9771—Observation car (not shown). 10¾ inches long...............$3.37

[7] **Diesel Switcher.** Automatic couplers at both ends. Electric motor. Die-cast metal chassis, wheels; plastic body. Headlamp. Oilless bronze bearings. Engine 10½ inches long.
49 N 9783—Shpg. wt. 2 lbs. 4 oz....$10.97

[8] **Automobile Carrier Car.** 2-deck rack on flat car carries 4 autos that detach to unload (each about 4 in. long). Plastic, steel. 9½ in. long.
49 N 9755—Shpg. wt. 12 oz........$3.27

[9] **Allstate Oil Car.** Adds realism to your freight set. Plastic and steel .. die-cast metal wheels. 8 inches long.
49 N 9759—Shpg. wt. 10 oz........$2.77

[10] **Interurban Car.** Built-in electric motor .. operates by remote control. Plastic and steel. Manual coupler .. die-cast wheels .. oilless bronze bearings. Car 11 inches long.
49 N 9784—Wt. 3 lbs. Was $6.97...$4.97

[11] **Cattle Car** ... with ramp, platform. Car stops, door opens. Cow comes out, draws back as train starts.
49 N 9763—9½ in. long. Wt. 1 lb....$3.37

[12] **Operating Crane, Wrecker Car.** Plastic cab and boom revolve on metal chassis. Crank wheels work boom. 12 inches long overall.
49 N 9786—Shpg. wt. 1 lb. 10 oz....$4.39

Cars above of heavy-duty plastic and steel .. feature remote control automatic couplers (except 10), two 4-wheel trucks, die-cast wheels. Engines, Hand Car, Interurban Car (1), (4), (7), (10) built with electric motors; couplers where needed.

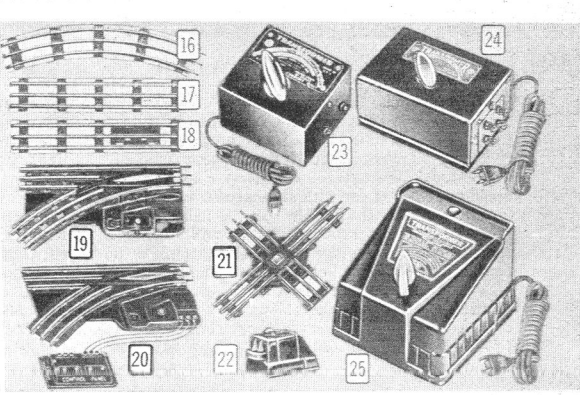

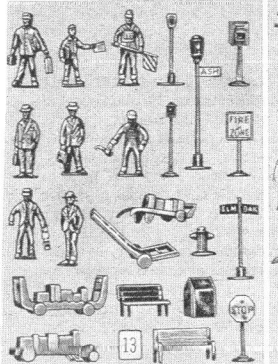

[13] **30-piece Railroad People and Accessory Kit.** Realistically molded plastic set. Includes 15 railroad people in various poses, 5 railroad accessories (hand truck, bench, freight wagon, etc.), 10 other accessories (mail box, trash can, etc.).
49 N 9772—Shipping weight 10 ounces................98c

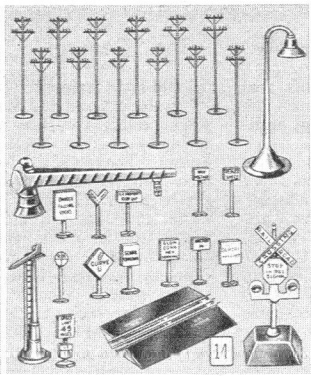

[14] **29-piece Railroad Accessories Set.** Carefully detailed to scale in sturdy plastic to add authentic railroading note. Set includes 12 seven-inch telegraph poles, 12 railroad right-of-way signs, and one each semaphore, lamp post, crossing gate, grade crossing sign and grade crossing plate. Track not included.
49 N 9750—Shipping weight 2 pounds............$2.59

[15] **Plastic Trestle Set.** 24 graduated trestles for up to 24 feet of track .. for figure 8 set-up with overpass or hilly road. Track not included.
49 N 9738—Shipping weight 2 pounds............$3.77

[16] **12½-inch Curved Track.** Big-radius, 5-tie type.
49 N 9723—Shipping weight 4 ounces........Each 13c

[17] **11¼-inch Straight Track.** Big-radius, 5-tie type.
49 N 9720—Shipping weight 4 ounces........Each 13c

[18] **Uncoupling Section.** With "Uncouple Here" sign. 11¼ inches long.
49 N 9749—Shipping weight 5 oz............79c

Track Connector (not shown). Carries electric power from transformer to track. Plastic, metal.
49 N 9709—Shipping weight 2 ounces...........12c

[19] **Manually Operated Switch Set.** One right, one left-hand switch.
49 N 9776—Shipping weight 2 pounds..........$4.37

[20] **Remote Control Switch Set.** Red, green light. Right, left-hand switch. Control panel incl.
49 N 9727—Shipping weight 2 lbs. 8 oz..........$8.37

[21] **Crossover Track.** 9¼x9¼ in. square. Wt. 8 oz.
49 N 9726—Big-radius type............Each $1.27

[22] **Lighted Dead-end Bumper.** Plastic. 2 in. high.
49 N 9707—Snap to end of spur. Shpg. wt. 4 oz..87c

[23] **50-watt Transformer.** 2 separate sets binding posts. (1) 7–13 volts controls train speeds; (2) 13 volts for accessories. Steel case.
49 N 9725—Shipping weight 3 pounds...........$5.47

[24] **Bigger 100-watt Transformer** for larger sets. 2 sets of binding posts. (1) 5–15 volts for train speeds; (2) 15 volts for accessories.
49 N 9777—Steel case. Shpg. wt. 4 lbs. 8 oz.....$8.27

[25] **Our Biggest ... Super-Powered 150-watt Transformer.** 2 sets binding posts; (1) 0–15 volts for train speeds; (2) 15 volts for accessories. Throttle-type control mechanism. Plastic case.
49 N 9764—Shipping weight 10 pounds.........$12.67

Big-radius track, switches fit ALLSTATE, HAPPI-TIME or MARX Electric Train sets. 5 cross tie track features .. wider curves for greater speeds. Circuit breaker transformers UL approved 110-120-volt, 60-cycle AC .. have safe low voltage, reset buttons.

LIONEL Electric Trains
Carloads of fun for Junior .. and Dad, too

7-Unit Diesel Train with Horn

[A] "Minneapolis & St. Louis GP-9" Diesel in red and white .. has sounding horn, powerful headlight, Magne-traction drive for greater pulling power. 6 cars: a helicopter car that launches a helicopter at the touch of a button, a Railway Express refrigeration car, a flat car with simulated transformer, a large gondola with 3 cable reels, a Lehigh Valley hopper car and a caboose. Plastic and steel. Run trains forward or reverse, fast or slow, couple or uncouple cars, blow the horn, all by remote control. 8 curved, 3 straight sections of "027" gauge track, 1 uncoupling section make 117-in. oval. 60-watt circuit-breaker transformer with horn control. UL approved 110–120-volt, 60-cycle AC. Shpg. wt. 16 lbs.
79 N 09665—Train 72¾ in. long. $4 down....Cash $39.79

6-Unit Freight with Whistle and Smoke

[B] Powerful 2-4-2 steam locomotive puffs real smoke and blows whistle as it roars down the line. Has realistic piston rod action and big headlight. Cars include a coal tender, a gondola which carries 3 canisters, a flat car with arch trestle bridge .. bridge can be removed and set up as a foot bridge . . . a box car and a caboose. Plastic and steel. Run train forward or back, fast or slow, blow whistle, couple or uncouple cars .. all by remote control. 8 sections of curved, 1 section of straight "027" gauge track, and 1 uncoupling section make 94-inch oval. 60-watt circuit-breaker transformer with whistle control UL approved for 110–120-volt, 60-cycle AC. Smoke fluid included. Shpg. wt. 14 lbs.
79 N 09664—Train 54 in. long. $3 down......Cash $29.79

The "General" .. from the Old West

[C] Old style train like those that blazed a trail west in the 70's and 80's. Engine has big balloon smokestack, headlight and long, pointed cowcatcher .. black, red and gold-color. A realistic replica of an old "woodburner." The rest of this 5-unit train consists of a tender, a "General" mail-baggage car, a "General" passenger car, and a "General" flat car that carries 6 plastic horses. Plastic and steel. Set also includes an 18-piece plastic frontier outfit with windmill, a building and animals to give a real frontier atmosphere. Manual couplers. Run train forward or back, fast or slow, by remote control. 8 curved and 2 straight sections of "027" gauge track make 94-in. oval. 45-watt transformer UL approved 110–120-volt, 60-cycle AC. Wt. 12 lbs.
79 N 09666—Train 52 in. long....................$25.89

USE SEARS EASY TERMS .. only 10% down on orders of $20 or more .. see page 294

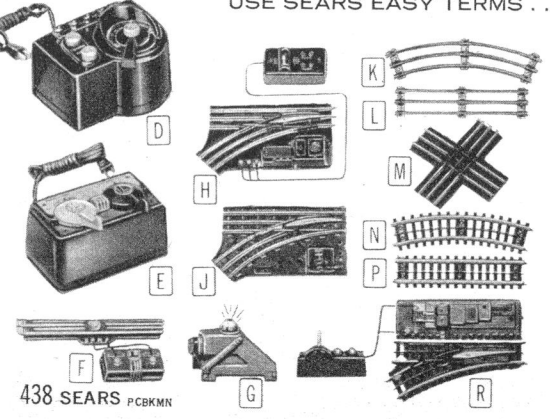

Railroading Accessories for Lionel "027" and Super "O"

(D), (E) Transformers. Built-in circuit breakers. UL approved 110–120-volt, 60-cycle AC.

[D] Type LW-125-watt. Full range of train speeds PLUS fixed 14 and 18-volt circuits for accessories. Whistle, direction controls.
49 N 9819—Shpg. wt. 6 lbs................$12.97

[E] Type TW-175-watt. 2 throttles: one controls the train speed; the other controls direction, sounds the whistle or horn on your train. 4 fixed accessory voltages: 14, 14, 18 and 25 volts. Two circuit breakers to protect train.
49 N 9842—Shpg. wt. 9 lbs. $2.50 down.....$20.97

[F] Magnetic Track Section. For remote control uncoupling and unloading. Control panel and wires are included with track.
49 N 9804—Shpg. wt. 1 lb................$3.97

[G] Lighted Bumper. For "027", super "O" gauges.
49 N 9859—Shpg. wt. 1 lb.............$1.98

[H] "027" Remote Control Switch Set. For non-derailing switching. Green, red control lights. One right, one left-hand switch. Control panel.
49 N 9806—Shipping weight 3 pounds........$13.57

[J] "027" Manual Switch Set. One right, one left hand switch. Non-derailing device.
49 N 9805—Shipping weight 2 pounds.........$5.97

[K] "027" Track Sections. Shpg. wt. each 3 oz.
49 N 9802—9½-in. curved section......Each 20c
(L) 49 N 9801—8⅞-inch straight section.....Each 20c

[M] "027" 7⅜-inch 90° Crossing.
49 N 9803—Shipping weight 8 oz........$1.54

[N] Super "O" Track Sections. Shpg. wt. each 4 oz.
49 N 9817—9-inch curved section........Each 39c
(P) 49 N 9816—9-inch straight section........Each 39c

[R] Super "O" Remote Control Switches. Non-derailing type. Right and left hand. Wt. 4 lbs.
49 N 9813—Illuminated indicators, wire....$19.97

LIONEL Atomic Age Set

With Rocket Launcher .. Target Box car

Complete Train Set $49.79 cash $5.00 down

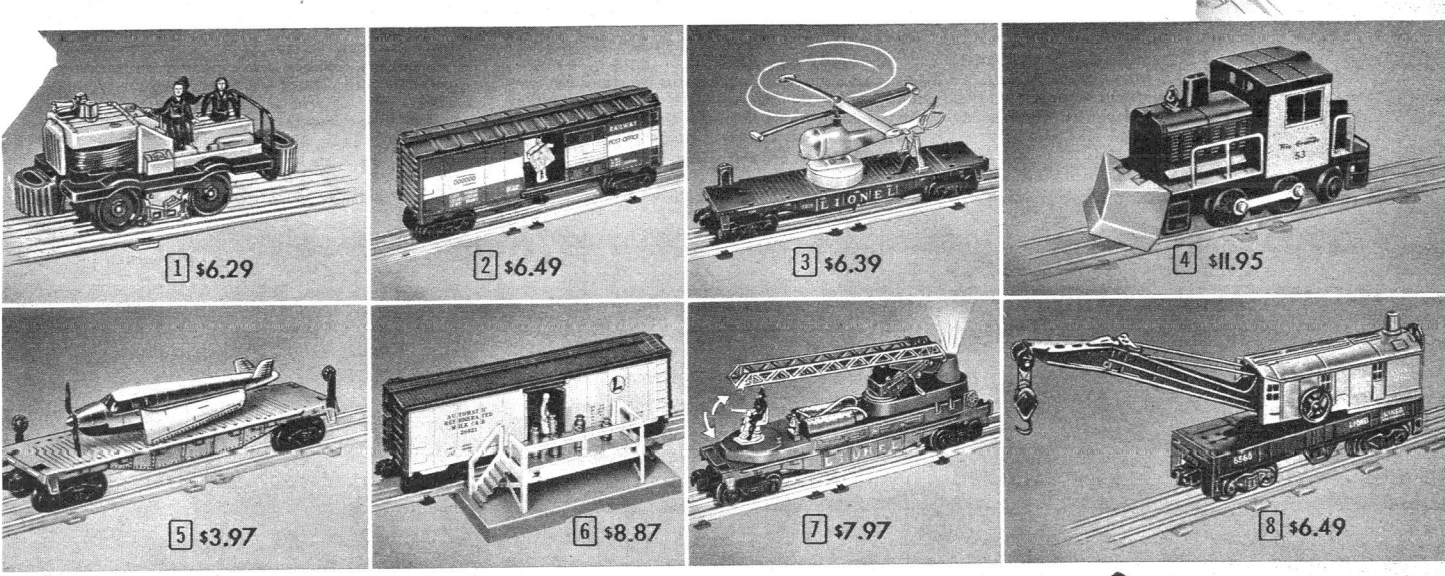

Atomic Super "O" Set that's packed with thrills ... combination diesel engine-mobile missile launcher fires 4 Little John missiles; IRBM missile launching car fires LaCrosse missile; exploding target car breaks apart when hit by missiles from first two cars; rocket-carrying flat car; Marine Corps car carries removable "Duck"; medical car has stretchers, stretcher-bearers, etc. Plastic and steel. Run train forward, back, fast or slow, couple and uncouple cars, fire missiles, all by remote control. Big stationary rocket launcher duplicates an earth satellite launching. Motorized launching tower moves on own track, carries safety foam nose rocket to platform, firing mechanism is then set from control panel, count down begins and rocket takes off. Set has 14 sections of Super "O" track. 60-watt circuit-breaker transformer UL approved 110–120-volt, 60-cycle AC.
79 N 09682K—Train 66 in. long. Shipping weight 21 lbs.... **$49.79**
49 N 9854—Rocket Launcher only. Shipping weight 7 lbs... **16.97**

[1] $6.29   [2] $6.49   [3] $6.39   [4] $11.95
[5] $3.97   [6] $8.87   [7] $7.97   [8] $6.49

Add more excitement to your Lionel train sets with these operating accessories

[1] **Operating Section Gang Car.** Built-in motor. Car and Gandy Dancer reverses automatically when buffer plate at either end strikes object. Plastic and steel. For "027" and "O" gauge, 6 inches long.
49 N 9846—Shipping wt. 2 lbs..... **$6.29**

[2] **Operating United States Mail Car.** Colorful red, white and blue mail car operated by remote control. At the touch of a button door slides open and a postal clerk tosses out a bundle of mail. Plastic and steel. 10½ inches long.
49 N 9853—Shipping wt. 2 lbs..... **$6.49**

[3] **Operating Helicopter Launching Car.** Wind spring on launching platform manually, set model helicopter in launching position. As car passes over remote control track, the touch of a button sends helicopter soaring into the air, its blades whirling. Car is plastic and steel .. 11 inches long. Plastic helicopter.
49 N 9856—Shpg. wt. 2 lbs....... **$6.39**

[4] **Locomotive with Snow Plow.** Modeled after the Vulcan. Simulated lights. Dummy bell. One operating coupler. Plastic and steel.
49 N 9870—8 in. long. Wt. 3 lbs..**$11.95**

[5] **Airplane-carrying Flat Car.** Plastic plane on flat car with wings retracted .. can be readied for a play "take off" by removing from flat car and extending wings. 10⅞-inch long flat car; remote control couplers, eight die-cast wheels. Car is plastic and steel.
49 N 9838—Shpg. wt. 1 lb. 10 oz.. **$3.97**

[6] **Operating Milk Car.** Milkman delivers cans onto platform. Hinged roof hatch allows reloading of cans into car. Car is 11 inches long .. plastic and steel. Also includes 7 milk cans, platform.
49 N 9858—Shipping wt. 3 lbs..... **$8.87**

[7] **Operating Fireman-and-Ladder Car.** As train moves, fireman at hose swivels to and fro as red light flashes. Ladder extends, pivots and can be raised or lowered with crank. Plastic and steel. 11 inches long.
49 N 9861—Shipping wt. 2 lbs..... **$7.97**

[8] **Operating Crane.** 2 hand wheels .. one raises and lowers boom .. one raises and lowers hook. Cab rotates. Die cast metal trucks. Plastic and steel. 7⅞ inches long.
49 N 9852—Shipping wt. 2 lbs..... **$6.49**

[9] **Automatic Shuttling Gateman.** Shuttles in and out of shack ... his lantern lights as the train goes by. Lighted shack is 7x5¾x4½ inches high. Plastic and steel construction.
49 N 9835—Shipping wt. 2 lbs....... **$5.87**

[10] **Illuminated Automatic Banjo Signal.** Signal lights as train approaches, "STOP" sign swings back and forth. 7½ inches high. Action stops automatically after the train has passed. Plastic and steel. Bulb, wires and connector are included.
49 N 9827—Shipping wt. 1 lb....... **$4.77**

[11] **Illuminated Automatic Block Signal.** Automatically stops train for time set. Plastic, steel. 7 inches high.
49 N 9808—Shipping wt. 1 lb....... **$5.87**

[12] **Automatic Crossing Gate.** Gate lowers and lights flash as train approaches grade crossing .. gate rises after train has passed. Plastic and steel construction. 9⅝ inches high.
49 N 9834—Shipping wt. 1 lb....... **$4.77**

[13] **Trestle Set.** 24 plastic piers. Use with Magne-traction locomotives to make over and under layouts.
49 N 9845—Shipping wt. 2 lbs....... **$4.79**

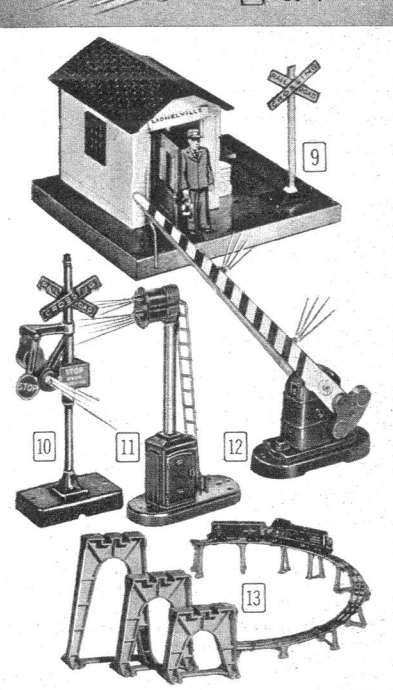

Engine and cars (except Gang Car) have remote control couplers

Hobby-size ALLSTATE® HO Electric

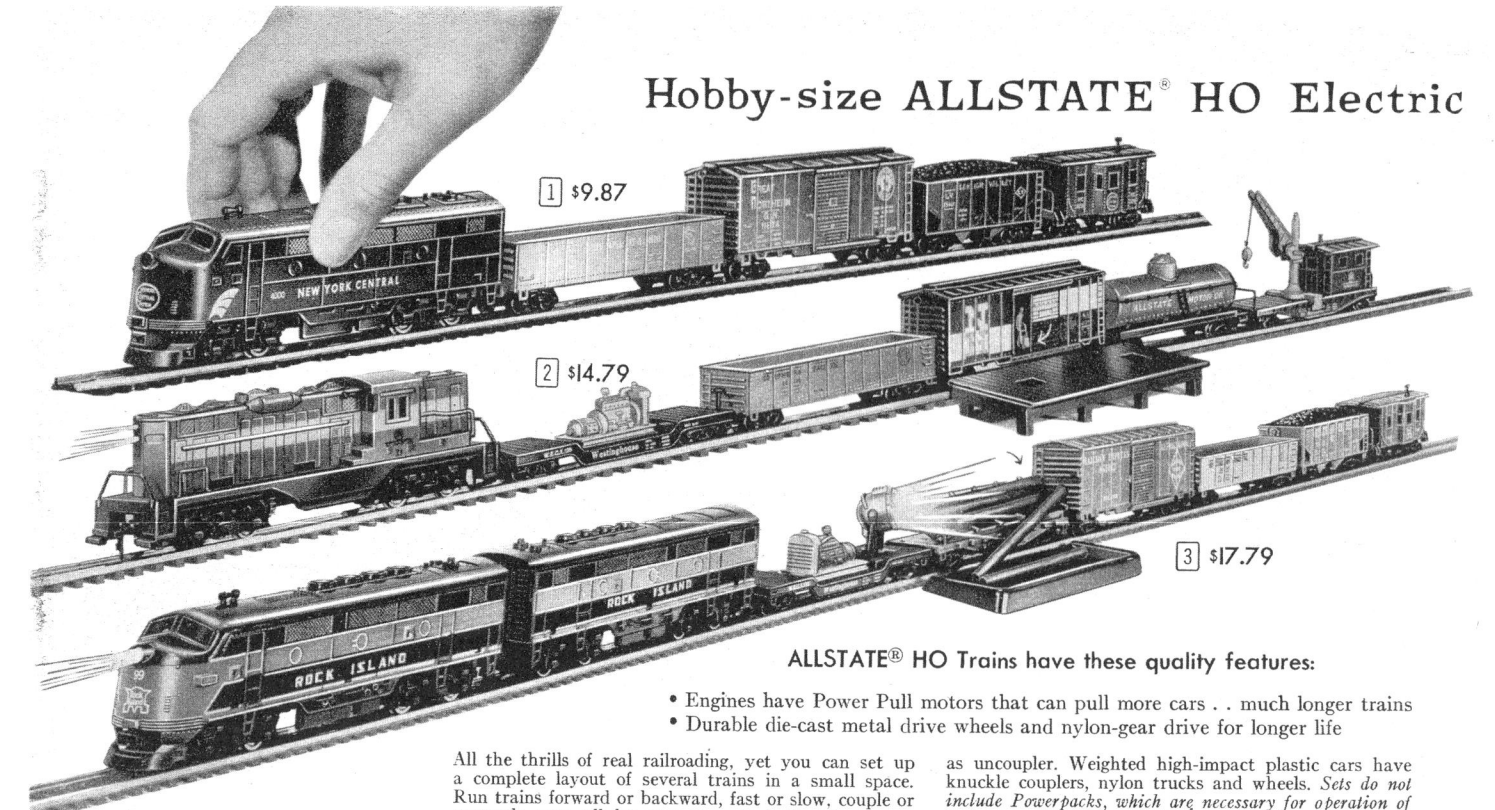

[1] $9.87

[2] $14.79

[3] $17.79

ALLSTATE® HO Trains have these quality features:

- Engines have Power Pull motors that can pull more cars .. much longer trains
- Durable die-cast metal drive wheels and nylon-gear drive for longer life

All the thrills of real railroading, yet you can set up a complete layout of several trains in a small space. Run trains forward or backward, fast or slow, couple or uncouple cars, all by remote control. Rerailer serves as uncoupler. Weighted high-impact plastic cars have knuckle couplers, nylon trucks and wheels. *Sets do not include Powerpacks, which are necessary for operation of trains .. order (17) or (18) separately below.*

[1] **New! 5-unit Freight Train.** The ideal starter set for the youngest railroader. New York Central diesel, coal car, box car, gondola and caboose. 12 sections curved, 1 section straight track, 1 rerailer uncoupler form 112-inch oval layout. Train 30 inches long. Track connector included.
49 N 9976—Shipping weight 2 lbs. 10 oz..........$9.87

[2] **New! 6-unit "Monon" Switcher Freight with operating Box Car**.. door opens.. man pops out. Diesel with light, generator car, tank car, gondola and work caboose with crane. 12 sections curved, 3 sections straight track, 1 rerailer uncoupler make 127-in. oval layout. Train 38 in. long.
49 N 9977—Track connector. Shpg. wt. 3 lbs. 6 oz..$14.79

[3] **8-unit Rock Island Twin Diesel Freight w/ operating Lumber Car**.. push button, watch logs roll into bin. Diesel with light, rear unit, gondola, Express car, electric searchlight car, hopper car, caboose. 15 sections track, 1 rerailer uncoupler form 127-in. oval. Train 49½ inches long.
49 N 9978—Track connector. Shpg. wt. 3 lbs. 12 oz...$17.79

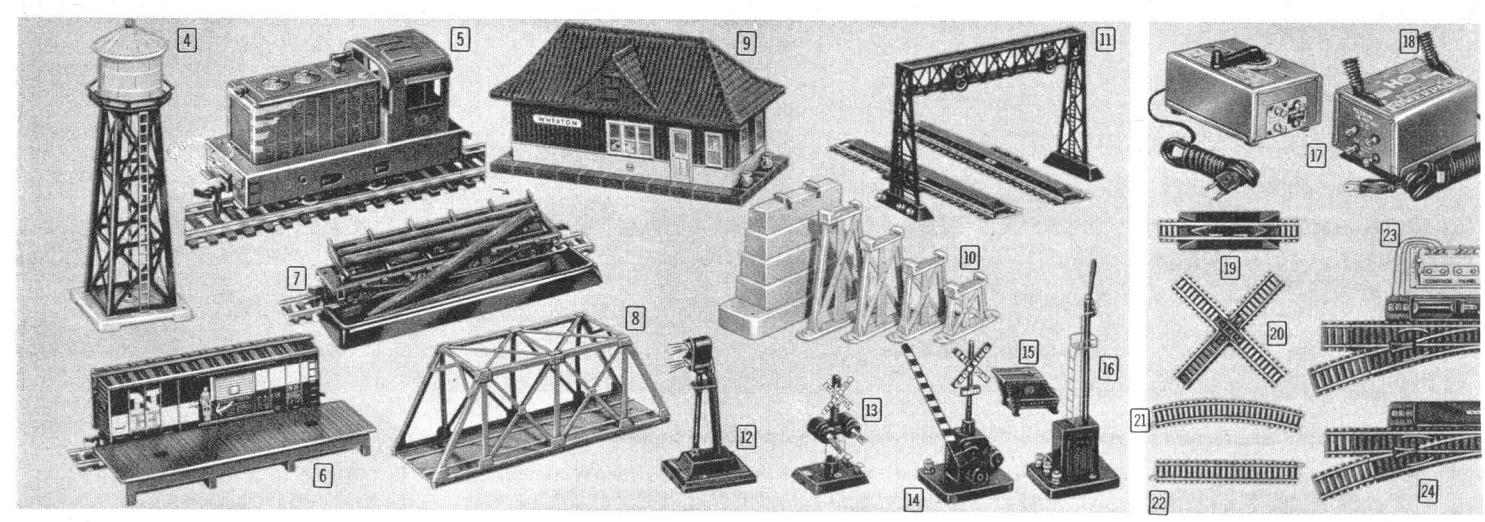

To complete your HO Hobby Train layout .. sturdy plastic accessories and extra cars for added realism and enjoyment

[4] **7½-in. Plastic Water Tower.** An inexpensive scenic piece youngsters will enjoy with their HO set. Light on top. Wiring included.
49 N 9986—Shipping weight 6 oz....$1.77

[5] **Diesel Switcher Locomotive.** 4x2x 1½ inches high. Nylon geared. 4-wheel drive. A versatile "workhorse" with brass wheels, knuckle couplers.
49 N 9997—Shipping weight 12 oz....$4.47

[6] **New! 6-inch Automatic Box Car.** Door opens.. trainman steps out onto plastic platform (included) and back into car.. door closes.
49 N 9945—Shipping weight 8 oz....$3.47

[7] **New! Automatic Lumber Car.** Dumps load of logs into tray by remote control. 6x1⅜x1¼ in. high. Plastic log bin 6¼ in. long. Includes special track section, wiring.
49 N 9946—Shipping weight 8 oz....$3.47

[8] **Trestle Bridge.** 8½x3¼x2¾ in. high. Plastic girder type. Makes a nice addition to any HO set.
49 N 9907—Shipping weight 8 oz....$1.17

[9] **Remote Control Whistling Station.** 8¼x3½x4 in. high. Steel and plastic. Authentic whistle. Includes control panel, wiring.
49 N 9919—Shpg. wt. 1 lb. 4 oz....$4.97

[10] **New! Trestle Set.** For figure 8, over and under layout. 30 graduated plastic trestles, 2 pillars.
49 N 9915—Shipping weight 10 oz....$2.57

[11] **New! Overhead Twin Signal Bridge.** Lights change from red to green as train approaches.. back to red. 4⅛ in. high, 6⅛ in. across. 2 special track sections, wiring included.
49 N 9917—Shipping weight 10 oz....$3.77

[12] **New! Automatic 2-light Block Signal.** One red, one green light. 2⅞ in. high. All necessary wiring.
49 N 9957—Shipping weight 8 oz....$2.77

[13] **New! Realistic Automatic Crossing Flasher.** Twin red lights flash alternately as train approaches. Easy to attach to your HO electric train. 2¼ in. high. Special track section and necessary wiring included.
49 N 9954—Shipping weight 6 oz....$2.67

[14] **New! Automatic Crossing Gate.** Gate arm raises, lowers automatically as train passes. Gate 3¾ inches long overall. Includes track section and all necessary wiring. Makes a wonderful addition to any train set.
49 N 9947—Shipping weight 6 oz......$2.67

[15] **New! Lighted Dead-end Bumper.** Attach to end of spur track. 1½x ½x¾ inches high. Constructed of sturdy black plastic.
49 N 9923—Shipping weight 5 ounces..87c

[16] **New! Lighted Semaphore Signal.** Flashes red or green. 4x1¼x1¼ inches high. Includes track section and all necessary wiring.
49 N 9955—Shipping weight 6 ounces $2.77

(17) (18) Powerpacks. UL approved 110–120-volt 60-cycle AC. With AC and DC binding posts, cord and plug.

[17] 49 N 9909—2 separate Circuit-Breakers 45-volt amps. output. Variable 0–14 volts DC for speed, fixed 15 volts AC for accessories. Shpg. wt. 5 lbs..............$9.39

[18] 49 N 9906—1½ amps. (no circuit breaker). 4–18 volts DC for speed, 18 volts AC for accessories. Total of 20-volt amps. Twin controls. Shpg. wt. 3 lbs.............$5.77

[19] **7½-in. Uncoupler Rerailer Track.**
49 N 9908—Shipping wt. 4 oz......47c

[20] **Crossover Track.** 7½x7½ in.
49 N 9911—Shpg. wt. 4 oz.....$1.47

[21] 49 N 9905—HO 8-inch curved track. Shipping weight 3 ounces..........13c

[22] 49 N 9904—HO 7-inch straight track. Shipping weight 3 ounces.........13c

(23) (24) Switches. One right, one left.
[23] 49 N 9983—Remote Control. Shipping weight 1 pound.....Pair $7.49

[24] 49 N 9982—Manual Control. Shipping weight 14 ounces....Pair 4.49

Trains Scale Detailed .. sold exclusively by Sears

New! HO ALLSTATE 6-unit Electric Freight with Figure-8 Trestle .. Smoking Locomotive

$19.87

Big 3-foot long train runs forward or backward, fast or slow, over, under and around on more than 15 feet of roadbed

A long roadbed filled with grades and curves, a brawny freight with cars you can couple and uncouple by remote control—here's railroading at its best! Die-cast metal Power Pull locomotive with headlight. Weighted, high-impact plastic coal tender, gondola, box car, tank car and caboose have nylon trucks and wheels. 2 pillars, girder bridge, 30 pieces of graduated plastic trestle *plus* 18 sections curved, 5 sections straight track and 1 rerailer uncoupler form 190-in. figure eight track layout. Train 36 in. long. Track connector, smoke refill included. Engine has Power Pull drive and puffs smoke. *Does not include Powerpack* .. order (17) or (18) on opposite page.
49 N 9979—Shipping weight 4 pounds...$19.87

Battery-powered or Wind-up Trains for Little "Engineers"

New! 18-inch Plastic Train with a "Brain". Set switches—battery-powered engine shuttles cars back and forth, uncoupling one at a time to pick up barrels from dock, then back to re-couple. Bumper trip makes it *all automatic!* 12 track sections, 2 switches make about 12 feet of track. Inexpensive fun for young railroaders; a long time favorite in play value.
49 N 9515—Uses 1 "D" Battery (not included, order below). Shpg. wt. 4 lbs.....$5.89

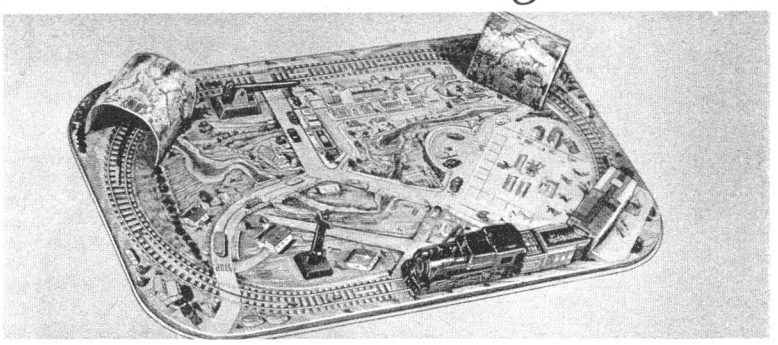

Wind-up Freight Train on Base. Plastic locomotive, powered by long-running spring motor, hauls 3 brightly colored metal cars around scenic metal base. Train speeds at high rate around grooved track through 2 tunnels; crossing gate and semaphore move up and down as it passes. Metal base has all-over scenic design. Train 11½ in. long and travels around track about 20 times on one winding.
49 N 9513—Base 21¾ in. long, 13 in. wide. Shipping weight 3 lbs............$2.79

Battery-powered Rocket Ship and Monorail Set. Give your youngster a realistic peep into this transportation future. Brightly colored metal rocket ship runs forward or backward suspended from a sturdy steel monorail, supported by 10 steel trestles. Ship is 10 in. long. 6 curved, 4 straight rails form 144-in. oval layout. Trestles are 5½ in. high. Uses "D" standard flashlight battery (not included, order below).
49 N 9516—Imported from Japan. Shipping weight 2 pounds..........$3.47
4 N 4650—"D" Batteries. Shipping weight 8 ounces..............2 for 33c

New! Colorful 4-unit Battery-powered Vinyl Freight Train. How he'll thrill to the sight of lively power of this old-fashioned steam-type locomotive as it pulls a coal tender, gondola and caboose around 92-inch oval layout! 8 sections curved, 2 sections straight track. Locomotive, cars and track all made of unbreakable vinyl plastic in realistic train colors. Train 31 in. long.
49 N 9514—Uses 1 "D" Battery (not included .. order at left). Shpg. wt. 2 lbs.........$2.87

SEARS CHRISTMAS CATALOG 1960

By 1960, electric trains were in their glory. Sears' Christmas Wishbook advertised trains on nine pages of their catalog that year, including one page in color showing off a complete H-O railroad empire for just $38.97... with $4 down. The set came with track already mounted on a landscaped plastic layout replete with tunnel. All you had to do was put the trains on the track, plug it in and go.

Another hint of the future was inserted into the 1960 train section: racing slot cars which would soon put a big dent into electric train sales. Also hopping onto the H-O bandwagon were non-train toy makers like Kenner, who offered H-O scale building sets designed to be used with toy trains.

Lots more H-O scale trains were available in 1960, and Sears' line also included H-O accessories. Lionel offered its own military-influenced O-27 set for $39.44 featuring a Boston & Maine Twin Diesel, Missile Car, Exploding Box Car, Submarine and Helicopter Cars and a Caboose.

$9.77

[1] Tractor only $13.77

[3] Tractor only $18.77

Tractor. A little farmer's delight! Sturdy steel construction. Bright red hood accented with white trim, red bucket seat and white wheels. Full steering wheel. Hitch for trailer. Pedal drive adjustable to 3 positions. Rubber pedals. 8-in. wheels. 1-in. semi-pneumatic front tires and 1-in. tractor tread tires in rear. Connecting straps with ball bearings for easy pedaling. 32 in. long, 19 in. wide.
79 N 8964L—Shipping weight 23 lbs...... $9.77

[1] **Our Better Quality Tractor.** Enclosed adjustable ball-bearing chain drive. Large tubular steel frame. Spring seat. Full circle turning. Semi-pneumatic tires mounted on ball-bearing wheels. 8-inch diameter in front, 10-inch diameter in rear. Yellow with red trim.
79N8967L—37x18x26 in. high. Shpg. wt. 26 lbs.. $13.77

[2] **Trailer.** Red and yellow. 7½-in. wheels. All-steel.
79N8968C—32x15x10 in. high. Wt. 10 lbs..... $5.77
79N8969L—Combination. Tractor and trailer listed above. Save $2.10. Shipping weight 35 pounds........ $17.44

[3] **Our Best.** Enclosed adjustable ball-bearing chain drive. Full circle turning. 4 plastic "spark plugs". Adjustable spring seat. Large semi-pneumatic tires on ball-bearing wheels 8 inches in front, 10 inches in rear. Vermilion, with white trim. Steel.
79 N 8922L—37x22x25 in. Shpg. wt. 34 lbs......... $18.77

[4] **Matching Dump Trac with seat.**
79 N 8917C—8-in. wheels. 33x15½ in. Wt. 16 lbs. $7.88
79 N 8925L2—Tractor and Dump Trac Combination. Save $1.77. Shpg. wt. 50 lbs. Only $2.50 down..... Cash $24.88

Casey Jones Locomotive
for tiny engineers

$**23**^{88}$ cash $2.50 down

All aboard for exciting railroadin' fun. Perfect for chuggin' and a puffin' in any backyard terminal or on any sidewalk railway. Engine sports a simulated headlight, make-believe old-time smoke stack, and rear bell. Adjustable pedal drive with ball-bearing hanger straps for smooth traveling. Engine rolls on big 10-inch wheels with 1-inch rubber tires. Engine color red with black and yellow trim. Black metal engine cab trimmed with yellow. Yellow cow-catcher. Engine is 37 inches long, 25 inches high.

Tender loaded with plenty of room for cargo or passengers. Red with yellow and black 7¼-in. wheels. Engine, tender together about 68 in. long. Shipping weight 44 pounds.
79 N 8971L—Engine and Tender........... $23.88

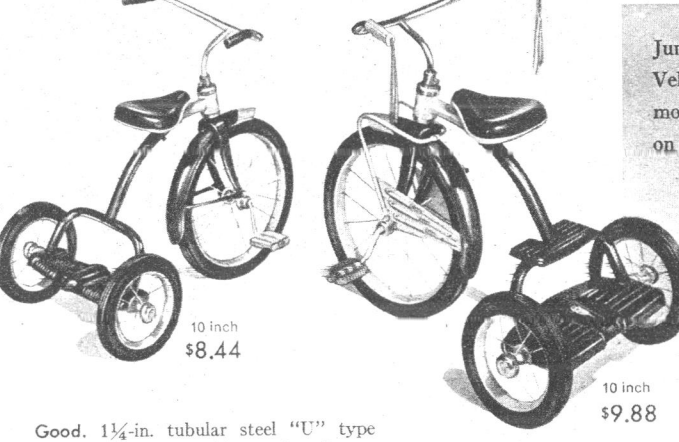

Junior steps right up on his Happi-Time Velocipede! Our Better and Best models have mount step plates in rear... makes getting on and off quick and easy, even for the smallest riders

Build your order up to $20 and order on Sears Easy Terms.. see page 294

10 inch $8.44

10 inch $9.88

10 inch $12.99

Good. 1¼-in. tubular steel "U" type frame for long, durable service. Large, adjustable steel seat. Ball-bearing front wheel with plain-bearing rear wheels. Semi-pneumatic 1⅝ in. tires. Auto type fender. Plastic pedals. ¾-in. tubular steel adjustable handlebars enameled white. Streamlined rear step-plate. Flamboyant blue body color with white trim. *See How to Measure leg reach on the opposite page.*
79 N 8720L—10-in. front wheel. Shipping weight 17 lbs.. $8.44
79 N 8721L—12-in. front wheel. Shipping weight 18 lbs.. 9.44
79 N 8722L—16-in. front wheel. Shipping weight 23 lbs.. 10.44

Our Better Model. Auto-type fender with truss rods and fender skirts. 1¼-inch "U" type steel frame; extra wide rear step plate and mounting step. Ball-bearing front wheel and plain-bearing rear wheels. Semi-pneumatic 1⅝ in. tires. Adjustable, chrome-plated handlebars with plastic grips and streamers. Stamped metal seat. 2-color plastic pedals. Flamboyant red with white trim.
See How to Measure leg reach on the opposite page. Size (below) is front wheel.
79 N 8730L—10-in. wheel. Shpg. wt. 18 lbs........ $ 9.88
79 N 8731L—12-in. wheel. Shpg. wt. 19 lbs........ 10.88
79 N 8732L—16-in. wheel. Shpg. wt. 24 lbs........ 12.88
79 N 8733L—20-in. wheel. Shpg. wt. 30 lbs........ 14.88

Our Best. The one all kids *OH* and *AH* at. Handsome deep well fender with chrome-plated truss rods, vinyl seat with 2 chrome-plated double-coil springs and crash rail, double-block vinyl pedals, saber-guard grips and streamers and, of course, white sidewall tires.. PLUS all the construction features of model at left. Turquoise with white trim. *See How to Measure leg reach on facing page.*
79 N 8750K—10-in. wheel. Shpg. wt. 21 lbs........ $12.99
79 N 8751L—12-in. wheel. Shpg. wt. 22 lbs........ 13.99
79 N 8752L—16-in. wheel. Shpg. wt. 27 lbs........ 14.99
79 N 8753L—20-in. wheel. Shpg. wt. 33 lbs........ 16.99

ALLSTATE HO TRAIN
with N.M.R.A. couplers

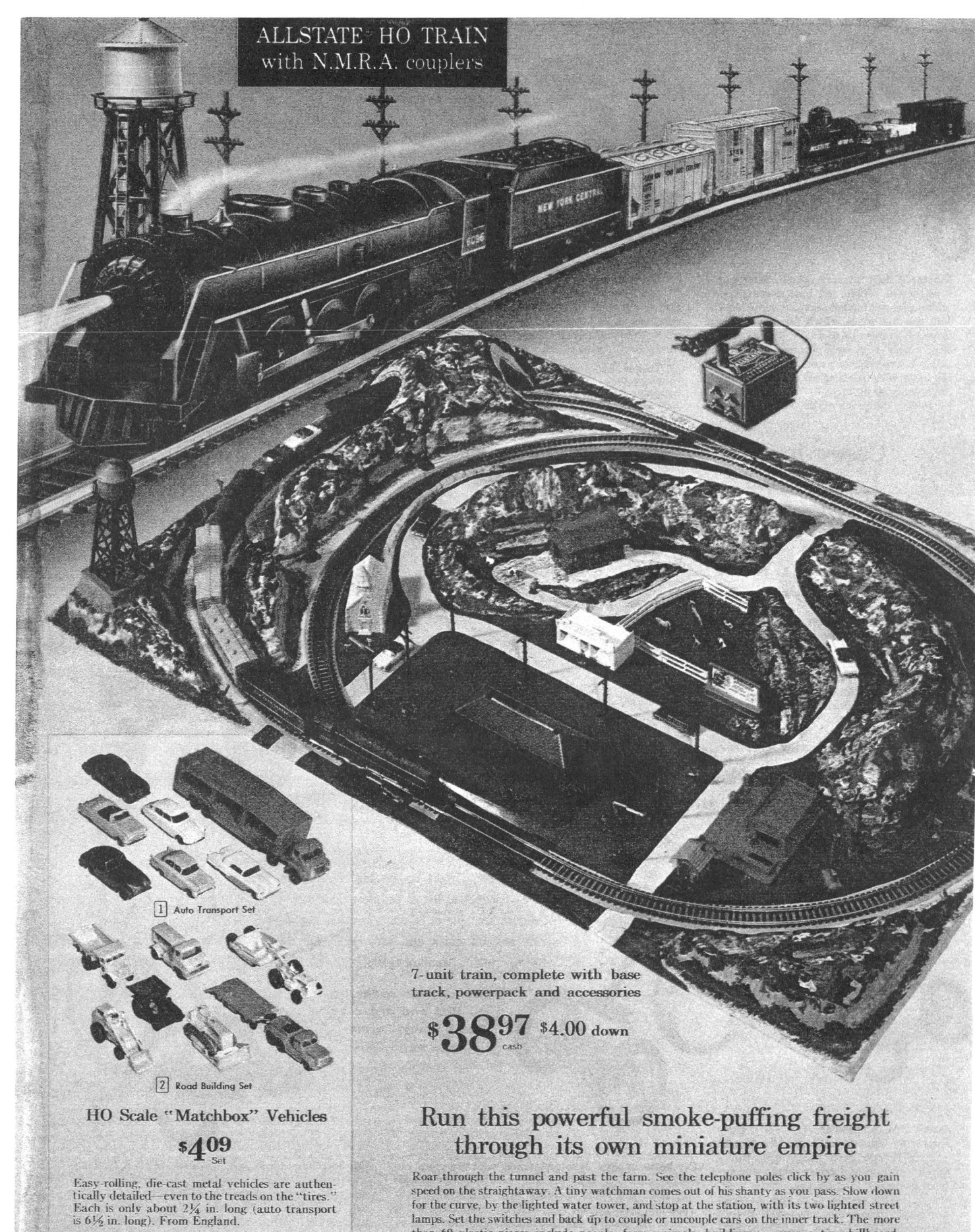

[1] Auto Transport Set

[2] Road Building Set

HO Scale "Matchbox" Vehicles

$4.09 Set

Easy-rolling, die-cast metal vehicles are authentically detailed—even to the treads on the "tires." Each is only about 2¼ in. long (auto transport is 6½ in. long). From England.

[1] **7-piece Auto Transport Set.**
49 N 2398—Shipping weight 14 ounces.... $4.09

[2] **7-piece Road Building Set.**
49 N 2397—Shipping weight 14 ounces.... 4.09

7-unit train, complete with base track, powerpack and accessories

$38.97 cash $4.00 down

Run this powerful smoke-puffing freight through its own miniature empire

Roar through the tunnel and past the farm. See the telephone poles click by as you gain speed on the straightaway. A tiny watchman comes out of his shanty as you pass. Slow down for the curve, by the lighted water tower, and stop at the station, with its two lighted street lamps. Set the switches and back up to couple or uncouple cars on the inner track. The more than 60 plastic pieces include people, farm animals, buildings . . . even a tiny billboard. Plastic, landscaped, 48x34-in. base. 18 sections of track with 2 manual switches form two (112 and 127-in.) ovals. *Uncoupler-rerailer.* "Powerpull" die-cast metal engine puffs real smoke; pulls plastic tender, cement car, box car, tank car, flat car with 2 autos, caboose—train 41 in. long. Cars have N.M.R.A. couplers to fit all standard HO cars. Uncouple cars, run it fast, slow, forward or reverse—all by remote control. 1½-amp power-pack *UL approved* for 110-120-volt, 60-cycle AC. With 4 posts; 4 to 18-volt DC for speed, 18-volt AC for accessories.
79 N 9963N2—Freight (rail or truck) or express. Shipping weight 17 pounds........ $38.97

436 SEARS SCPBKMN AMDLG

BRAKE for the turn

It takes skill to win this Remote-control Auto Race

28-piece set $42.95 cash $4.50 down

If you take the corner too fast, your car will jump the track. Ease up on the hand control and let your car swing around the turn, then down with your thumb to accelerate on the straightaway.

The hand controls work like a real throttle—with your thumb you can make the molded plastic car (1/30 scale size) go from a slow crawl up to 130 scale miles per hour. Held to the track groove by a nylon guide pin, the cars skid and spin realistically at the turns—with practice you can drive them like a professional. Set contains 19 rubber sections for figure eight track, 2 grand prix cars, 2 hand controls, 4 plastic fence sections, lubricating oil. NOTE: To operate set, you will need a Powerpack (not included). Made in England.
79 N 9530C—Size set up about 7x2½ ft. wide. Shpg. wt. 14 lbs... $42.95
49 N 9936—Powerpack. U.L. approved—110-120-volt, 60-cycle A.C. with AC and DC binding posts 1½ amps output. 4 to 18-volt DC for speed. Shipping weight 3 pounds.................................$5.33

Build HO Scale Models

605-pc. combination set builds roads, bridges and buildings $7.44

Start with a framework of girders, add prefab wall, window and roof panels. Run superhighways across bridges. Possibilities are unlimited with this huge combination set. Plastic parts snap together—you can pick up the most elaborate structures and move them anywhere. Actually HO scale, use them with your O gauge train layout, too. Parts are interchangeable. Vehicles not included, see facing page.
79 N 2323C—605-pc. Bridge, turnpike, building set. Shpg. wt. 8 lbs. $7.44
79 N 2395C—543-pc. Bridge, turnpike set only. Shpg. wt. 7 lbs..... 6.98
49 N 2322—330-pc. Bridge, turnpike set only. Shpg. wt. 4 lbs..... 4.49
49 N 2393—287-pc. Building set only. Shpg. wt. 3 lbs. 14 oz....... 5.29
49 N 2320—189-pc. Building set only. Shpg. wt. 2 lbs. 10 oz....... 2.88

HO Scale-detailed

- Power-pull motor pulls longer trains .. lets you add cars later
- Nylon gear drive .. won't slip or age .. gives extra long life
- Die-cast metal drive wheels on engine give sure traction
- New roadbed track with all trains shown on this page .. rails fixed in strong plastic base, molded to look like railroad cinder bed

Plus .. remote control lets you run trains forward, reverse, fast or slow—even couple or uncouple cars. High-impact plastic cars are weighted .. cling to the track. And, every ALLSTATE® HO train *has NMRA operating couplers to fit any standard HO scale cars.* NOTE: Sets do not include a Powerpack, which is necessary to operate your train. *Be sure to order (5) or (6) separately below.*

[1] **4-unit Diesel Freight.** N.Y. Central diesel, hopper, gondola, caboose. 13 track sections plus uncoupler form 112-in. oval.
49 N 9958—23½-in. train. Wt. 3 lbs........ **$8.97**

[2] **5-unit Switcher Freight.** Yard switcher pulls generator car, box car, hopper, caboose. 13 track sections plus uncoupler form 112-in. oval.
49 N 9959—26½-in. train. Shpg. wt. 3 lbs....... **$11.47**

[3] **6-unit Diesel Switcher Freight.** "Monon" Switcher engine has bright headlight. Flat car has 2 autos to unload. Box car, covered hopper, tanker car, caboose with working crane. 15 track sections plus rerailer-uncoupler track form oval 127 inches around.
49 N 9960—36¾-in. train. Wt. 4 lbs...... **$14.95**

[4] **7-unit Triple Diesel Freight.** Workman pops out of automatic box car when train stops .. draws back as train starts. Rock Island diesel has bright headlight. Carrier has ramp to unload 4 autos; wrecker crane car, work caboose. 15 sections of track plus uncoupler form 127-in. oval.
49N9961—46¾-in.train.Wt. 5 lbs. $2.00 down. Cash **$19.79**

Powerpacks. UL listed for 110–120 volt, 60-cycle AC. Delivers DC for train, AC for accessories.

[5] **Super size.** 45-volt amp output with 2 circuit breakers to safeguard unit. Easy one-lever control. Delivers 0 to 14-volt 1¼-amp DC .. and 15-volt 1¼-amp AC.
49 N 9937—Shpg. wt. 5 lbs..... **$8.88**

[6] **Standard size.** 20-volt amp output. No circuit breakers. 2 control levers. Gives 4 to 18-volt 1¼ amp DC .. 18-volt 1¼-amp AC.
49 N 9936—Shpg. wt. 3 lbs.....**$5.33**

New HO Roadbed Track
Track sections mounted on nearly unbreakable plastic roadbed to resemble realistic cinder roadbed.

[7] **Rerailer-uncoupler.** 7½ in.
49 N 9926—Shpg. wt. 5 oz....**76c**

[8] **90° Crossover.** 7½x7½ in.
49N9927—Shpg. wt. 8 oz..**$1.37**

[9] **Curved Track.** 8¼ in. long.
49N9925—Shpg. wt. 4 oz...**19c**

[10] **Straight Track.** 7½ in. long.
49N9924—Shpg. wt. 4 oz...**19c**

(11) (12) **Switches.** Sold in pairs only—1 right, 1 left.

[11] 49N9929—Remote Control. Shipping wt. 1 lb. Pair **$6.99**

[12] 49N9928—Manual Control. Shipping wt. 14 oz...Pair **4.49**

HO Plastic Accessories for realistic train layouts

[13] **Lighted Dead-end Bumper.** Attach to end of spur track .. prevents cars from rolling off. Sturdy black plastic with red light. 1½x½x¾ in. high.
49 N 9923—Shpg. wt. 5 oz..........**76c**

[14] **Semaphore Signal.** Color filter in arm flashes green, turns red as train passes. Track, wiring included.
49 N 9955—4 in. high. Wt. 6 oz....**$2.37**

[15] **Automatic Crossing Gate.** Arm raises, lowers automatically as train passes. 3¾-in. long. Track, wiring included.
49 N 9947—Shpg. wt. 6 oz.........**$2.67**

[16] **Automatic Crossing Flasher.** Lights flash alternately as train approaches. Track, wiring included. 2¼ in. high.
49 N 9954—Shpg. wt. 6 oz.........**$2.37**

[17] **Automatic 2-light Block Signal.** Light changes from green to red as train passes. Wiring included.
49 N 9957—2⅞ in. high. Wt. 6 oz.**$2.37**

[18] **Trestle Set.** For figure 8, over and under layout. 30 graduated plastic trestle, 2 bridge piers.
49 N 9915—Shpg. wt. 12 oz......**$2.57**

[19] **Remote Control Whistling Station.** Press button on control panel, hear loud train whistle. Steel, plastic. Wiring included. 8 in. long.
49 N 9919—Shpg. wt. 1 lb. 4 oz..**$4.97**

[20] **Overhead Twin Signal Bridge.** Lights turn green as train approaches, then to red. 4 in. high, 6 in. across. 2 track sections included.
49 N 9917—Shpg. wt. 10 oz......**$3.69**

438 SEARS PCBKMN

ALLSTATE® Electric Train Sets come complete with track

HOBBY-SIZE "HO" GAUGE

7-unit Freight .. with over 15 feet of track $17.88

Thrill at watching this brawny "Power Pull" diesel pull its load up grades and around the curves of the figure 8 trestle track. Run it fast or slow, forward or reverse, couple and uncouple cars—*all by remote control.* Weighted, high-impact plastic cars hold to the track even at high speeds. *Cars have NMRA (National Model Railroad Association) operating couplers to fit all standard HO gauge cars.*

Set includes engine with headlight, auto carrier with 4 cars, 2 box cars, hopper, tank car, caboose, complete 190-inch track layout of 18 curved and 5 straight sections, rerailer-uncoupler, 30 graduated trestles, 2 pillars and girder bridge. **NOTE:** Powerpack not included, necessary for operating train—*order (5) or (6) on opposite page.*
49 N 9966—42-inch long train. Shipping weight 5 pounds $17.88

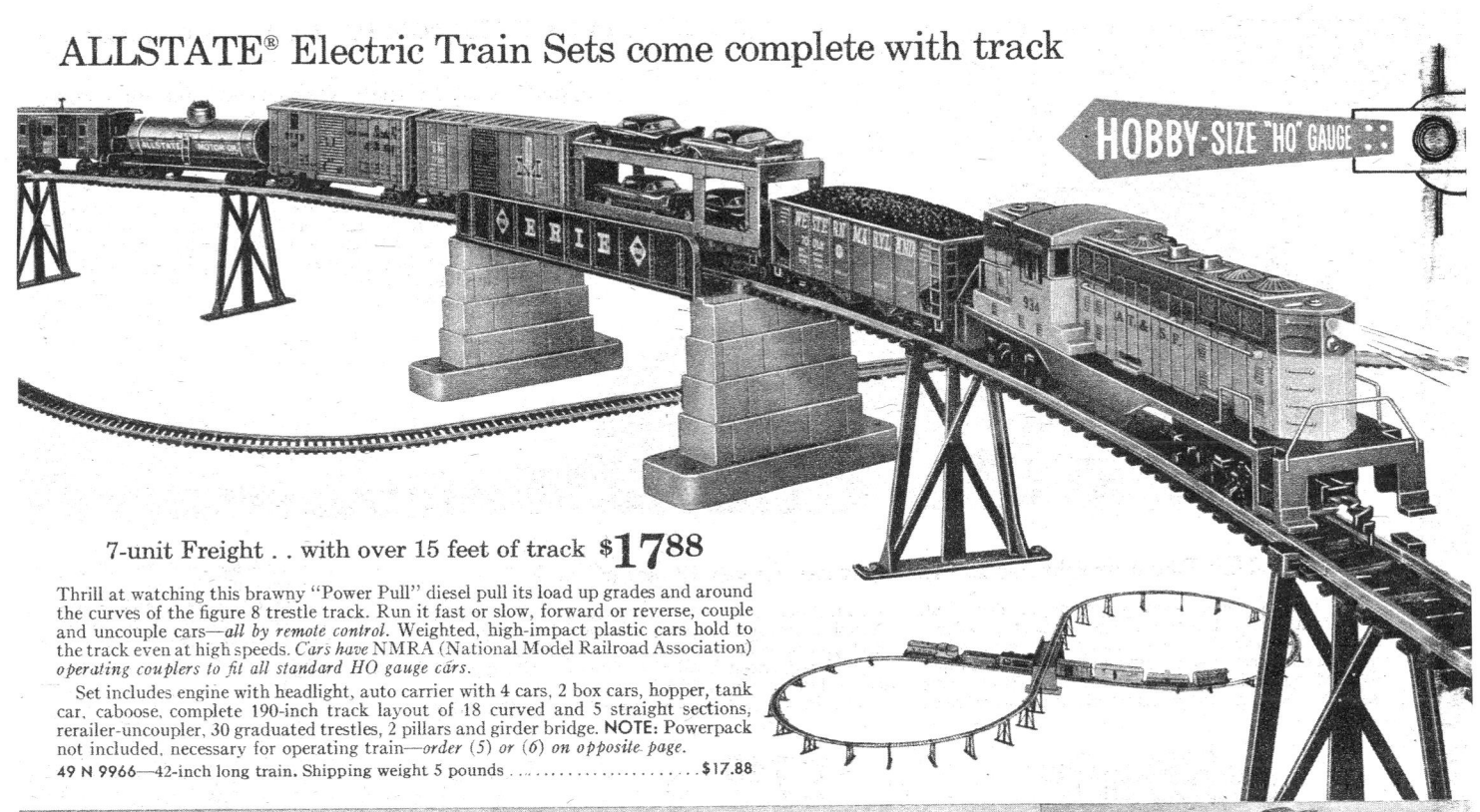

Add these Plastic Cars to your HO Train .. all have NMRA operating couplers

[1] Diesel Switcher R.R. Workhorse. Nylon gears, 4-wheel drive. Brass wheels. Knuckle couplers front and back for moving cars. 4x2x1½ in. high.
49 N 9997—Shpg. wt. 12 oz. $4.33

[2] Industrial Yard Steam Switcher. Plastic with die-cast chassis, 4-wheel gear drive. Knuckle couplers front, back. 4¾x 1½x2 in. high.
49 N 9939—Shpg. wt. 1 lb. $5.79

[3] Automatic Lumber Car. Dumps load of logs into tray by remote control. 6 inches long. Plastic log bin. Special track section and wiring incl.
49 N 9946—Shpg. wt. 8 oz. $2.97

[4] Automatic Box Car. Door opens, man steps out onto plastic platform (included) when train stops. Returns when train starts, door closes.
49 N 9945—6 in. long. Wt. 8 oz. . $2.97

[5] Automobile Car with 4 cars. Lower the ramp to roll the scale model cars up to the upper deck. 4-wheel double nylon trucks. 6½ in. long.
49 N 9576—Shpg. wt. 8 oz. $1.97

[6] Operating Crane Car. Two hand wheels .. one to raise and lower 4-inch boom .. one to raise and lower hook. Cab rotates. 5 in. long.
49 N 9938—Shpg. wt. 8 oz. $2.97

Set of 4 Standard Cars

Make your train longer, carry more cargo .. all for one low price. Set includes 6-in. automobile carrier with 2 scale model cars; 6¼-in. refrigerator car; 5½-in. cement car and 6½-in. gondola. Markings exact duplicates of real-life counterparts. All cars of weighted high-impact plastic; with long-wearing nylon trucks. wheels. All have NMRA operating couplers.
49 N 9965—Shpg. wt. 1 lb. 8 oz. $4.99

---

[7] Landscape Mats. Flocked-on fiber, paper-backed .. can be cut for any effect. True colors.
79 N 9571C—50x99 in. Grass Mat. Wt. 3 lbs. ... $2.79
79 N 9572C—33x48 in. Earth Mat. Wt. 1 lb. 89c

[8] Trees and Shrubbery. A variety of scale-size trees for model landscaping. Includes a generous amount of lichen for natural shrubbery.
49 N 9573—True colors. Shpg. wt. 12 oz. $2.79

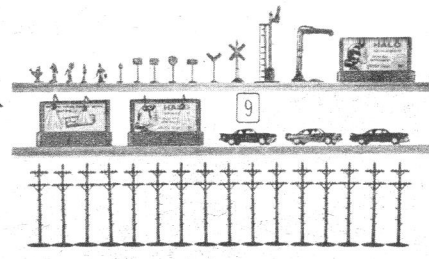

[9] 39-pc. Plastic Accessory Set. Includes two lighted billboards, 4 scale model cars, 5 posed figures, 18 telegraph poles and 10 railroad signs.
49 N 9964—Shipping weight 1 lb. $2.98

[10] 24-pc. Plastic Building Set. Switch tower, suburban station, coaling station, 3 houses, 12 telephone poles, farm buildings, animals, figures.
79 N 9967C—Shipping weight 2 lbs. $5.98

SEARS 439

REGULAR GAUGE

ALLSTATE® Electric Trains complete

5-Unit Smoking Freight with over 10 feet of track

$14.98

The electric headlight locomotive puffs harmless smoke as it chugs along on 4-wheel drive, pulling tender, refrigerator car, gondola and caboose. Run it forward or reverse, fast or slow, couple and uncouple cars—all by remote control. Locomotive and cars are scale-detailed in high-impact plastic, with die-cast metal wheels. 8 sections curved, 1 section straight big-radius track, and uncoupler unit form 129-inch oval track layout. 50-watt circuit breaker transformer, UL approved for 110-120-volt, 60-cycle AC. Smoke refill liquid included. Train 40½ inches long over-all.
49 N 9613—Shipping weight 9 pounds.....................$14.98

6-Unit Diesel Freight has Rocket-firing car, almost 13 feet of track

Diesel Locomotive has powerful headlight, Power-pull engine with oilless bronze bearings for greater traction. Pulls Rocket car that really fires a miniature rocket, gondola plus box car, tank car and caboose. Realistically-detailed locomotive and cars are sturdily built of plastic and steel, have die-cast metal wheels. Run it forward or back, fast or slow, couple or uncouple cars—all by remote control. 3 sections straight, 8 sections curved big-radius track and uncoupler track unit form 152-inch oval layout. 50-watt circuit breaker transformer, UL approved for 110-120-volt, 60-cycle AC.
79 N 9614C—Train 55 in. long over-all. Wt. 11 lbs...$17.45

$17.45

Big-radius track is included with all trains on these two pages. 5 ties per section make firm layouts with gentle curves for fast speeds.

Extra-long 9-Unit Freight puffs smoke as it speeds along

[1] With 152-in. Oval Layout
$24.99 cash $2.50 down

[2] With 172-in. Switch Layout
$29.45 cash $3 down

A real railroading beauty .. and it's over 6½ feet long. Steam-type die cast metal locomotive puffs real smoke, has 4-wheel drive, pony truck, two guide wheels. Husky Power-pull engine. Plastic and steel coal-tender, tank car, automobile car with 4 autos, piggy-back car with truck, crane car, box car, girder car and wrecker caboose. 82 in. long over-all. Run it fast or slow, forward or back, couple or uncouple cars all by remote control. 100-watt circuit breaker transformer, UL approved for 110-120-volt, 60-cycle AC. Smoke refill included.

[1] **With Oval Track Layout.** 3 straight, 8 curved sections big-radius track, plus uncoupler section form 152-inch oval layout.
79 N 9634C—Shipping weight 13 pounds.....................$24.99

[2] **With Switch Track Layout.** 3 straight, 10 curved sections big-radius track, plus uncoupler unit and 2 manual operated switches form outer oval 172 inches, inner oval 152 inches around.
79 N 9643C—Shipping weight 16 pounds.....................$29.45

with 5-tie Track and Transformer

$18.88 cash $2 down

6-Unit Freight with Figure 8 trestle track

Watch this smoke-puffing freight push its bright headlight over nearly 27 feet of grades and curves. Power-pull engine has oilless bronze bearings. Pulls tender, gondola, tank car, refrigerator car, caboose. All plastic and steel with die-cast metal wheels.

Run it fast or slow, forward or back, couple and uncouple cars .. all by remote control. 11 sections straight, 12 sections curved, big-radius track, uncoupler unit give 319 inches of track. 22 trestles, plastic viaduct. 50-watt circuit-breaker transformer UL approved. 110-120-volt, 60-cycle AC. Smoke refill included.
79 N 9615C—Train 48¼ in. long over-all. Shpg. wt. 15 lbs...$18.88

Run fast or slow by remote control

5-unit trains.. take your pick Only $9.77 each

[1] **5-Unit Passenger Train.** Plastic and steel switcher engine pulls metal mail car, two passenger coaches and observation car. Manual couplers. 8 sections curved, 2 sections straight big-radius track form 129½-in. oval. 25-watt transformer. Train 35½ in. long.
49 N 9607—Shpg. wt. 6 lbs.........$9.77

Your Choice of Locomotive. Plastic steam-type or twin-diesel metal engine pulls plastic tender, tank car, tractor car, caboose. Manual couplers. 8 sections curved, 2 sections straight big-radius track form 129½ in. oval. 25 watt transformer.

[2] **5-Unit Steam-type Freight.** Train 40 in. long over-all.
49 N 9610—Shpg. wt. 6 lbs.........$9.77

[3] **5-Unit Twin-diesel Freight.** Train 41 in. long over-all.
49 N 9611—Shpg. wt. 6 lbs.........$9.77

NOTE: Transformers for above trains are UL approved for 110-120-volt, 60-cycle AC.

Old-style Woodburner .. add an authentic model to your collection

Train only $12.89

Here it comes, 'round the bend, chugging and puffing real smoke, its drive pistons pounding back and forth. The plastic engine is scale-detailed—even has an old-fashioned cow-catcher. Oilless bronze bearings for smooth running. Tender shows huge molded-on logs. Combination baggage-passenger car and passenger car. Remote-control couplers. 31 in. long over-all. Ideal extra train for your own track layout, or buy track and transformer on following page. *Track and transformer not included* .. runs on any O gauge, 027 or Allstate 5-tie track layout.
49 N 9642—Shpg. wt. 3 lbs. 12 oz...$12.89

Build a working Railroad Empire with Accessories

Motorized Cars run by remote control

[1] **Twin Diesel.** Powerful headlamp lights up the track ahead. Equipped with automatic coupler. Electric motor has oilless bronze bearings. High-impact plastic; die cast metal wheels. 24½ inches long.
49 N 9782—Wt. 3 lbs. 12 oz. **$11.97**

[2] **Handcar.** Two railroaders pump the crossbars as the little car scoots around the track. Electric motor, oilless bronze bearings. Steel and plastic, die cast metal wheels. 6¼ in. long.
49 N 9753—Shpg. wt. 12 oz. **$3.27**

[3] **Diesel Switcher** makes rhythmic diesel motor noise. Bright headlight. Automatic couplers front, rear. Electric motor, oilless bronze bearings. Steel and plastic, die cast wheels. 10½ in. long.
49 N 9783—Wt. 2 lbs. 4 oz. **$9.97**

[4] **Interurban Car.** Lights up to show riders silhouetted in windows. Manual couplers. Electric motor has oilless bronze bearings. Plastic and steel, with die cast metal wheels. 11 inches long.
49 N 9784—Shpg. wt. 3 lbs. **$4.97**

Allstate Oil Car. Realistically colored and marked, with details such as a tiny ladder and miniature domes. Plastic and steel with 4-wheel trucks, die-cast metal wheels. Automatic couplers. 8 inches long.
49 N 9759—Shpg. wt. 8 oz. **$2.77**

Tractor Car. The two scale model tractors are detachable, have rolling wheels. Tractors and car of high-impact plastic. Car has 4-wheel trucks, die-cast metal wheels. Automatic couplers. 9½ inches long.
49 N 9773—Shpg. wt. 8 oz. **$2.77**

Lighted Passenger Cars. Riders silhouetted in windows. Shiny metal. Automatic couplers. Wt. each 1 lb.
49 N 9770—Astrodome Car (shown). 11 in. long. **$3.37**
49 N 9771—Observation Car (not shown). 10¾ in. long. **$3.37**

Make life-like countryside with Scene-O-Rama Kit

Create a 4x8-foot scenic landscape for your train to scoot around. Kit includes 15 natural-looking trees of true-color lichen in 3 shades; also makes shrubbery. Flocked-on fiber green color grass and earth color mats form roads, paths and contrast. Can be cut or draped for dozens of effects. Snow-capped plastic tunnel fits O or HO gauge trains. 3 tiny lampposts light up realistically, are wired to attach to any electric track. Easy-to-follow instructions.
79 N 9713L—Shpg. wt. 5 lbs. **$7.89**

Operating Cars add action

[5] **Automatic Lumber Car.** Dumps load of 5 logs into plastic bin by remote control. Plastic and steel car with 4-wheel trucks, die-cast metal wheels. Automatic couplers. Car is 8¼ in. long. Control panel, necessary wiring, special track section included.
49 N 9761—Shpg. wt. 12 oz. **$3.97**

[6] **Wrecker-crane Car.** Two hand wheels .. one to operate boom, one to raise and lower hook. Cab and boom rotate in full circle. Heavy-duty plastic and steel with 4-wheel trucks, die-cast metal wheels. Automatic couplers. 12 inches long over-all.
49 N 9786—Shpg. wt. 1 lb. 8 oz. **$3.97**

[7] **Cattle Car.** Door opens, and cow comes out when train stops, draws back when train starts up again. Plastic ramp and platform included. High-impact plastic with 4-wheel trucks and die-cast metal wheels. Automatic couplers. 9½ inches long.
49 N 9763—Shpg. wt. 1 lb. **$3.37**

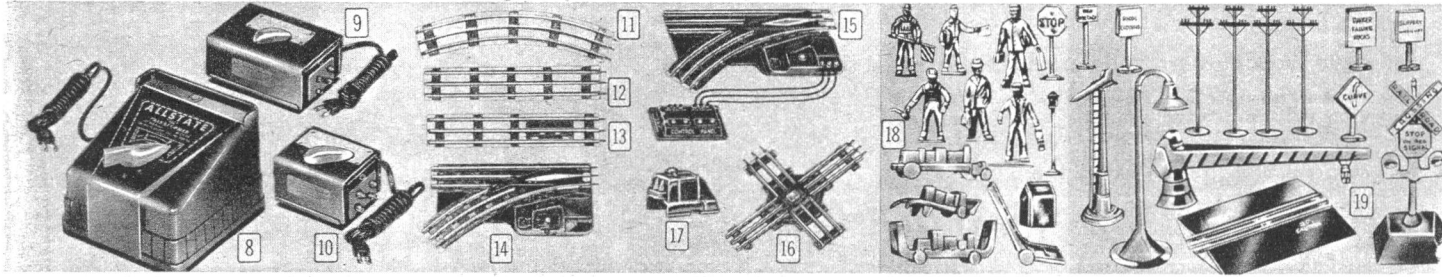

Circuit-breaker Transformers have low, safe voltage, reset buttons. Throttle-type variable speed control UL approved 110-120-volt, 60-cycle AC only.

[8] **150-Watt** .. our biggest, most powerful. Two sets binding posts: 1 (15 volts) for accessories; 1 (0-15 volts) for variable speed. Plastic case.
49 N 9724—Shipping weight 10 lbs. 4 oz. **$11.99**

[9] **100-Watt.** Two sets binding posts: 1 (15 volts) for accessories; 1 (5-15 volts) for variable speed.
49 N 9722—Steel case. Shpg. wt. 4 lbs. 4 oz. **$8.27**

[10] **50-Watt.** Two sets binding posts: 1 (13 volts) for accessories; 1 (7-13 volts) for variable speed.
49 N 9721—Steel case. Shpg. wt. 3 lbs. **$5.47**

Big Radius Track. 5-tie sections make firmer track; wider curves. Fit Allstate, Happi-Time or Marx electric train sets.
(11) 49 N 9723—Curved Track. 12½ in. long. Wt. 4 oz. **21c**
(12) 49 N 9720—Straight Track. 11¼ in. long. Wt. 4 oz. **21c**

[13] **Uncoupling Section.** "Uncouple Here" sign included.
49 N 9749—11¼ inches long. Shpg. wt. 4 oz. **79c**

[14] **Manually operated Switches.** One right, one left.
49 N 9776—Shipping weight 1 lb. 12 oz. **$4.37**

[15] **Remote Control Switches.** One right, one left. Red, green lights. Control panel and wiring included.
49 N 9727—Shipping weight 2 pounds **$7.99**

[16] **Crossover Track.** 9¼x9¼ inches.
49 N 9726—Shipping weight 4 ounces **$1.27**

[17] **Lighted Dead-end Bumper.** Snap to end of spur. Plastic.
49 N 9707—2 inches high. Shipping weight 4 oz. **87c**

[18] **30-pc. Accessory Set.** Molded plastic. 15 railroaders in various poses; 5 railroad accessories (freight wagon, hand cart, etc.) and 10 other accessories (mail box, trash can, etc.).
49 N 9772—Shpg. wt. 10 oz. **98c**

[19] **29-pc. Railroad Layout Kit.** Ideal for your regular size electric or mechanical train layout. Molded plastic. Includes 12 telephone poles, 12 railroad right-of-way signs, and one semaphore, lamppost, crossing gate, sign; grade crossing for autos to roll over track (track not included).
49 N 9750—Wt. 1 lb. 12 oz. **$2.59**

for your ALLSTATE Train

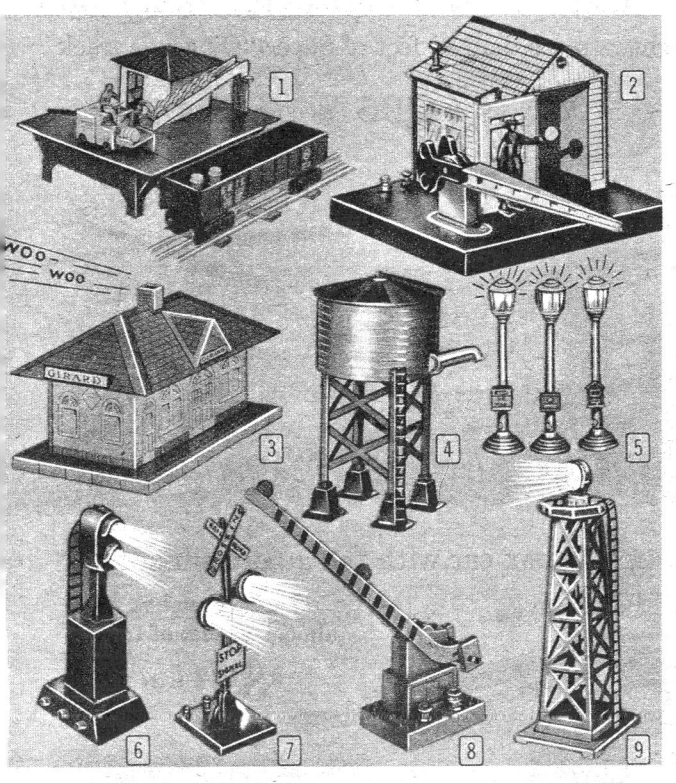

Watch the "Train with a Brain" perform $5.44

The tiny engine chugs back and forth, loading and unloading miniature barrels, coupling and uncoupling its cars .. the bumper trip makes it all automatic! 3-dimensional plastic trainman looks on. The battery-operated plastic engine pulls two plastic gondolas .. train is 18 inches long overall. 12 track sections, 2 switches make about 12 feet of track. 6 plastic barrels, bumper loading chute. Uses 1 "D" battery, not included, order separately below.
49 N 9515—Shipping weight 3 pounds 4 ounces $5.44
34 N 4650—2 "D" Batteries. Shipping weight 8 oz. .... 2 for 30c

Working Pieces make a train layout more exciting

[1] **Remote Control Barrel Loader.** Press a button, truck takes barrel from loading chute to car (not incl.). Plastic, 8¾x8x5 in. high. Plastic barrels, push button control panel, necessary wiring included.
49 N 9779—Wt. 1 lb. 6 oz.—$4.49

[2] **Automatic Grade-crossing Shack and Watchman.** As train nears, watchman comes out with stop sign, gate lowers. Steel shack 4½ in. high. Base 7x6½ in. Wires included.
49 N 9760—Shpg. wt. 2 lbs...$3.37

[3] **Remote Control Whistling Station.** Steel, 9x5½x5 in. high. Push button on control panel, hear loud train whistle.
49 N 9739—Shpg. wt. 2 lbs...$3.97

[4] **Plastic Water Tower.** Adjustable spout. 8¼ in. high, 4¼-in. diam.
49 N 9731—Shpg. wt. 8 oz.....84c

[5] **Three Lighted Lamp Posts.** Plastic, 6 in. high. Wires included.
49 N 9737—Shpg. wt. 10 oz...$1.87

[6] **Automatic 2-light Block Signal.** Train stops on red, goes on green. Manual switch. Plastic, 7½ in. high. 2 track sections included.
49 N 9745—Shpg. wt. 8 oz....$1.77

[7] **Automatic Crossing Flasher.** 2 lights flash alternately as train passes. Plastic, 7 in. high.
49 N 9742—Shpg. wt. 8 oz....$1.77

[8] **Crossing Gate.** 8-in. arm lowers as train passes. Plastic. Wires.
49 N 9743—Shpg. wt. 8 oz....$1.67

[9] **Lighted Revolving Beacon.** Beams red one direction, green the other. Plastic, 12½ in. high.
49 N 9740—Shpg. wt. 12 oz...$1.67

Battery-operated Freight $2.87

[14] Ideal for tots because all parts are of almost unbreakable vinyl plastic. Old-fashioned steam-type locomotive pulls coal tender, gondola and caboose around 92-in. oval track layout. Realistic train colors. 8 sections curved, 2 sections straight track. Train 31 in. long. Uses 1 "D" battery, not included, order below.
49 N 9514—Shpg. wt. 2 lbs......$2.87
34 N 4650—2 "D" Batteries.
Shpg. wt. 8 oz..............2 for 30c

Wind-up Freight Train $3.94

[15] Husky steam-type locomotive, powered by long-running keywind clock motor, emits harmless sparks. Has speed governor so train runs at even speed. On-off lever. Made of high-impact plastic, it pulls plastic tender, colorful lithographed metal gondola, box car and caboose .. train is 34½ inches long overall. 8 sections curved and 2 sections straight track form oval 102 inches around.
49 N 9512—Shpg. wt. 3 lbs. 4 oz..$3.94

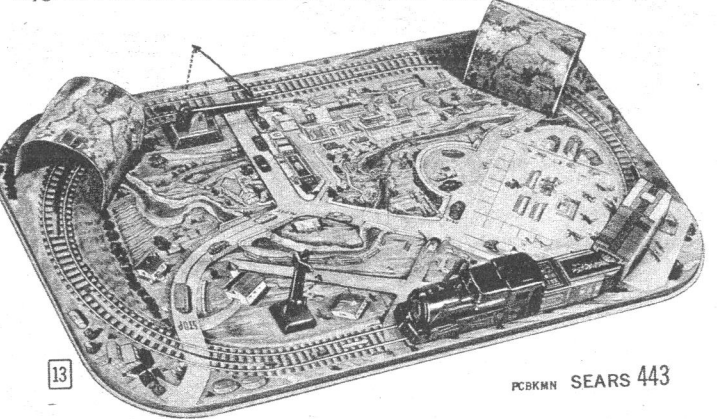

[10] **Railroad Trestle Bridge.** Accurately embossed. Steel, 18 inches long.
49 N 9732—Shpg. wt. 2 lbs......$1.87

[11] **10-inch Metal Tunnel.** Realistic mountain scene.
49 N 9729—Shpg. wt. 1 lb........84c

[12] **Plastic Trestle Set.** 24 graduated trestles will hold up to 24 feet of track. Create figure 8 layout or hilly road with grades and curves. ½ inch to 4½ inches high.
49 N 9738—Shpg. wt. 2 lbs.$3.37

Wind-up Freight Train with scenic base

[13] Plastic locomotive powered by long-running spring motor, hauls three brightly colored metal cars around decorated metal base. Train speeds at high rate around grooved track through two tunnels. Crossing gate and semaphore move up and down as it passes. Train is 11½ inches long and travels around track about 20 times on one winding. Base is about 22 inches long and 13 inches wide.
79 N 9513C—Shipping weight 3 pounds......................... $2.79

Press a button .. the helicopter takes off
7-unit Freight .. more than 10 feet of Super "O" gauge track

$48.95 cash $5.00 down

Famous Lionel Electric Trains
Complete with Track and Transformer

All transformers included with trains are UL approved for 110-120-volt, 60-cycle AC

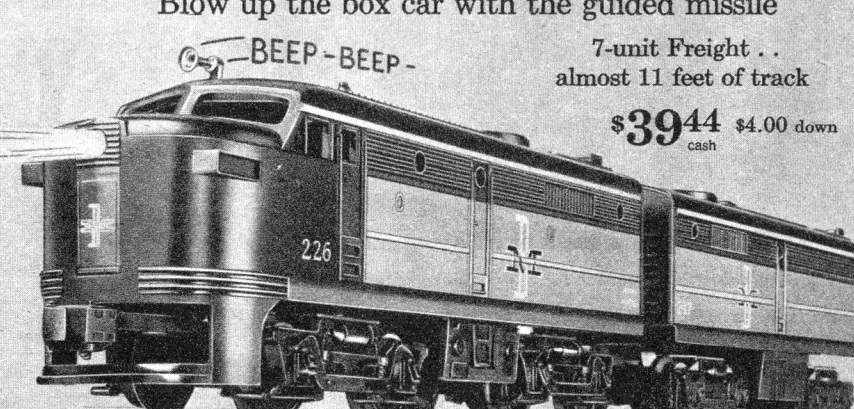

Blow up the box car with the guided missile
7-unit Freight .. almost 11 feet of track

$39.44 cash $4.00 down

6-unit Steam Freight with whistle and smoke

$29.44 cash $3.00 down

Smoke-puffing 2-4-2-steam locomotive sounds two-tone whistle as it clips down the track, drive rods pounding. Track-scanning headlight. Pulls tender, gondola with 3 cable reels, box car, flat car with trestle bridge, caboose. Run train forward, backward, fast, slow, sound whistle, couple or uncouple cars .. all by remote control. 11 "027" track sections and uncoupler form 117-in. oval. 75-watt transformer has whistle control, circuit breaker. Smoke fluid incl.
49 N 9653—Train 57 in. long over-all. Shipping weight 11 lbs........$29.44

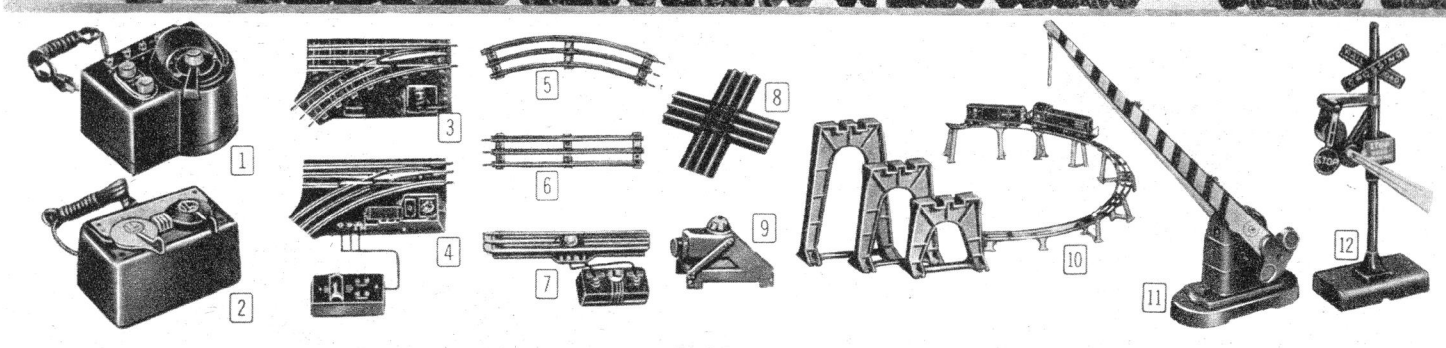

Transformers. Built-in circuit breaker for added safety. UL approved for 110–120-volt, 60-cycle AC.

[1] **Type LW-125-watt.** Fixed 14, 18-volt accessory circuits. Horn or whistle, direction controls.
49 N 9819—Speed throttle. Shipping weight 5 lbs..$12.88

[2] **Type TW-175-watt.** 2 throttles: one for speed, other for direction, whistle or horn control of your train. 4 fixed accessory voltages, 14, 14, 18 and 25 volts.
49 N 9842—Shpg. wt. 9 lbs...$2.00 down. Cash $19.97

[3] **Manual "027" Switches.** 1 right, 1 left.
49 N 9805—Shipping weight 2 lbs....$5.27

[4] **Remote Control "027" Switches.** Green, red control lights. Control panel, wires. 1 right, 1 left.
49 N 9806—Shipping weight 3 lbs.....$12.88

"027" Track Sections. Shpg. wt. each 7 oz.
(5) 49 N 9802—9⅛-in. curved section....19c
(6) 49 N 9801—8⅞-in. straight section....19c

[7] **"027" Magnetic Track.** For coupling, unloading. Remote control panel, wires.
49 N 9804—Shipping weight 1 lb......$3.97

[8] **"027" 7⅜-inch 90° Crossing.**
49 N 9803—Shipping weight 1 pound......$1.44

[9] **Lighted Bumper** for "027" or Super "O."
49 N 9859—Shipping weight 7 oz..........1.97

[10] **24 Plastic Trestles** make over, under layouts.
49 N 9845—Shipping weight 2 pounds......$4.44

[11] **Automatic Crossing Gate** lowers, flashes lights as train passes, then rises. Plastic and steel.
49 N 9834—9⅝ inches long. Shpg. wt. 1 lb....$4.44

[12] **Automatic Banjo Signal.** Signal lights, "STOP" sign swings as train passes. Plastic and steel.
49 N 9827—7½ inches high. Shpg. wt. 1 lb.....$4.44

Just press a button and the helicopter, blade whirling, soars into the air. And that's not all. As the train roars down the track, a red light flashes and a fireman holding a hose swivels on the fireman-and-ladder car; a cop chases a hobo around the animated gondola car. The Santa Fe twin diesel sounds its deep-tone "horn," shines its bright headlight. Powerful motor with Magne-Traction also pulls Allis Chalmers tractor-dozer car and caboose. Diesel engine and cars are made of plastic and steel. Run train forward or reverse, fast or slow, sound horn, couple or uncouple cars, operate the helicopter-launching car .. all by remote control. 14 sections of super "O" track with 16 ties per section make 126-inch oval. Includes 75-watt transformer with circuit breaker and horn control.
49 N 9693—Train 74 in. long. Shpg. wt. 13 lbs.... **$48.95**

Remote Control Helicopter Car. Plastic, steel. 11 in.
49N9856—Wt. 1 lb. .. **$5.97**

Fireman and Ladder Car. Plastic and steel. 11 in. long.
49N9861—Wt. 1 lb. .. **$7.97**

SUPER "O" GAUGE

[1] Super "O" Track Sections. 9 in. long. Wt. each 8 oz.
49N9817-Curved Section 27c 49N9816-Straight Sec. 27c

[2] 49 N 9807—90° Super "O" Crossover. Shipping weight 10 ounces.................**$1.94**

[3] Manual Super "O" Switches. Built-in safety device stops train on "open" switch. One right, one left.
49 N 9818—Shipping weight 3 pounds............**$8.88**

[4] Remote Control Super "O" Switches. Non-derailing device. Lighted indicators. One right, one left.
49 N 9813—Wiring included. Shpg. wt. 4 lbs..... **$17.97**

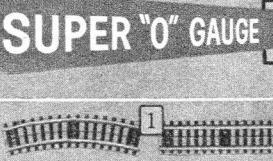

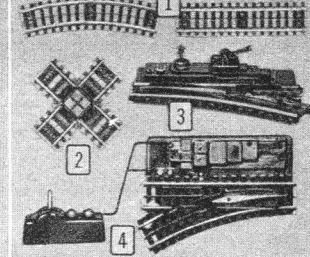

Press on the launching pad .. the IRBM missile soars straight at the target box car .. and the box car "explodes!" Another remote control button releases the helicopter, blade whirling. These exciting cars are headed up by Boston & Maine twin diesel with its deep-throated horn and powerful headlight. The brawny motor with Magne-Traction has super pulling power. It also pulls a flat car carrying a detachable submarine and a caboose. All cars are made of plastic and steel. Run the train forward or reverse, fast or slow, blow the horn, couple or uncouple cars, operate the 3 cars .. all by remote control. 13 sections of "027" gauge track plus uncoupling section form oval about 130 inches around. 75-watt circuit breaker transformer with horn control.
49 N 9654—Train 73 in. long over-all. Shipping weight 12 pounds....... **$39.44**

Exploding Target Car. Reassembles easily. Plastic, steel, 10½ in. long.
49 N 9823—Shpg. wt. 1 lb...... **$4.47**

Submarine Car. Removable submarine. Plastic and steel. Car 11 in. long.
49 N 9824—Shpg. wt. 1 lb...... **$4.47**

IRBM Missile Launching Car. Fire by remote control. Plastic and steel.
49 N 9825—11 in. long. Wt. 1 lb. **$5.97**

"027" GAUGE

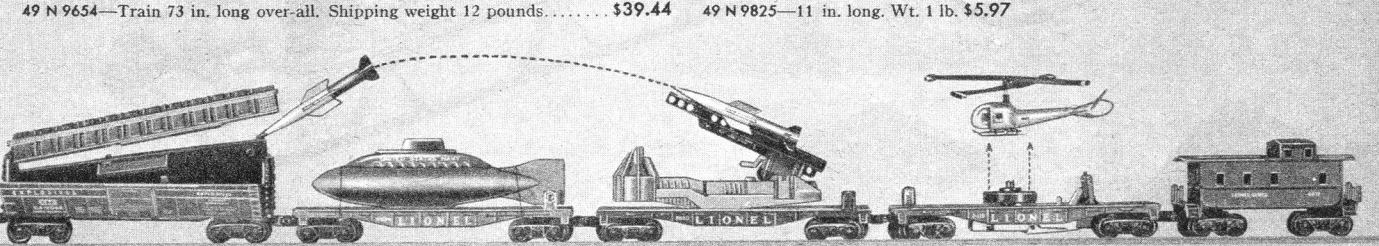

6-unit Diesel Work Train .. nearly 8 feet of track

$25.97 cash
$3.00 down

Shining its powerful headlight on the track ahead, the Chesapeake & Ohio diesel is equipped with Magne-Traction for heavy loads and steep grades. It pulls a timber transport loaded with tree trunks, a track maintenance car for overhead repairs, an Allis Chalmers motor scraper car, a manually operated derrick car and a work caboose. Run the train forward or back, fast or slow, couple or uncouple cars, all by remote control. 9 sections of "027" track plus uncoupling unit make 94-inch oval. 45-watt transformer.
49 N 9652—Train 63 in. long over-all. Plastic and steel. Shipping weight 11 lbs......... **$25.97**

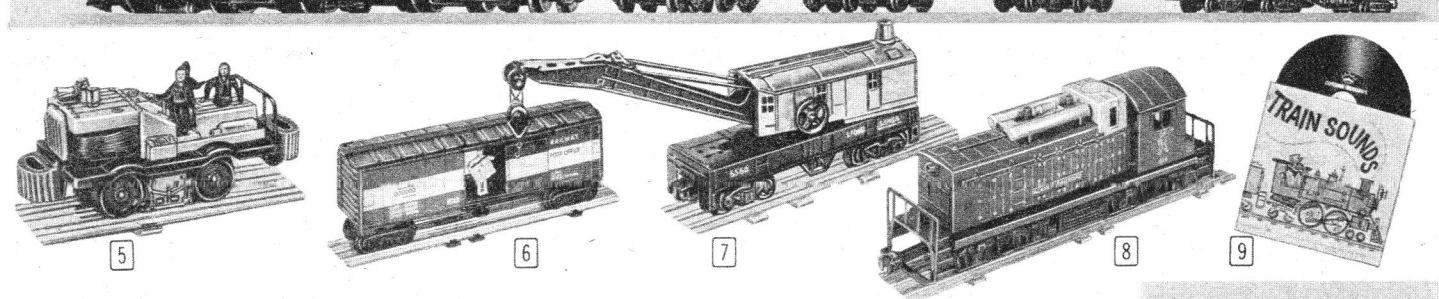

[5] Operating Section Gang Car. Built-in motor. Car and Gandy Dancer reverses automatically when buffer plate at either end strikes object. Plastic and steel. For "027" and "O" gauge.
49 N 9846—6 in. long. Shpg. wt. 2 lbs....... **$5.97**

[6] Operating United States Mail Car. Red, white and blue mail car operated by remote control. At the touch of a button door slides open, postal clerk tosses out a bundle of mail. Plastic and steel.
49 N 9853—10½ in. long. Shpg. wt. 1 lb..... **$5.97**

[7] Operating Crane Car. Rotating cab has two hand wheels .. one to raise and lower boom, one to raise and lower hook and pulley. Sturdily constructed of plastic and steel.
49 N 9852—7⅞ in. long. Shpg. wt. 2 lbs....... **$5.97**

[8] Alaska Diesel Switcher. Magne-Traction. Motor can take big loads up steep grades. Powerful headlight. Automatic couplers front and rear for moving cars. Plastic and steel.
49 N 9894—12 in. long. Shpg. wt. 3 lbs. **$12.97**

[9] Railroad Sounds Record. 45 rpm. Brings railroading to life.
49N9899—Wt. 2 oz. **59c**

[10] Automatic Gateman. Shuttles in and out of his shack, lantern lit. Lighted shack. Plastic, steel. Shack 7 in. long.
49N9835—Wt. 2 lbs.. **$5.66**

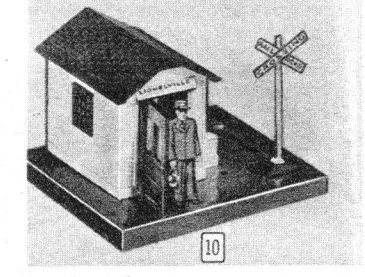

All cars and engines on this page (except Gang Car) have remote control couplers. Items (6), (7), (8) for "027" and "O" gauge

SEARS CHRISTMAS CATALOG

1961

There was something for everybody in the 1961 Sears Wishbook. Marx Trains, sold mostly under the Allstate name, were extremely popular allowing customers to take home Lionel look-a-likes at much lower prices. These trains were offered in Steam and Diesel versions and now had lots of extra features added like remote control cars and track switches.

H-O trains had more variety by 1961 and continued to gain market share. Allstate added another, slightly less expensive version of its pre-packaged and landscaped H-O layout. For just $7.88, one could buy the scenic base only.

But train makers, seeing the big new interest in slot cars (which boys felt offered them more hands-on control than old-fashioned trains) were looking for ways to tie the two concepts together. The result: the $28.95 Train and Turnpike Thriller where an H-O train could criss-cross a race track. Think of all those wonderful accidents that could be staged!

Mobile Crane Truck
$6⁹³

Giant 26-in. steel girder-type boom with real 4½ in. clam bucket. Bucket closes on load, then trip lever releases load. Boom folds back for moving to another site. Demolition ball and 2 workers included. 16½ in. long.
49 N 5622—Shpg. wt. 10 lbs..$6.93

Steel Construction Toys .. set of four $9⁹⁹

[1]-[4] **Save $3.72 on Complete Set.** Individual prices total $13.71. Baked-on, rust-resistant enamel over heavy-gauge steel. 4-pc. set includes:
Hi-Lift Loader (1) with giant scoop .. digs, scrapes, lifts and dumps load.
Road Grader (2) with steering wheel that works. Blade raises, lowers, turns.
Power Shovel (3) with automatic scooping and bucket-release action. Crank controls raising, lowering, loading and unloading. Cab revolves in full circle.
Hydraulic Dump Truck (4) with lever-operated hydraulic cylinder to dump load.
79 N 5421L—Complete Set. Includes (1), (2), (3), (4). Shpg. wt. 14 lbs......$9.99
(1) 49 N 5484—High-Lift Loader 15½ inches long. Shpg. wt. 3 lbs............2.93
(2) 49 N 5614—Road Grader. 17 inches long. Shpg. wt. 5 lbs.................2.92
(3) 49 N 5646—Power Shovel. 18 inches long. Rubber treads. Shpg. wt. 4 lbs...4.94
(4) 49 N 5661—Dump Truck. 15 inches long. Rubber wheels. Wt. 2 lbs. 12 oz...2.92

Camping-Boating Outfit for roughing it in style

[5] All the comforts of home! Steel truck has built-in living quarters with sliding windows, fold-away rear steps. High-impact plastic cruiser has twin outboards, rides on 2-wheel trailer. Truck has spring-suspension front wheels, lower separately.
49 N 5478—24 in. long overall. Whitewall tires. Shpg. wt. 3 lbs. 12 oz......$4.94

Bells clang .. ladders raise .. water squirts

[6]-[7] **Save $2.69 on Set of Two.** Individual prices total $15.46. Exciting working parts add to the fun. Rust-resistant enamel over steel. Plastic cab on pumper. Set includes: *Pumper Fire Truck* (7) that actually sprays water. Just hook hydrant to garden hose and turn valve. Has hook-on ladder, dummy plastic searchlight, hydrant and 3 firemen. *Hook and Ladder* (6) with main ladder on a full-radius swivel .. raises by mechanical hydraulic action. Crank elevates 2 other ladders a full 5 feet. Removable tillerman's seat.
79 N 5437L—Set. Includes (6), (7). Shipping weight 17 pounds...........$12.77
(6) 79 N 5570L—Hook and Ladder. 3 feet long. Shpg. wt. 12 lbs............8.89
(7) 79 N 5663C—Pumper Fire Truck. 22 inches long. Shpg. wt. 7 lbs........6.57

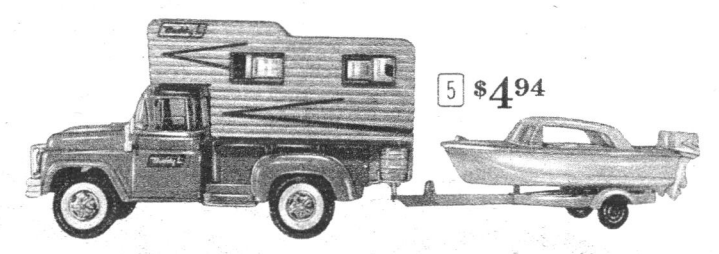

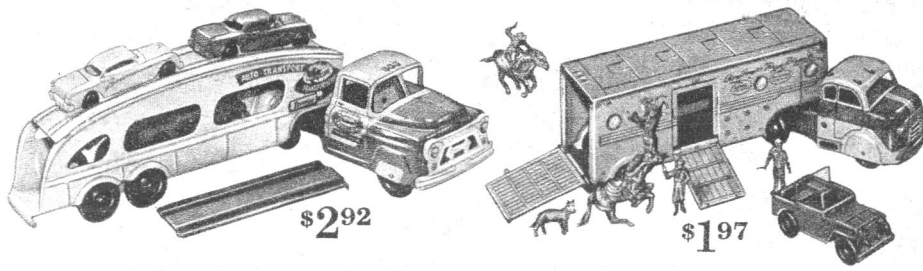

[5] $4⁹⁴

[7] $6⁵⁷

[6] $8⁸⁹

$2⁹² $1⁹⁷ $2⁹²

Big Steel Haulers built to last, give "loads" of fun

Auto Transport. Carries four 5½-in. plastic sedans cross country to dealer's showroom. Ramp attaches to upper or lower deck. Cab detaches easily from van. 9 heavy duty rubber wheels.
49 N 5582—23 in. over-all. Wt. 4 lbs..$2.92

Roy Rogers Hauler and Trailer. Roy and all his gang in 3-dimensional plastic. Dale Evans, Pat Brady and his jeep Nellybelle and Bullet. Trailer has side and rear gate ramps for easy loading.
49 N 5557—15½ in. long. Wt. 2 lbs..$1.97

Cattle Van with Livestock and Corral. Nineteen pieces of plastic livestock ride comfortably in all-steel truck and trailer. Drop tailgate serves as loading ramp. 17½ inches long.
49 N 5609—Shipping weight 3 lbs...$2.92

PCB2 SEARS 393

Regular Gauge "Gauge" refers to size. Locomotives are about 4 inches high, track 1¼ inches wide.

ALLSTATE® Regular-gauge Electric Train Sets are

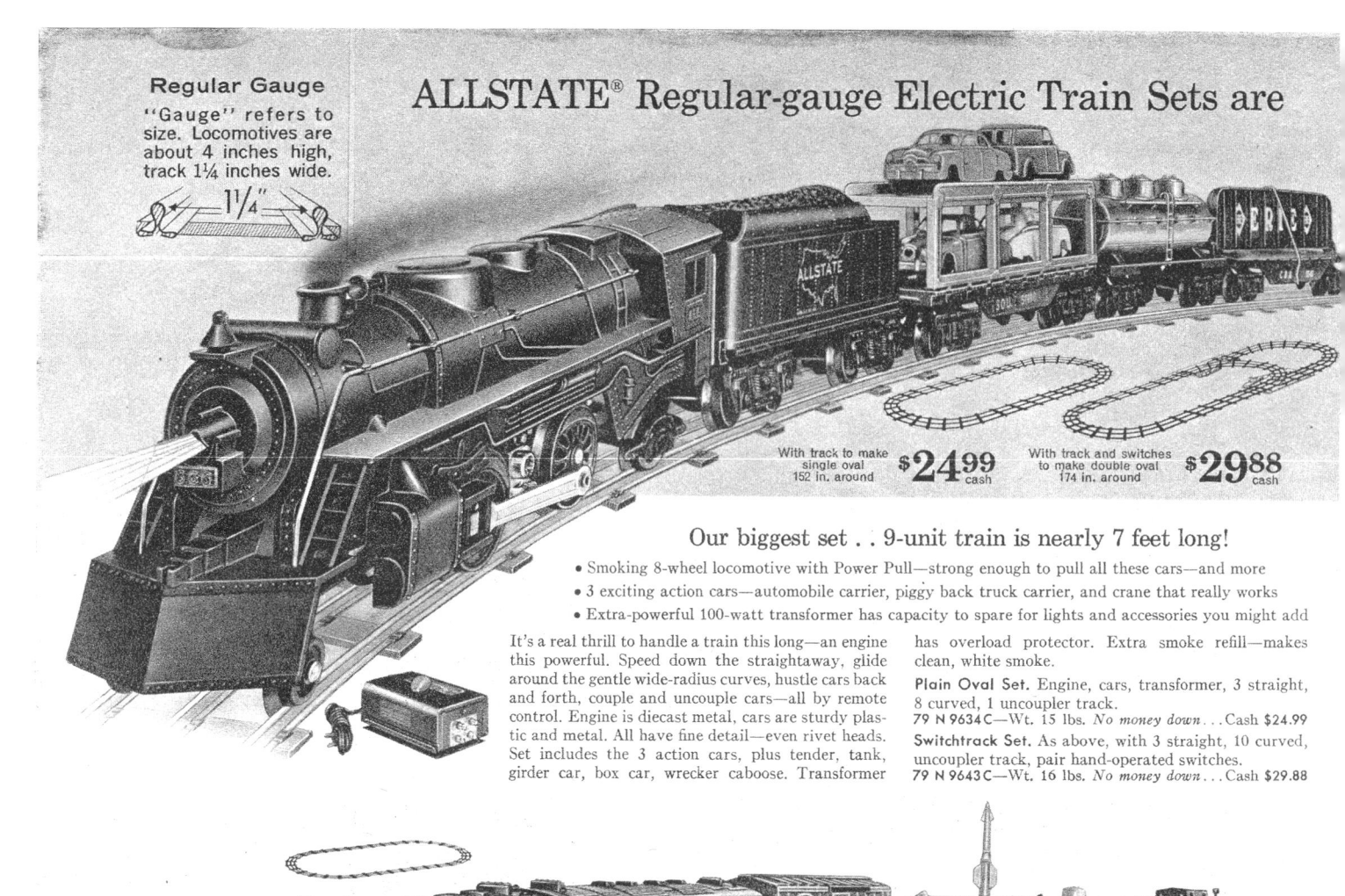

With track to make single oval 152 in. around **$24.99** cash

With track and switches to make double oval 174 in. around **$29.88** cash

Our biggest set.. 9-unit train is nearly 7 feet long!

- Smoking 8-wheel locomotive with Power Pull—strong enough to pull all these cars—and more
- 3 exciting action cars—automobile carrier, piggy back truck carrier, and crane that really works
- Extra-powerful 100-watt transformer has capacity to spare for lights and accessories you might add

It's a real thrill to handle a train this long—an engine this powerful. Speed down the straightaway, glide around the gentle wide-radius curves, hustle cars back and forth, couple and uncouple cars—all by remote control. Engine is diecast metal, cars are sturdy plastic and metal. All have fine detail—even rivet heads. Set includes the 3 action cars, plus tender, tank, girder car, box car, wrecker caboose. Transformer has overload protector. Extra smoke refill—makes clean, white smoke.

Plain Oval Set. Engine, cars, transformer, 3 straight, 8 curved, 1 uncoupler track.
79 N 9634C—Wt. 15 lbs. *No money down*...Cash $24.99

Switchtrack Set. As above, with 3 straight, 10 curved, uncoupler track, pair hand-operated switches.
79 N 9643C—Wt. 16 lbs. *No money down*...Cash $29.88

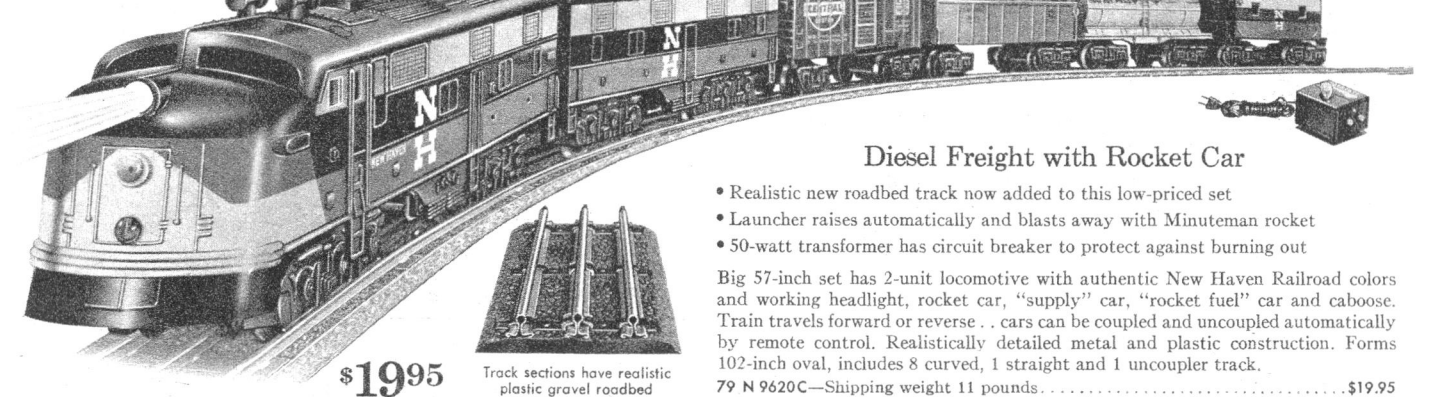

Diesel Freight with Rocket Car

- Realistic new roadbed track now added to this low-priced set
- Launcher raises automatically and blasts away with Minuteman rocket
- 50-watt transformer has circuit breaker to protect against burning out

Big 57-inch set has 2-unit locomotive with authentic New Haven Railroad colors and working headlight, rocket car, "supply" car, "rocket fuel" car and caboose. Train travels forward or reverse.. cars can be coupled and uncoupled automatically by remote control. Realistically detailed metal and plastic construction. Forms 102-inch oval, includes 8 curved, 1 straight and 1 uncoupler track.
79 N 9620C—Shipping weight 11 pounds............$19.95

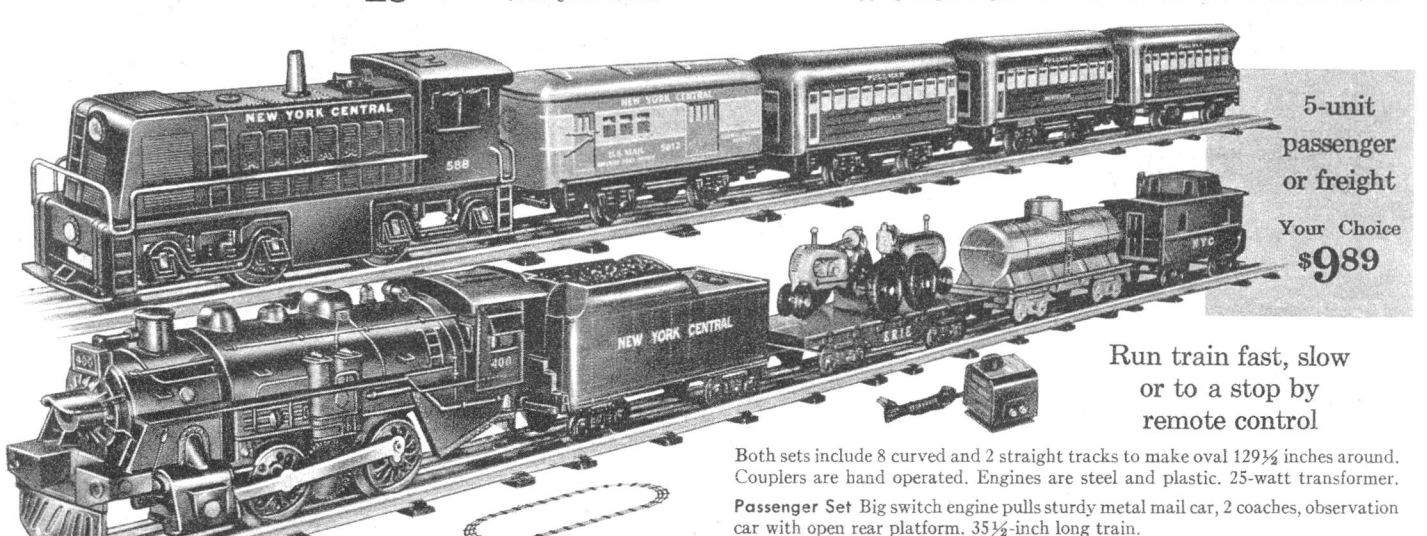

$19.95 Track sections have realistic plastic gravel roadbed

5-unit passenger or freight
Your Choice **$9.89**

Run train fast, slow or to a stop by remote control

Both sets include 8 curved and 2 straight tracks to make oval 129½ inches around. Couplers are hand operated. Engines are steel and plastic. 25-watt transformer.

Passenger Set. Big switch engine pulls sturdy metal mail car, 2 coaches, observation car with open rear platform. 35½-inch long train.
49 N 9607—Locomotive, cars, track, transformer. Shipping weight 6 lbs.......$9.89

Freight Set. Steam type locomotive pulls plastic tender, tank car, flatcar with tractors, caboose. Train is 40 inches long overall.
49 N 9610—Locomotive, cars, track, transformer. Shipping weight 6 lbs.......$9.89

TRANSFORMERS: All sets on these two pages include transformers to start and stop, also to control speed of trains.. *UL approved* for 110–120-volt, 60-cycle AC.

made extra sturdy .. simple to set up

Detailed scale models of real railroad equipment with plenty of action

Train as shown **$16³⁷**

40½ in. 5-unit Freight Train .. 2 types

- 8-wheel engine puffs smoke from stack, steam from cylinders
- New roadbed 3-tie track gives added realism .. 50-watt circuit-breaker transformer is UL approved, 110–120-v, 60-cycle AC

Run train fast or slow, forward or reverse .. couple or uncouple cars—all by remote control. Clean smoke and cool steam puffs as train travels—made by an automatic vaporizer in engine. Plastic and steel, highly detailed. Includes engine and tender, gondola, refrigerator car and caboose. All cars have automatic couplers. 10 sections of track form oval 102 in. around.
49 N 9617—Shipping weight 9 pounds..................$16.37

Economy-priced Train. Same as above but engine puffs smoke from stack only. 5-tie wide-radius track forms oval 129 in. around; no roadbed.
49 N 9613—Not illustrated. Shipping weight 9 pounds..................$14.98

Track sections have realistic gravel roadbed

Complete Set **$19⁹⁸** cash NO MONEY DOWN

Diesel engine pulls 4 ACTION cars .. Train 46 in. long

- Do all these fascinating things by remote control—run train fast or slow, forward or reverse ... couple and uncouple cars ... unload logs from lumber car ... stop cattle car and box car at loading platform, watch door open automatically and men pop out—then go back in as train moves on
- Light the big searchlight on worktrain caboose
- Powerful Diesel modeled after Union Pacific engines

Most action-packed train set we've ever offered under $20. New roadbed-type track (small view above) adds to the realism, includes 8 curved, 3 straight and 1 uncoupler track to form oval 120 inches around.

Rolling stock is highly detailed plastic and steel construction. Powerful 50-watt circuit-breaker transformer is UL approved for 110–120-volt 60-cycle AC.
79 N 9621C—Shipping weight 10 pounds..........$19.98

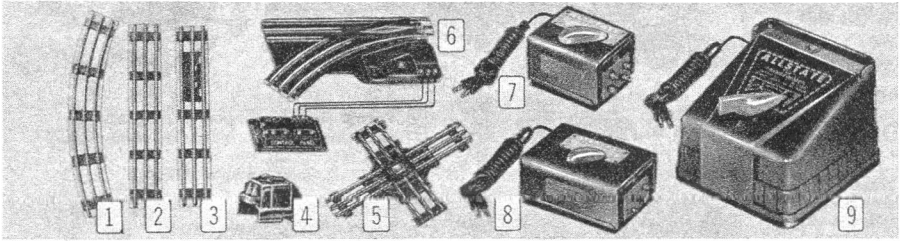

NEW Roadbed 3-tie Track

Each section is mounted on plastic molded base to look like the gravel roadbed of real railroads. Use with Marx or ALL-STATE trains.

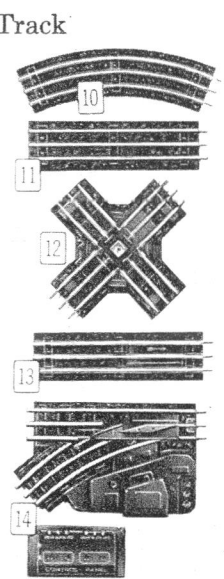

[10] **9½-inch Curved.**
49 N 9702—Wt. 4 oz...27c

[11] **8⅞-inch Straight.**
49 N 9701—Wt. 4 oz...27c

[12] **Crossover** for figure 8's.
49 N 9703—7½x7½ in.
Shipping weight 4 oz....$1.39

[13] **Uncoupling Track.** Use in place of straight track to uncouple cars having automatic couplers. 8⅞ in. long.
49 N 9710—Shpg. wt. 4 oz..94c

[14] **Electric Switches.** Push-button control panel, wires. Signal lights show position. Sold in pairs.
49 N 9706—Wt. 2 lbs...$6.87

Hand-operated Switches. Lever control (not shown). Pair.
49 N 9704—Wt.1 lb. 12 oz.$3.88

---

[1]-[2] **Wide-radius Track.** Has 5 ties instead of 3. Curves are gentle—trains can round curves at full speed. Also fits Marx trains.
(1) 49 N 9723—12½-in. Curved. Wt. 4 oz......22c
(2) 49 N 9720—11¼-in. Straight. Wt. 4 oz.....22c

[3] **Uncoupling Track.** Replaces straight section to uncouple cars equipped with automatic couplers. "Uncouple here" sign incl.
49 N 9749—Shipping weight 4 oz............79c

[4] **End-of-track Bumper.** Keeps trains from running off dead-end siding. With light.
49 N 9707—2 in. high, plastic. Shpg. wt. 4 oz..89c

[5] **Crossover.** Build exciting figure-eight layouts. Each track 9¼ inches long.
49 N 9726—Shipping weight 4 oz............$1.29

[6] **Electric Switches.** Push-button controls and wires included. Signal lights show position.
49 N 9727—1 right, 1 left. Shpg. wt. 2 lbs...$7.99
49 N 9776—Hand operated, no signals (not shown). 1 right, 1 left. Shpg. wt. 1 lb. 12 oz......$4.44

Transformers. Extra and larger transformers for big layouts. All have circuit breakers, 2 sets of binding posts. UL listed, 110–120v, 60c. AC.

[7] **50-watt.** 7–13 volt for train speed, 13 volt for accessories. Steel case.
49 N 9721—Shipping weight 3 lbs..........$5.47

[8] **100-watt.** 5–15 volt train circuit, 15 volt accessory circuit. Steel case.
49 N 9722—Shipping weight 4 lbs..........$7.99

[9] **150-watt.** 0–15 volt train circuit, 15 volt accessory circuit. Throttle handle. Plastic case.
49 N 9724—Shipping weight 10 lbs. 4 oz....$11.99

No MONEY DOWN on Easy Terms. See page 226 for details.

PCB SEARS 395

Regular Gauge Cars, engines, accessories for Allstate regular gauge or any sets with 1¼-in. wide track

Add these Regular-gauge Accessories

$11.99 $9.99 $3.37

Motorized Cars run by remote control

Twin Diesel. Headlamp lights up the track ahead. Equipped with automatic coupler. Electric motor has oilless bronze bearings. High-impact plastic; die-cast metal wheels. 24½ in. long. Wt. 3 lbs. 12 oz.
49 N 9782.........$11.99

Diesel Switcher makes rhythmic diesel noise. Headlight. Automatic couplers on both ends. Electric motor, bronze bearings. Steel and plastic; die-cast metal wheels. 10½ in. long. Wt. 2 lbs. 4 oz.
49 N 9783.........$9.99

Handcar. Two workmen pump the crossbars as car goes around track. Electric motor, oilless bronze bearings. Plastic and steel; die-cast metal wheels. 6¼ in. long. Wt. 12 oz.
49 N 9753.........$3.37

Make landscape with Scene-O-Rama Kit $7.89

Create a 4x8-foot life-like countryside for your train to scoot around. Kit includes: true-color lichen in 3 shades to make 15 natural-looking trees, lots of shrubbery. Grass-color and earth-color mats of flocked-on fiber to form roads, paths and contrast .. can be cut or draped for dozens of effects. Snow-capped plastic tunnel fits HO, O or Regular gauge trains, 3 tiny lamp posts light up, are wired to attach to any electric track.
79 N 9713C—With easy-to-follow instructions. Shipping weight 5 lbs.....$7.89

Operating Cars add action to your train

[1] **Log Car.** Touch button to unload 5 logs into plastic bin. Controls, wiring, special track section included. Plastic and steel car, 8¼ inches long.
49 N 9761—Shipping wt. 12 oz. .. $4.37

[2] **Wrecker-crane** .. ready to roll in emergencies. Hand wheels control boom and cable. Cab swivels. 12 inches long, plastic and steel construction.
49 N 9786—Shpg. wt. 1 lb. 8 oz. ...$3.99

[3] **Lighted Passenger Cars.** Haul commuters. Riders silhouetted in windows. Shiny metal. Astradome shown. Shpg. wt. each, 1 lb.
49 N 9770—11-inch Astradome... $3.44
49 N 9771—10¾-inch Observation.. 3.44

[4] **Cattle Car.** As train stops, door slides open, steer steps out, climbs back aboard when train starts. Car, track, wiring, plastic ramp included. 9½-in. long plastic and steel car.
49 N 9763—Shipping wt. 1 lb...... $3.44

All cars have automatic couplers to match Allstate Regular Gauge sets, die-cast metal wheels

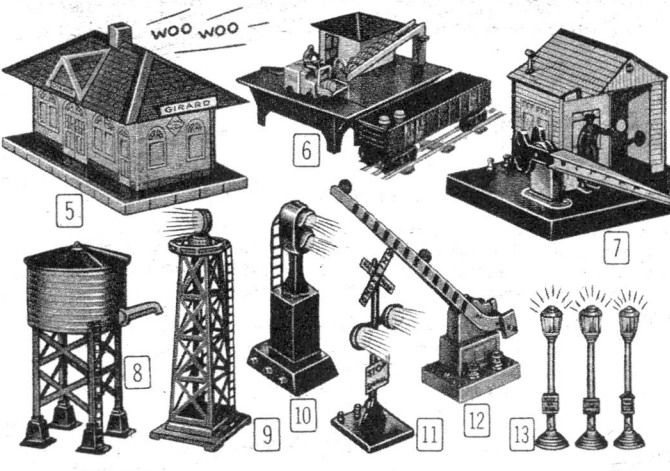

Working Pieces make a train layout more exciting

[5] **Remote Control Whistling Station.** Steel, 9x5½x5 in. high. Push button on control panel, hear loud train whistle.
49 N 9739—Shpg. wt. 2 lbs... $3.99

[6] **Remote Control Barrel Loader.** Press a button, truck takes barrel from loading chute to car (not incl.). Plastic, 8¾x8x5 in. high. Plastic barrels, push button control panel, necessary wiring included.
49 N 9779—Wt. 1 lb. 6 oz..... $3.99

[7] **Automatic Grade-crossing Shack and Watchman.** As train nears, watchman comes out with stop sign, gate lowers. Steel shack 4½ in. high. Base 7x6½ in. Wires incl.
49 N 9760—Shpg. wt. 2 lbs... $3.37

[8] **Plastic Water Tower.** Adjustable spout. 8¼ in. high, 4¼-in. diam.
49 N 9731—Shpg. wt. 8 oz..... 87c

[9] **Lighted Revolving Beacon.** Beams red one direction, green the other. Plastic, 12½ in. high.
49 N 9740—Shpg. wt. 12 oz....$1.87

[10] **Automatic 2-Light Block Signal.** Train stops on red, goes on green. Manual switch. Plastic, 7½ in. high. 2 track sections included.
49 N 9745—Shpg. wt. 8 oz.....$1.87

[11] **Automatic Crossing Flasher.** 2 lights flash alternately as train passes. Plastic, 7 in. high.
49 N 9742—Shpg. wt. 8 oz.....$1.87

[12] **Crossing Gate.** 8-in. arm lowers as train passes. Plastic. Wires.
49 N 9743—Shpg. wt. 8 oz.....$1.87

[13] **Three Lighted Lamp Posts.** Plastic, 6 in. high. Wires included.
49 N 9737—Shpg. wt. 10 oz....$1.89

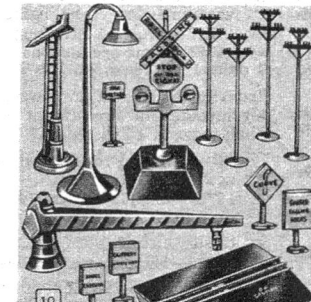

[14] **Trestle Bridge.** Embossed rivet-head detail, finished in bright aluminum finish steel. 18 inches long.
49 N 9732—Shipping weight 2 lbs...... $1.89

[15] **Tunnel.** Decorated with landscape scene. Colorfully lithographed steel.
49 N 9729—10 in. long. Shpg. wt. 1 lb... 87c

[16] **Trestle-Viaduct Set.** Create an exciting 2-level figure-8 layout with grades and curves. 24 graduated trestles and viaduct will hold up to 22 feet of track. ½ to 4¼ inches high. Plastic construction.
49 N 9741—Shipping weight 2 lbs...... $3.87

[17] **30-piece Accessory Set.** 15 workmen, passengers, in various poses; freight wagons, hand carts, signs, etc. Plastic.
49 N 9772—Shipping weight 10 oz........ 98c

[18] **29-pc. Railroad Kit.** Ideal for any regular-size train layout. Includes 12 telephone poles, 12 railroad right-of-way signs, semaphore, signal, crossing gate, lamp post and grade crossing for autos (track not incl.). For scenery .. molded plastic.
49 N 9750—Shipping weight 1 lb. 12 oz....$2.79

← Turn back a page for complete sets

HO provides realistic railroading, fine detail, action

HO rolling stock has N.M.R.A.* operating automatic couplers.

Add these exciting, plastic Scale Cars and Diesel Workhorse to your HO train

Set of 4 Extra Cars .. to make longer trains and add more realism and dispatching fun. All are high-impact plastic and have 8 nylon wheels (4 each on 2 nylon trucks), operating couplers, authentic R.R. markings. Box, cement cars; flat car with 2 autos; gondola .. 5 to 6 in. long.
49 N 9965—Wt. 1 lb. *Was $4.99.*$3.99

[1] **Automatic Lumber Car.** Unload logs by tapping a push-button. 6-in. car, log bin, special track, wiring.
49 N 9946—Shipping weight 8 oz.....$3.27

[2] **Operating Crane Car.** 2 hand wheels .. one raises and lowers boom, other lifts and lowers hook. Rotating cab.
49 N 9938—5-in. car. Shpg. wt. 8 oz..$3.27

[3] **Automatic Box Car.** Train stops, door opens, man steps onto platform, jumps back in as train leaves.
49 N 9945—6-in. car. Wt. 8 oz...$3.27

[4] **Auto Carrier.** Drive 4 scale model autos up the loading ramp. 2 levels. 6½-in. carrier.
49 N 9576—Shipping wt. 4 oz....$1.88

Diesel Industrial Switcher. Yard switching is real fun with this powerful, compact unit. Operating couplers on front, back. Brass wheels. Powerful 4-wheel drive. 4 in. long.
49 N 9997—Shpg. wt. 8 oz.....$4.39

*National Model Railroad Association couplers on all cars. See the following page for more details.

Plastic HO Accessories

[5] **Crossing Gate.** As train approaches, gate swings down, raises after train passes. Special track, wiring included.
49 N 9947—3¾ in. long. Wt. 4 oz..$2.49

[6] **Crossing Flasher.** Lights flash alternately as train approaches. Special track, wiring included.
49 N 9954—2¼ in. high. Wt. 4 oz..$2.49

[7] **2-light Block Signal.** Green light changes to red as train passes. Special track, wiring included.
49 N 9957—2⅞ in. high. Wt. 6 oz..$2.49

[8] **Semaphore.** Arm lowers and light changes from green to red as train passes. Special track, wiring included.
49 N 9955—4 in. high. Wt. 6 oz...$2.49

[9] **Trestle Set.** 30 graduated trestles, plus bridge piers. Build over and under figure 8's, or add hills.
49 N 9915—Plastic. Wt. 12 oz.....$2.67

Remote Control Whistling Station. Press push-button on panel, hear loud train "woo-woo". Plastic and steel. 8 inches long. Wiring included. Shipping weight 1 pound 4 ounces.
49 N 9919.....................$4.98

Landscape Materials

Build mountains, roads, trees, shrubs with easy-to-use materials. No special tools or skills needed.

[10] **Grass and Earth Mats.** Colored fiber glued to heavy paper.
79 N 9571C—Grass. 50x99 in. Shpg. wt. 3 lbs...$2.79
79 N 9572C—Earth. 33x48 in. Shpg. wt. 1 lb.....92c

[11] **Tree and Shrub Material.** Lichen plants treated to stay soft, flexible. True-to-life colors.
49 N 9573—Shipping weight 12 ounces..........$2.79

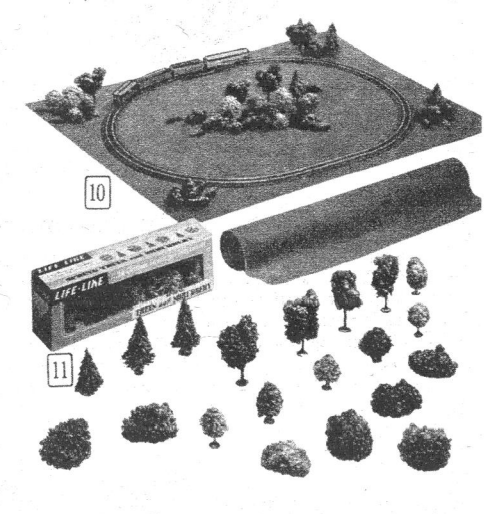

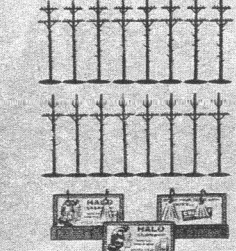

Battery-powered HO-gauge Beginner's Set

$4.97 without batteries

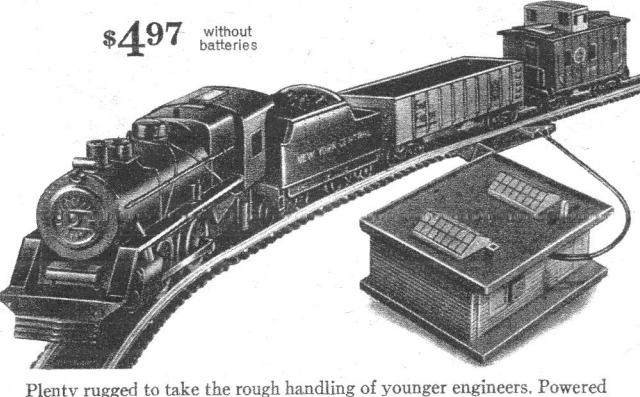

Plenty rugged to take the rough handling of younger engineers. Powered by 3 flashlight batteries that fit into passenger station. Lever on roof stops, starts, reverses train. Set includes high-impact plastic locomotive, tender, gondola and caboose. 12 curved sections, 1 straight, 1 re-railer-terminal. Track makes 35½x30¼-in. oval. 21¾-in. train.
49 N 9517M—Use 3 "D" batteries, order below. Shpg. wt. 2 lbs.....$4.97
49 N 4662M—"D" batteries. Shipping weight two, 8 oz.........2 for 39c

Plastic Rail and Road Scenery Set. About 39 pieces in all. Includes railroad signs, billboards, 18 telephone poles, people, and 4 cars, plus semaphore signal and watering station. All built to HO scale.
49 N 9964—Shpg wt. 1 lb.......$2.99

Plastic Building Set. About 43 pieces in all. Fine detail and realistic coloring. Includes switch tower, station, coal tower, 3 houses, 12 telephone poles, farm buildings, animals, figures. Buildings snap together. All HO Scale.
79 N 9967C—Shpg. wt. 2 lbs......$5.97

Turn the page for complete HO Sets

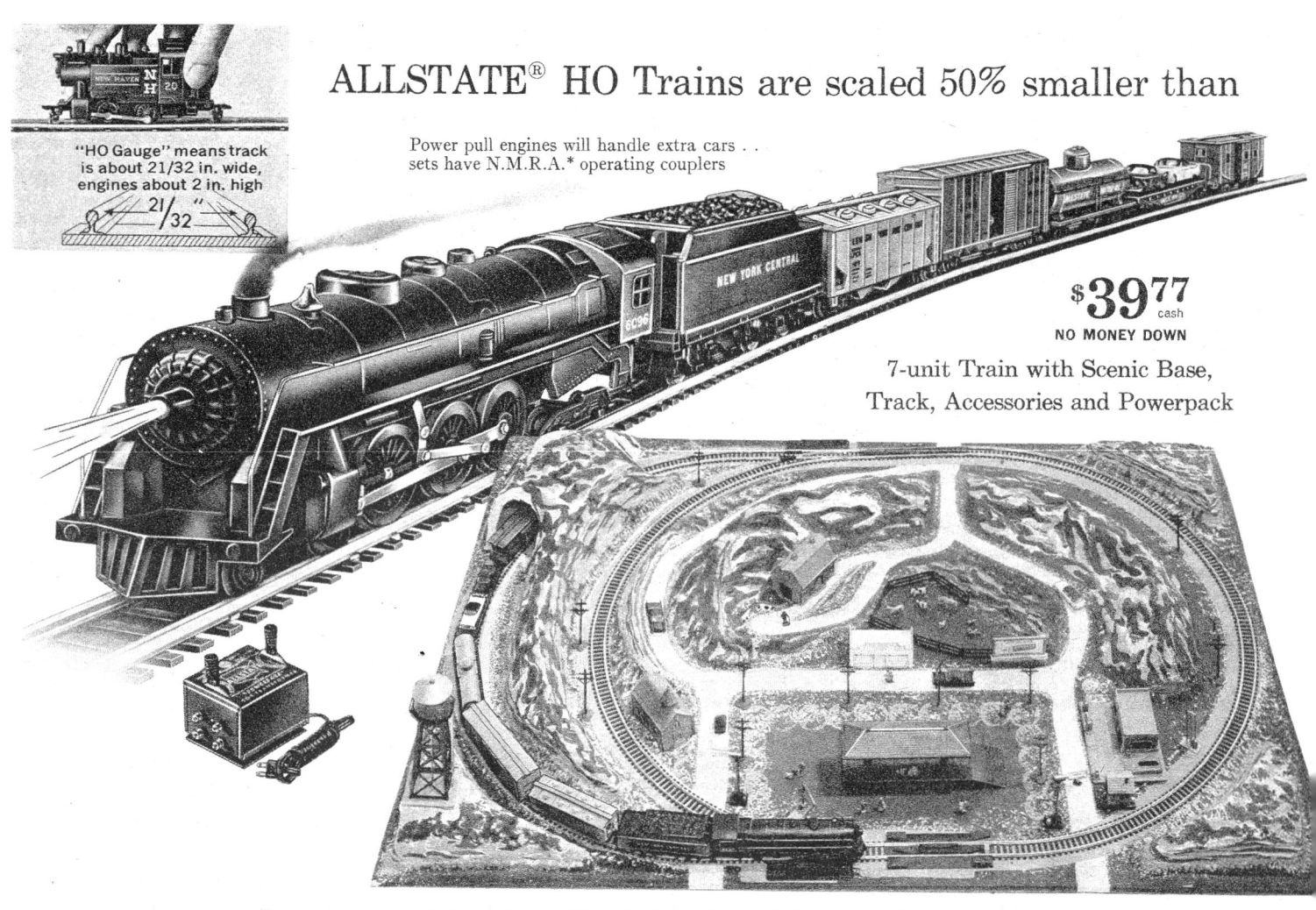

"HO Gauge" means track is about 21/32 in. wide, engines about 2 in. high

ALLSTATE® HO Trains are scaled 50% smaller than

Power pull engines will handle extra cars .. sets have N.M.R.A.* operating couplers

$39.77 cash
NO MONEY DOWN

7-unit Train with Scenic Base, Track, Accessories and Powerpack

Run this powerful smoke-puffing freight through its own miniature empire

Roar through the tunnel and past the farm. See the tiny watchman come out of his shanty as you flash by. Slow down for the curve by the lighted water tower. Stop at the station with its two lighted street lamps. Set the switches and back up to uncouple or couple cars on the inner track. Engine puffs real smoke, has big working headlight, goes fast, slow, forward or reverse by remote control. Rolling stock includes tender, cement hopper car, box car, tank car, flat car with two automobiles, and caboose .. all have nylon trucks and wheels.

Molded plastic, landscaped base is 48x34 inches. The more than 60 plastic pieces include station, church, gas station, farm building, store, people, animals. 18 sections of track with 2 manual switches for 112 and 127-inch ovals. Uncoupler-railer operates N.M.R.A.* couplers, helps put cars on track. Engine is die-cast metal, cars are plastic. 1¼-amp powerpack UL approved for 110-120-volt, 60-cycle AC. With 4 posts, 4 to 18-volt DC for speed, 18-volt AC for accessories.
79 N 9963N2—Freight (rail or truck) or express. Shpg. wt. 17 lbs..........$39.77

"SEARS DOES MORE"

You get a complete HO layout with 7-pc. Switcher Set, Scenic Base, Track, Accessories and Powerpack..

Only **$26.77 cash**
NO MONEY DOWN

◀ HO Accessories on preceding page

Everything you need for a scenic railroad at a minimum of cost and work. You can uncouple cars, run it fast, slow, forward or reverse .. by remote control. Switcher pulls hopper, sliding door box car, piggyback truck hauler on 6-inch flat car, gondola, tank car and caboose. Plastic and metal construction.
Track includes 1 uncoupler-railer and 15 other sections. Base is formed plastic, detailed with tunnel, mountains, roads. Accessories include station, trees, telephone poles, people, semaphore, etc. 1-amp powerpack, UL approved for 110-120-volt, 60-cycle AC. Freight (rail or truck) or express.
79 N 9942N2—38-inch Train. Shpg. wt. 16 lbs....$26.77

Scenic Base only. Same as base with set at left but does not include any track or accessories. Suitable for use with any ALLSTATE or Marx HO train. Base can hold up to 12 curved and 4 straight tracks. Shipped by freight (rail or truck) or express.
79 N 9943N—Shpg. wt. 8 lbs.......$7.88

*N.M.R.A. (National Model Railroad Assoc.) standard operating couplers used on every ALLSTATE HO train and will fit any standard make of HO gauge car.

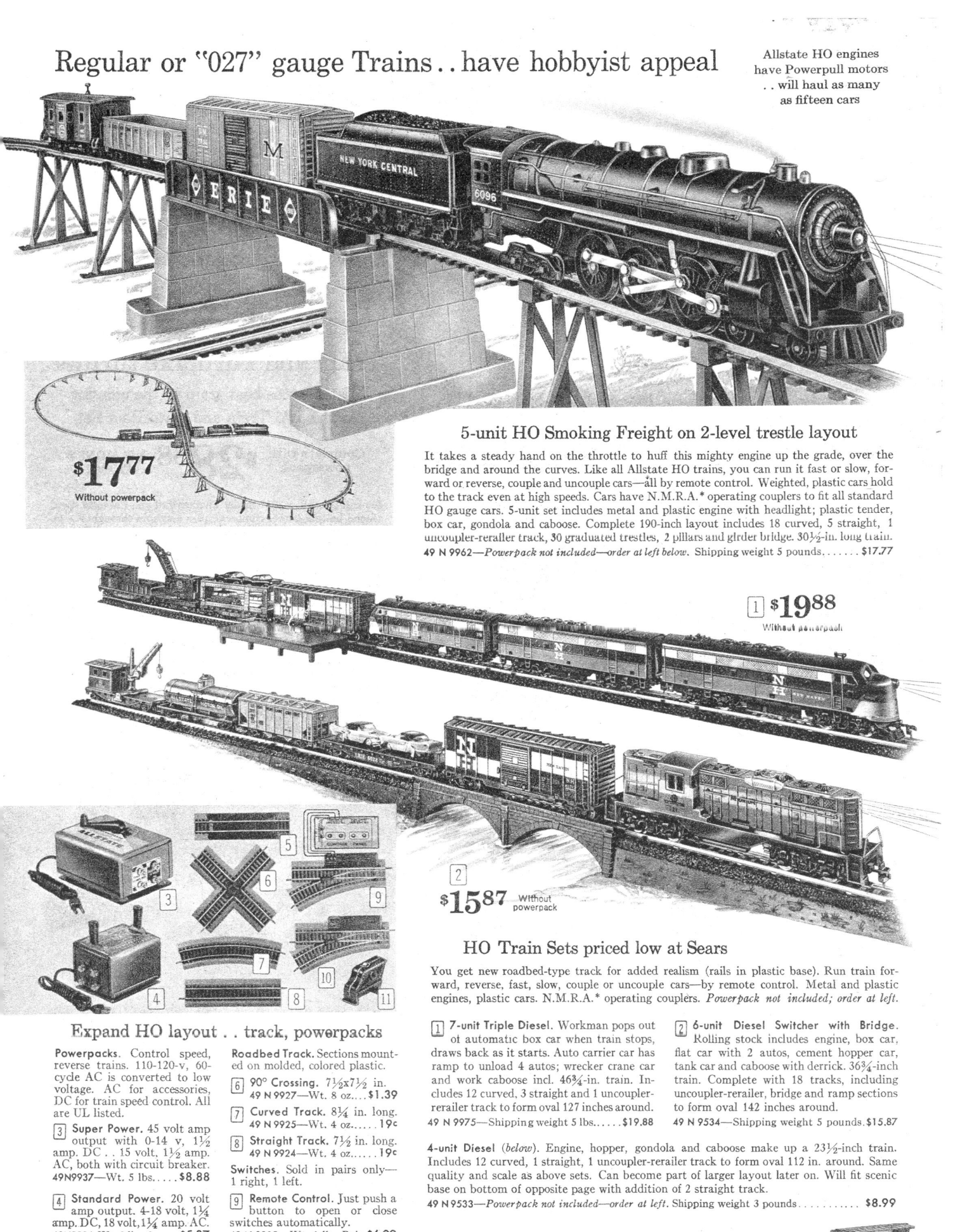

Regular or "027" gauge Trains.. have hobbyist appeal

Allstate HO engines have Powerpull motors .. will haul as many as fifteen cars

$17.77 Without powerpack

5-unit HO Smoking Freight on 2-level trestle layout

It takes a steady hand on the throttle to huff this mighty engine up the grade, over the bridge and around the curves. Like all Allstate HO trains, you can run it fast or slow, forward or reverse, couple and uncouple cars—all by remote control. Weighted, plastic cars hold to the track even at high speeds. Cars have N.M.R.A.* operating couplers to fit all standard HO gauge cars. 5-unit set includes metal and plastic engine with headlight; plastic tender, box car, gondola and caboose. Complete 190-inch layout includes 18 curved, 5 straight, 1 uncoupler-rerailer track, 30 graduated trestles, 2 pillars and girder bridge. 30½-in. long train.
49 N 9962—Powerpack not included—order at left below. Shipping weight 5 pounds......$17.77

[1] **$19.88** Without powerpack

[2] **$15.87** Without powerpack

HO Train Sets priced low at Sears

You get new roadbed-type track for added realism (rails in plastic base). Run train forward, reverse, fast, slow, couple or uncouple cars—by remote control. Metal and plastic engines, plastic cars. N.M.R.A.* operating couplers. *Powerpack not included; order at left.*

[1] **7-unit Triple Diesel.** Workman pops out of automatic box car when train stops, draws back as it starts. Auto carrier car has ramp to unload 4 autos; wrecker crane car and work caboose incl. 46¾-in. train. Includes 12 curved, 3 straight and 1 uncoupler-rerailer track to form oval 127 inches around.
49 N 9975—Shipping weight 5 lbs......$19.88

[2] **6-unit Diesel Switcher with Bridge.** Rolling stock includes engine, box car, flat car with 2 autos, cement hopper car, tank car and caboose with derrick. 36¾-inch train. Complete with 18 tracks, including uncoupler-rerailer, bridge and ramp sections to form oval 142 inches around.
49 N 9534—Shipping weight 5 pounds. $15.87

4-unit Diesel (*below*). Engine, hopper, gondola and caboose make up a 23½-inch train. Includes 12 curved, 1 straight, 1 uncoupler-rerailer track to form oval 112 in. around. Same quality and scale as above sets. Can become part of larger layout later on. Will fit scenic base on bottom of opposite page with addition of 2 straight track.
49 N 9533—Powerpack not included—order at left. Shipping weight 3 pounds..........$8.99

Expand HO layout .. track, powerpacks

Powerpacks. Control speed, reverse trains. 110-120-v, 60-cycle AC is converted to low voltage. AC for accessories, DC for train speed control. All are UL listed.

[3] **Super Power.** 45 volt amp output with 0-14 v, 1½ amp. DC .. 15 volt, 1½ amp. AC, both with circuit breaker.
49N9937—Wt. 5 lbs..... $8.88

[4] **Standard Power.** 20 volt amp output. 4-18 volt, 1¼ amp. DC, 18 volt, 1¼ amp. AC.
49N9936-Wt. 2 lbs. 8 oz... $5.37

[5] **Uncoupler-Rerailer.** Operates NMRA couplers, helps rerail cars. Serves as vehicle crossing. 7½ in. long.
49 N 9926—Wt. 4 oz......77c

Roadbed Track. Sections mounted on molded, colored plastic.

[6] **90° Crossing.** 7½x7½ in. 49 N 9927—Wt. 8 oz... $1.39

[7] **Curved Track.** 8¼ in. long. 49 N 9925—Wt. 4 oz......19c

[8] **Straight Track.** 7½ in. long. 49 N 9924—Wt. 4 oz......19c

Switches. Sold in pairs only—1 right, 1 left.

[9] **Remote Control.** Just push a button to open or close switches automatically.
49 N 9929—Wt. 1 lb..Pair $6.99

[10] **Manual Lever Control.**
49N9928-Wt. 8 oz. Pair $4.59

[11] **Lighted Dead-end Bumper.** Black plastic, red light.
49N9923-3¾ in. high. Wt. 2 oz..77c

PCB SEARS 399

Train and Turnpike thriller

Watch autos beat train to the crossing in this HO Train and Auto Race Set

Complete with powerpack $28.88 cash **NO MONEY DOWN**

Look at 'em go .. 1961-model Thunderbird and Corvette speed around hairpin curve, climb overpass and spin through 3 more curves. Union Pacific diesel freight highballs it toward grade crossing. Autos must race the train or .. *Hit the brake!* Locomotive roars through crossing, its headlamp beaming. Coal hopper car, cement car, tank car and finally the caboose pass by. Off speed the autos again—right down the straightaway.

HO scale plastic autos, 2¼ in. long, have electric motors, nylon guide pins on front. Two speed controls operate each auto independently. 15 plastic road sections with metal contact strips snap together to form 12-foot turnpike, 8 plastic trestles.

HO train is 28 in. long. Plastic engine pulls plastic cars with N.M.R.A. couplers, nylon wheels. Run train fast, slow or in reverse—by remote control. 15 track sections plus rerailer grade crossing for turnpike form 127-inch oval. 1½-amp powerpack with circuit breaker, 18-volt AC-DC.
79 N 9523C—Train and Turnpike Set. Shpg. wt. 9 lbs.....$28.88

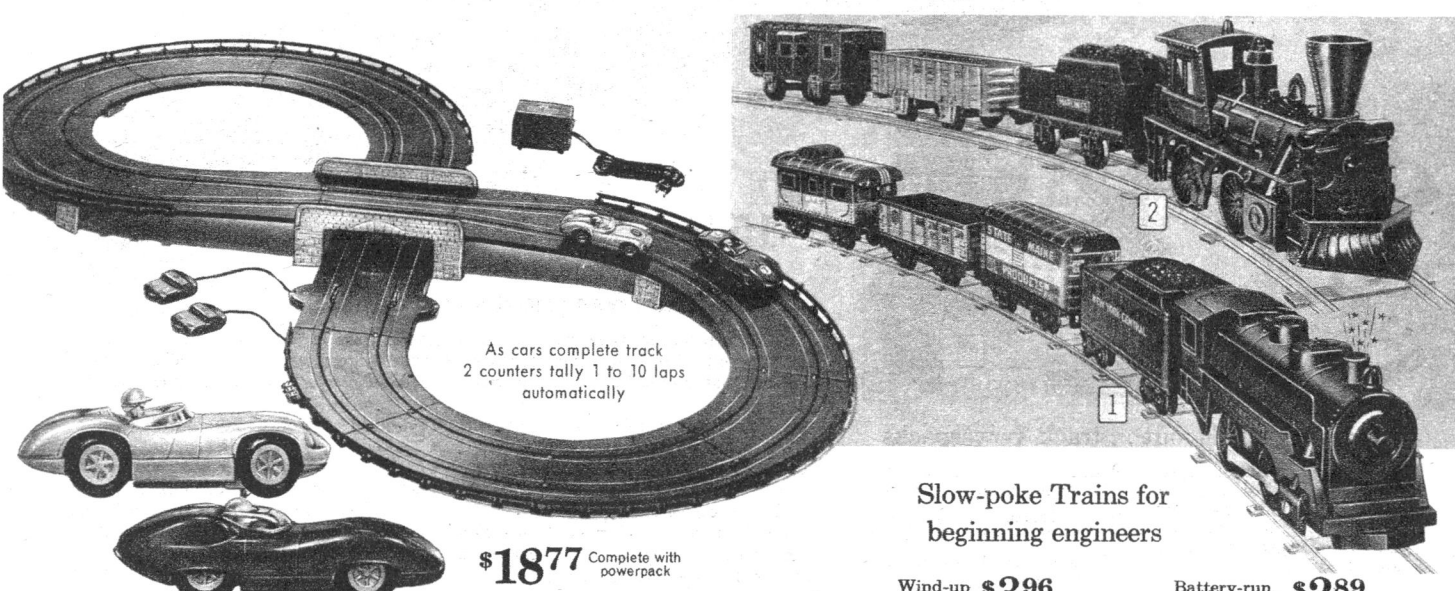

Powerpack works both train and autos. UL approved. 110-120-volt, 60-cycle AC

As cars complete track 2 counters tally 1 to 10 laps automatically

$18.77 Complete with powerpack

International Sports Car Race counts each lap around

Brake for the turns and at top of overpass. Bridge narrows so only one car can pass at a time, an obstacle that requires daredevil skill to avoid collision. Lap-counter section tallies 1 to 10 laps as each racer rounds the figure-8, over-and-under track.

Miniature Aston Martin and Lister Jaguar racers are molded plastic and ride on metal contact strips. Actually skid around curves .. held in grooves by nylon guide pins. 2 hand throttles control speed. 15 plastic sections plus narrow overpass snap together .. form a 5-foot figure 8 with 15½-foot lap. 4 plastic trestles. 1-amp 18-volt D.C. powerpack.
49 N 9521—UL approved for 110–120-volt, 60-cycle AC. Shpg. wt. 8 lbs............$18.77

Slow-poke Trains for beginning engineers

Wind-up motor $3.96

[1] Husky, steam-type locomotive is powered by long-running, keywind clock motor. Emits harmless sparks. Speed governor runs train at even speed. On-off lever. High-impact plastic engine and coal tender pull colorfully decorated metal gondola, box car and caboose. Train 34 in. long. 8 curved and 2 straight track form 102-in. oval.
49 N 9512—Wt. 3 lbs. 4 oz. $3.96

Battery-run motor $2.89

[2] Ideal for tots because all parts are of soft, flexible vinyl plastic. Old-fashioned steam-type locomotive pulls coal tender, gondola and caboose. 31-in. long train. 10 sections of flexible vinyl track form a 92-inch oval. Uses 1 "D" battery .. order below.
49N9514M—Wt. 1 lb. 12 oz .$2.89
49N4662M—"D" batteries. Shpg. wt. two, 8 oz............2 for 39c

Speed .. spins .. thrills

Like real speedway driving! Travel as much as 20 feet around many different layouts

Complete with powerpack $29.88 cash **NO MONEY DOWN**

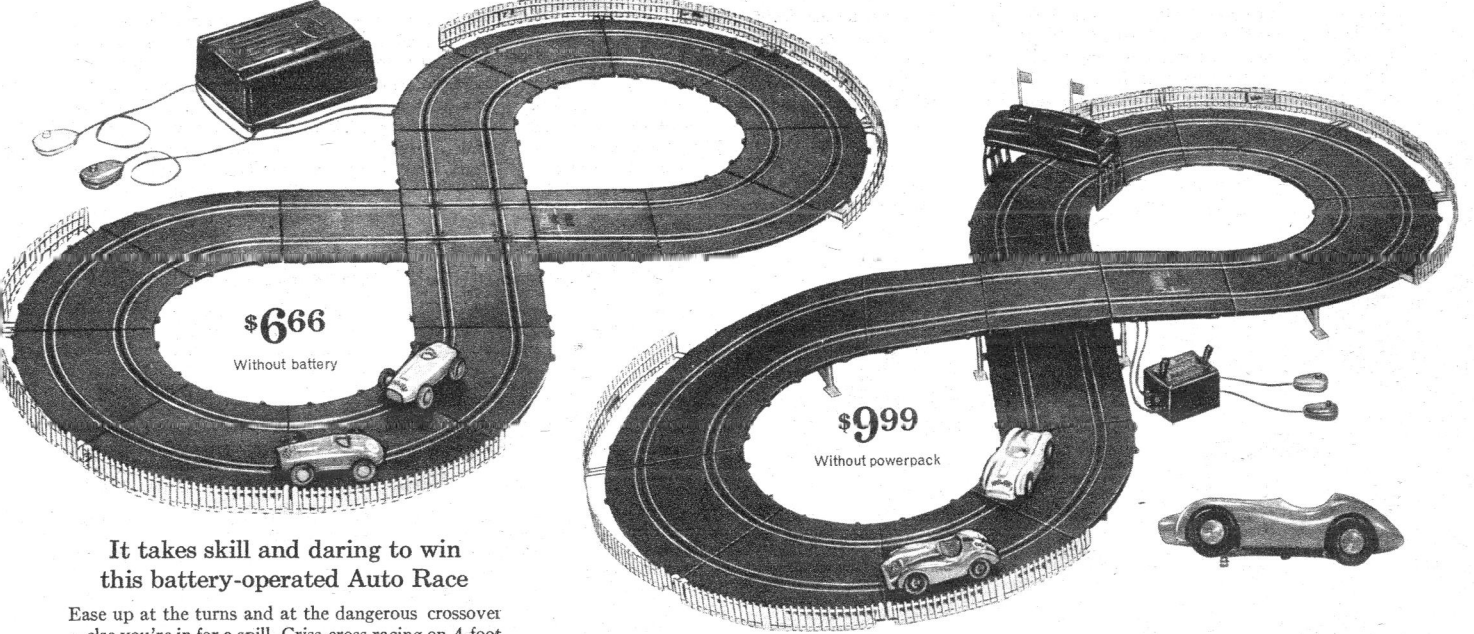

Experience the fast pace, quick decisions and daredevil chances that top-notch drivers take on 6 great American speedways. Set up a new track layout—meet a new challenge every time.

Fun to watch .. more fun to run. Feel the surge of power as you press your control throttle. Wheels spin. Your car races wildly, neck and neck with your opponent. Ease up! Here's that hair-pin curve. Watch that Jag! He's out of control! He's spun out!

Ferrari Testa Rosa and D-Jaguar are 1/32-scale molded plastic, 5½ inches long. Ready to run with heavy-duty electric racing motors. Nylon pins guide them along track grooves between aluminum contact strips. Watch them skid and spin realistically at the turns. Independently controlled by 2 push-button hand throttles.

22 plastic sections (10 straight, 12 curved) slip together like train tracks. Form a 6-foot figure 8, a 6½-foot Hour Glass, an 8½-foot Lake Garnett, or other famous track layouts. Instruction manual shows you how. 12 plastic trestles let you build overpass. 12 plastic fence sections protect racers along the curves. Set includes 1¼-amp powerpack with twin 7½-volt DC circuits, circuit breaker, on-off switch. UL approved. 110–120-volt, 60-cycle AC.
49 N 9532—Electric Road Race Set. Shpg. wt. 9 lbs..........$29.88

Make any of these famous track layouts with this set

Palm Springs, Calif. — Lake Garnett, Kansas — Daytona International — Hour Glass, La Jolla — Montgomery, Alabama

$6.66 Without battery

It takes skill and daring to win this battery-operated Auto Race

Ease up at the turns and at the dangerous crossover —else you're in for a spill. Criss-cross racing on 4-foot figure 8 is sure to be full of suspense and near-accidents. Two 4-inch molded plastic racers have prewired electric motors, ride metal contact strips. They skid and spin .. held to track grooves by plastic guide pins. Two on-off control buttons govern speed.

17 plastic road sections, 8 fence sections snap together. Battery box, connecting wires. Battery not included. Order one 1½-volt dry cell battery below.
79 N 9540CM—Shipping weight 4 lbs..........$6.66
79 N 4701M—1½-volt Battery. Wt. 2 lbs. 5 oz....95c

$9.99 Without powerpack

Flag lowers automatically as winning car speeds across finish line

Plastic tower counts each lap around. When your racer goes 9 laps tiny flag goes up .. when you cross finish line on 10th lap flag goes down, marking winner. Two 4-inch molded plastic racers travel over and under a 4-foot figure 8. Racers have 12-volt direct drive motors, plastic guide pins .. ride on metal conductors. Speed governed by 2 on-off hand controls. 24 plastic road sections and 8 fence sections snap together. 8 plastic trestles.
79 N 9525C—Powerpack not included. Wt. 5 lbs. $9.99
49 N 9936—1¼-amp Powerpack. 4 to 18-volt DC. UL listed, 110–120-volt, 60-cycle AC.
Shipping weight 2 lbs. 8 oz.................$5.37

PCB SEARS 401

Lionel "027" Gauge Electric Train Sets..

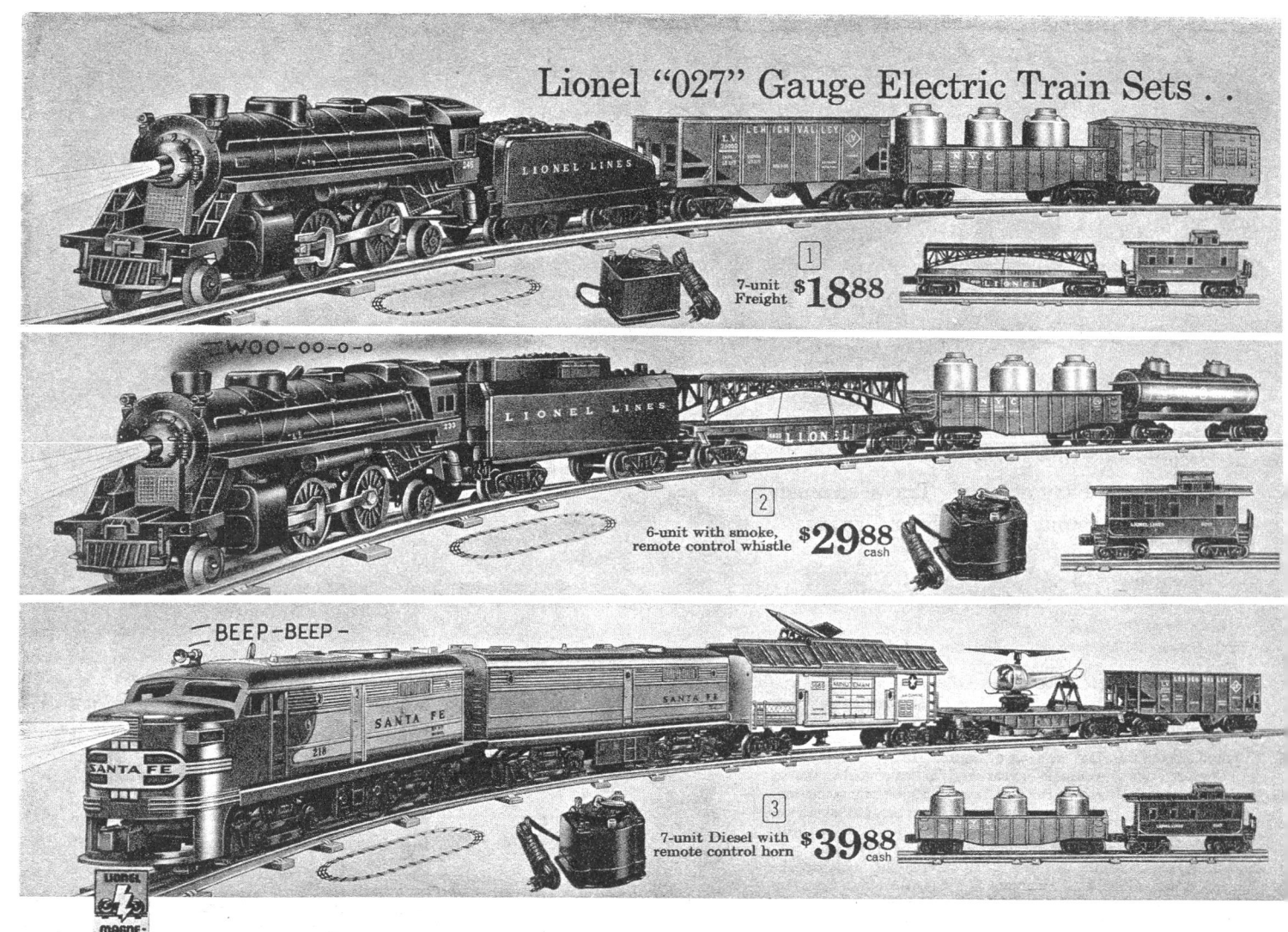

[1] 7-unit Freight **$18.88**

[2] 6-unit with smoke, remote control whistle **$29.88** cash

[3] 7-unit Diesel with remote control horn **$39.88** cash

Imagine! Lionel Trains with Magne-Traction and remote-control uncoupling—at prices so low

"027" gauge trains have 3-rail track with 3 cross ties, 1¼ in. between outer rails. Engines powered by Magne-Traction drive for greater pulling power. Run forward or reverse, fast or slow, even uncouple cars—all by remote control. Cars of plastic and steel. Connecting wires, Lockon unit, lubricant and instructions included. All 3 sets have a circuit-breaker transformer .. UL approved for 110-120-volt, 60-cycle AC.

[1] **7-unit Steam-type Freight.** Powerful 8-wheel locomotive with slope-back coal tender. Bright headlight. Rolling stock includes hopper car; gondola with 3 canisters; Savings Bank car (deposit coins toward purchase of additional cars and accessories); flat car with arched trestle bridge; caboose. 8 curved, 1 straight and 1 remote-control uncoupling track form 27x36-inch oval. Train is 63½ inches long. 35-watt transformer.
49 N 9670—Shipping weight 8 lbs. 12 oz......$18.88

[2] **6-unit Steam Freight.** When engine has a full head of steam it billows real smoke. Headlight shines, whistle gives warning when you want. Couple on a real load .. coal tender; flat car with arched trestle bridge; gondola with 3 canisters; twin-dome tank car; caboose. 8 curved, 3 straight and 1 remote-control uncoupling track form 27x45-inch oval. Train is 56 inches long. 75-watt transformer has whistle control. With smoke fluid.
49 N 9672—Wt. 12 lbs. *No money down.*..Cash $29.88

[3] **7-unit Diesel Freight.** Double unit diesel with headlight, horn. Two cars work by remote control .. Minuteman Missile Launching car opens roof, raises launcher, fires missile .. Helicopter Launching car soars spring-powered 'copter by push-button. Hopper car, gondola with 3 canisters, caboose. 8 curved, 5 straight and 1 remote-control uncoupling track form 27x54-inch oval. Train is 72 inches long. 75-watt transformer with horn control.
49 N 9673—Wt. 14 lbs. *No money down.*..Cash $39.88

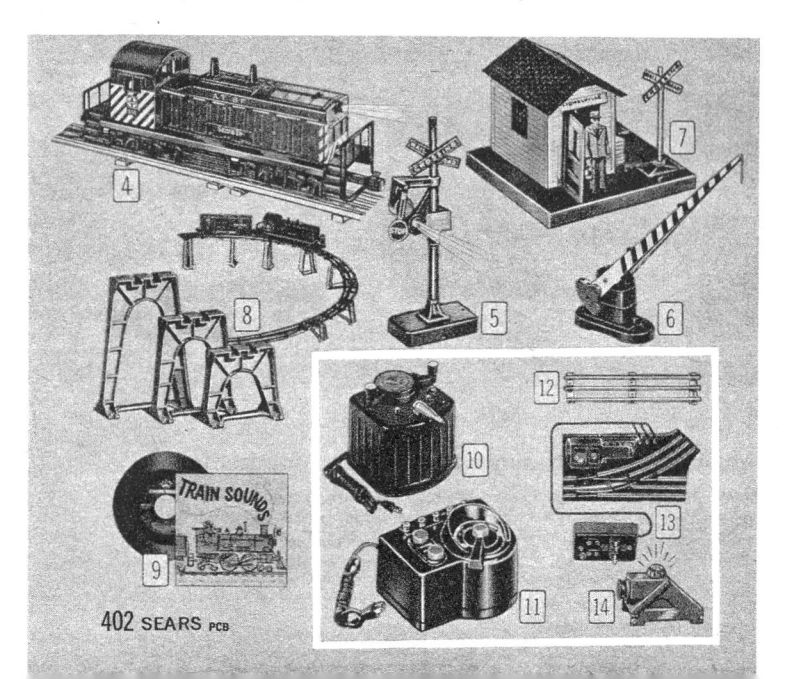

"027" plastic-and-metal accessories .. extra track

[4] **Santa Fe Switcher.** Has working headlight, horn, Magne-Traction and couplers on front and rear.
49N9814—12¼ in. Wt. 3 lbs. 8 oz. $23.66

[5] **Banjo Signal.** Flashing lights and swinging stop sign go into action as train passes. Operates automatically. Shpg. wt. 12 oz.
49 N 9827—7½ in. high......$4.57

[6] **Crossing Gate.** Gate swings down as train nears crossing, raises after train has passed. Flashing lights on gate arm.
49N9834—9⅝ in. long. Wt. 1 lb. $4.57

[7] **Gateman.** Man rushes out of shanty swinging lantern to warn of approaching train, returns to shack when train is gone. Wt. 2 lbs.
49 N 9835—4½ in. high........$5.66

[8] **Trestle Set.** For over-and-under figure 8's. 24 trestles, 3/16 to 4¾ inches high. All plastic.
49 N 9845—Shpg. wt. 2 lbs. Set $4.67

[9] **Sound Effects Record.** 45 rpm.
49 N 9899—Shpg. wt. 2 oz. 59c

Transformers. Reduce house current (110-v. 60c. AC) to low voltage for trains. Circuit breakers protect against overload. Horn, whistle, directional controls. UL approved.

[10] **190-w. Type KW Dual Control.** For 2-train layouts. Two speed controls, plus fixed voltage for accessories. 7¼x6⅝x7½ in. high.
49 N 9821—Shpg. wt. 11 lbs.. $24.77

[11] **125-w. Type LW.** Speed control, 2 accessory circuits.
49 N 9819—Shpg. wt. 5 lbs. 8 oz. $13.17

[12] **"027" Track.** Shpg. wt. ea. 3 oz.
49 N 9801—8¾-in. straight...19c
49 N 9802—9½-in. curved....19c
90° Crossover. For figure-8 set-up.
49N9803—7⅜x7⅜ in. Wt. 11 oz. $1.49

[13] **Remote-control Switches.** 1 left, 1 right. Has red, green signal lights. Control panel, wiring.
49N9806—Shpg. wt. 3 lbs. Pair $13.77
49 N 9805—Hand switches. No signals. 1 left, 1 right. Wt. 2 lbs....Pair $5.77

[14] **Lighted Deadend Bumper.**
49 N 9859—Shpg. wt. 8 oz...$1.97

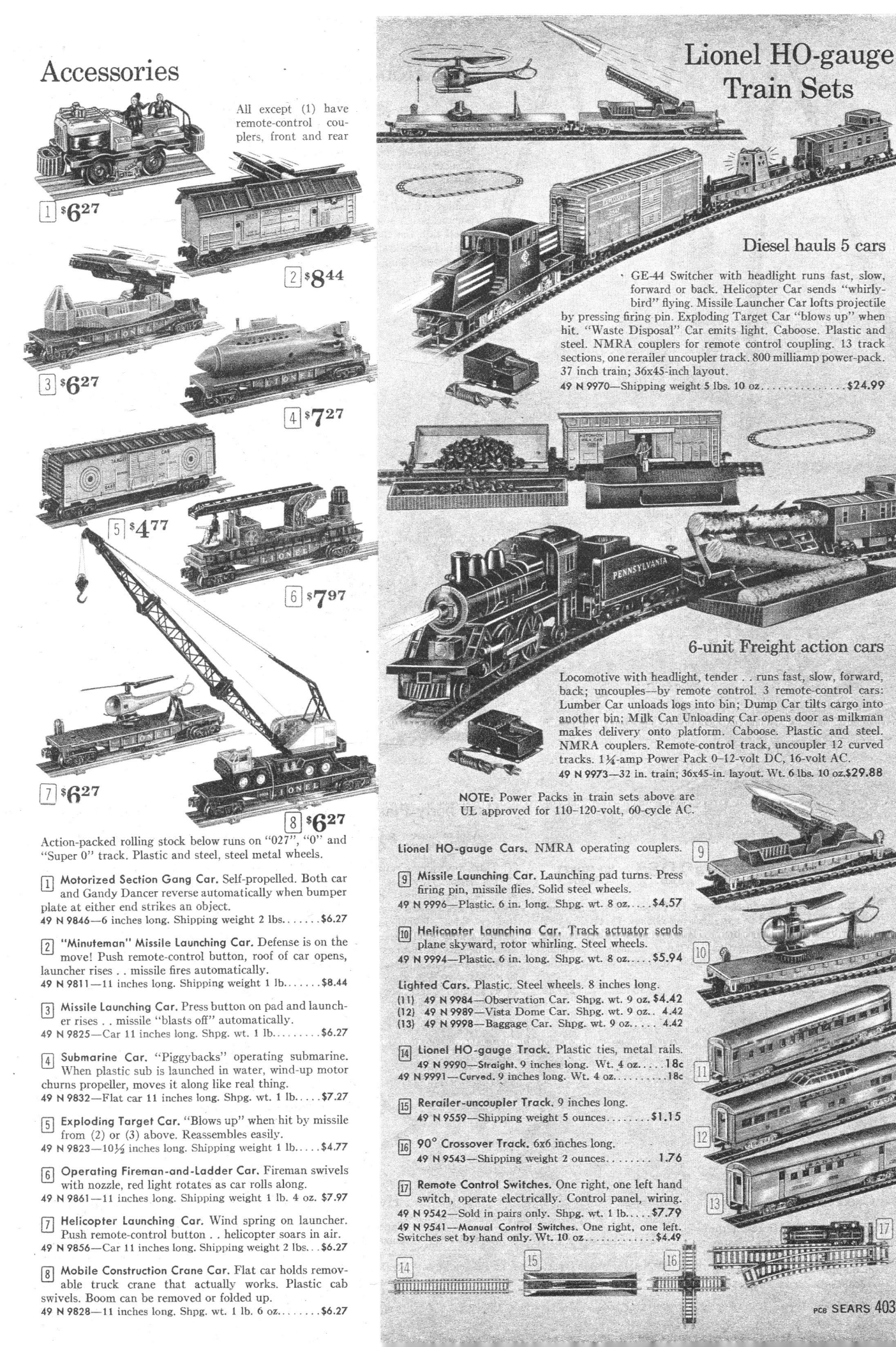

Accessories

All except (1) have remote-control couplers, front and rear

[1] $6.27
[2] $8.44
[3] $6.27
[4] $7.27
[5] $4.77
[6] $7.97
[7] $6.27
[8] $6.27

Action-packed rolling stock below runs on "027", "0" and "Super 0" track. Plastic and steel, steel metal wheels.

[1] **Motorized Section Gang Car.** Self-propelled. Both car and Gandy Dancer reverse automatically when bumper plate at either end strikes an object.
49 N 9846—6 inches long. Shipping weight 2 lbs.......$6.27

[2] **"Minuteman" Missile Launching Car.** Defense is on the move! Push remote-control button, roof of car opens, launcher rises .. missile fires automatically.
49 N 9811—11 inches long. Shipping weight 1 lb.......$8.44

[3] **Missile Launching Car.** Press button on pad and launcher rises .. missile "blasts off" automatically.
49 N 9825—Car 11 inches long. Shpg. wt. 1 lb.........$6.27

[4] **Submarine Car.** "Piggybacks" operating submarine. When plastic sub is launched in water, wind-up motor churns propeller, moves it along like real thing.
49 N 9832—Flat car 11 inches long. Shpg. wt. 1 lb.....$7.27

[5] **Exploding Target Car.** "Blows up" when hit by missile from (2) or (3) above. Reassembles easily.
49 N 9823—10½ inches long. Shipping weight 1 lb.....$4.77

[6] **Operating Fireman-and-Ladder Car.** Fireman swivels with nozzle, red light rotates as car rolls along.
49 N 9861—11 inches long. Shipping weight 1 lb. 4 oz. $7.97

[7] **Helicopter Launching Car.** Wind spring on launcher. Push remote-control button .. helicopter soars in air.
49 N 9856—Car 11 inches long. Shipping weight 2 lbs...$6.27

[8] **Mobile Construction Crane Car.** Flat car holds removable truck crane that actually works. Plastic cab swivels. Boom can be removed or folded up.
49 N 9828—11 inches long. Shpg. wt. 1 lb. 6 oz........$6.27

Lionel HO-gauge Train Sets

Diesel hauls 5 cars

GE-44 Switcher with headlight runs fast, slow, forward or back. Helicopter Car sends "whirlybird" flying. Missile Launcher Car lofts projectile by pressing firing pin. Exploding Target Car "blows up" when hit. "Waste Disposal" Car emits light. Caboose. Plastic and steel. NMRA couplers for remote control coupling. 13 track sections, one rerailer uncoupler track. 800 milliamp power-pack. 37 inch train; 36x45-inch layout.
49 N 9970—Shipping weight 5 lbs. 10 oz..............$24.99

6-unit Freight action cars

Locomotive with headlight, tender .. runs fast, slow, forward, back; uncouples—by remote control. 3 remote-control cars: Lumber Car unloads logs into bin; Dump Car tilts cargo into another bin; Milk Can Unloading Car opens door as milkman makes delivery onto platform. Caboose. Plastic and steel. NMRA couplers. Remote-control track, uncoupler 12 curved tracks. 1¼-amp Power Pack 0–12-volt DC, 16-volt AC.
49 N 9973—32 in. train; 36x45-in. layout. Wt. 6 lbs. 10 oz. $29.88

NOTE: Power Packs in train sets above are UL approved for 110-120-volt, 60-cycle AC.

Lionel HO-gauge Cars. NMRA operating couplers.

[9] **Missile Launching Car.** Launching pad turns. Press firing pin, missile flies. Solid steel wheels.
49 N 9996—Plastic. 6 in. long. Shpg. wt. 8 oz.....$4.57

[10] **Helicopter Launching Car.** Track actuator sends plane skyward, rotor whirling. Steel wheels.
49 N 9994—Plastic. 6 in. long. Shpg. wt. 8 oz.....$5.94

Lighted Cars. Plastic. Steel wheels. 8 inches long.
(11) 49 N 9984—Observation Car. Shpg. wt. 9 oz. $4.42
(12) 49 N 9989—Vista Dome Car. Shpg. wt. 9 oz.. 4.42
(13) 49 N 9998—Baggage Car. Shpg. wt. 9 oz..... 4.42

[14] **Lionel HO-gauge Track.** Plastic ties, metal rails.
49 N 9990—Straight. 9 inches long. Wt. 4 oz.....18c
49 N 9991—Curved. 9 inches long. Wt. 4 oz.......18c

[15] **Rerailer-uncoupler Track.** 9 inches long.
49 N 9559—Shipping weight 5 ounces........$1.15

[16] **90° Crossover Track.** 6x6 inches long.
49 N 9543—Shipping weight 2 ounces........ 1.76

[17] **Remote Control Switches.** One right, one left hand switch, operate electrically. Control panel, wiring.
49 N 9542—Sold in pairs only. Shpg. wt. 1 lb.....$7.79
49 N 9541—Manual Control Switches. One right, one left. Switches set by hand only. Wt. 10 oz............$4.49

PCB SEARS 403

SEARS CHRISTMAS CATALOG 1962

Electric train manufacturers realized by 1962 that their products needed more action and user-involvement if they were to sell.

Both Lionel and Marx released items to make trains more exciting and to compete with slot cars. Even toy monorails were adding competition! Among Lionel's Space-Age action accessories were the new "Minuteman" Launcher Car, which fired a missile from an ordinary looking box car, the Aerial Target Car that kept a target balloon hovering above the car as it circled the tracks, and the new Mercury Capsule Launching Car which could shoot a miniature astronaut into the space above your home layout.

Prices of trains actually seemed to drop a little in 1962. Allstate offered your choice of two complete sets, with remote control features, for just $19.88. Lionel quietly offered its first H-O scale train sets, alongside their regular O-27 gauge trains.

Lots of Action
Racers zoom around curves, roar over and under bridge

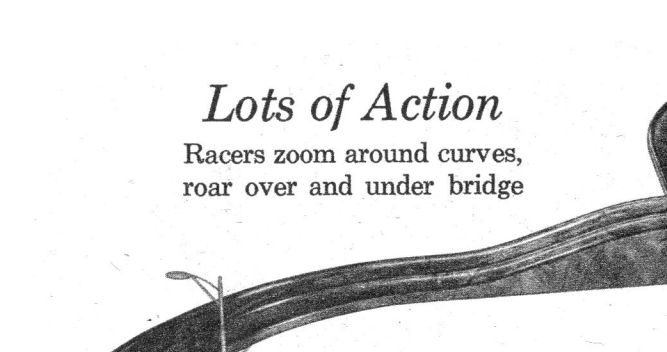

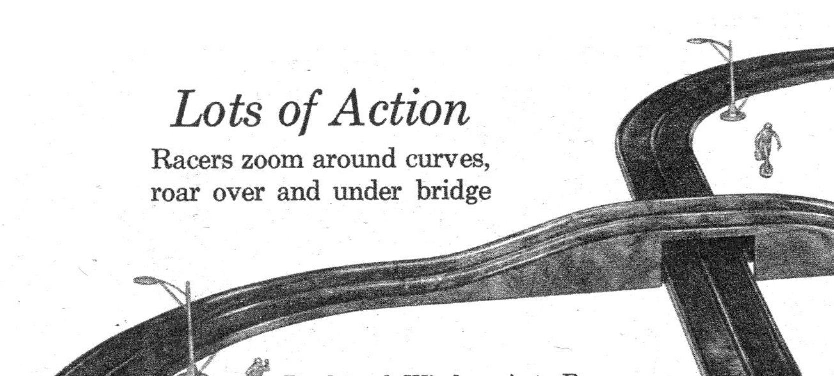

Dual-track Wind-up Auto Race .. nearly 5 feet long

$3.89

Cars zip down the straightaway, fighting for the lead. Speed under the bridge and around the 56x25-inch figure-8 track. Travel so fast over the bridge it almost looks like they'll fly in the air. Two 4-inch steel racers with long-running clock-spring motors, stop levers. Molded plastic track sections snap together. Includes plastic lamp posts, plastic figures in action poses.
49 N 5782—Shipping weight 2 pounds 8 ounces.................$3.89

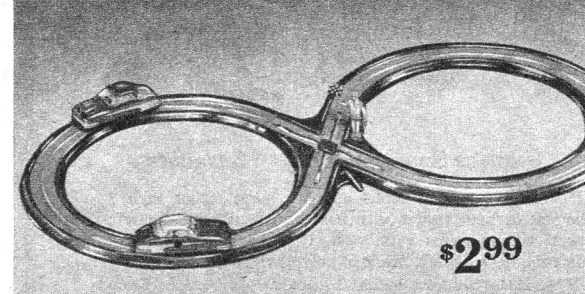

$2.99

Single-track Wind-up Auto Race

Starter waves his flag—they're off. Two 4-inch steel cars speed around 29x14-inch figure-8 track. Never collide at intersection .. one stops automatically, then continues. Clock-spring motors. Steel track snaps together. From West Germany.
49 N 4220—Shipping weight 1 pound 14 ounces.................$2.99

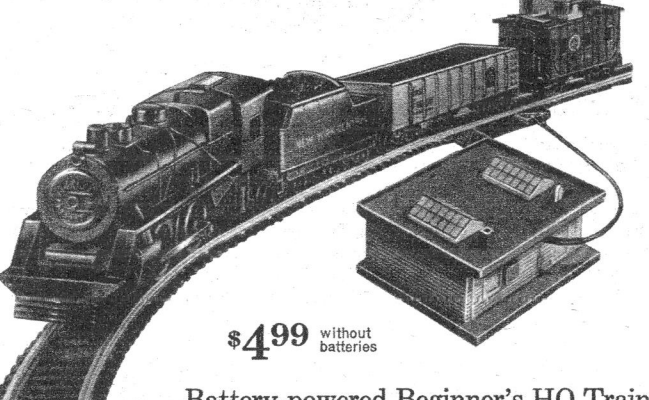

$4.99 without batteries

Battery-powered Beginner's HO Train Set

Rugged—takes rough handling. Runs on 3 batteries. Lever on station roof starts, stops, reverses train. Plastic engine, tender, gondola, caboose. 12 curved tracks, 1 straight, 1 rerailer make 35x30-inch oval track layout. Train 21¾ inches long.
49 N 9517—Train Set (*order 3 "D" batteries below*). Shpg. wt. 2 lbs.........$4.99
49 N 4660—"D" batteries. Shipping weight 4 ounces. Each 16c.........4 for 60c

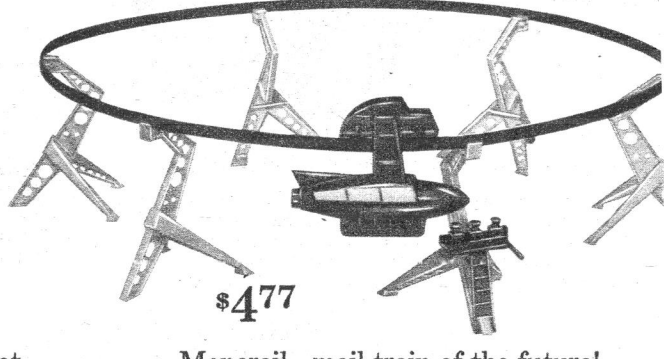

$4.77

Monorail—mail train of the future!

Just turn a knob—car travels .. push lever to load, unload mail bags while car is still in motion. 7-inch car runs on elevated fiber track about 9 ft. around. Order 1 "D" battery left. 6 plastic track supports, baggage platform, "mail bags."
49 N 9520—Shipping weight 1 lb. 9 oz.................$4.77

Wind-up Clock-motor Trains travel over big 102-inch oval tracks

$4.97

[1] "Western style" engine with huge cow catcher of plastic and steel. Colorful steel tender, baggage car and passenger coach. Train 32½ inches long. 8 curved, 2 straight track form 102-inch oval.
49 N 9516—Wt. 3 lbs.....$4.97

$3.97

[2] Husky plastic steam-type engine with tender emits harmless sparks. Metal gondola, box car, caboose. Motor has speed governor, on-off switch. 34 in. long. 8 curved, 2 straight track form 102 in. oval.
49 N 9512—Wt. 3 lbs. 4 oz..$3.97

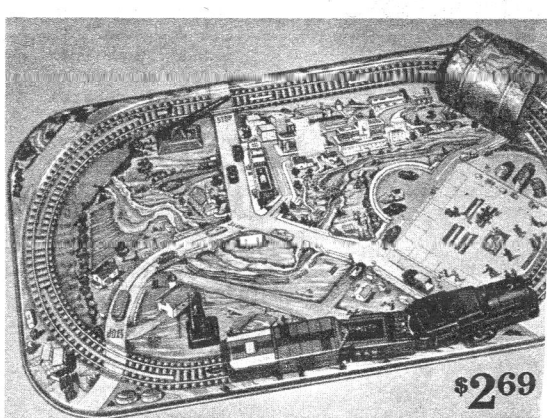

$2.69

Wind-up Train on Scenic Base

Look at it go! Speeds around curves, through a tunnel and a land of colorful scenery. Train energizes the railroad crossing—sempahore moves up and down as train passes. Grooved track guides train. Travels about 20 times around base on one winding—or over 100 feet of travel. Plastic locomotive with attached key, spring-wind motor .. lithographed metal tender and car. Colorfully decorated metal base about 22x13 inches wide; train about 11 inches long.
79 N 9511C—Shipping weight 3 pounds................$2.69

Lionel Matching Outfits

"027"-gauge 8-unit Train $49.77 cash NO MONEY DOWN

HO-gauge 8-unit Train $44.77 cash NO MONEY DOWN

"027" — Outside rails 1¼ in. apart. Engine about 4 in. high

HO-gauge — Rails 21/32 in. apart. Engine about 2 in. high

"027"-gauge 7-unit Train $39.77 cash NO MONEY DOWN

HO-gauge 7-unit Train $38.77 cash NO MONEY DOWN

8 units with whistle .. smoke .. 3 action cars

Freight whistles by remote control, speeds ahead puffing smoke .. headlamp beams. Pulls tender, "gold" bullion car, "log" car, "battling sheriff-and-outlaw" car, giraffe car, car with bobbing horses, caboose. Plastic, steel. UL listed transformer or powerpack for 110-120-v, 60-cycle AC. Uncoupling track. Both uncouple by remote control; HO has N.M.R.A. couplers.

75-in. "027"-gauge Train. Die-cast Magne-Traction engine. 12 tracks make 27x45-in. oval. 75-w. circuit-breaker transformer.
49 N 9657—Shipping weight 15 lbs...$49.77

47-inch HO-gauge Train. 8 tracks .. 36x45-in. oval. 1¼-amp. DC-AC powerpack.
79 N 9906C–Wt. 11 lbs. $44.77

7-unit Twin Diesel with horn .. 4 action cars!

Twin diesel locomotive has bright headlamp, wailing horn. Action-packed cars let you launch a helicopter, fire a "Minuteman" missile, blow up target car, fire "Turbo" missile. Caboose. Run train fast, slow, forward or backward .. uncouple cars, sound horn—all by remote control. Plastic and steel. UL listed transformer or powerpack for 110-120-volt, 60-cycle AC is included with set.

72-in."027"-ga.Train. Power unit diesel. Magne-Traction drive, more pull power. 12 tracks .. 27x45-in. oval. 60-w circuit break transformer.
49 N 9656—Shipping weight 13 lbs......$39.77

45-inch HO-gauge Train. 8 tracks .. 36x45-inch oval. 800-milliamp DC-AC powerpack.
79 N 9905C–Wt. 9 lbs. $38.77

Extra Lionel Cars and Accessories of plastic and steel

[1] "027" Crossing Signal, 7½ in. high. Light flashes, arm swings as the train passes by.
49 N 9827—Wt. 8 oz......$4.59
HO Crossing Signal, 4⅛ in. high. "Stop" arm swings as the train goes by.
49 N 9591—Wt. 4 oz......$4.59

[2] "027" "Minuteman" Switcher. 7½ inches long. Hauls, couples cars, both ends.
49 N 9857—Wt. 2 lbs. $11.97
HO "Minuteman" Switcher. 4 inches long; headlamp. Couplers at both ends.
49 N 9592—Wt. 8 oz....$4.59

Note: Rolling stock has working couplers

[3] "Turbo" Missile Launcher. Press firing pin. Missile whirls off at top speed .. blows apart exploding box car sold below. Spare missile.
"027"-gauge Car. 9 in. long.
49 N 9851—Wt. 1 lb...$5.69
HO-gauge Car. 5½ in. long.
49 N 9908—Wt. 8 oz....$5.49

[4] Cop and Hobo Car. Cop chases hobo. Hobo leaps to trestle. As train passes trestle again cop leaps to trestle but hobo escapes to car.
"027"-gauge Car. 9 in. long.
49 N 9855—Wt. 1 lb...$6.44
HO-gauge Car. 6 in. long.
49 N 9909—Wt. 8 oz....$5.77

[5] "Minuteman" Launcher. Roof opens, missile rises, fires to explode target car sold at right.
"027"-ga. Car. 10 in. long.
49 N 9811—Wt. 1 lb....$7.94
HO-gauge Car. About 6 in.
49 N 9911—Wt. 8 oz....$7.77

[6] "027"-gauge Trestle Set. 22 plastic piers, graduated from 3/16 to 4¾ inches high.
49 N 9845—Wt. 1 lb. 10 oz. $4.69
HO-gauge Trestle Set for over and under figure 8 layouts. 46 piers plus arch.
49 N 9979—Wt. 14 oz....$2.99

[7] Exploding Target Range Car. "Explodes" when hit with "Minuteman" or "Turbo" missile. Re-assembles.
"027"-gauge Car. 11 in. long.
49 N 9823—Wt. 1 lb....$4.79
HO-gauge Car. 6 in. long.
49 N 9920—Wt. 8 oz....$3.88

[8] Helicopter Launching Car. Spring-powered "whirlybird" soars into air at a touch of release button.
"027"-gauge Car. 10 in. long.
49 N 9856—Wt. 1 lb....$6.39
HO-gauge Car. 6 in. long.
49 N 9994—Wt. 1 lb....$5.77

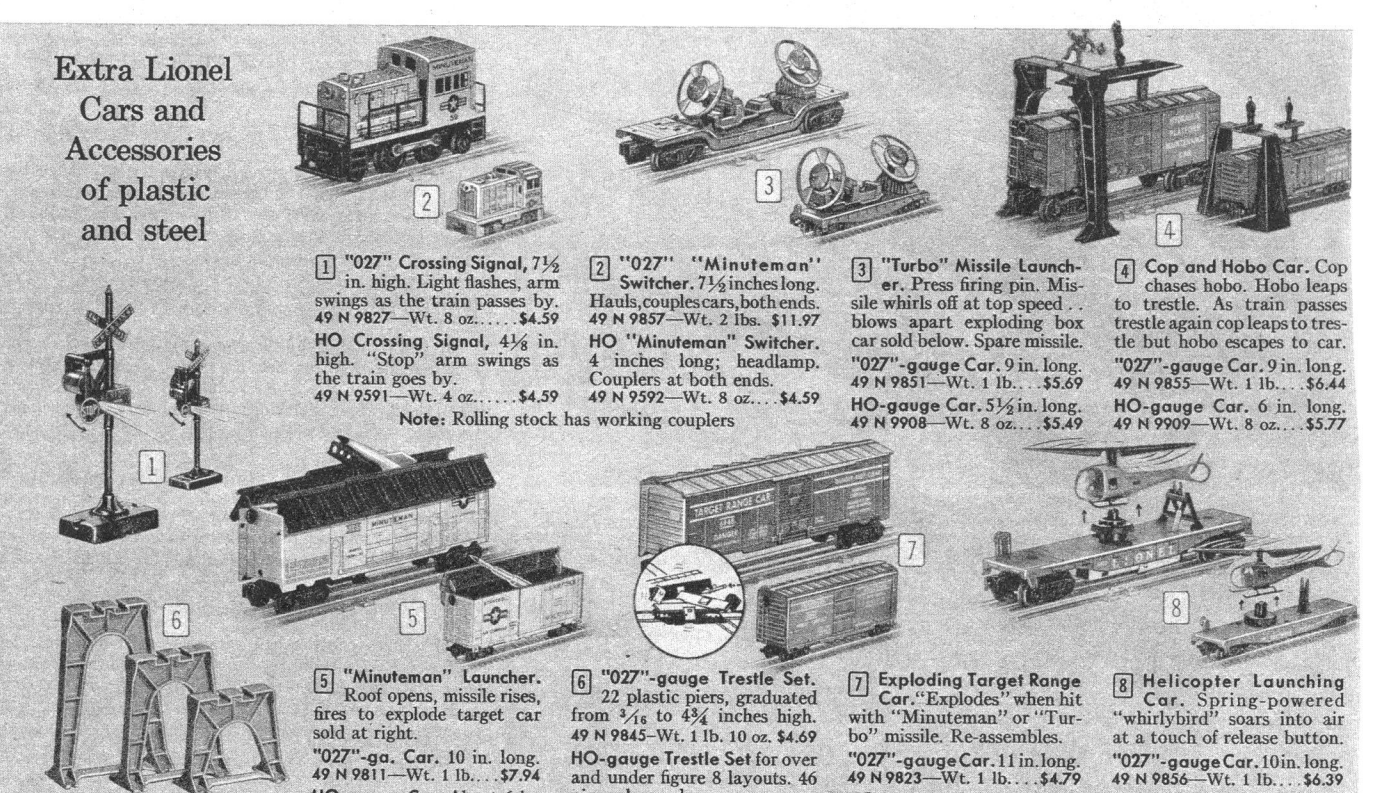

Lionel Accessories and Rolling Stock for "027", "O" and "Super O"-gauge layouts .. metal, plastic

HO-gauge 6-unit Train
$28.66 cash
NO MONEY DOWN

"027"-gauge 6-unit Train
$29.75 cash
NO MONEY DOWN

6-unit Diesel with "Space Age" cars. Fire the missile— target car "blows up"

Powerful GP-7 diesel locomotive with headlight hauls "space age" cars. Runs forward, backward, fast or slow .. couples or uncouples cars all by remote control .. even fires Turbo missiles. Box car "explodes" when hit, reassembles easily. Plastic, steel. UL listed transformer or powerpack for 110-120-volt, 60-cycle AC.

62-inch "027"-gauge Train. Has Magne-Traction diesel. 10 tracks make 27x36-inch oval. Includes 35-watt circuit-breaker transformer.
49 N 9655—Shpg. wt. 12 lbs. ... $29.75

38-inch HO-gauge Train. 8 tracks make 36x45-inch oval. Includes 800-milliamp DC-AC powerpack.
79N9904C—Wt. 7 lbs. $28.66

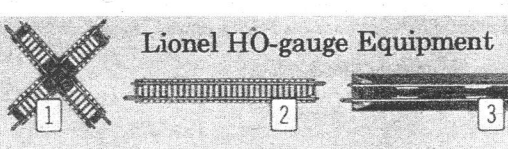

Lionel HO-gauge Equipment

[1] **6-inch 90° Crossover Track.** Plastic ties, metal rails.
49 N 9543—Shipping weight 2 ounces. ... $1.77

[2] **9-inch Straight Track Section.** Plastic ties, metal rails.
49 N 9990—Shipping weight 4 ounces. ... 19c
9-in. Curved Track Section. Plastic ties, metal rails. (Not shown.)
49 N 9991—Shipping weight 4 ounces. ... 19c

[3] **9-inch Rerailer-Uncoupler Track Section.** Operates N.M.R.A.* couplers, rerails cars.
49 N 9559—Shipping weight 5 ounces. ... $1.17

*All HO rolling stock have N.M.R.A. (National Railroad Association) standard operating couplers

Remote-control Switch Set: 1 right-hand, 1 left-hand. Sold in sets only. Work electrically. Push button to open or close. Control panel and wiring included.
49N9542—Wt. 1 lb. Set $7.67

Manual-control Switch Set: 1 right-hand, 1 left-hand. Open and close by hand.
49N9541—Wt. 10 oz. Set $4.47

"Multi-Volt" 2½-amp. Powerpack. Reduces 110-120-volt, 60-cycle AC current to low voltage to operate HO-gauge train. Supplies 2½ amps. at 0-14 volts DC to run train at varying speeds. Switch reverses train direction. AC circuit supplies 16 volts AC for accessories. Self-resetting circuit breaker protects against overload damage. UL listed.
49 N 9563—Shpg. wt. 4 lbs. $13.77

New Motorized Hand Car. 6 in. long. Self-propelled with continuous action! As the car moves along the track, gangmen raise and lower their arms in a realistic pumping motion. Shipping weight 1 pound 2 ounces.
49 N 9812 ... $7.89

Motorized Section Gang Car. Self-propelled. 5 in. long. When car strikes bumper or other object, it reverses direction and one of the gangmen moves to other side of car. Action is continuous. Shipping weight 1 pound 8 ounces.
49 N 9846 ... $6.39

Santa Fe Diesel Switcher. 12¼ in. long. Designed after the GM "SW2". Working headlight and horn. Front and rear couplers. Magne-Traction for greater pulling power. Ideal for switching operation. Shipping weight 3 pounds 8 ounces.
49 N 9814 ... $23.79

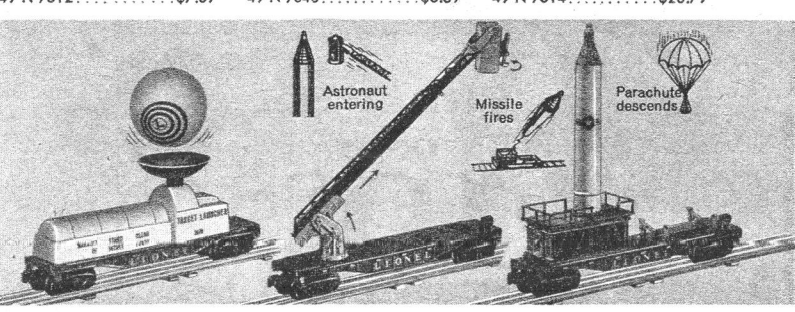

11-in. Aerial Target Car. Compressor generates air, keeps balloon aloft above traveling car. Remains aloft until hit. Uses 2 "D" batteries, order below.
49 N 9829—Wt. 1 lb. $7.89
"D" Battery. Wt. ea. 4 oz.
49 N 4660—Ea. 16c; 4 for 60c

New Cherry Picker Car. 11 in. long. Needed for space launchings! Ladder raises and extends, astronaut swivels out in full view. Use with car at right to give effect of astronaut being loaded into capsule.
49 N 9815—Wt. 1 lb. $5.66

New Mercury Capsule Launching Car. 11 in. long. Fires space capsule by remote control. Missile falls to earth. Mercury capsule continues to soar, then turns upside down, gracefully parachutes down.
49 N 9826—Wt. 1 lb. $7.89

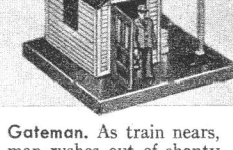

Sound Effects Record. 45 rpm. Adds realistic train sounds (clangs, whoos, clicks and steam sounds) to your railroading fun. Shipping weight 2 ounces.
49 N 9899 ... 59c

Gateman. As train nears, man rushes out of shanty swinging lantern. After train passes, man returns to shanty. 4½ in. high. Shipping weight 1 lb. 10 oz.
49 N 9835 ... $6.39

9-in. Highway Crossing Gate. As train passes, red lights go on, arm comes down. Lights go off, arm goes up automatically. Shipping weight 12 ounces.
49 N 9831 ... $6.39

"027" Track, Switches and Transformers

[4] **Straight Section "027" Track.** 8⅞ in. long.
49 N 9801—Shipping weight 3 ounces ... 19c
Curved Section of "027" Track. 9½ in. long.
49 N 9802—Shipping weight 3 ounces ... 19c
90° Crossover Track. "027"-ga. 7⅜x7⅜ in.
49 N 9803—Shipping weight 11 ounces ... $1.52

[5] **Remote-control Switch Set:** 1 right, 1 left-hand switch. Open, close electrically. Red, green signal lights. Control panel, wiring incl.
49 N 9806—Shipping weight 3 pounds. Set $13.79
Hand-operated Switch Set: 1 right-hand and 1 left-hand switch. No lights.
49 N 9805—Shipping weight 2 pounds. Set $5.79

[6] **Lighted Dead-end Bumper.** Red light.
49 N 9859—Shipping weight 8 ounces ... $1.97

Transformers. UL listed. Reduce 110-120-volt, 60-cycle AC to low voltage for trains. Circuit breaker protects against overloads.

[7] **125-Watt type LW for 1 train.** Throttle controls speed. Two buttons control train direction, horn or whistle. Two fixed accessory voltages. Lighted dial. "Shorts" indicator. Wt. 5 lbs.
49 N 9819 ... $14.49

[8] **130-watt type SW for 2 trains.** Separate throttles control speed and directions of each train. Button controls horn or whistle on 1 train. Circuit breaker. "Power-on" light. Wt. 5 lbs.
49 N 9840 ... $19.77

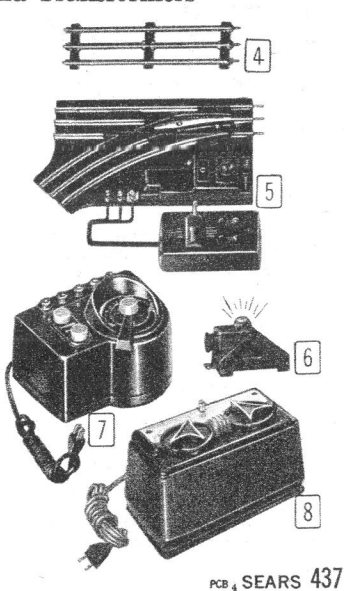

ALLSTATE®
Regular Gauge Electric Trains

Huge 8-unit set.. remote control.. Plus almost 14 feet of track

Stretch out this sprawling switch track railway.. and really cut loose. From straightaway to sharp curves, you're in command. Move the 65-inch train fast or slow, forward or reverse, even couple or uncouple cars by remote control.. or set your manually-operated switches from outer to inner oval.

Look what you get at this low price: 4-wheel-drive locomotive with light and chug-chug sound; tender, tank car, hopper, refrigerator car, 2 gondolas and caboose. 1 right, 1 left manual switch. Roadbed track includes 10 curved, 3 straight and 1 uncoupler section. 50-watt transformer with circuit breaker.
79 N 9624C—Shipping weight 11 pounds.....................Set $19.88

Either Set ONLY $19.88 cash
NO MONEY DOWN

6-unit Train includes 3 action cars.. scanning searchlight, rocket launcher and cattle car

Watch husky locomotive puff clean smoke and cool steam, its headlight beaming the way along almost 10 feet of track. Suddenly, launching car hits a "count-down" lever. You see Minuteman missile spring up for "blast off." Whoosh!, it's on its way.. and you follow rocket's path with searchlight. Back cattle car along loading platform. Door opens and a steer moves from car to platform.. pops back in as train moves on. Tender and gondola. Remote Control uncoupling; directional and speed control. Includes 8 curved, 3 straight, 1 uncoupler roadbed track, 50-watt transformer with circuit breaker. Train approximately 52 inches long.
79 N 9619C—Shipping weight 10 pounds......................Set $19.88

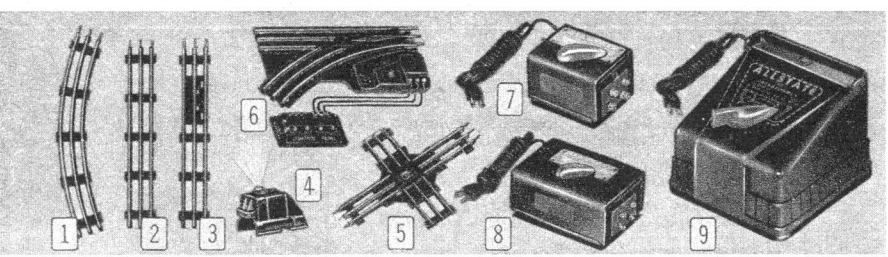

Wide-radius Track. Has 5 ties instead of 3, makes larger roadbed. Curves are gentle—trains can take curves at full speed. Fits all "ALLSTATE" and MARX electric trains.
(1) 49 N 9723—12½-in. Curved. Wt. 4 oz.....23c
(2) 49 N 9720—11¼-in. Straight. Wt. 4 oz....23c

[3] **Uncoupling Track.** For cars equipped with automatic couplers. "Uncouple here" sign. Also serves as road crossing. 11¼ in. long.
49 N 9749—Shipping weight 4 ounces........79c

[4] **End-of-track Bumper.** Blocks end of dead-end track. Has light. 2 in. high, plastic.
49 N 9707—Shipping weight 4 ounces.........87c

[5] **Crossover.** Build exciting figure-eight layouts. Each track 9¼ inches long.
49 N 9726—Shipping weight 4 ounces......$1.33

[6] **Electric Switch Set.** Remote controls and wires included. Lights signal position. One right-hand and one left-hand switch.
49 N 9727—Shipping weight 2 lbs.........$8.29

Manual Switch Set. No lights, etc. (not shown).
49N9776—1 right, 1 left. Wt. 1 lb. 12 oz...$4.49

Transformers. All have circuit breakers, 2 sets of binding posts, one for train, other for accessories. UL listed for 110-120-volt 60-cycle AC.

[7] **50 watt.** 7-13-volt for train speed, 13-volt for accessories. Steel case.
49 N 9721—Shipping weight 3 lbs........$5.47

[8] **100 watt.** 5-15-volt train circuit, 15-volt accessory circuit. Steel case.
49 N 9722—Shipping weight 4 lbs........$7.99

[9] **150 watt.** 0-15-volt train circuit. 15-v accessories. Throttle handle. Plastic case.
49 N 9724—Shipping wt. 10 lbs..........$11.99

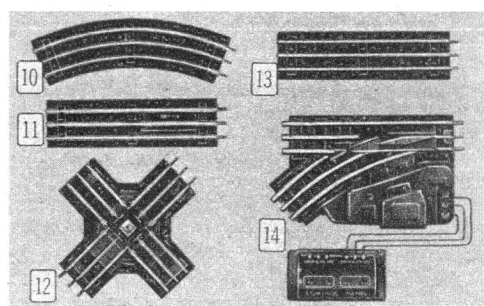

"Gravel roadbed" 3-tie Track

Same realistic track as used in Allstate regular gauge sets on these 2 pages. Use also with Marx trains.

[10] **9½-inch Curved.**
49N9702—Wt. 4 oz.........28c

[11] **8⅞-in. Straight.**
49N9701—Wt. 4 oz.........28c

[12] **Crossover.** 7½x7½ in.
49N9703—Wt. 4 oz. $1.39

[13] **8⅞-in. Uncoupling Track** to uncouple Allstate or Marx cars with automatic couplers. Add one or more to your layout.
49N9710—Wt. 4 oz....97c

[14] **Electric Switches.** Push button control panel. Signal lights show position. Complete with wires, panel. 1 left and 1 right switch. Shipping weight 2 lbs.
49 N 9706............$6.88

Manual Switches. Lever control. No light. (Not shown.) 1 left, 1 right switch. Shpg. wt. 1 lb. 12 oz.
49 N 9704............$3.89

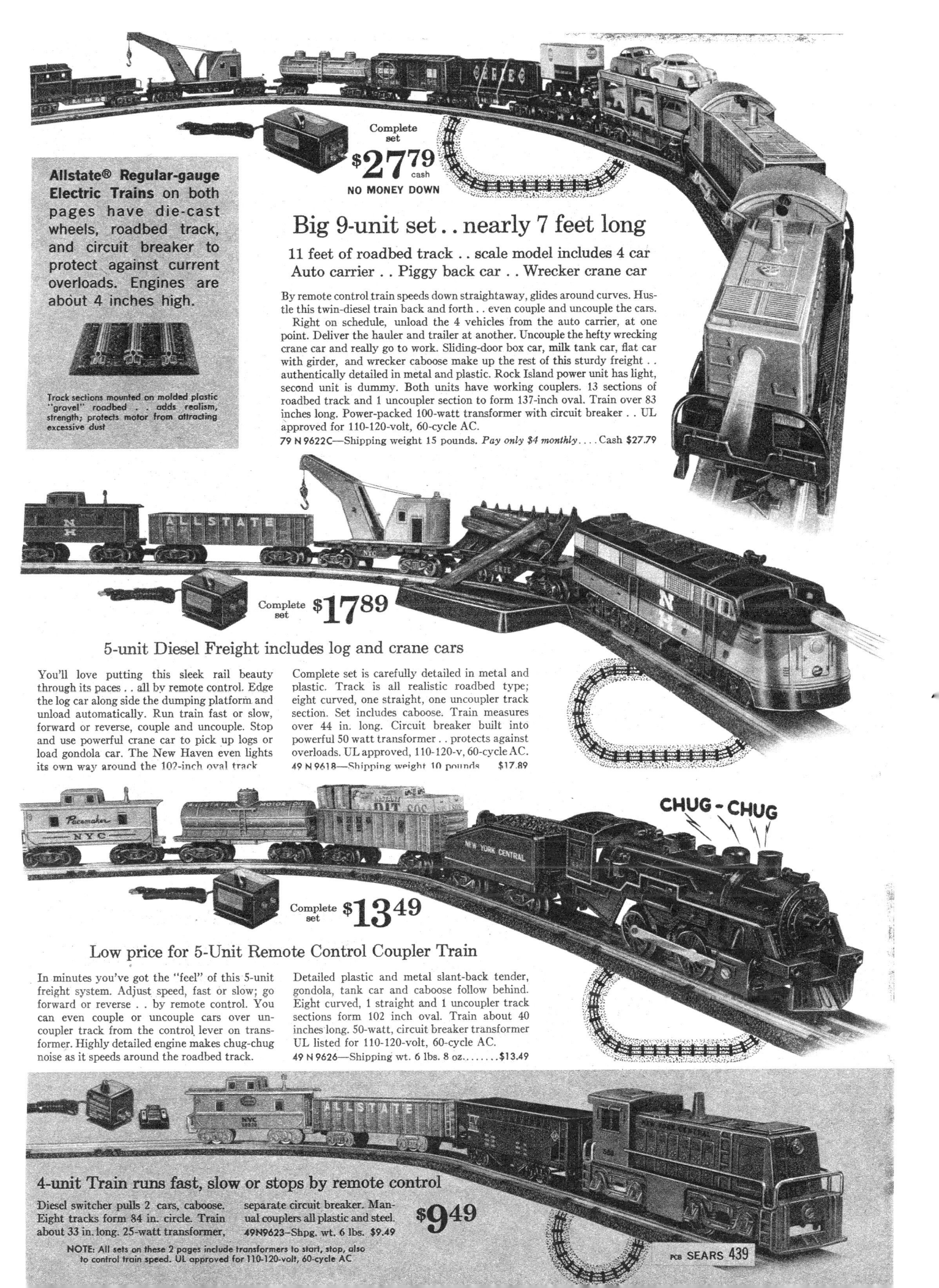

Allstate® Regular-gauge Electric Trains on both pages have die-cast wheels, roadbed track, and circuit breaker to protect against current overloads. Engines are about 4 inches high.

Track sections mounted on molded plastic "gravel" roadbed .. adds realism, strength; protects motor from attracting excessive dust

Complete set **$27.79** cash
NO MONEY DOWN

Big 9-unit set .. nearly 7 feet long

11 feet of roadbed track .. scale model includes 4 car Auto carrier .. Piggy back car .. Wrecker crane car

By remote control train speeds down straightaway, glides around curves. Hustle this twin-diesel train back and forth .. even couple and uncouple the cars.

Right on schedule, unload the 4 vehicles from the auto carrier, at one point. Deliver the hauler and trailer at another. Uncouple the hefty wrecking crane car and really go to work. Sliding-door box car, milk tank car, flat car with girder, and wrecker caboose make up the rest of this sturdy freight .. authentically detailed in metal and plastic. Rock Island power unit has light, second unit is dummy. Both units have working couplers. 13 sections of roadbed track and 1 uncoupler section to form 137-inch oval. Train over 83 inches long. Power-packed 100-watt transformer with circuit breaker .. UL approved for 110-120-volt, 60-cycle AC.
79 N 9622C—Shipping weight 15 pounds. *Pay only $4 monthly....Cash $27.79*

Complete set **$17.89**

5-unit Diesel Freight includes log and crane cars

You'll love putting this sleek rail beauty through its paces .. all by remote control. Edge the log car along side the dumping platform and unload automatically. Run train fast or slow, forward or reverse, couple and uncouple. Stop and use powerful crane car to pick up logs or load gondola car. The New Haven even lights its own way around the 102-inch oval track.

Complete set is carefully detailed in metal and plastic. Track is all realistic roadbed type; eight curved, one straight, one uncoupler track section. Set includes caboose. Train measures over 44 in. long. Circuit breaker built into powerful 50 watt transformer .. protects against overloads. UL approved, 110-120-v, 60-cycle AC.
49 N 9618—Shipping weight 10 pounds $17.89

CHUG - CHUG

Complete set **$13.49**

Low price for 5-Unit Remote Control Coupler Train

In minutes you've got the "feel" of this 5-unit freight system. Adjust speed, fast or slow; go forward or reverse .. by remote control. You can even couple or uncouple cars over uncoupler track from the control lever on transformer. Highly detailed engine makes chug-chug noise as it speeds around the roadbed track.

Detailed plastic and metal slant-back tender, gondola, tank car and caboose follow behind. Eight curved, 1 straight and 1 uncoupler track sections form 102 inch oval. Train about 40 inches long. 50-watt, circuit breaker transformer UL listed for 110-120-volt, 60-cycle AC.
49 N 9626—Shipping wt. 6 lbs. 8 oz........$13.49

4-unit Train runs fast, slow or stops by remote control

Diesel switcher pulls 2 cars, caboose. Eight tracks form 84 in. circle. Train about 33 in. long. 25-watt transformer, separate circuit breaker. Manual couplers all plastic and steel.
49N9623—Shpg. wt. 6 lbs. $9.49

$9.49

NOTE: All sets on these 2 pages include transformers to start, stop, also to control train speed. UL approved for 110-120-volt, 60-cycle AC

PCB SEARS 439

HO Gauge means track is about 2½ in. wide, engine about 2 in. high

7-unit H O Diesel Freight..
2-level scenic base.. over 20 ft. of track
..*plus* 65 other play pieces

Greatest array of features, most exciting action we've ever offered in an HO set at this low price

Complete with powerpack **$29.98** Cash   NO MONEY DOWN

Hobby size—scaled 50% smaller than regular or "027"-gauge trains—yet every bit as exciting. Seven-unit Diesel freight, 42 in. long, roars through the tunnel, past mountains and farm land as it streaks up and down the scenic layout. Locomotive has New Haven markings, gleaming headlamp. Runs fast or slow, forward or reverse, couples and uncouples its cars—all by remote control!

Scenic layout measures 45x55x5 inches high. Includes 65 lifelike plastic play pieces—trees, farm house, animals, telephone poles, etc. About 260 in. of running trackage with 33 sections of track giving continuous over-and-under rail system. Uncoupler-rerailer operates N.M.R.A.* couplers, puts cars back on track. Plastic cars include coal hopper, tank car, flat car with boat, flat car with two automobiles, sliding-door box car, caboose. UL listed 1½-amp. powerpack (110–120-volt, 60-cycle AC) has 4 posts; gives 4 to 18-volt DC to run train, 18-volt AC for accessories. Sent freight (rail or truck) or express.
79 N 9940N2—Shipping weight 21 pounds.....................Complete $29.98

HO Train and Turnpike Thriller

Combines the excitement of railroad and superhighway traffic in one big play set. Two autos speed along superhighway, stop to let 5-unit train roar by. It's all by remote control!

Complete with powerpack **$39.98** Cash   NO MONEY DOWN

Three youngsters can play at same time. One highballs the mighty Union Pacific Diesel freight under viaducts, through tunnels on the big 46x48-in. scenic mountain base with trees and plastic roadguards. Two other youngsters can race 1962 T-bird and Corvette, *each with its own speed control.*

Plastic-and-metal 28-inch train includes locomotive, hopper car, tank car, cement car, caboose. Run train fast or slow, stop or start—*all by remote control*. 112-inch track (15 track sections plus crossover).

The two plastic automobiles are 2¾ in. long and are powered by electric motors. Race along 129¾-in. 13-section turnpike. UL listed powerpack with circuit breaker reduces 110–120-volt, 60-cycle AC to 18-volt AC-DC. Sent freight (rail or truck) or express.
79 N 9548N2—Shipping weight 20 pounds.........Complete $39.98

6-unit ALLSTATE HO Freight..
19 feet of 2-level trestle track!

Lumbers up the grade .. across the high bridge ..
then down again. Hugs curves even at high speeds

$13.98 without powerpack

It takes a steady hand on the throttle to huff this mighty freight up the grade and across the trestle. Run train fast or slow, forward or back .. couple and uncouple cars— *all by remote control.*

Weighted plastic cars have NMRA* couplers to fit standard HO-gauge cars. Nylon trucks and wheels. Six-unit train is about 33 in. long. Includes metal-and-plastic switcher engine (dummy headlight), plastic hopper car, lumber car, cable car, low-side gondola, caboose.

Giant 229-inch trestle over-and-under track measures 34x45 in. Includes 23 sections of curved track, 5 sections of straight track, plus rerailer-uncoupler section, 30 graduated trestles, 2 bridge pillars. Powerpack not included; order below.
49 N 9956—Shipping weight 4 pounds 12 ounces............$13.98

All ALLSTATE® HO engines have Power-pull motors, will haul up to 15 cars. Rolling stock has NMRA* standard operating couplers.

[3] $19.88 without powerpack

[1] $8.88 without powerpack

[2] $15.95 without powerpack

ALLSTATE HO-gauge Freight Trains travel on realistic track with plastic roadbed

[1] **4-unit Industrial Switcher.** Just 20¾ in. long, but loads of fun! Run train fast or slow, couple or uncouple cars *by remote control.* New Haven switcher does not have headlamp that lights. Plastic cars have NMRA* couplers; include hopper, gondola and caboose. 112 inches of oval track (12 curved, 1 straight, 1 uncoupler-rerailer section). Powerpack not included; order below.
49 N 9950—Shipping weight 3 pounds.......$8.88

[2] **6-unit Diesel with bridge, track.** 36¾-in. train has engine with headlamp that lights, box car, flat car with 2 tractors, cement car, tank car, caboose. Runs forward or back, fast or slow, couples and uncouples cars. Over 10 feet of track (10 curved, 2 straight), also uncoupler-rerailer, ramps, and bridge. Metal and plastic. NMRA* couplers. Powerpack not included; order below.
49 N 9930—Shipping weight 5 pounds......$15.95

[3] **8-unit Steam-type Freight.** *Die-cast metal locomotive puffs smoke, has bright headlamp.* Plastic tender, auto car with 2 autos, box car, flat car with lumber, crane car, gondola, caboose—all with NMRA* operating couplers. Run 41-in. train fast or slow, forward or back, couple and uncouple cars *by remote control.* 112-in. oval track (12 curved, 3 straight, 1 rerailer-uncoupler). Order powerpack below (not incl.).
49 N 9968—Shipping weight 4 lbs. 10 oz.......$19.88

†NMRA. (National Model Railroad Association) standard operating couplers used on every ALLSTATE HO train will fit any standard make of HO gauge car.

[4] **7½-inch HO Uncoupler-Rerailer Track.** Operates NMRA* couplers and rerail cars.
49 N 9926—Shipping weight 4 ounces...75c

[5] **90° HO Crossover Track.** 7½ x 7½ in.
49 N 9927—Shipping wt. 8 oz.....$1.39

[6] **8¼-inch Curved Track.** HO gauge.
49 N 9925—Shipping weight 3 oz... 19c

[7] **7½-inch Straight Track.** HO gauge.
49 N 9924—Shipping weight 3 oz... 19c

[8] **Remote-control HO Switch Set:** one left, one right-hand. Push button to operate switch. With panel, wiring.
49 N 9929—Shipping wt. 1 lb....Set $6.99

[9] **Hand-operated HO Switch Set:** one left, one right-hand. Lever controls.
49 N 9928—Shpg. wt. 8 oz.....Set $4.59

[10] **Lighted Dead-end Bumper** with red light. Black plastic. ¾ inches high.
49 N 9923—Shipping weight 2 oz....78c

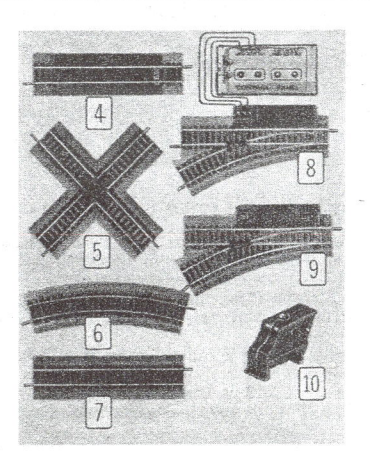

ALLSTATE HO Powerpacks. Convert 110–120-volt 60-cycle AC to low voltage needed. *UL listed.* All have circuit breaker to prevent shorts. 49N9922 and 49N9937 have 2 sets of binding posts: AC for accessories, DC for controlling train speed, direction and uncoupling operations.

[11] **Low priced.** Operates train only. 1 amp. 18-volt AC. 7.5-watt output.
49 N 9921—Shpg. wt. 1 lb. 10 oz....$4.49

[12] **Standard.** 1½ amp...4 to 18-volt DC for train, 18-volt for accessories.
49 N 9922—Shpg. wt. 2 lbs. 8 oz....$5.79

[13] **Our Best.** Has 2 circuit breakers and output of 45 volt-amperes. 0 to 14-volt DC for train control and 15-volt AC for accessories.
49 N 9937—Shpg. wt. 5 lbs..........$8.98

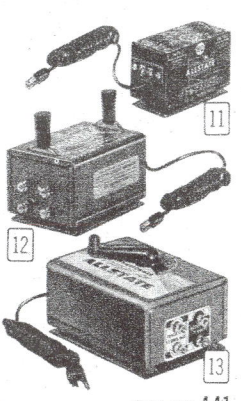

Create a giant 4-by-8 foot life-like countryside for your trains

SCENE-O-RAMA

Only $7.89 Complete outfit with instructions

Build your own train settings. True-color lichen in 3 shades make 15 trees, lots of shrubbery. Grass and earth color mats of flocked-on fiber to make roads, paths .. can be cut or draped. Snow-capped plastic tunnel. 3 lamps light .. are wired to hook up to track of your own electric train. Use with HO or regular gauge trains.
79 N 9713C—Shipping weight 5 lbs............$7.89

REGULAR GAUGE Accessories for ALLSTATE® or Marx Electric Trains

30-piece Station Set
Realistically molded plastic set includes: 15 railroad people in various poses, 5 station accessories (truck, bench, freight wagon, etc.); 10 other items (mail box, trash can, etc.). Men about 2 in. high.
49 N 9772—Shpg. wt. 10 oz....98c

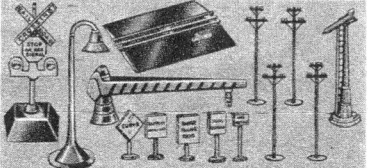

29-piece Railroad Scenery Set
Ideal for any regular-size train layout .. carefully detailed to scale in sturdy plastic. Set includes 12 seven-inch telegraph poles, 12 railroad right-of-way signs, one semaphore, lamp post, crossing gate, grade crossing sign, and crossing plate. Track not included.
49 N 9750—Shipping wt. 1 lb. 12 oz......$2.89

Trestle Bridge .. Tunnel
[1] Sturdy steel bridge has realistic rivet-head detail. Finished in bright aluminum color. 18 in. long.
49 N 9732—Shipping wt. 2 lbs.....$1.89
[2] Metal Tunnel. Colorfully decorated with landscape scene. 9x7x10 in. long.
49 N 9729—Shipping wt. 1 lb........84c

Plastic Trestle Set
[3] Create exciting layouts with grades and curves. 24 trestles and viaduct hold up to 22 feet of regular gauge track. Trestles graduate from ½ to 4¼ in. high.
49 N 9741—Wt. 2 lbs...$3.89

Whistling Station. Push button on control panel and hear loud train whistle. Detailed steel station is 9x5x5 in. high. Includes panel and necessary wires. Shipping weight 2 lbs.
49 N 9739......$3.97

Barrel Loader. Press remote button, truck takes barrel from loading chute to car (not included). Plastic about 9x8x5 in. high. With barrels, control and wiring. Shpg. wt. 1 lb. 6 oz.
49 N 9779......$3.99

Grade-crossing Shack. Watchman comes out, automatically, as the train nears. He holds stop sign as gate lowers. Steel shack 4½ in. high; base is 7x6½ in. Wires included. Shipping weight 2 lbs.
49 N 9760......$3.49

[4] **Plastic Water Tower.** Has girder-type construction to look like the real thing. Adjustable spout lowers for the "fill." Measures 8 in. high, 4 inches in diameter. Wide base legs. Shipping weight 8 ounces.
49 N 9731.........94c

[5] **Revolving Beacon.** Beams red and green lights. Plastic, 12 in. high. With wires. Wt. 12 oz.
49 N 9740.........$1.89
[6] **Crossing Flasher.** As train passes, lights flash. 7 in. high. Sturdy plastic. Wires. Wt. 8 oz.
49 N 9742.........$1.89

[7] **Crossing Gate.** 8-in. arm lowers, raises automatically as train passes. Plastic. Wires, track clips included.
49N9743—Wt. 8 oz. $1.87
[8] **Lighted Lamp Posts.** Set of 3. Plastic, 6 inches high. Wires.
49N9737—Wt. 10 oz. $1.94

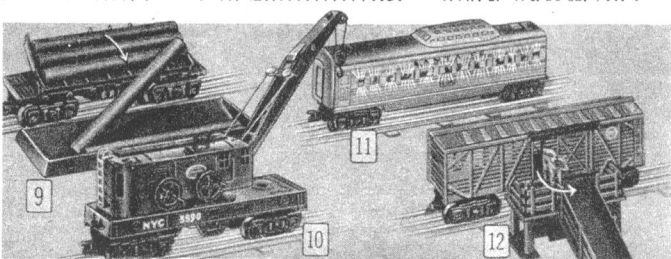

Engines and Hand Car run by remote control .. all have automatic couplers where needed

Handcar. Two workmen pump cross-bars as car goes around track. Electric motor, no couplers. Plastic and steel, 6 inches long. Shipping weight 12 oz.
49 N 9753........$3.39

Sleek Twin Diesel. Headlamp lights up. Electric motor in power unit, rear unit has coupler. Oilless bronze bearings.
Made of steel and plastic; die-cast wheels. 24 inches long. Shipping wt. 3 lbs 12 oz.
49 N 9782.........$11.97

Diesel Switcher. Makes rhythmic diesel noise. Detailed steel and plastic, 10 in. long. Electric motor, oilless bronze bearings. Headlight. Coupler on both ends. Shipping weight 2 pounds 4 ounces.
49 N 9783......$10.79

[9] **Log Car.** Touch button to unload 5 logs into plastic bin. Controls, wiring, special track section included. Plastic and steel. Shipping wt. 12 oz.
49 N 9761—Shipping wt. 12 oz....$4.39

[10] **Wrecker Crane.** Hand wheels control boom and cable. Cab swivels. 12 in. long, plastic and steel.
49 N 9786—Shpg. wt. 1 lb. 8 oz...$4.29

[11] **Lighted Passenger Cars.** Metal. Astrodome shown. Wt. ea. 1 lb.
49N9770—11-in. Astrodome...$3.47
49N9771—10¾ in. Observation 3.47

[12] **9-inch Cattle Car.** Back car to loading platform. Door opens; steer comes out .. pops in as train starts. With ramp. Plastic; steel.
49 N 9763—Wt. 1 lb........$3.47

Finely-detailed Buildings..
scaled to HO train and race sets
Only 88¢ Each

All of high-impact plastic .. sections simply "snap" together, no tools, no glue, no mess

Community Church
"Stone" look .. 8 in. high to steeple. 3¾x5 in. long.
49 N 9524—Wt. 6 oz...88c

School House
Red "brick" school house, gray "shingled" roof. 6½ in. long, 3 in. high, 2⅝ in. wide. Shpg. wt. 6 oz.
49 N 9527............88c

Suburban Station
With freight platform, luggage and accessories. 5½ inches long, 2 in. high, 3 in. wide. Shpg. wt. 6 oz.
49 N 9535............88c

Service Station
Modern highway service station with car, gas pumps. Building is 6 in. long, 3¾ inches high., 3½ in. wide.
49 N 9536—Wt. 6 oz...88c

Colonial House
Complete with awnings, shutters, even "colonial" pillars. 4½ inches long, 2½ in. high, 3 inches wide. Shpg. wt. 6 oz.
49 N 9537............88c

Barn with Silo
Real-looking barn with attractive "wood" siding, a "shingled" roof. Has attached shed and silo. 5 inches long, 4 inches high, 2⅝ inches wide.
49 N 9538—Shpg. wt. 6 oz.....88c

HO GAUGE Accessories and cars for sets with 21/32-inch wide track

Whistling Station. Press remote control button, hear "woo-woo" whistle inside plastic and steel station. 8 inches long. Wiring is included. Shipping weight 1 pound 4 ounces.
49 N 9919......$4.98

Build mountains, roads, trees and shrubs with easy-to-use materials. No special tools needed.

[1] **Grass and Earth Mats.** Colored fiber glued to heavy paper. Cut or drape in variety of shapes.
79 N 9571C—Grass. 50x99 in. Weight 3 lbs..$2.79
79 N 9572C—Earth. 33x48 in. Weight 1 lb.....94c

[2] **Tree and Shrub Material.** Lichen plants treated to stay soft, flexible. Natural colors.
49 N 9573—Shipping weight 12 ounces.....$2.79

Signal and Crossing Accessories. Approaching train activates unit .. each with special track and wiring.

[3] **Crossing Gate.** Arm swings down, raises as train passes. Gate is 3¾ inches long.
49 N 9947—Weight 4 oz.$2.49

[4] **Crossing Flasher.** Lights alternately. 2¼ in. high.
49 N 9954—Weight 4 oz.$2.37

[5] **Block Signal.** Red, green lights change.
49 N 9957—Wt. 6 oz.$2.59

[6] **Semaphore.** Arm lowers; red, green lights change. 4 in. high.
49 N 9955—Wt. 6 oz.$2.49

[7] **Trestle Set.** Includes 30 graduated trestles, and 2 viaducts. Build over and under figure 8's with your HO system. Plastic. Shipping weight 12 ounces.
49 N 9915—Set $2.69

HO Scenery Set 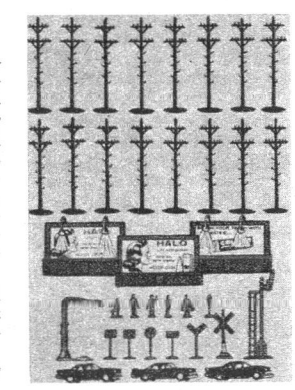
Rail and Road Scenery Set. Basic parts to any rural or suburban "atmosphere". Gives your HO train layout added realism. About 39 pieces in all .. includes railroad signs, billboards, 18 telephone poles, people, 4 cars, plus semaphore signal and watering station.

Each piece constructed of break-resistant plastic to small, HO scale. Shipping weight 1 lb.
49 N 9964.........$2.99

Huge 43-piece Railroad Accessory Set .. scaled to HO size

Snap together the plastic sections of this finely detailed set. Sturdy, colorful buildings and scenery .. plus people and accessories to round out most train layouts .. all in this one set.

See what's included at this low, low price. For the railyard .. a giant coaling station; a suburban and freight station with 3 people, accessories, switching tower and extras.

For the barnyard .. red barn with silo; ranch house; 4 farm buildings with 16 animals. Also, you get a gas station with car and pumps, a Cape Cod house and 12 telephone poles. All HO scaled in high-impact plastic.
49 N 9918—Shpg. wt. 1 lbs. 8 oz. $5.89

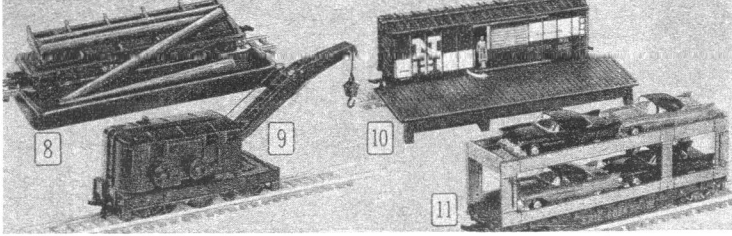

HO Scale Rolling Stock .. high-impact plastic .. all with NMRA* automatic operating couplers

Box Car. Build huge freight trains with this basic unit. 8 nylon wheels .. couplers. 5½ inches long.
49 N 9539—Wt. each 6 oz.
Ea. $1.00........3 for $2.79

*National Model Railroad Association couplers fit any standard make of HO gauge car.

[8] **Automatic Lumber Car.** Unload logs by pushing remote control button. Comes complete with 6-inch car, log bin, special track section and necessary wires.
49 N 9946—Shipping weight 8 oz......$3.29

[9] **Operating Crane Car.** Two hand wheels .. one raises and lowers boom, other lifts and lowers the hook. Cab swivels. 5-inch car.
49 N 9938—Shipping weight 8 oz.......$3.29

[10] **Automatic Box Car.** Train stops, door opens, man moves onto platform and jumps back in as train begins to roll. Car is 6 inches long.
49 N 9945—Shipping weight 8 oz....$3.29

[11] **Auto Carrier.** Drive 4 scale-model autos up the loading ramp. The 6½-inch long carrier has 2 levels.
49 N 9576—Shipping weight 4 oz...$1.88

Diesel Industrial Switcher. Yard switching is fun with powerful, compact unit. Scoot it busily around, couple and uncouple from front or rear. Plastic and metal. 4 wheel drive. 4 inches long.
49 N 9997—Shipping wt. 8 oz.$4.49

PCB SEARS 443

SEARS CHRISTMAS CATALOG 1963

When Sears' Christmas Wishbook arrived in homes in 1963, it was clear that the electric train market was way off.

Even the better selling H-O trains were being pushed out of the spotlight by fast, flashy slot cars. One train company, Marx, jumped on the bandwagon and released the $39.88 "Train and Speedway" set which combined an H-O train and two slot cars, a Thunderbird and a Corvette.

Sadly, Lionel barely managed to hang in and had only one train set offered in 1963. Adding insult to injury, Lionel's wonderful 9-unit set pulled by Santa Fe #218 Twin Diesels was forced to compete with a cheap Allstate set... "Your choice for $29.88".

Sears also offered several variations on its popular "all in one" H-O train sets with the pre-landscaped plastic bases.

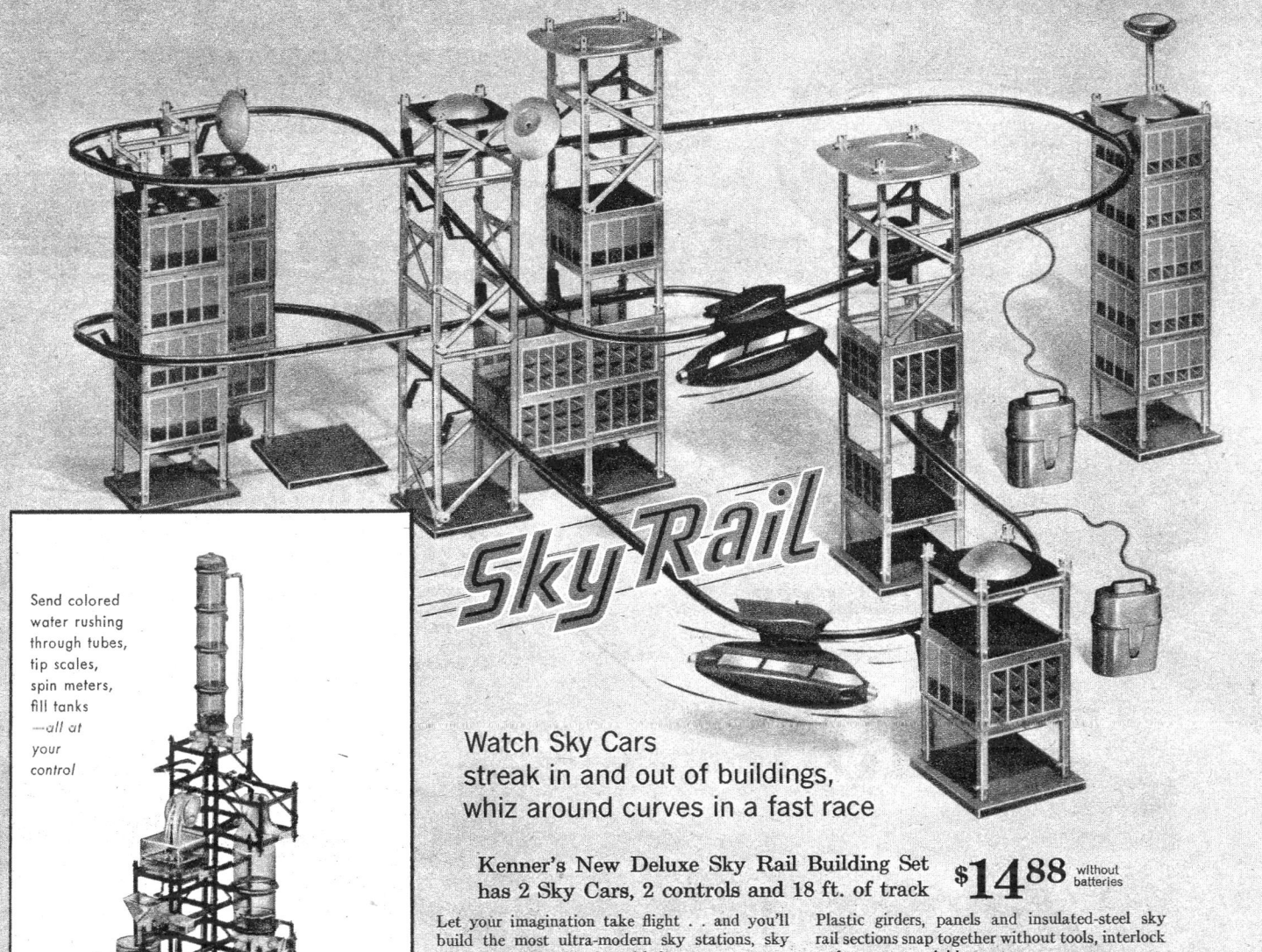

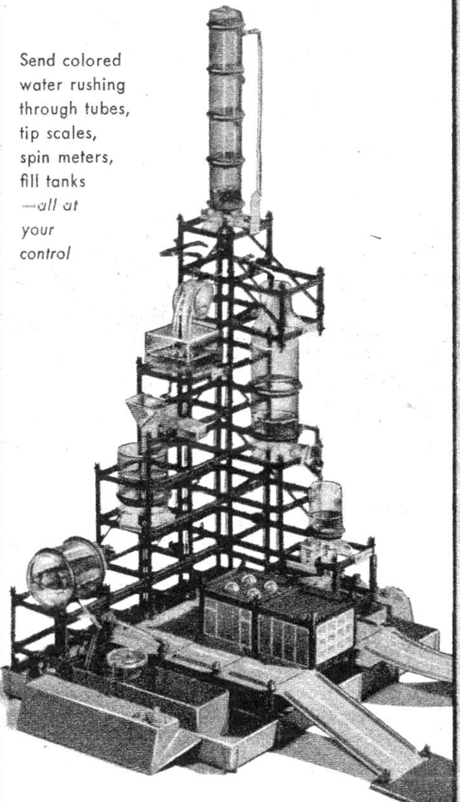

Sky Rail

Watch Sky Cars streak in and out of buildings, whiz around curves in a fast race

Kenner's New Deluxe Sky Rail Building Set has 2 Sky Cars, 2 controls and 18 ft. of track — **$14.88** without batteries

Let your imagination take flight . . and you'll build the most ultra-modern sky stations, sky ports, towers, terminals and heliports.

Two separate remote control units mean that Sky Cars can be operated at the same time by one child or two. Cars go forward or reverse . . even have headlights to add to the excitement.

Plastic girders, panels and insulated-steel sky rail sections snap together without tools, interlock to form strong, rigid structures.

Can be used in combination with any Kenner Girder and Panel set. 753 pieces plus project book. Uses 4 "D" batteries (sold below left).
79 N 1958C—Shipping weight 8 lbs $14.88

Sky Rail Set with 1 Sky Car, 1 control, 9-ft. track — **$9.66** without batteries

Offers the same fun and excitement of our Deluxe Set above but on a smaller scale . . 481 pieces.
Uses 2 "D" batteries (sold below left).
79 N 1965C—Shipping weight 6 lbs $9.66

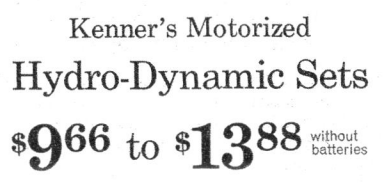

Send colored water rushing through tubes, tip scales, spin meters, fill tanks —all at your control

Kenner's Motorized Hydro-Dynamic Sets

$9.66 to $13.88 without batteries

Design and build industrial plants, refineries, chemical plants, purification systems up to 2½ feet high. Regulate flow of water with control pumps and valves. Watch water change color as it circulates . . just put color tablets in different tanks. Colorful, sturdy plastic parts snap together in a jiffy—without tools. Sets include plastic tray base and illustrated instructions. Motorized pumps operate on "D" batteries . . not included, order below.

Two Motor 634-pc. Set. 3 lights, 10 ft. of tubing, 20x13-in. base. Order 4 batteries.
79 N 1912L—Shipping wt. 9 lbs $13.88

One Motor 437-pc. Set. 6 ft. of tubing, 18x13-in. base. Order 2 batteries.
79 N 1911C—Shipping wt. 6 lbs $9.66

"D" Batteries. Shpg. wt. each 4 oz.
79 N 4660 . . . . Each 16c; 4 for 60c

Build a Kenner Subdivision . . erect 6 houses at one time or design your own mansion

Kenner's 410-piece set has patios, carport, swimming pools, chimneys, TV antennas. Design 8-inch high Cape Cod, Colonial, Ranch-style and other homes.

Add the finishing touch of landscaping with trees, shrubs, trellises. Plastic frames, panels are break resistant. Six Masonite Presdwood foundations (four, 8x9 in., two, 9x11 in.). Illustrated plans book.
79 N 6327C—Shipping wt. 8 lbs $7.99

SEARS 181

ALLSTATE
Regular Gauge Electric Trains

Either set Only $19.88

Huge 9-unit Set
Diesel-type locomotive with headlight .. automatic coupler .. over 14 ft. of track

Train so long engine just misses caboose at crossover. You can run it fast or slow .. run it in reverse to any point along the sprawling figure-8 roadside track .. couple or uncouple cars—all by remote control. Big New Haven locomotive lights its own way around the 176-inch track circumference. Locomotive and cars scaled to look like the real thing. Includes 5 straight, 12 curved track with roadbed, 90° crossover, 1 uncoupler section, 1 "Uncouple Here" sign and 1 track connector. Train measures approximately 79 inches long. Track makes layout about 63x27 inches wide. 50-watt circuit-breaker transformer. UL approved for 110-120-volt, 60-cycle AC.
79 N 9757C—Shipping weight 13 pounds.........Set $19.88

6-unit Train
Scanning searchlight, rocket launcher and cattle car

Locomotive puffs clean smoke, cool steam. Headlight beams along almost 10 feet of track. Suddenly, launching car hits "countdown" lever—Minuteman missile springs up for "blast off" .. and whoosh! It's on its way! Follow rocket with searchlight! Back cattle car along loading platform. Door opens and a steer moves from car to platform, pops in as train moves on. Tender and gondola. Remote control uncoupling; directional and speed control. 8 curves, 3 straight, 1 uncoupler track, 50-watt transformer with circuit breaker. Train about 52 inches long.
79 N 9619C—Shipping weight 10 pounds.........Set $19.88

Complete Set $14.97

5-unit Diesel Freight Train with unloading log car

Powerful Union Pacific diesel pulls an Allstate tank car, gondola, log car and caboose around 8½-foot track. Press lever .. log car dumps its load in roadside bin. Detailed metal and plastic train is about 43 inches long.

28x37-inch oval includes 10 sections of roadbed track with attached uncoupling ramp. "Uncouple Here" sign, too. 25-watt transformer is UL approved for 110-120-volt, 60-cycle AC.
79 N 9716C—Shipping wt. 10 lbs. Set $14.97

5-Unit "chug-chug" Freight Train with automatic log car

Steam-type engine makes chug-chug noise as it speeds along. Headlight casts a bright beam. Adjust speed fast or slow. Ease log car alongside bin and unload logs automatically. 8 curved, 2 straight track, 1 track connector form 102-inch oval. Train measures about 41 inches long. Includes 25-watt transformer UL approved for 110-120-volt, 60-cycle AC.
49 N 9715—Shpg. wt. 6 lbs. 4 oz....Set $8.97

Complete Set $8.97

ALLSTATE 6-unit Set

Switch cars into sidings . . couple and uncouple them by remote control . . load and unload them with derrick

Engine puffs smoke, cool steam, has bright headlamp. Couple or uncouple cars by remote control. Switch cars into siding, use trailer-truck and autos separately—many other fun possibilities. Set has 8 straight, 8 curved roadbed tracks; 2 uncoupling tracks, 2 "Uncouple Here" signs, 2 switches, bridge, 8 telephone poles, 2 lighted lamp posts, billboard, 2 dead end bumpers, station with figures, 6 autos, 20 empty cartons, track connector, smoke refill. Train 48 in. long; track about 28x64 in. 50-watt transformer, circuit breaker, UL approved, 110–120-volt, 60-cycle AC.
79 N 9719L—Shipping weight 18 pounds.....................Set $29.88

Regular Gauge Electric Trains

Either set $29.88 cash NO MONEY DOWN

LIONEL 9-unit Set

Powerful double-unit engine pulls 7 cars at terrific speeds without jumping track

If you like the excitement of a long train coming down the line and rounding the curves at high speed, then this is for you. Magne-Traction holds train securely to track. Big "AA" Santa Fe diesel unit with headlight . . plus a realistic diesel horn you operate by remote control. Couple and uncouple cars by remote control. Two box cars; hopper car; animated rodeo car; miscellaneous car; tank car; caboose. 5 straight, 8 curved tracks; 1 uncoupling straight track. Train is 87 inches long. Track 130 inches; forms 28x56-inch oval. Includes 60-watt transformer with circuit breaker, horn controller . . UL approved for 110–120-volt, 60-cycle AC.
49 N 9730—Shipping weight 13 pounds.....................Set $29.88

REGULAR GAUGE TRAINS ON BOTH PAGES

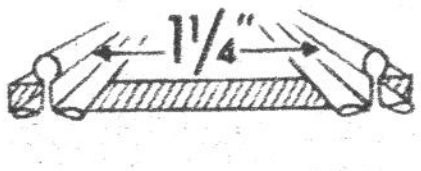

All trains on these two pages have die-cast wheels, three-rail 1¼-in. wide tracks, and circuit breaker to protect against current overloads. Engines about 4 inches high.

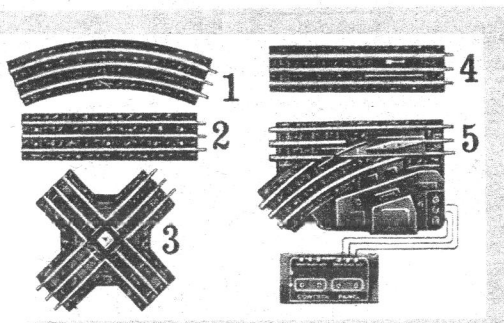

Whistling Station

Push button on control panel and hear whistle as train speeds along. Made of steel, 9x5x5 in. high. With wires.
49 N 9739—Wt. 2 lbs..$3.97

"Gravel roadbed" 3-tie Track

For Allstate or Marx regular gauge sets. Metal, plastic.

1. **Curved Track.** 9½ inches long.
   49 N 9702—Shipping weight 4 ounces..........28c
2. **Straight Track.** 8⅝ inches long.
   49 N 9701—Shipping weight 4 ounces..........28c
3. **Crossover Track.** 7½x7½ inches long.
   49 N 9703—Shipping weight 4 ounces..........$1.39
4. **Uncoupling Track.** 8⅜ inches long.
   49 N 9710—Shipping weight 4 ounces..........97c
5. **Electric Switches.** Push-button control panel. Lights signal position. 1 left and 1 right switch. Wires.
   49 N 9706—Shipping weight 2 pounds........Set $6.88
   Manual Switches. Lever control, no light. 1 left, 1 right.
   49 N 9704—(Not shown.) Shpg. wt. 1 lb. 12 oz. Set $3.89

Regular-gauge Transformers. Steel cases. Circuit breakers. UL listed. 110–120-v, 60-c. AC.
6. 50 watt. 7–13-v. for train, 13-volt for accessories.
   49 N 9721—Wt. 3 lbs..$5.47
7. 100 watt. 5–15-v. for train, 15-volt for accessories.
   49 N 9722—Wt. 4 lbs..$7.99

$7.89 Complete

Create a giant 4x8-ft. countryside layout

SCENE-O-RAMA

Picture your train or road race in a natural setting like this. Or arrange any way you like. True-color lichen in 3 shades make 15 trees, lots of shrubbery. Grass and earth mats of flocked-on fiber make roads, paths . . can be cut or draped. Snow-capped plastic tunnel. 3 lamps light up . . wired to hook up to track of your electric train or road race set . . HO or regular gauge. Instructions.
79 N 9713C—Shpg. wt. 4 lbs..$7.89

Grass and Earth Mats. Colored fiber glued to heavy paper. Cut or drape in variety of shapes. (Not shown.)

Grass Mat. 99x50 inches wide.
79 N 9571C—Shpg. wt. 3 lbs..$2.79
Earth Mat. 48x33 inches wide.
79 N 9572C—Shipping wt. 1 lb. 94c

Our Biggest HO-gauge Train and Track Layout

7-unit Diesel Freight .. 2-level scenic board 4½ feet long, almost 22 feet of track .. *plus* 65 other plastic play pieces

Complete with powerpack **$29.88** cash **NO MONEY DOWN**

HO size—scaled 50% smaller than regular or "027"-gauge trains—yet every bit as exciting. 7-unit train, 43 in. long, roars through the tunnel, past mountains and farmland, as it streaks up and down the scenic layout. Runs fast or slow, forward or reverse. Couples and uncouples cars—all by remote control. Plastic layout measures 47x54x5¾ in. high. Includes 65 lifelike plastic play-pieces .. trees, telephone poles, farm set, service station with cars. 263-in. spiral track has 33 sections giving a continuous over-and-under rail system. Uncoupler-rerailer operates coupler, lines up wheels on track. Plastic cars include Diesel locomotive with headlight, Diesel dummy "B" unit, flatcar carrying 2 automobiles, chemical fuel tank car, hopper car, boxcar, caboose. UL listed 1½-amp. powerpack (110-120-volt, 60-cycle AC) has 4 posts; gives 4 to 18-volt DC to run train, 18-volt AC for accessories. Sent freight (rail or truck) or express.
79 N 9949N2—Wt. 22 lbs. Complete $29.88

43-pc. Railroad Accessory Set .. scaled to HO size. Plastic sections snap together. Includes: for the rail-yard .. a giant coaling station, a suburban and freight station with 3 people, accessories, switching tower and extras. Also red barn, silo, ranch house, 4 farm buildings with 16 animals, gas station with car and pumps, Cape Cod house, 12 telephone poles.
49 N 9918—Shpg. wt. 1 lb. 8 oz. $5.89

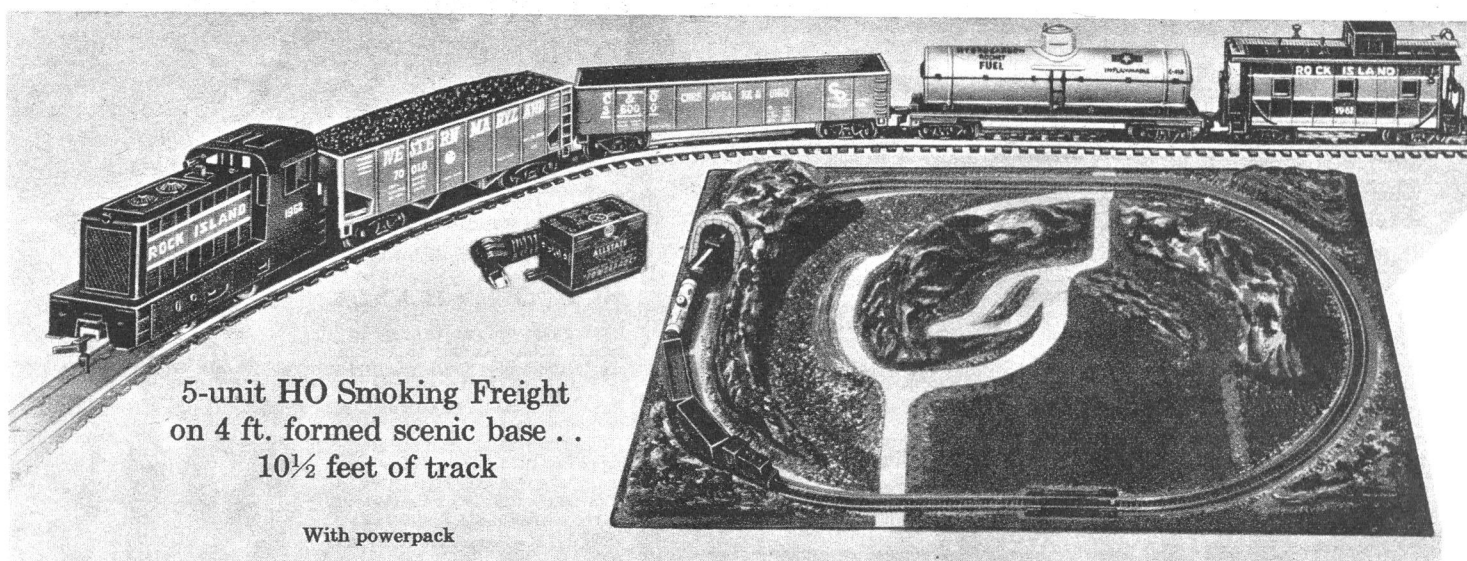

5-unit HO Smoking Freight on 4 ft. formed scenic base .. 10½ feet of track

With powerpack
$19.88

Create your own scenic railroad layout at a minimum of cost and work. You can uncouple cars, run 26½-in. train fast, slow, forward, reverse .. all by remote control. Rock Island Diesel switcher pulls chemical tank car, hopper, gondola, caboose. Plastic, metal construction. 127-in. oval track includes one uncoupler-rerailer, 15 track sections. 48x34-in. base is plastic detailed with tunnel, mountains, roads. You can add own accessories for more detail (see accessory set above). Powerpack has circuit breaker (reduces 110-120-volt, 60-cycle AC to 18-volt DC). UL approved. Sent freight (rail or truck) or express.
79 N 9632N2—Shpg. wt. 18 lbs. .... Set $19.88

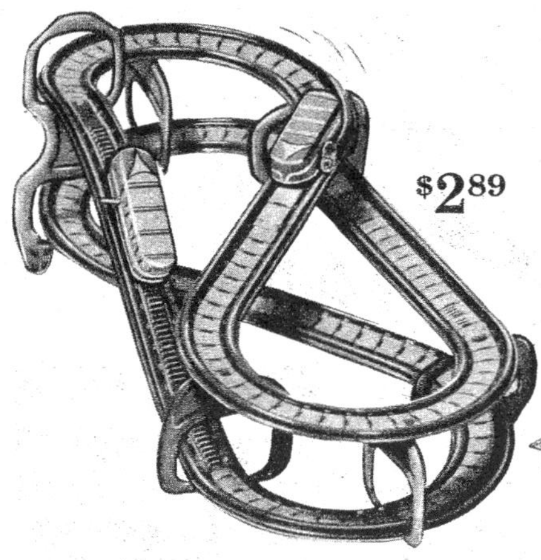

Battery-powered HO Train Set—
locomotive smokes, whistles..
cars uncouple automatically

Wind-up Roller Coaster
$2.89

Exciting amusement park and all you have to do is wind it up. Cars zip around 92-inch track .. "shooting the chute" on two levels at once.

Each car has people painted at the windows to make it more realistic. Both cars 3¼ in. long; all metal. Track easily set up, 10 in. high. From Japan.
49 N 4246—Shpg. wt. 1 lb. 12 oz. $2.89

Traffic Control Set by OHIO ART
$2.99

Cars wind up, run along the roads, around curves, into parking areas .. and you control them with 4 hand-operated levers. Set includes three cars, each 3⅜ inches long. Board is generous 14x19½ inches long. Entire unit is all metal to make it last. Painted cities and parks add travel interest.
79 N 5701L—Shpg. wt. 3 lbs.....$2.99

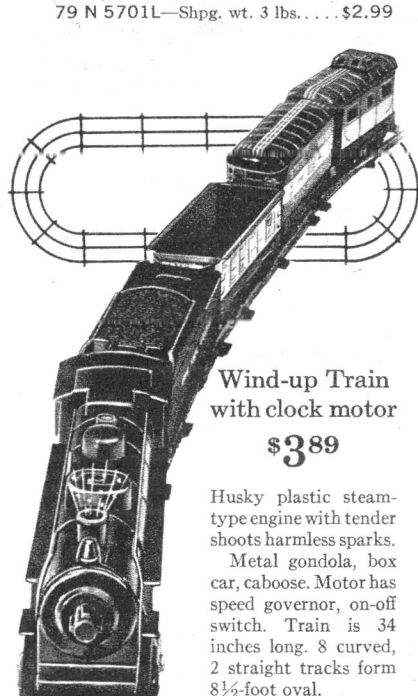

Wind-up Train with clock motor
$3.89

Husky plastic steam-type engine with tender shoots harmless sparks. Metal gondola, box car, caboose. Motor has speed governor, on-off switch. Train is 34 inches long. 8 curved, 2 straight tracks form 8½-foot oval.
Shpg. wt. 3 lbs. 2 oz.
49 N 5731....$3.89

All steel and only $4.89 without batteries

Hear it whistle, see it smoke as it chugs around the 8-foot oval track. Includes steam locomotive, coal tender, Santa Fe freight car, New York Central gondola, steel "power pack" control tower. 14 pieces HO-gauge track. From Japan. Order 4 "D" batteries below.
49 N 5777—Shipping weight 2 pounds 8 ounces.........Set $4.89
49 N 4660—"D" Battery. Shpg. wt. ea. 4 oz. Each 16c.... 4 for 60c

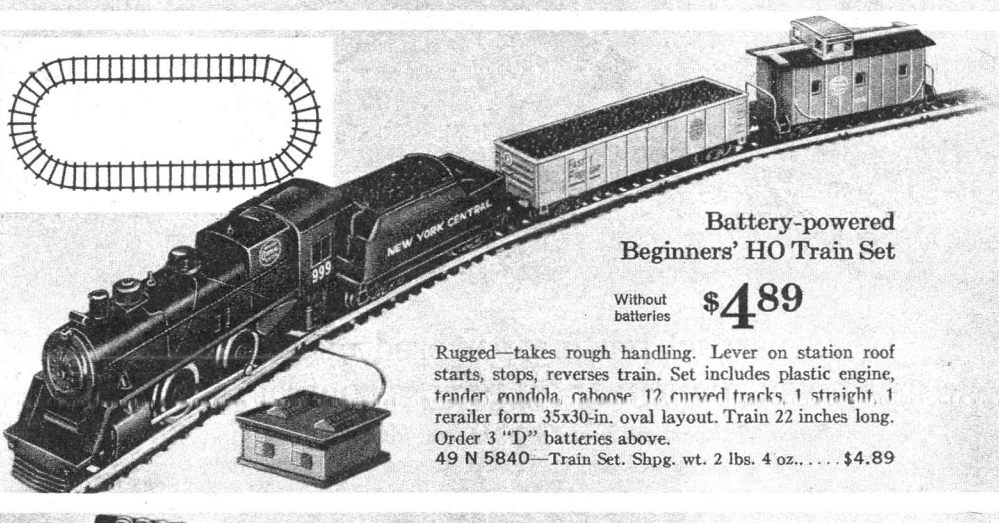

Battery-powered Beginners' HO Train Set
Without batteries $4.89

Rugged—takes rough handling. Lever on station roof starts, stops, reverses train. Set includes plastic engine, tender, gondola, caboose, 12 curved tracks, 1 straight, 1 rerailer form 35x30-in. oval layout. Train 22 inches long. Order 3 "D" batteries above.
49 N 5840—Train Set. Shpg. wt. 2 lbs. 4 oz.....$4.89

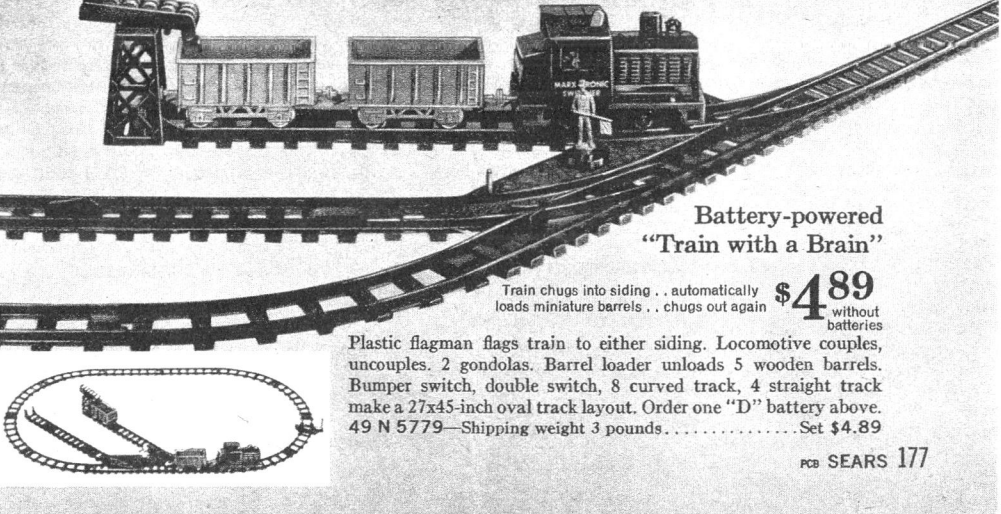

Battery-powered "Train with a Brain"
$4.89 without batteries

Train chugs into siding .. automatically loads miniature barrels .. chugs out again

Plastic flagman flags train to either siding. Locomotive couples, uncouples. 2 gondolas. Barrel loader unloads 5 wooden barrels. Bumper switch, double switch, 8 curved track, 4 straight track make a 27x45-inch oval track layout. Order one "D" battery above.
49 N 5779—Shipping weight 3 pounds............Set $4.89

SEARS 177

Train and Speedway thrills galore
Separate controls for split-second timing

5-unit HO Diesel plus two 2½-inch jet-speed racers zoom around hairpin curves .. 112-inch track, 130-inch speedway track

By MARX

Complete with powerpack $39.88 cash **NO MONEY DOWN**

Scenic plastic base 46x48x4⅜ inches with 16 movable trees and 6 movable fence sections provides the background for this exciting train and turnpike set.

28-inch train of plastic and metal. Diesel-switcher locomotive, tank car, hopper car, cement car and caboose. Runs fast or slow, stops or starts—all by remote control. 112-inch track has 13 sections plus grade crossing.

1963 plastic Thunderbird and Corvette Sting Ray automobiles each 2½ inches long. Powered by electric motors, each has its own speed control to send it racing along the 130-inch, 13-section turnpike track.

UL listed powerpack with circuit breaker reduces 110-120-volt, 60-cycle AC to 18-volt AC-DC. Set assembles easily. Shipped freight (rail or truck) or express.
79 N 9602N2—Shipping wt. 19 lbs........Set $39.88

---

17 pieces of asphalt-black track form 2x4-foot figure 8
By ELDON
$9.97 with powerpack

9 ft. of track .. 15 pieces with 2 lane changers
By MARX
$14.88 with powerpack

Over-and-under track with sharp curves challenge two 1/32-scale 5-inch racers

Test your racing skill in keeping the cars from skidding off those tight curves as they speed around the grooved track. 5-inch plastic cars are modeled after famous Indianapolis racers and each has its own pre-wired push-lever throttle .. lets you control amount of speed. Stop, start, slow down or speed up, just like you were driving. 17 pieces of pre-wired track fit together in minutes without the use of glue or tools. 6 cross-over supports hold track steady. 8 sections of polyethylene fence, decal set and instructions for assembling included. 6-volt powerpack UL approved for safety. (Input 110-120-volt, 60-cycle AC; output 3-volt DC, 1.5 amp.)
49 N 9513—Shipping weight 5 pounds 8 ounces................Set $9.97

Two 1/32-scale 5-inch racers speed around over-under track with dangerous crossovers

You'll thrill to the excitement of a near-miss when the Mercedes and Jaguar meet at the tricky lane changers. 3 pieces of narrow (chicane) track at the bridge test your skill in maneuvering through obstacles. 5-inch plastic cars are held in the metal track grooves by plastic guide pins. Each car has its own push button control powered by the UL listed powerpack (input 110-120-volt, 60-cycle AC; output 3-volt DC. 2 amp.). Instructions, 4 extra pickup shoes, 2 high trestles, 2 low trestles, bridge sides and 12 fence sections included.
49 N 9630—Shipping weight 7 pounds 8 ounces................Set $14.88

SEARS CHRISTMAS CATALOG 1964

Thankfully, electric trains made a bit of a comeback in the 1964 Sears Christmas Wishbook.

Trains offered ranged from a $2.99 battery-powered tin set "with light" up to a combo H-O Road Race and Train Set by Marx for $39.88. Gone were the $50 deluxe Lionel locomotives and fancy accessories of years past.

In order to rescue its market share, Lionel came up with several action-oriented O-27 sets and received two full pages in the catalog.

These sets included the Military Freighter set complete with "Long Tom" missile, army soldiers and exploding box car; the Trestle Set, which featured an over-and-under track plan and whirling satellite launching car; and the Giant Steam Freighter Set at $29.99 which included the famous Lionel Culvert Pipe Loader accessory, one of the more valuable collector's items today.

Just set lever, car unloads automatically

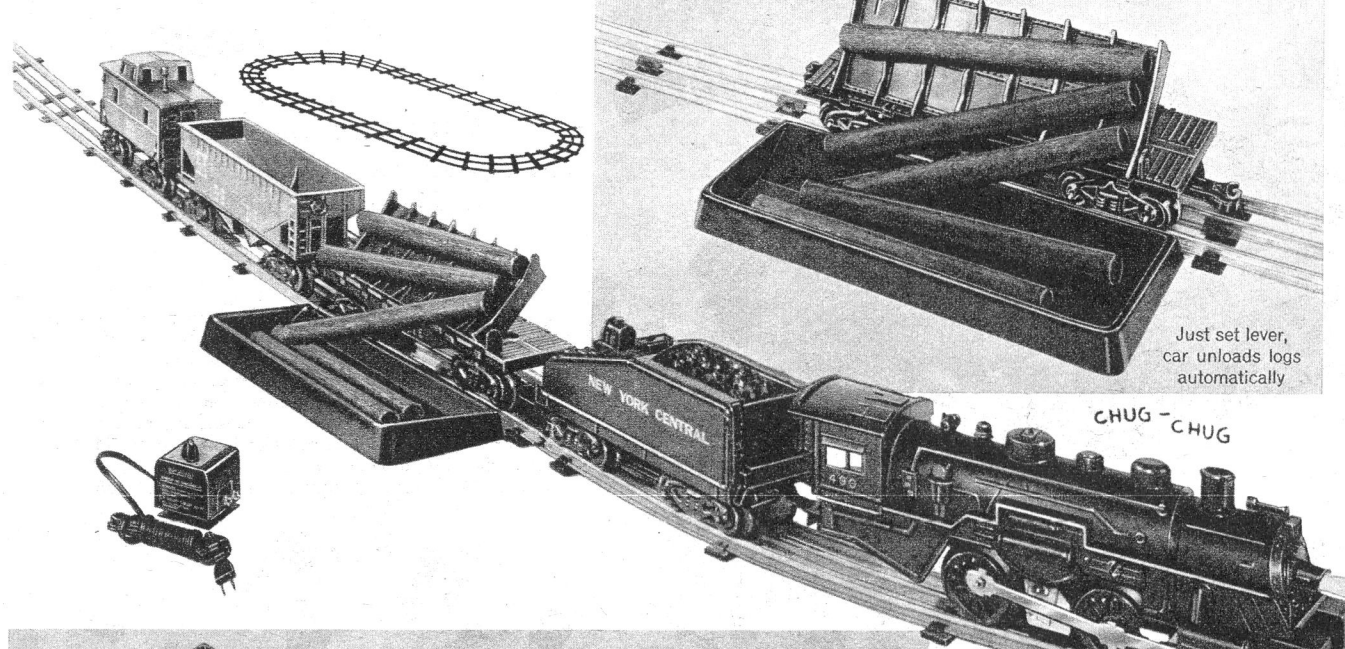

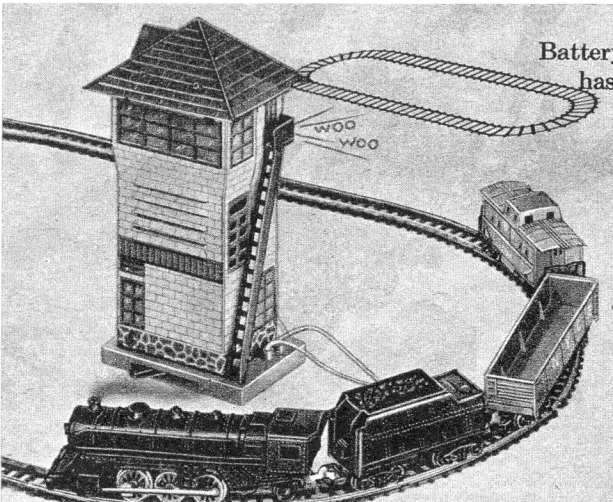

CHUG-CHUG

Battery-powered HO Train Set has locomotive that smokes, realistic whistle sound, automatic car couplers

$4.89 without batteries

Watch smoke rings rise as a "steam" locomotive puffs over 9 feet of track. 22-in. train has a coal tender, gondola and caboose of high-impact plastic.

Hear the realistic whistle wail as it passes by special track section. Everything has been faithfully reproduced and scaled down. 9-in. control tower holds 4 "D" batteries (not included); order below. From Japan.
Shipping weight 2 lbs. 4 oz.
49 N 5822............$4.89

Train with a brain .. automatically chugs into 2 sidings to load barrels, uncouple cars

$5.47 without battery

See a battery-operated locomotive, with 2 gondolas, switch cars .. couple .. and change direction automatically. Plastic flagman signals train to either siding. Train is 18 inches long. Metal track covers 120 inches around. Get: train, cars, track, bumper switch, flagman, barrel loader with 5 wooden barrels. Order one "D" battery below.
49 N 5779—Wt. 4 lbs...$5.47

"D" Battery. Shpg. wt. ea. 4 oz.
49N4660—Each 16c; 4 for 60c

Battery-powered Train with light

$2.99 without batteries

Big 6-wheel locomotive barrels down the track hauling a coal tender, open freight car, tank car and a caboose. It's powerful headlight casts a long beam into the darkest night. All metal; train 25 in. long. Comes with 8 sections of track, 92 inches around. Made in Japan. Powered by 2 "D" batteries (not included); order above.
49 N 4289—Shpg. wt. 2 lbs. 4 oz...$2.99

Five-unit Electric Train with log car that unloads

Midnight Freight "chugs" along as headlight throws beam up-ahead

$9.97

Steam-type engine makes a chug-chug noise as it speeds along .. adjust speed fast or slow. Ease log car alongside bin and logs tumble out automatically. Slant-back coal tender carries realistic embossed "coal." Gondola and caboose tag behind. Big 027-gauge train is 41 in. long. Track includes 8 curved, 2 straight sections .. forms 102-inch oval. Plastic and metal. 25-watt transformer, track connector. UL listed, 110–120-v, 60-c. AC.
49 N 9715C—Shpg. wt. 6 lbs. 12 oz....$9.97

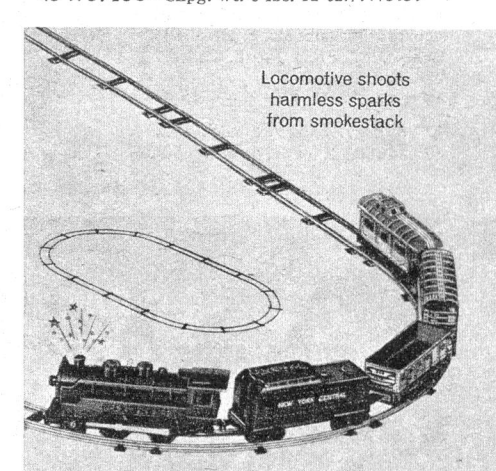

Locomotive shoots harmless sparks from smokestack

Just wind up this husky Train .. see it run for over 2 minutes

$3.89

Steam-type plastic engine gets all its power from a long-running, wind-up clock motor. Motor has speed governor and on-off switch. Highly decorated coal tender, gondola, box car and caboose all metal. Eight curved and 2 straight tracks form a 102-inch oval. Complete train is 34 in. long.
49 N 5731—Shpg. wt. 3 lbs. 6 oz...$3.89

ALLSTATE 6-unit Electric Train on Trestle

Locomotive smokes, steams, shines light

Complete with transformer $19.89

Belches smoke as it chugs up grade, sweeps around curves of 20 foot track

Authentic? You bet. Locomotive pours out the smoke, steam comes out of the mighty pistons and a headlight casts a strong beam. Hauls a tender, tank car, boxcar and caboose.

Track, in straight and curved sections, rambles in two circles with an over-and-under bridge. Trestle set in gradual heights gives your engine hills to test its "muscles."

50-w transformer with circuit breaker lets you control all action. UL approved for 110-120-v, 60-c AC. Bottle of smoke-making fluid. Train 4 ft. long. Over 20 ft. of track.
49 N 9822C—Shipping weight 13 pounds........Set $19.89

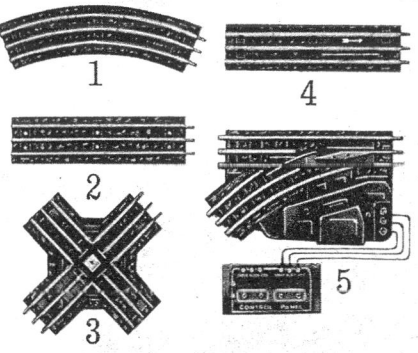

"Gravel roadbed" 3-tie Track

For ALLSTATE or MARX regular gauge sets. Metal and plastic.

1. **Curved Track.** 9½ inches long.
   49 N 9702—Shipping weight 4 oz. 28c
2. **Straight Track.** 8⅞ inches long.
   49 N 9701—Shipping weight 4 oz. 28c
3. **Crossover Track.** 7½ x 7½ inches.
   49N9703—Shipping weight 4 oz. $1.39
4. **Uncoupling Track.** 8⅞ in. long.
   49 N 9710—Shipping weight 4 oz. 97c
5. **Electric Switches.** Push-button control panel. 1 right and 1 left. Wires.
   49 N 9706—Shipping wt. 2 lbs. Set $6.88
   Manual Switches. Lever-control action. 1 left and 1 right. (Not shown.)
   49 N 9704—Wt. 1 lb. 12 oz. Set $3.89

Transformers for regular gauge

Steel cases. Circuit breakers. UL listed, 110-120-volt, 60 cycle AC.

6. **50-watt.** 7-13-v for train, accessories.
   49 N 9721—Shipping wt. 3 lbs. $5.47
7. **100-watt.** 5-15-v for train, accessories.
   49 N 9722—Wt. 4 lbs. 4 oz. ... $7.99

Complete with transformer $29.89 cash
NO MONEY DOWN

Run an ALLSTATE 9-unit Electric Train, 6 feet long

Switch cars into sidings.. couple and uncouple them by remote control .. load and unload them with derrick

Highballing down the track, this freight puffs a trail of smoke from the stack and cool steam from the piston cylinders as headlight pierces the darkness ahead. Locomotive speeds up or reverses .. pulls tender, piggyback car with truck, gondola and side-rack flat car with cartons, boxcar, hopper, tank car and caboose. Station with figures, 6 autos, poles, lamp posts, billboard and derrick add realism to the 55x28-inch layout. Over 11 feet of roadbed track include 8 curved, 8 straight, 2 uncoupling sections, 2 manual switches. 2 bumpers, bridge. Plastic and metal. 50-watt transformer with circuit breaker, track connector. UL approved, 110-120-v, 60-c AC.
79N9825L—Wt. 19 lbs. ... Set $29.89

NOTE: *All items on this page are regular gauge, have 3-rail, 1¼-in. wide tracks*

BLAST OFF!

Fire a "Long Tom" missile by remote control—a direct hit explodes the Target Range Car

New Military Freighter by LIONEL $19.89

Put yourself in command of this exciting military freight train. It's .027 regular gauge. Steam locomotive has headlight, puffs smoke. Pulls tender, flat car with removable army tank, exploding target car, Long Tom remote-control firing car and first-aid caboose. At the first sign of an enemy ambush, push remote-control button.. roof of firing car separates and Long Tom cannon rises to firing position. Cannon blasts off automatically, shooting a plastic shell. Load rocket-firing installation, then push button, plastic shells take off at once. Direct hit explodes target car (reassembles quickly). Includes 8 curved, 5 straight track with 1 remote-control track. 6-car train is 4 ft. 10 in. long; 11 ft. of running track. Includes set of soldiers and smoke fluid for locomotive. Plastic and steel. 45-watt transformer with circuit breaker. UL approved for 110-120-volt, 60-cycle AC.

Shipping weight 9 pounds.
49 N 9820.....................$19.89

Fire a whirling satellite in Trestle Set by LIONEL
$9.97

Steam engine and tender speed up, down, and around slopes.. pulling Turbo-missile firing car, gondola car, caboose. Put satellite into space by pressing button on firing car. Change angle for a high-powered missile.

Figure-8 "over and under" track arrangement is only one of layouts you can make with 6 straight, 12 curved sections of .027 gauge track. Train is 42 in. long. Track 14½ feet. Includes graduated trestle set, billboard set, and 25-watt transformer. Plastic and steel. UL approved for 110-120-volt, 60-cycle AC.
49 N 9813—Wt. 8 lbs........$9.97

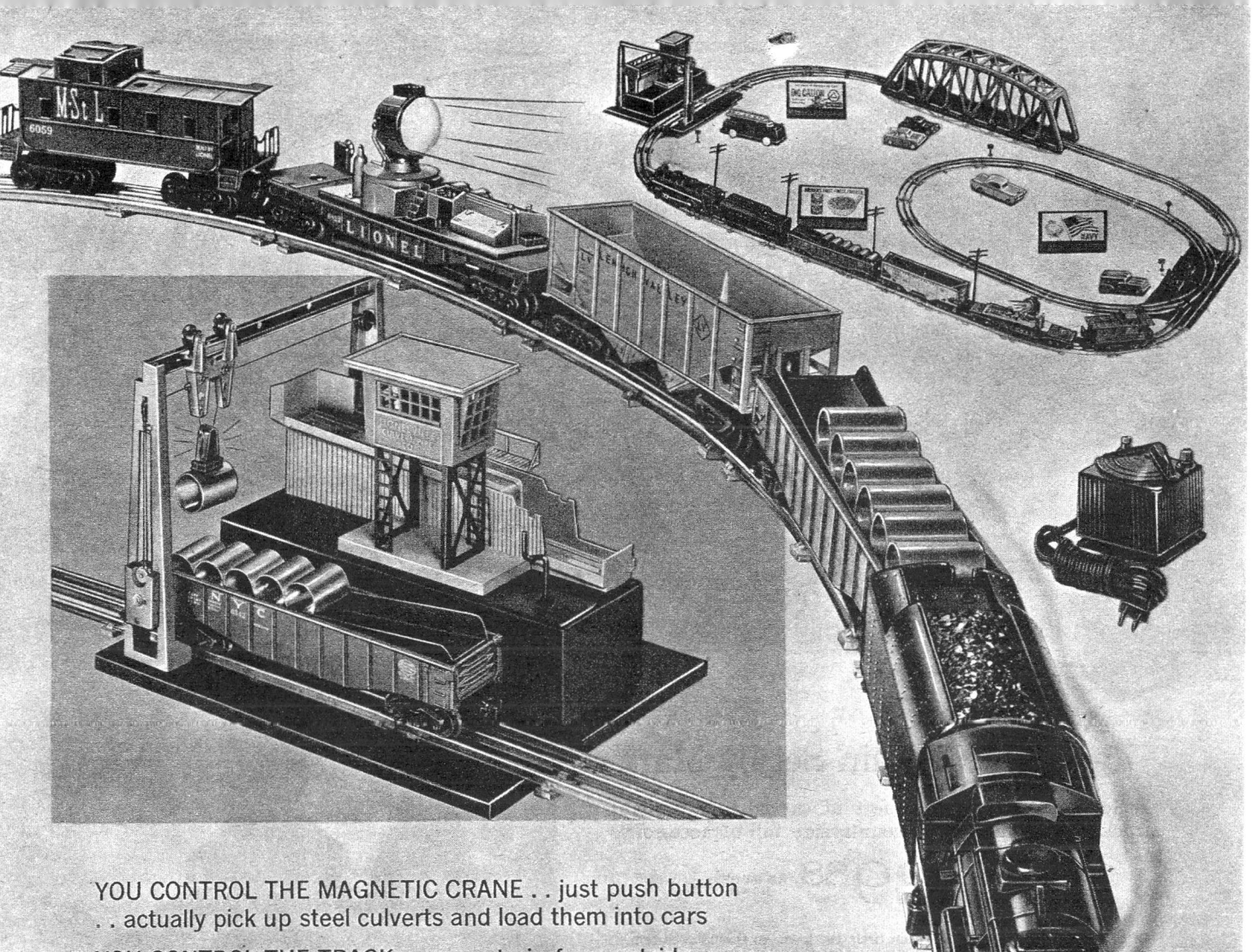

YOU CONTROL THE MAGNETIC CRANE .. just push button
.. actually pick up steel culverts and load them into cars

YOU CONTROL THE TRACK .. move train from outside
to inside loop with manually-operated switches

YOU CONTROL THE TRAIN .. couple and uncouple cars,
go forward or reverse, all by remote control

Giant Steam Freighter Set by Lionel

6-unit electric train complete with 23-foot twin-oval track, transformer, and two manual switches   **$29.99** cash   NO MONEY DOWN

Get ready for plenty of railroading fun as this big freighter barrels around a curve. Powerful steam locomotive will always keep this .027 regular gauge train on schedule. Has headlight, puffs real smoke. Pulls tender, hopper car, searchlight car, culvert pipe car and caboose. Guide train from one loop to the other with pair of manual switches. Move culvert pipe car into position under crane, push remote control button and watch as crane loads pipe by magnetic action. 11 straight, 14 curved and a remote control track let you build many track layouts. Add the trestle bridge and billboards for added realism. Freight train measures about 55 inches long, 23 feet of running track. 45-watt transformer with circuit breaker is UL listed for 110–120-volt, 60-cycle AC.
79 N 9807L—Shipping weight 21 pounds...$29.99

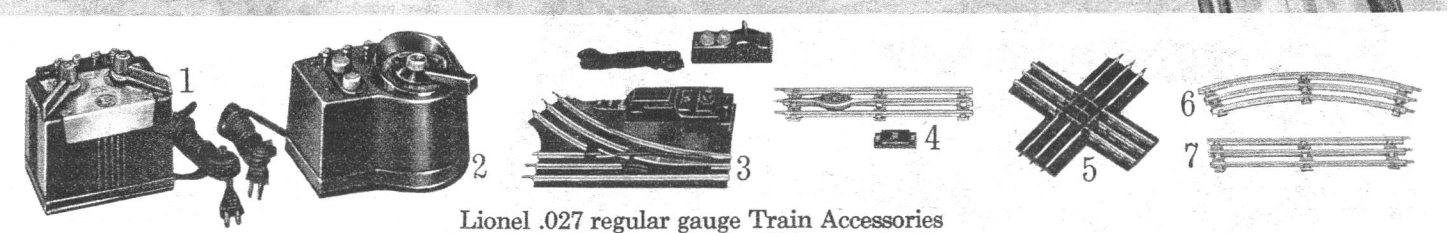

Lionel .027 regular gauge Train Accessories

1 90-watt Transformer. As below, except 7–13-volt for train, 13-volt for accessories.
49 N 9758—Shipping weight 4 lbs. 6 oz. $10.95

2 125-watt Transformer. Phenolic case, steel base. Circuit breaker. UL listed for 110–120-v., 60-c. AC. 5–15 v. for train, 15-v. accessories.
49 N 9756—Shipping weight 4 lbs. 10 oz. $15.95

3 Right-hand Manual Switch. 10½ in. long.
49 N 9752—Shipping weight 1 lb. 6 oz. $2.99

Left-hand Manual Switch. 10½ in. (Not shown.)
49 N 9746—Shipping weight 1 lb. 6 oz. ...$2.99

4 Uncoupling Track. 8⅞ inches long.
49 N 9744—Shipping weight 4 ounces.. 2.39

5 Crossover Track. 6⅞x6⅞ inches long.
49 N 9745—Shipping weight 6 ounces.. 1.59

Track Sections. Metal rails with 3 plastic ties.

6 Curved Track. 9½ inches long.
49 N 9759—Shipping weight 2 oz....... 29c

7 Straight Track. 8⅞ inches long.
49 N 9762—Shipping weight 2 oz....... 29c

75-piece HO Train Set by Marx

Includes 6-unit train, 34 feet of curved and straight track, 3-D scenic base, a countryside full of accessories

Complete with power pack **$29.88** cash NO MONEY DOWN

What excitement to watch the train circle the town, go through the tunnel, stop for delivery of a truck or a sleek new car. Realistic, vacuum-formed plastic terrain is 47x54x5¾ inches. Freight train of plastic and metal is 34 inches long. Consists of 1 industrial switcher locomotive with New Haven design, 1 each flat car with 2 automobiles, piggy back car with hauler and trailer, lumber car, New Haven caboose, boat car with boat.

Also: 8 sections straight track, 1 half section straight track, 24 sections curved track, 1 uncoupler-rerailer track. 16 polyethylene trees add charm to the little town. More realism is added with 1 traffic set, 12 telephone poles, 1 each plastic accessory set, farm set, service station with cars. UL approved 1½-amp. power pack with circuit breaker (110-120-v., 60-c. AC).
79 N 9830N2—Shipping weight 23 pounds..................Set $29.88

SHIPPING NOTE: Both sets on page sent freight (rail or truck) or express.

HO Scale Road Race and Train Set by Marx

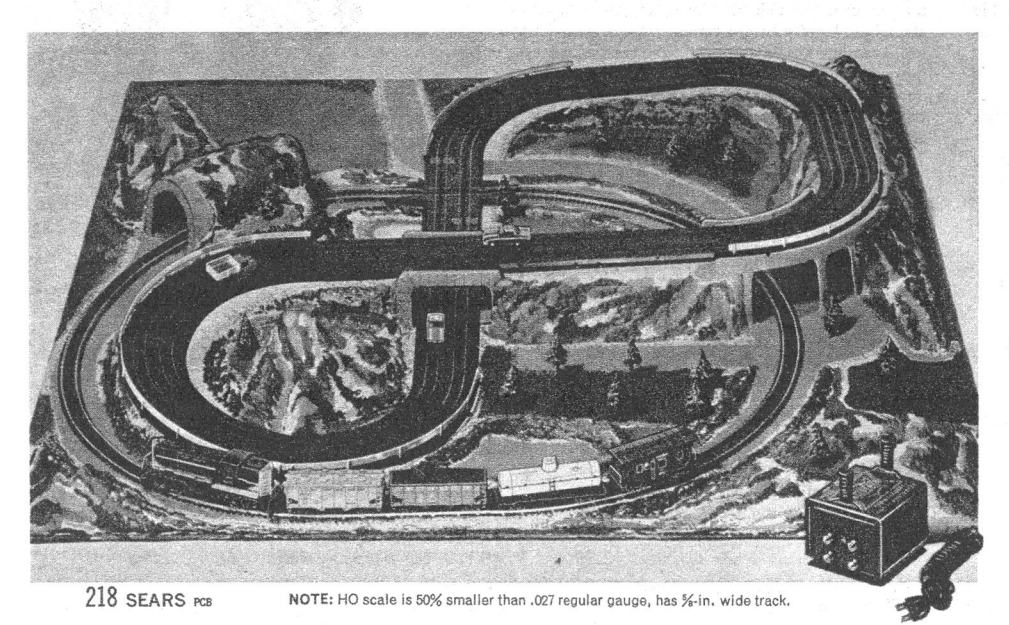

5-unit HO Diesel and two 2½-inch vehicles zip through the grade crossing .. 9⅓-foot train track, 10⅔-foot roadway—on 3-D base

Complete with power pack **$39.88** cash NO MONEY DOWN

Mountainous country terrain provides the background for this exciting train and turnpike set. Watch Northern Pacific diesel switcher speed through tunnel—light beaming. Pulls rocket fuel tank car, hopper car, Portland cement car and caboose. Train is 28 inches long. Track includes 12 curved, 1 straight section and 1 grade crossing.

Roadway has '64 T-bird car with extra Corvette Sting Ray body and a dump truck with extra stake truck body. Roadway sections include 7 straight, 5 curved and 1 curved terminal track. Also 2 speed controls, 6 fence sections, 16 trees, track connector. Train, road race and base are plastic with metal parts. Power pack, 1½ amps. with circuit breaker. UL approved for 110-120-volt, 60-cycle AC.
79 N 9832N2—Shipping wt. 19 lbs. Set $39.88

NOTE: HO scale is 50% smaller than .027 regular gauge, has ⅝-in. wide track.

SEARS CHRISTMAS CATALOG 1965

If you were a kid who could hardly wait for your 1965 Sears Wishbook to arrive so you could dream about the latest electric trains, 1965 was a grim year for you. Not a single train was featured in the catalog! Slot cars had finally taken over.

The catalog featured pages and pages of slot car sets in every imaginable variety. Of these, the most glamorous was the James Bond 007 Road Race at $34.44, featuring an authentic model of Bond's customized Aston Martin. Anticipating a big seller the toy's display ad took up two full pages. The set was made up of six interlocking plastic panels which formed a Swiss Alp landscape for high speed getaways.

Spy toys were huge in 1965. At one point Lionel prepared sketches of a proposed 007 Spy Train replete with special effects, but either could not license the James Bond rights or was unable to get the brand new design to market fast enough.

James Bond 007

Featuring an authentic model of his customized

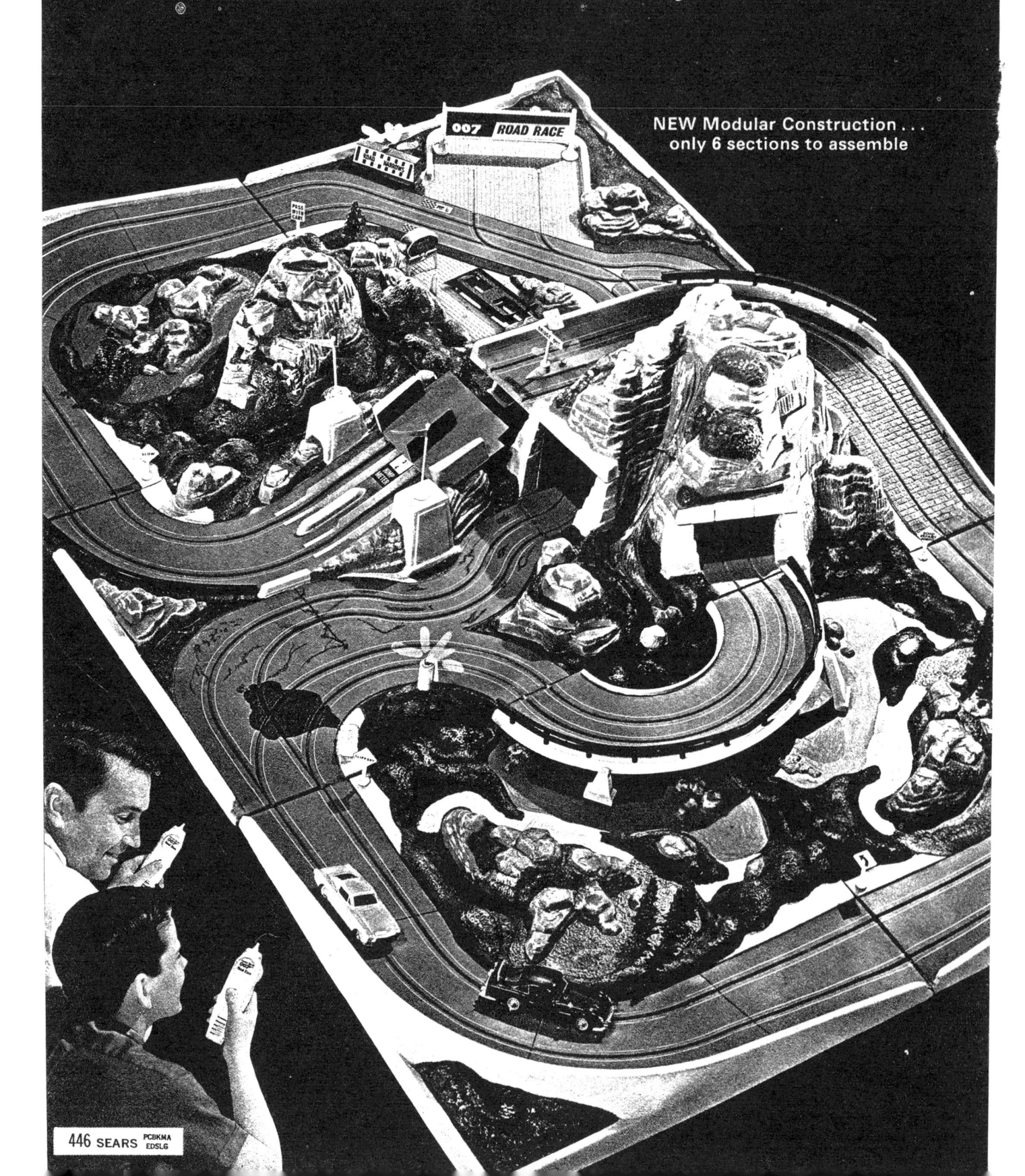

NEW Modular Construction...
only 6 sections to assemble

007 ROAD RACE

Road Race
Aston Martin DB5

Roar from LeMans start into double-exit tunnel .. which route will your car take?

Varied-speed motor sounds
Bullet shield
Tire "cutters"
"Machine guns"

Danger! Use your skill to zig-zag over winding road, spin around an oil slick

Fly past warning lights and make daredevil leap over "washed-out" bridge

Hug the banked curve, then climb up the 40° steep hill with its "slippery bricks"

plus..

Amazingly realistic roads that wind through majestic scenery .. lap counters, switches, even 3 flashing lights at danger points

COMPLETE SET includes 51x34-inch roadway, 2 cars, speed controls and power pack

$34.44

Assemble it in just minutes

Slide together 6 fully landscaped, fully wired, fully contoured tiles. Strong 4-prong "trees" lock them in place. Even the power pack hides under a hill. Each tile 17x17 inches, colorful injection-molded plastic.

James Bond's "Aston Martin" parks next to a Mustang Fastback. A scuffle, then a "shot." The Mustang roars off, James Bond follows in pursuit. Into the tunnel with surprise exits .. one car takes the short zig-zag route, the other a long "S" curve. Spin past an oil slick and 2 banked curves. Climb the hill (the slippery bricks look treacherous). Wind around the mountain .. a flashing warning light—bridge "washed out". Both cars chance it—and make it (span adjusts to 4 positions as skill increases). Will James Bond catch his quarry? It's up to you—and your daring.

Set has 3-dimensional roadway, two 3⅝-inch motorized plastic cars, 2 controls, 12-volt power pack. UL listed. 110-120-v. 60-c. AC.
79 N 7666L—Shipping weight 15 lbs. $34.44

Extra Cars to interchange with cars in set. Sturdy plastic. 3⅝ in. long. Wt. each 4 oz.
49 N 7667—Jaguar XK-E............$2.99
49 N 7668—Ferrari 250 GTO........ 2.99

Spare Parts Kit. Contains 2 tires, pick-ups, 1 front guide pin, gear plate, axle face gear.
49 N 7669—Shpg. wt. 3 oz.........Kit 99c

No Money Down on anything Sears sells

74-piece set $3.97

Union Station by Remco

Make people "walk".. trains, cars and buses roll by "magnetic power". All the hustle, and bustle of a busy terminal .. 24x24 inches square.

All aboard for Union Station! Suddenly you're the engineer of a streamlined train .. or the bus driver who gets his passengers there just before the train pulls out .. or the man behind the wheel of a hurrying sedan. Just wave (maneuver) your magnetic wand *under* the station and a whole city of action opens up for you. Complete with 11 magnetic-motion items, street signs, furnished train and bus station, ticket office, sweet shop and more. Sets up quickly .. just snap buildings onto base.
79 N 6080C—Shipping weight 6 pounds............$3.97

Invasion of the monstrous insects

Hamilton's Invaders
by Remco

17-piece set $8.97   12-piece set $5.87

Their claws ready to snap, 11-in. Horrible Hamilton, 9-in. Hamilton Spider and 3 mini-monsters crawl from their cave to grasp for the very lives of your 9 men. Whirling above, special helicopter drops its deadly plastic bombs .. your mighty tank rolls in, shells the invaders. Horrible, Spider, copter, tank spring-motorized .. just pull cords. Battle-tough plastic lets you, your men and Horrible meet again and again.
49 N 5815C—17-pc. set. Shipping weight 3 lbs......$8.97

12-pc. Set. With Horrible, 6 men, copter, mini-monsters.
49 N 5814—Shipping weight 2 pounds............$5.87

Just say "Charge It" when you phone your order

Torpedo-firing sub cruises just below surface .. real grappling arm on sea crawler scoops up "treasure."

VOYAGE TO THE BOTTOM OF THE SEA

12-piece set $4.99

Admiral Nelson welcomes you aboard for some fantastic voyages you yourself can skipper. In bathtub, at beach, you'll wind 18-in. Seaview sub and watch it dive 'til conning tower alone shows. Order down exploring Mini-sled, too. Then you can alert the Domed Sea-Crawler to find the octopus and monster. Assisted by 2 divers, 2 torpedos you're set for adventure. Plastic.
49 N 6082—Shipping weight 3 lbs. 8 oz.......$4.99

SEARS CHRISTMAS CATALOG 1966

There was a brief comeback for electric trains in the 1966 Sears Christmas Catalog.

Sears offered a bare bones electric set for just $9.95 and a battery-operated tin set for $5.99. Lionel managed to get one train advertised, a stripped down O-27 steam set with a tender and three cars for $19.99.

For the first time in recent years, Sears offered a Gilbert brand set (makers of American Flyer trains). It incorporated the interlocking panel design of the best-selling slot car outfits of the day and utilized American Flyer's two rail track.

In a reverse move, successful slot car newcomer Eldon made available their Little Big Train outfit, a Western-themed H-O variation. As interest in slot cars waned over the next couple of years, Eldon would be one of the first casualties.

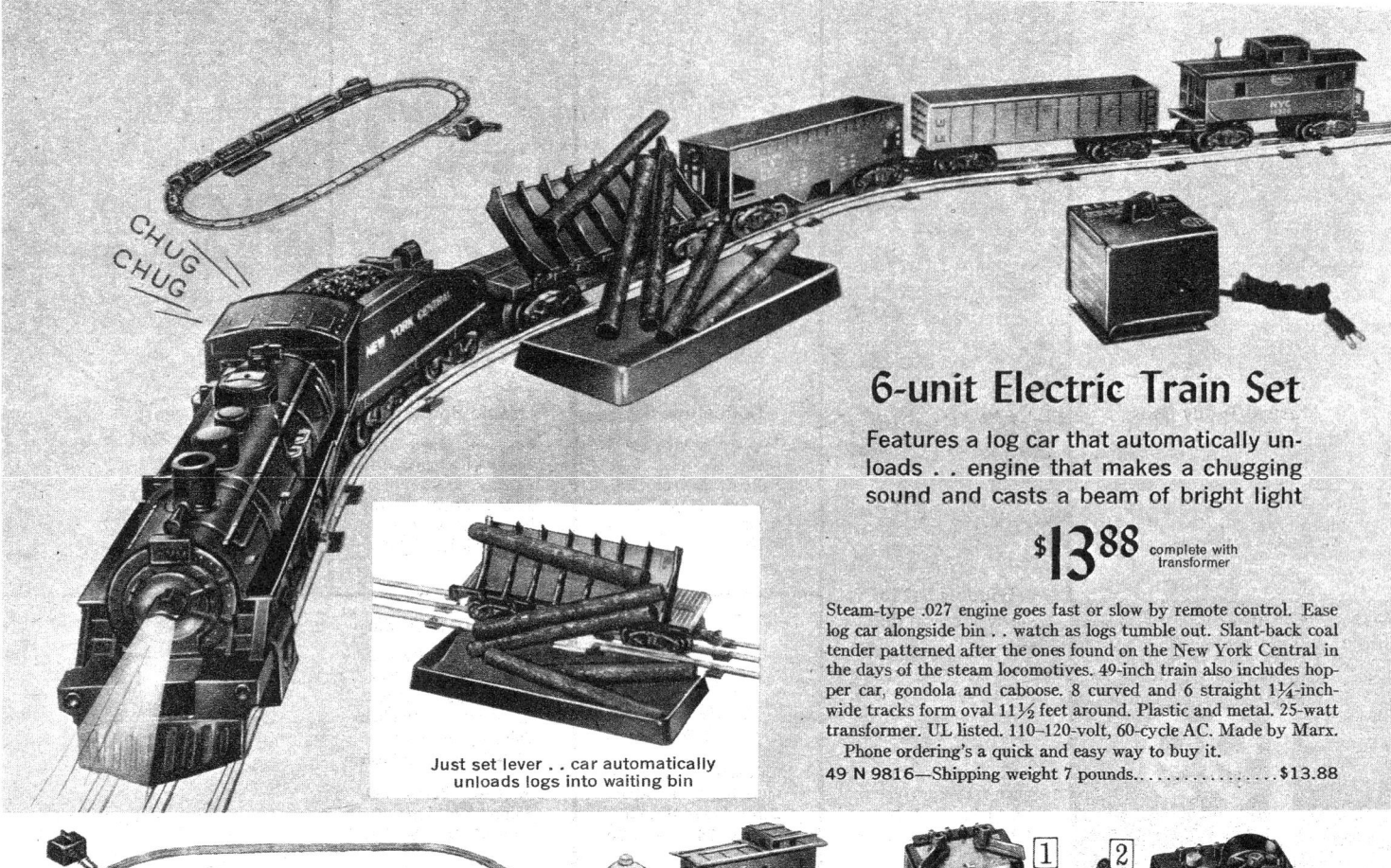

6-unit Electric Train Set

Features a log car that automatically unloads . . engine that makes a chugging sound and casts a beam of bright light

$13.88 complete with transformer

Steam-type .027 engine goes fast or slow by remote control. Ease log car alongside bin . . watch as logs tumble out. Slant-back coal tender patterned after the ones found on the New York Central in the days of the steam locomotives. 49-inch train also includes hopper car, gondola and caboose. 8 curved and 6 straight 1¼-inch-wide tracks form oval 11½ feet around. Plastic and metal. 25-watt transformer. UL listed. 110–120-volt, 60-cycle AC. Made by Marx. Phone ordering's a quick and easy way to buy it.
49 N 9816—Shipping weight 7 pounds..............$13.88

Just set lever . . car automatically unloads logs into waiting bin

More than 16 feet of track with this Lionel Electric Train Set

$19.99 complete with transformer

Watch the 5-unit train zip along the track pulled by .027 steam-type locomotive. Cars include coal tender, hopper car, gondola with 2 cannisters and caboose. 8 straight and 10 curved tracks . . plus 2 manual switches to form double loop layout. Watchman's shanty has a crossing gate that can be lowered manually. Yard set includes crossing signs. Powerful 45-watt transformer lets you make train go fast or slow, forward or reverse. Train is 42 inches long. UL listed. 110–120-volt, 60-cycle AC.
49 N 9808—Shipping weight 10 pounds $19.99

Lionel .027 regular gauge Accessories

1 **90-watt Transformer.** Circuit breaker. UL listed. 110–120-v., 60-cycle AC. 7–13 volts for train, 13 volts for accessories.
49 N 9758—Shipping weight 4 lbs. 4 oz......$10.95

2 **125-watt Transformer.** Same as above except 5–15 volts for train, 15 volts for accessories. 2 buttons control horn or whistle.
49 N 9756—Shipping weight 4 lbs. 12 oz......$9.39

3 **Manual Switches.** 10 in. long. Shpg. wt. each 1 lb.
49 N 9752—Right-hand Switch...........$2.99
49 N 9746—Left-hand Switch................ 2.99

4 **Crossover Track.** 6⅞x6⅞ inches long.
49 N 9745—Shipping weight 6 oz.......... 1.59

5 **Curved Track.** 10½ in. long. 3 steel ties.
49 N 9759—Shipping weight 2 oz...........29c

6 **Straight Track.** 8⅞ inches long. 3 ties.
49 N 9762—Shipping weight 2 oz...........29c

Our lowest-priced Electric Train Set

$9.99 with transformer

Steam-type .027 engine goes fast or slow by remote control. Slant-back coal tender, gondola, hopper car, caboose. 5-unit train is 41 in. long. 4 straight and 8 curved tracks form oval 10 ft. around. 25-watt transformer. UL listed. 110–120-v., 60-c. AC. Made by Marx.
49 N 9815—Shipping wt. 5 lbs. 4 oz............$9.99

Battery-operated Train Set

$5.99 without batteries

Locomotive puffs out smoke rings and whistles automatically. Steam locomotive, coal tender, freight car and caboose. High-impact plastic. 43 inches of HO-gauge track. Station house holds batteries. Order 4 "D" batteries on page 482.
49 N 5748—Shipping wt. 2 lbs............$5.99

Gilbert All Aboard Train Set

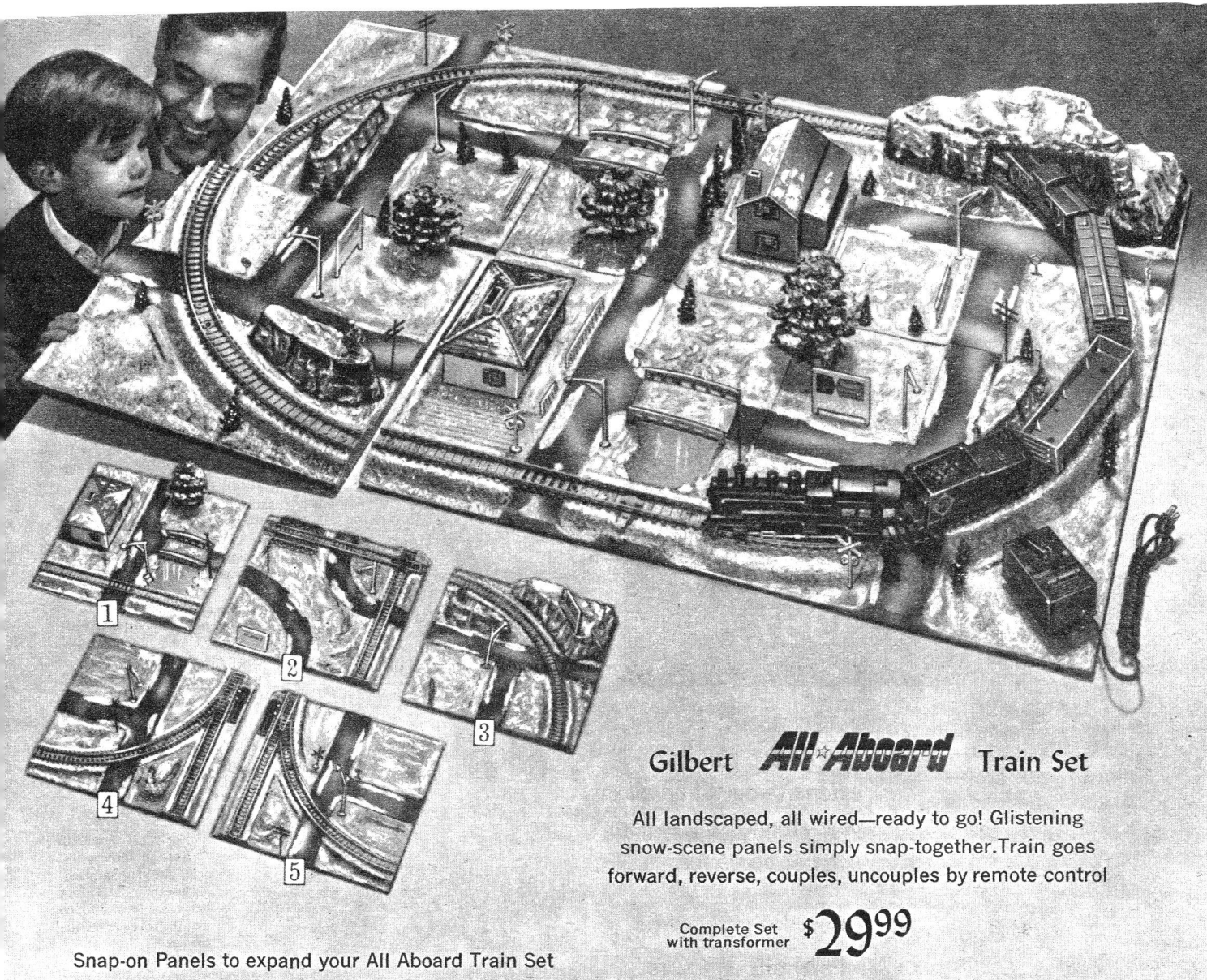

All landscaped, all wired—ready to go! Glistening snow-scene panels simply snap-together. Train goes forward, reverse, couples, uncouples by remote control

Complete Set with transformer **$29.99**

Takes only minutes to assemble. Just snap-together six scenic molded plastic panels of lakes, roads, ravines—even a tunnel. Freight train travels through landscaped area surrounded by houses, street lamps, signs, trees, bridges and billboards. 5-unit, standard gauge train consists of steam locomotive, tender, box car, coal car and caboose. 122 inches of track. Entire layout measures 51x34 inches wide. 25-watt transformer gives you remote-control starting, stopping and reversing. Train couples and uncouples automatically. Extra add-on panels sold at left. UL listed. 110-120-volt, 60-cycle AC. Phone ordering's a quick and easy way to buy it.
79 N 9803L—Shipping weight 17 pounds.....................Set $29.99

Snap-on Panels to expand your All Aboard Train Set

Snow-covered panels with pre-wired, built-in train track. All with contoured landscaping touched with icy glitter that looks like snow. Each panel decorated with fencing, signs, one or more trees, telegraph pole, street lamp and more. Colorful plastic and metal. 17x17 inches. Shipping weight each 4 pounds.

(1) 79 N 9711C—**Straight track.** With house, footbridge, big tree.....$4.97
(2) 79 N 9714C—**Crossover track.** With lake, bridge, billboard, tree... 4.97
(3) 79 N 9709C—**Curved track.** Also with billboard, hill, 3 trees...... 4.97
(4) 79 N 9712C—**Right switch track.** Remote controlled. With signs..... 6.99
(5) 79 N 9713C—**Left switch track.** Remote controlled. With signs..... 6.99

Eldon's LITTLE BIG TRAIN carries supplies to the U. S. Cavalry as the battle begins

Set with transformer **$18.99**

Place 1-piece plastic base on floor or table top. Over 7 feet of track—all pre-mounted. The Rawhide and Hangtown Railroad passes through decorated hills of sage brush, over a trestle bridge and through a removable mountain. Sound whistle on locomotive and take the side track to the trading post. Then unload needed cannon from flat car. 5-piece train with box car, log car with removable logs, caboose. 30x30-in. base has place for train storage. All figures ¾ in. tall. Indians with bows and arrows take on cavalry with guns. Horses, flag, teepees, corral. 12-v. transformer for forward, reverse. UL listed. 110-120-v., 60-c. AC. Sent freight (rail or truck) or express.
79 N 9809N—Shipping weight 5 pounds...$18.99

No Money Down on anything Sears sells . . see page 266

Sears 465

SEARS CHRISTMAS CATALOG 1967

The 1967 edition of the Sears Wishbook Christmas Catalog showed a mind-boggling array of slot cars and accessories, but only two pages of electric trains. Still, this must have proved that there was still some market for the wonderful toys.

A new manufacturer, Tyco, debuted with its line of H-O gauge sets. Available as four, six or eight-unit consists, each came with a different locomotive and 12 feet of track.

Continuing to be available, though not in the variations of past years, was a Sears H-O gauge set on a pre-built plastic base.

Lionel featured two O-27 sets: a 5-unit Union Pacific Diesel Freighter and a 6-unit set with a #1061 Steam locomotive.

Sears' own brand made up the remainder of trains for sale ranging in price from $14.77 down to $3.99 for a battery-operated O-27 set.

Revell Cars
$4.99 each

1/32 and 1/24 scale .. all ready to race on commercial or home raceways

(5 thru 9) Choose from 2 American or 3 European cars, including Grand Prix and Grand Touring racers. All boast super-detailed molded plastic bodies, Delrin® plastic chassis with swing pickups, hi-torque 12-v. motors. Rubber tires, chrome-color trim, windscreens and driver. (5 and 6) are 1/32 scale, about 5½ inches long; (7 thru 9) are 1/24 scale, about 6 inches long. 1/24-scale cars will run on 1/32-scale track (see page 515).

So easy to buy when you just use the phone.
(5) 49 N 7664—*Camaro SS350*. Be a sport!
(6) 49 N 7665—*Mustang 2+2*. Set the pace.
(7) 49 N 7670—*GP Ferrari Squalo 555*.
(8) 49 N 7671—*Porsche RS-60*. Sleek GT.
(9) 49 N 7672—*Lotus 23*. Super-fast GT.
Shipping weight each 8 ounces........Each $4.99

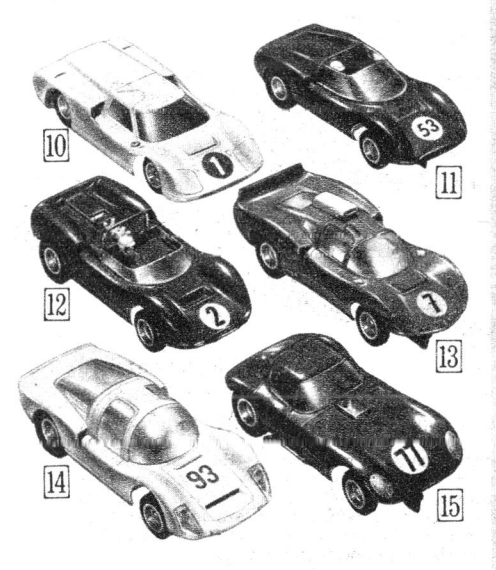

Strombecker Cars
For 1/32-scale home raceways $4.39 each

All authentically detailed. Snap together in seconds with instant-action fasteners. Each with high-impact plastic body, powerful 12-volt motor. Delrin/metal chassis with independently rotating front wheels. Sturdy rubber tires, aluminum wheels, decals and driver. Each about 5½ in. long. Ready to race.

(10) 49 N 20896—*Ford J*. One of Ford's fastest.
(11) 49 N 20897—*Dino Ferrari*. A sensation!
(12) 49 N 20898—*McLaren Mark II*. Latest design.
(13) 49 N 20899—*American Roadster*. Thrilling.
(14) 49 N 7649—*Porsche Carrera*. Fast and hot!
(15) 49 N 7651—*Cheetah*. A real challenger.
Shipping weight each 6 ounces........Each $4.39

Strombecker Car Repair Kit. For 1/32 scale. Be sure to have one for "pit stops." Includes 4 tires, 4 pickup wires and guide pin.
49 N 7627—Shipping weight 2 oz........Kit 99c

$10.99 1/24 scale, ready to race

Cox new La Cucaracha Slot Racer boasts a Nascar 40,000-rpm motor only at Sears

Hugs the track at meteoric speeds!

The super-sport car of tomorrow! One of the fastest ready-to-race car on any slot raceway .. everything about La Cucaracha is designed to win. Iso-Fulcrum self-compensating aluminum chassis reduces speed-retarding vibration and road shock. Low center of gravity (only 5/16-inch off the roadway). Body molded of super-light, super-tough polypropylene with a "cow catcher" front end that keeps it from going airborne at high speeds. Speed profile front tires, super-soft spongy rear tires. Self-centering quick-connect guide—no screws.

La Cucaracha 1/24 scale. Measures 6¾ in. long.
49 N 20891—Shipping weight 1 pound......$10.99
La Cucaracha 1/32 scale. Measures 5 inches long.
49 N 20892—Shipping weight 1 pound......$8.44

Jim Hall's Chaparral 2-E .. 1/24-scale Slot Car with Nascar 40,000-rpm motor and a rear spoiler that works
$10.99

One of the most exciting ready-to-race models in history. Take it to a commercial slot raceway and watch it perform. The full-length aluminum chassis serves as one big swinging guide arm that actually operates the elevated spoiler—lowers it going into the turns, raises it coming out on the straightaway. Tough, injection-molded plastic body. 6¾ inches long. Made by Cox.
49 N 20893—Shipping weight 1 pound.............$10.99

Solder metal
Electric tool also cuts, welds plastic

Repair slot cars or scratch-build one of your own design! Electric tool has copper tip for soldering (20 in. of flux wire included). Also 3 brass tips for plastic reshaping, smoothing, cutting. 23½-watt heating unit. Has 6 styrene rods. 110-120-v., 60-c. AC. UL listed.
Shpg. wt. 8 oz.
49 N 20830.....$2.99

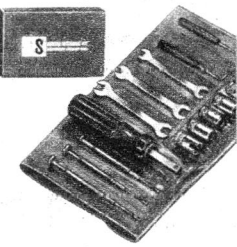

16-pc. Tool Set
for cars, hobbies

Great help in building slot racer, tiny models of all kinds. Bayonet-type handle takes 3/48, 7/40, 7/48-inch socket wrenches and socket attachments for 3 and 2-prong hubs. Straight and 90° Allen head wrenches, 3 screwdrivers, 3 end wrenches. Compact blue plastic fold-out case.
Shipping wt. 12 oz.
49 N 20832.....$2.66

Cox 15-ohm Mark 4 Controller
Gives instant response to most slot racers

$6.44

One of the finest, most sensitive made .. so rugged it outwears many others. A taper-wound resistor even handles super-fast 6 and 12-volt motors. High-impact plastic case is cool to touch—vented on 4 sides. Comfortable 4½-inch grip for steady racing. Dynamic brakes react when you let up on the plunger. Fuse wire protected. Has no-tangle power cord with 3 alligator clips.
Shipping wt. 7 oz.
49 N 20821.....$6.44

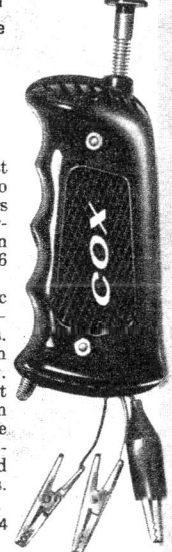

Classic Gamma Ray .. the first 1/24-scale Slot Racer with functional disc brakes

$11.99

Most futuristic-looking streak of light seen around any slot raceway. Noses its way close to the ground .. speeds deeper into the turns and through zigzags. Stops fast because its disc brake mechanism clamps to rear wheels when your controller slows car down. Boasts pan-type aluminum chassis, independently rotating front wheels, 3-volt motor. All ready to race. Light plastic body, 7½ inches long.
49 N 20894—Shipping weight 13 oz.....$11.99

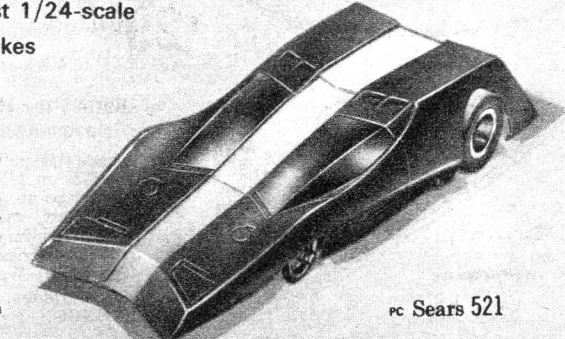

SEARS HO-GAUGE TRAIN SET

...run 5-unit diesel freight cross country, through the tunnel, around the town on its own scenic board with 12 feet of track, 2 switches and 65-piece plastic town

Available only at Sears $34.66 cash $5.00 monthly Complete with powerpack

HO size—scaled 50% smaller than regular or "027"-gauge trains for exciting miniature realism. Detailed 5-unit plastic and metal train runs fast or slow, forward or reverse. Cars couple, uncouple.

Train pulled by diesel switcher locomotive. Beautifully detailed cars include flatcar with 2 autos, hopper, boxcar and caboose. Plastic layout measures 47x34x4 in. high. Includes station, houses, people, animals, trees and other plastic accessories.

Set also includes track and 2 manual switches. UL listed 1-amp. powerpack (110–120-v., 60-c. AC) has 2 posts; gives 4 to 18-v. DC to run train. Sent freight (rail, truck), express.
79 N 9716N—Shipping weight 15 lbs....$34.66

"TRAINS DON'T STOP AT NIGHT, YA KNOW."

[2] $24.66
[1] $17.88

Authentically-detailed TYCO HO-gauge Train Sets..
each with 12-ft. track, 17-piece bridge and trestle, powerpack

Just like the hardworking yard hustlers that haul goods across the land. Each set comes with track for 45x36-in. oval with rerailer section that may be used anywhere in the loop. *Plus* 17-piece plastic bridge and trestle set (not shown) you can set up over "rough terrain." All engines are reversible.. trains run forward and backwards. Plastic and metal. UL listed power pack (110–120-v., 60-c. AC). Japan. Dyna-balanced 5-pole motor. Nylon worm and gear. Precision ground wheel bearings.

1 **Four-unit Set.** Powered by F9 diesel engine with working headlight. Set also includes refrigerator car, cable reel car and caboose. Makes a perfect HO starter set.
49 N 9719—Shipping weight 5 lbs. 8 oz. *$3.00 monthly*............Cash $17.88

2 **Six-unit Set.** Alco 430 Century diesel engine with operating headlight pulls tanker, refrigerator car, flatcar with load of cable reels, hopper and caboose.
79 N 9718C—Shipping weight 8 pounds. *$4.00 monthly*............Cash $24.66

[3] $29.66

3 **Eight-unit Set.** Pacific 4-6-2 steam locomotive with operating headlight pulls long haul tender, gondola, skid flatcar, boxcar, tanker, covered hopper and caboose.
79 N 9717C—Shipping weight 8 pounds. *$4.00 monthly*............Cash $29.66

$5.99 without batteries

Battery-run HO Train with working locomotive and station house

Locomotive puffs out smoke rings, stops on track in front of station, bell rings, train starts up again. Cars include tender, freight car, caboose. 110-in. HO-gauge track. High-impact plastic. Japan. Uses 4 "D" batteries, order 1 pkg. below.
49 N 9738—Wt. 2 lbs. 3 oz.....$5.99
"D" Batteries. Package of 2.
49 N 4660—Wt. pkg. 8 oz.....Pkg. 36c

HO-gauge Accessories

4 **Straight Track.** 9 inches long. Package of 4.
49 N 9903—Shipping weight pkg. 4 oz...........Pkg. 96c
5 **Curved Track.** 18 inches long. Package of 4.
49 N 9912—Shipping weight pkg. 4 oz...........Pkg. 96c
6 **Remote Control Switch.** Shipping weight each 5 oz.
49N9901-Lt. Hand.Ea. $3.99 49N9902-Rt. Hand. Ea. $3.99

Only at Sears will you find these LIONEL 027 regular-gauge Train Sets .. each with 8 feet of track and transformer

[1] **$22.50**

[2] **$18.44**

5-unit Diesel Freighter runs forward and reverse .. cars couple and uncouple by remote control

1. Colorful Union Pacific diesel switcher engine heads this train. Headlight blazes ahead. Uncouple a car or two, run train forward, reverse and couple waiting cars. Train sings along the rails .. box car doors slide open and close, cable reel flat car, hopper and work caboose. Set track in oval or circle. UL listed transformer. 110-120-volt, 60-cycle AC. Train made of plastic and metal.
To order the easiest way, look in your phone book white pages under "Sears, Roebuck and Co., Catalog Sales" for number to call. Shipping weight 7 pounds.
49 N 9724—$4.00 monthly......................Cash $22.50

Steam locomotive with headlight leads 6-unit freighter with 2 loaded cars

2. Just like the old Iron Horses that supplied the pioneers.. this rugged plastic and metal train is pulled by a solid steam locomotive. Just right for a young engineer. Locomotive has shining headlight. Cars include coal tender, hopper, flat car, cable reel car and caboose. Flat car transports husky load of timber. Cable reel car carries giant plastic reels. Haul other playset pieces on the cars, too. Complete with track and transformer. UL listed. 110-120-volt, 60-cycle AC. Shipping weight 6 pounds 8 ounces.
49 N 9723..$18.44

No Money Down on anything Sears sells

$9.88 with track and transformer

Our lowest-priced Electric Train runs fast or slow

Steam-type 027 engine travels around its own 84-in. circle of track. Coal tender, gondola and caboose all realistically decorated. Haul plastic Indians and troop supplies in the gondola. Plastic and metal train. 25-w. transformer. UL listed. 110-120-v., 60-c. AC.
49 N 9725—Shipping weight 6 pounds............$9.88

$14.77 with track and transformer

Log car automatically unloads .. locomotive chugs, headlight shines ahead for this 6-unit Electric Train Set

This train comes straight from the northwoods with a load of timber. Steam-type 027 engine pulls log car beside bin .. set lever .. watch logs tumble out. Train runs fast, slow. Includes slant-back coal tender, hopper, gondola, caboose. Track forms 11½-foot oval. Plastic and metal. 25-watt transformer. UL listed. 110-120-volt, 60-cycle AC.
49 N 9816—Shipping weight 7 pounds............$14.77

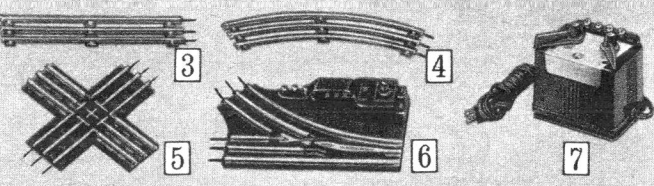

027 Regular-Gauge Accessories

(3) 49 N 9731—**Straight Track**. 9½ in. Pkg. of 4. Wt. 8 oz. Pkg. $1.09
(4) 49 N 9730—**Curved Track**. 10½ in. Pkg. of 4. Wt. 8 oz. Pkg. 1.09
(5) 49 N 9745—**Crossover Track**. 6⅞x6⅞ in. Shpg. wt. 6 oz. Ea. 1.66
[6] 49N9752—Right-hand Manual Switch. 10 in. long. Wt. 1 lb. .$3.44
49N9746—Left-hand Manual Switch (not shown). Wt. 1 lb. . 3.44
[7] 90-w. **Transformer**. Circuit breaker. UL listed. 110-120-v., 60-c., AC.
49 N 9758—Shipping weight 4 pounds 4 ounces........$11.99

$3.99 without batteries

Battery-run 4-unit Train switches on its 9-foot track

027 locomotive with shining headlight leads this hard working little train. Cars include tender, gondola, caboose. Track may be arranged in oval shape with switcher or in continuous-travel figure 8. Plastic and metal train. In colorful gift box. Uses 2 "C" batteries, order 1 package below.
49 N 9720—Shipping weight 1 pound 4 ounces...............$3.99
49 N 4665—"C" Batteries. Package of 2. Shpg. wt. 4 oz........Pkg. 36c

SEARS CHRISTMAS CATALOG 1968

The big news for electric train buffs in the 1968 Sears Christmas Catalog was the debut of the tiny new N-gauge.

The Wishbook advertising that year explained that N-gauge "Micro Trains" took up about one-fourth the space used for H-O gauge trains. Two new brands were shown, Aurora and Revell, both toy model companies who had recently expanded into the electric train market.

Of primary interest was Sears' Play 'N Carry train set, which was a full N-gauge train layout that actually folded up into a 14 x 18-inch briefcase! This set could fit on the smallest card table. Now electric trains were truly portable.

One H-O set with a Western theme was featured as were three generic-looking Sears brand O-27 sets.

CORGI
Crime-fighting Cars
Made in England

James Bond DB5
1 New Aston Martin has revolving license plates, remote-controlled ejector seat, screen, and extending override bumpers. Includes James Bond, 2 spies and 007 badge. 4 in. long. Die-cast metal and plastic.
49 N 54026—Wt. 5 oz..$3.47

Green Hornet's Black Beauty
2 Touch of a lever lowers radiator grill, and a switch releases flying radar scanner. Green plastic windows conceal driver. 5 in. long. Die-cast metal and plastic construction. Green Hornet and Kato included.
49 N 54029—Wt. 8 oz..$3.97

Batmobile and Batboat
3 Batmobile has features like you've seen on TV. 10½ in. long.
Removable trailer holds Batboat that actually floats. 5½ in. long. Both Batmobile and Batboat made of die-cast steel with plastic accessories. Hand-painted figures of Batman and Robin. Batmobile badge included.
49N54024—Wt. 12 oz.$5.97

Batmobile only. Batman and Robin figures incl.
49N54025—Wt. 8 oz.$3.97

Aerial Hook and Ladder Rescue Fire Engine
Raise, lower, and rotate ladder 360°. Main aerial ladder extends to 16½ inches; six 4-inch extensions included. Cab detaches. 6 firemen. Die-cast metal and plastic construction. 11 inches long. Made in England.
49 N 54028—Wt. 1 lb. 5 oz.....$8.88

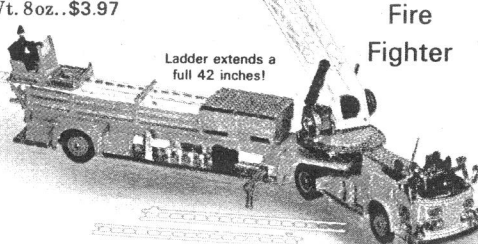

CORGI Fire Fighter
Ladder extends a full 42 inches!

Corgi model of the jungle Landrover $1.97
Just look at this super realistic model of Daktari's camouflaged jungle Landrover (3¾ inches long). Dr. Marsh Tracy holds Judy the Chimp, daughter Paula Tracy sits on Clarence the cross-eyed lion, and a convalescing Tiger rests on the Landrover's hood. Landrover of die-cast metal, plastic figures. Made in England.
49 N 54027—Shipping wt. 5 oz........$1.97

SOLIDO—die-cast metal, spring-suspension cars $1.79
(4 and 5) Touch control steering. Doors open to show completely detailed interior.

4 **Chaparral with stabilizer.** 3⅝ inches long. Dummy headlights, dummy rear lights.
49 N 54031—Shipping wt. 6 oz.........$1.79

5 **Lamborghine.** Measures 4 inches long. Hood tilts back or removes. Dummy rear lights.
49 N 54032—Shipping wt. 6 oz.........$1.79

SUPER CITY HELIPORT
Only at Sears.. $9.88
complete set with carry case that opens into landing field

Imagine a helicopter zooming in over buildings you've designed and built! Set has over 260 pieces so you can build all buildings here and more

Twin rotor blades of the 7-inch plastic helicopter whiz around as you direct the landing.. tie one end of the string onto the landing field and hold onto the other. Vinyl case opens into a big 31x23-inch field. As an architect, you design the buildings and plan the layout.. an exciting and rewarding challenge.

Units incl. 50 full frames, 8 half frames and 6 triangle frames, all plastic, to give you variety in shapes.

Among the other construction pieces are full columns, half columns, travertine inserts, building extenders, brick-look inserts and gravel inserts.

To keep your designs interesting you'll find skylight domes, a bay window, colonial door, a clock with hands you can turn manually, and fluted inserts. Miniature plastic truck and 10 figures included.
49 N 44177—Shpg. wt. 4 lbs. 4 oz...........$9.88

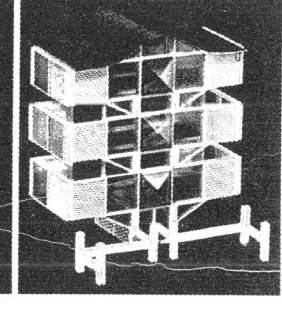

Accessory Helicopter and 2 colored Searchlights
$2.49 without batteries

Helicopter comes in on string you direct (complete description at left). Searchlights use two "D" batteries—order below.
49 N 44176—Wt. 7 oz.....$2.49
"D" Batteries. Package of 2.
49 N 4660—Wt. 8 oz.. Pkg. 38c

Play 'N' Carry—*realistic 3-D railroad layout—opens to 24x36-inch card-table size .. ready to set up operation for N-ga. trains sold below*

Vinyl carry-about case holds complete N-gauge operation, ready for fascinating mini-train fun. Setting with track lanes, tunnel, buildings, hills and landscaped effect. Made of heat-sealed, vacuum-formed vinyl. Buildings with hinged tops serve to store trains, track and powerpack. Measures 14x18 in. closed. (Train set not included, order below.)
79 N 96009C—Shpg. wt. 4 lbs......$7.88

$7.88
Without train set, powerpack, track

Case holds complete N-gauge set-up

N-gauge Micro Trains take about one-fourth the space used for HO-gauge

N-gauge electric outfits
include trains, track, power

1 **7-unit Cannonball by Aurora.** Just 1/160th scale—tiny yet authentic .. tough and powerful. And though the mighty diesel is only 5 inches long, it could pull 24 cars.
Set has 8-wheel drive diesel, boxcar, gondola, cattle car, coal hopper, refrigerator car, caboose. Metal and plastic. Also has 16 assorted pieces of chrome-plated metal track. One-amp powerpack*.
49 N 96006—Wt. 3 lbs. 8 oz......$24.88

2 **5-unit "The Powerhouse" by Revell.** Workhorse 8-wheel drive, hood-type diesel with light pulls boxcar, gondola car, tank car and caboose. 16x24 in. oval, black and nickel-plated track. 6-amp powerpack*. Metal and plastic.
49 N 96005 Wt. 2 lbs. 11 oz......$19.88

3 **4-unit "The Load King" by Revell.** Cab-type diesel with light. Three popular freight cars: tank car, billboard refrigerator car, caboose. Metal and plastic. 16x24 in. oval, black and nickel-plated track plus the .6-amp powerpack*.
49N96004 Shpg. wt. 2 lbs. 10 oz...$15.88

*NOTE: 110-120-volt. 60-cycle AC operation. UL listed

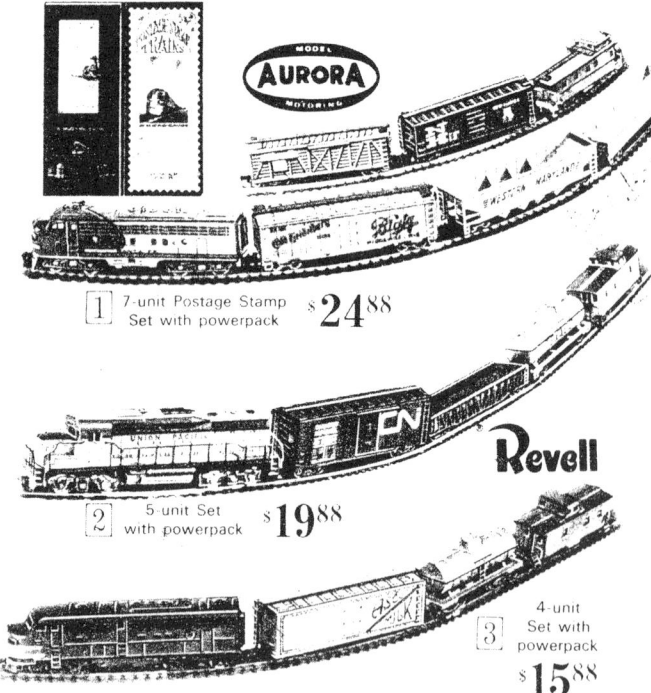

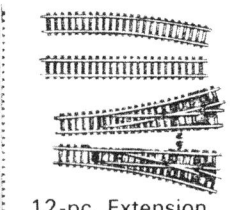

12-pc. Extension Kit adds switch-action interest to Revell N-gauge train set-up
$6.99

Convert basic track layout that comes with Revell N-gauge train set to a variety of switching arrangements. Micro-track sections include a pair of manual switches, two pieces 17-in. 15° radius curved track and 8-pieces straight track. Forged from railroad tempered steel; black nickel plate finish.
Wt. 4 oz.
49 N 96003..Kit $6.99

[1] 7-unit Postage Stamp Set with powerpack $24.88

[2] 5-unit Set with powerpack $19.88

[3] 4-unit Set with powerpack $15.88

HO-gauge WILD WEST TINY TRAIN
takes only 28x28-in. area for set up
$9.88 including powerpack

Place this 5-unit supply train on floor or on table top. Over 7 feet of track to lay out for the Rawhide and Hangtown Railroad to circle. Sound the whistle on the locomotive and take the side track to the trading post. Then unload the long-awaited cargo from the flat car, box car and log car. Plastic play figures are ¾ inches tall. Horses, caboose and corral incl. 12-v. transformer is UL listed, 110-120-v., 60-c. AC.
49 N 96008—Shipping weight 2 lbs. 2 oz...........$9.88

6-unit Train with trestle
22 sections of track combine to make 16 feet of 027 track— plus a 50-watt transformer

Listen to that locomotive as it comes around the bend .. look for the headlight on the rails. Authentic? You bet! Big, 10-inch locomotive makes "chug-chug" sound, has moving drive arm and a headlight that sends out a strong beam.

Other cars include a coal tender, boxcar, gondola, tank car and caboose. Forms a train 4 feet long. Also included are 10 sections straight track, 12 sections curved. Trestle sections in graduated heights. 50-watt transformer UL listed, 110–120-v., 60-c. AC. Plastic and metal. Instructions.
79N95016C—Shpg. wt. 12 lbs. Set $22.50

$22.50

027 GAUGE Electric Trains and accessories

4-unit Train with 8 sections of track .. 25-watt transformer $9.99

Steam-type engine travels an 84-inch circle. Coal tender, gondola and caboose realistically detailed. Plastic, metal train. Transformer UL listed. 110–120-v., 60-c. AC.
49 N 9725—Shipping weight 5 pounds....... Set $9.99

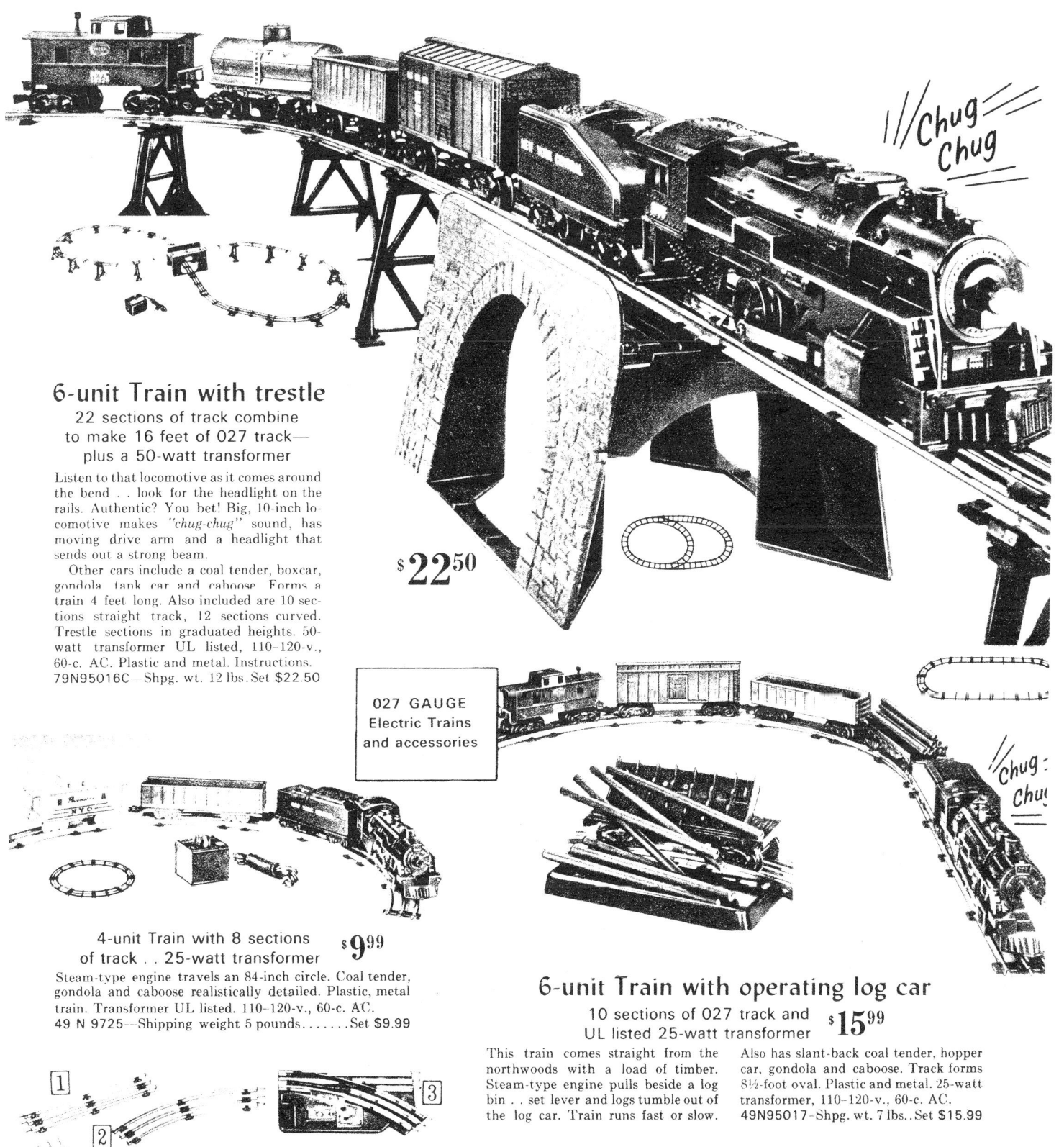

6-unit Train with operating log car
10 sections of 027 track and UL listed 25-watt transformer $15.99

This train comes straight from the northwoods with a load of timber. Steam-type engine pulls beside a log bin .. set lever and logs tumble out of the log car. Train runs fast or slow.

Also has slant-back coal tender, hopper car, gondola and caboose. Track forms 8½-foot oval. Plastic and metal. 25-watt transformer, 110–120-v., 60-c. AC.
49N95017—Shpg. wt. 7 lbs.. Set $15.99

027 straight, curved track sold in package of 4.
(1) 49N96114—**Straight**. Wt. 7 oz..Pkg. 99c
(2) 49N96115—**Curved**. Wt. 7 oz..Pkg. 99c
(3) **Manual Switches**. 1 R and L, 027 gauge.
   49 N 96117—Wt. 1 lb. 4 oz...Set $4.44
(4) 49 N 96116—**Crossover**. Wt. 6 oz. 1.19

Wind-up 4-unit Tot Train runs for 2 full minutes
$4.99

Ideal for the young railroader! Engine has wind-up clock motor with speed governor, on-off switch. Includes coal tender, box car and caboose. Train is metal. Instructions included.
49N9740-Wt. 2 lbs. 12 oz.$4.99

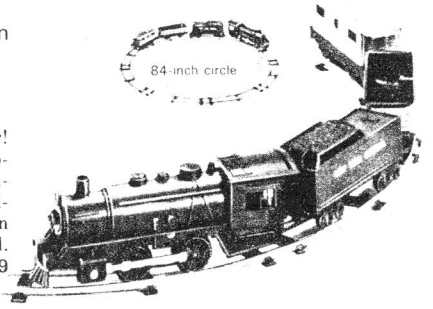

84-inch circle

BATTERY-RUN 4-UNIT TRAIN
with switch tracks, 9 ft. of track

Engine is 5¼ in. long with working drive arms. Cars include coal tender, gondola and caboose. Plastic track forms a 33x16½-inch layout. Comes with one manual switch and one universal switch. Train is plastic and metal, 16 in. long. From Japan. Uses 2 "C" batteries, order 1 package below.
49 N 9505—Shpg. wt. 1 lb. 1 oz....... Set $3.99
"C" Batteries. Package of 2.
49 N 4665—Shipping wt. 4 oz......... Pkg. 38c

$3.99 without batteries

PC Sears 521

SEARS CHRISTMAS CATALOG 1969

It seems fitting that after twenty good and bad years for Wishbook trains, the 1969 Sears Christmas Catalog ended this golden era with a hint of optimism.

Although O and O-27 gauge trains had been nearly forgotten by mass marketers like Sears, H-O scale trains continued to be popular with new, younger customers. The 1969 catalog displayed a nice line-up of H-O trains, including an impressive 8-unit freight set by Tyco, pulled by a lighted 4-6-2 locomotive. The set featured a Piggyback trailer dock and an Auto Carrier.

As happened in the 1950's when O-gauge proliferated, now advanced H-O model railroaders could purchase individual engines and elaborate accessories from Sears. An illuminated GP 20 Diesel and a 2-6-2 Prairie locomotive and tender were for sale for $9.99 and $13.99 respectively. N-gauge followed suit too, borrowing the original H-O idea of a Styrofoam pre-landscaped platform which folded neatly away.

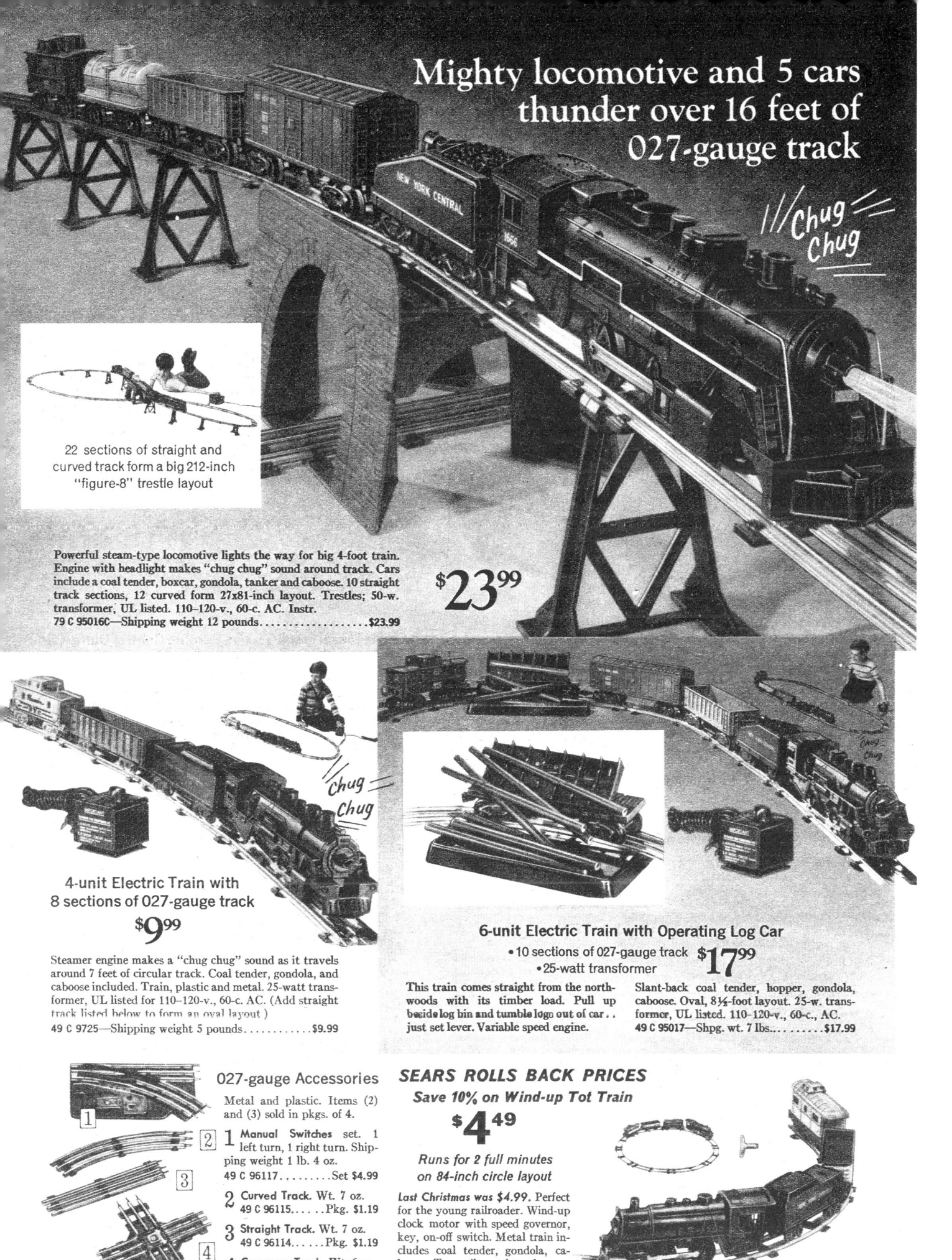

Mighty locomotive and 5 cars thunder over 16 feet of O27-gauge track

Chug Chug

22 sections of straight and curved track form a big 212-inch "figure-8" trestle layout

Powerful steam-type locomotive lights the way for big 4-foot train. Engine with headlight makes "chug chug" sound around track. Cars include a coal tender, boxcar, gondola, tanker and caboose. 10 straight track sections, 12 curved form 27x81-inch layout. Trestles; 50-w. transformer, UL listed. 110–120-v., 60-c. AC. Instr.
79 C 95016C—Shipping weight 12 pounds.....................$23.99

$23.99

4-unit Electric Train with 8 sections of O27-gauge track
$9.99

Chug Chug

Steamer engine makes a "chug chug" sound as it travels around 7 feet of circular track. Coal tender, gondola, and caboose included. Train, plastic and metal. 25-watt transformer, UL listed for 110–120-v., 60-c. AC. (Add straight track listed below to form an oval layout.)
49 C 9725—Shipping weight 5 pounds............$9.99

6-unit Electric Train with Operating Log Car
- 10 sections of O27-gauge track
- 25-watt transformer

$17.99

This train comes straight from the north-woods with its timber load. Pull up beside log bin and tumble logs out of car .. just set lever. Variable speed engine. Slant-back coal tender, hopper, gondola, caboose. Oval, 8½-foot layout. 25-w. transformer, UL listed. 110–120-v., 60-c., AC.
49 C 95017—Shpg. wt. 7 lbs..........$17.99

O27-gauge Accessories
Metal and plastic. Items (2) and (3) sold in pkgs. of 4.

1. **Manual Switches** set. 1 left turn, 1 right turn. Shipping weight 1 lb. 4 oz.
49 C 96117........Set $4.99
2. **Curved Track.** Wt. 7 oz.
49 C 96115......Pkg. $1.19
3. **Straight Track.** Wt. 7 oz.
49 C 96114......Pkg. $1.19
4. **Crossover Track.** Wt. 6 oz.
49 C 96116......Each $1.29

SEARS ROLLS BACK PRICES
Save 10% on Wind-up Tot Train
$4.49

Runs for 2 full minutes on 84-inch circle layout

Last Christmas was $4.99. Perfect for the young railroader. Wind-up clock motor with speed governor, key, on-off switch. Metal train includes coal tender, gondola, caboose. Two-rail metal track.
49 C 9740—Wt. 2 lbs. 12 oz. $4.49

TYCO HO-scale Electric Trains

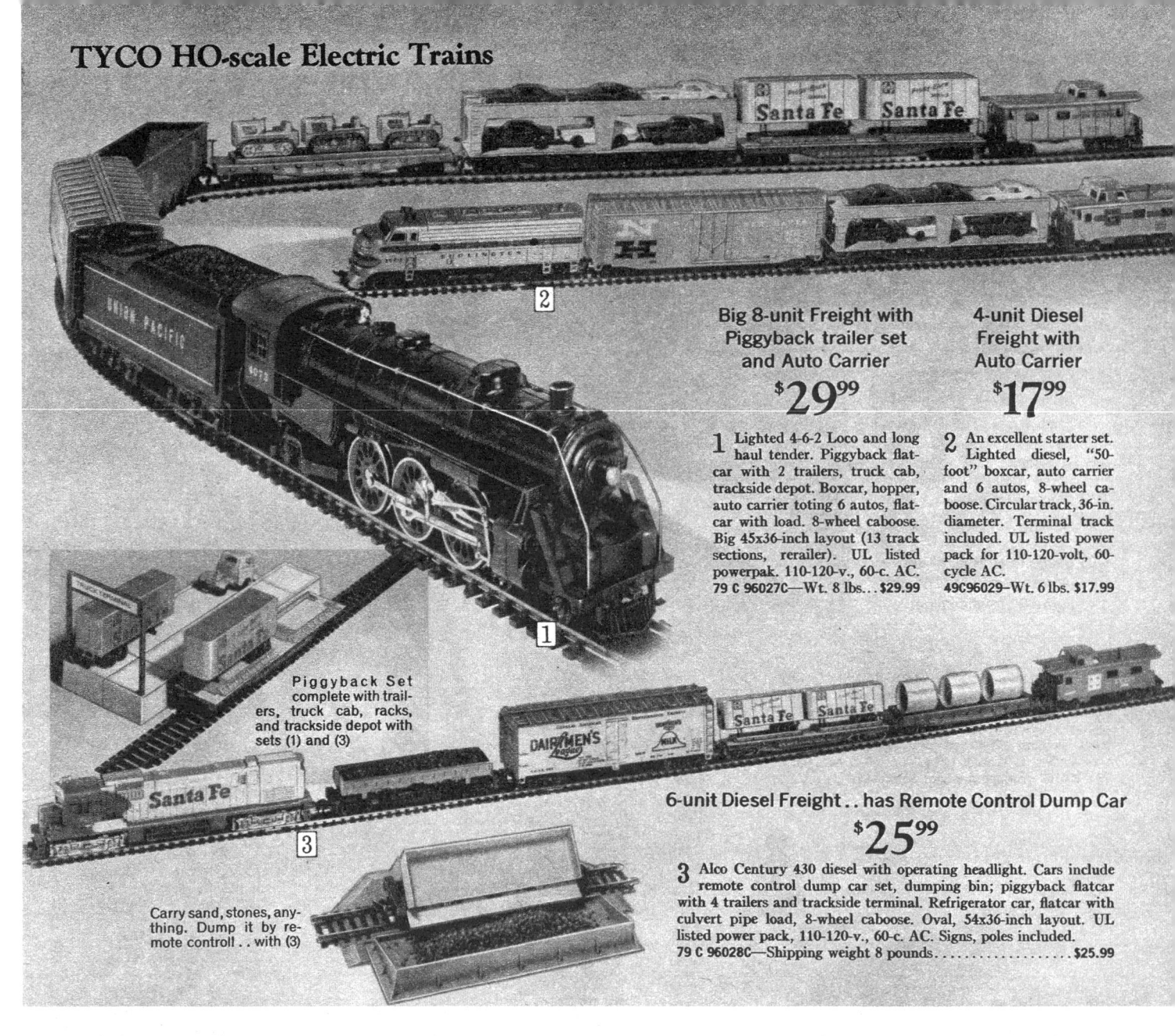

Big 8-unit Freight with Piggyback trailer set and Auto Carrier
$29.99

1 Lighted 4-6-2 Loco and long haul tender. Piggyback flatcar with 2 trailers, truck cab, trackside depot. Boxcar, hopper, auto carrier toting 6 autos, flatcar with load. 8-wheel caboose. Big 45x36-inch layout (13 track sections, rerailer). UL listed powerpak. 110-120-v., 60-c. AC.
79 C 96027C—Wt. 8 lbs... $29.99

4-unit Diesel Freight with Auto Carrier
$17.99

2 An excellent starter set. Lighted diesel, "50-foot" boxcar, auto carrier and 6 autos, 8-wheel caboose. Circular track, 36-in. diameter. Terminal track included. UL listed power pack for 110-120-volt, 60-cycle AC.
49C96029—Wt. 6 lbs. $17.99

Piggyback Set complete with trailers, truck cab, racks, and trackside depot with sets (1) and (3)

Carry sand, stones, anything. Dump it by remote control!.. with (3)

6-unit Diesel Freight.. has Remote Control Dump Car
$25.99

3 Alco Century 430 diesel with operating headlight. Cars include remote control dump car set, dumping bin; piggyback flatcar with 4 trailers and trackside terminal. Refrigerator car, flatcar with culvert pipe load, 8-wheel caboose. Oval, 54x36-inch layout. UL listed power pack, 110-120-v., 60-c. AC. Signs, poles included.
79 C 96028C—Shipping weight 8 pounds.................. $25.99

Powerful HO Locomotives and Railroad Utility Cars

4 **Lighted GP 20 Diesel Loco.** Smooth operating dynabalance 5-pole motor. Nylon worm gear drive. Stainless steel handrails.
49 C 96032–Wt. 1 lb. 1 oz. $9.99

5 **2-6-2 "Prairie" Locomotive and Tender.** Operating headlight. "Valvegear" works.
49 C 96031–Wt. 15 oz... $13.99

6 **Log Transport.** Authentic detail. Realistic wooden logs secured with "sturdy" metal link chain.
49 C 96033—Wt. 6 oz.... $1.49

7 **Flatcar with Load.** Detailed Western Maryland car toting realistic tractors.
49 C 96034—Wt. 11 oz... $1.49

8 **Piggyback Set.** "50-foot" flatcar with 2 trailers, truck cab and terminal. Wt. 15 oz.
49 C 96036......... Set $3.49

9 **Remote Control Log Dump Set.** Has logs, receiving bin, operating track, controller.
49 C 96035—Wt. 1 lb. 3 oz. $5.99

HO Layout Accessories add railroading realism

10 **Lighted Freight Station.** Lifelike trackside structure with realistic old wood design. Hand painted. Includes workers and cargo.
49 C 96037—Wt. 10 oz. $4.99

11 **Operating Crossing Gate.** Safety gate drops as train approaches, raises after all cars clear. Automatic.
49 C 96038—Wt. 5 oz... $4.99

Extra Track, Switches
Convert basic layouts to a variety of shapes, sizes.

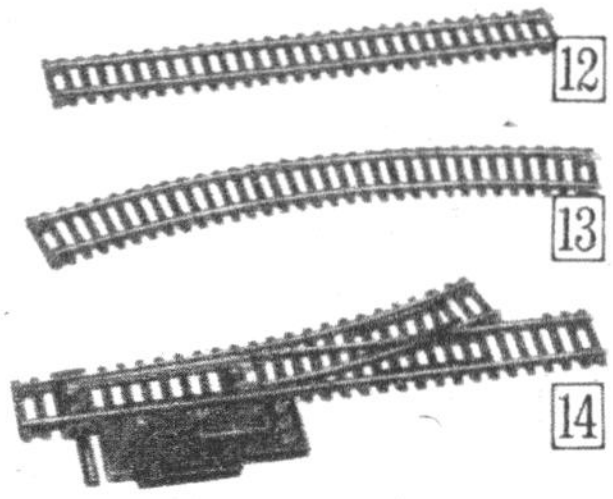

12 **Straight Track.** 9-inch pcs. Pkg. of 4. Wt. 3 oz.
49 C 9903......... Pkg. 99c

13 **Curved Track.** 18-inch radius. Pkg. of 4. Wt. 3 oz.
49 C 9912......... Pkg. 99c

14 **Remote Control Switches.**
49 C 9901—Left Turn
49 C 9902—Right Turn
Shpg. wt. 4 oz.... Each $4.19

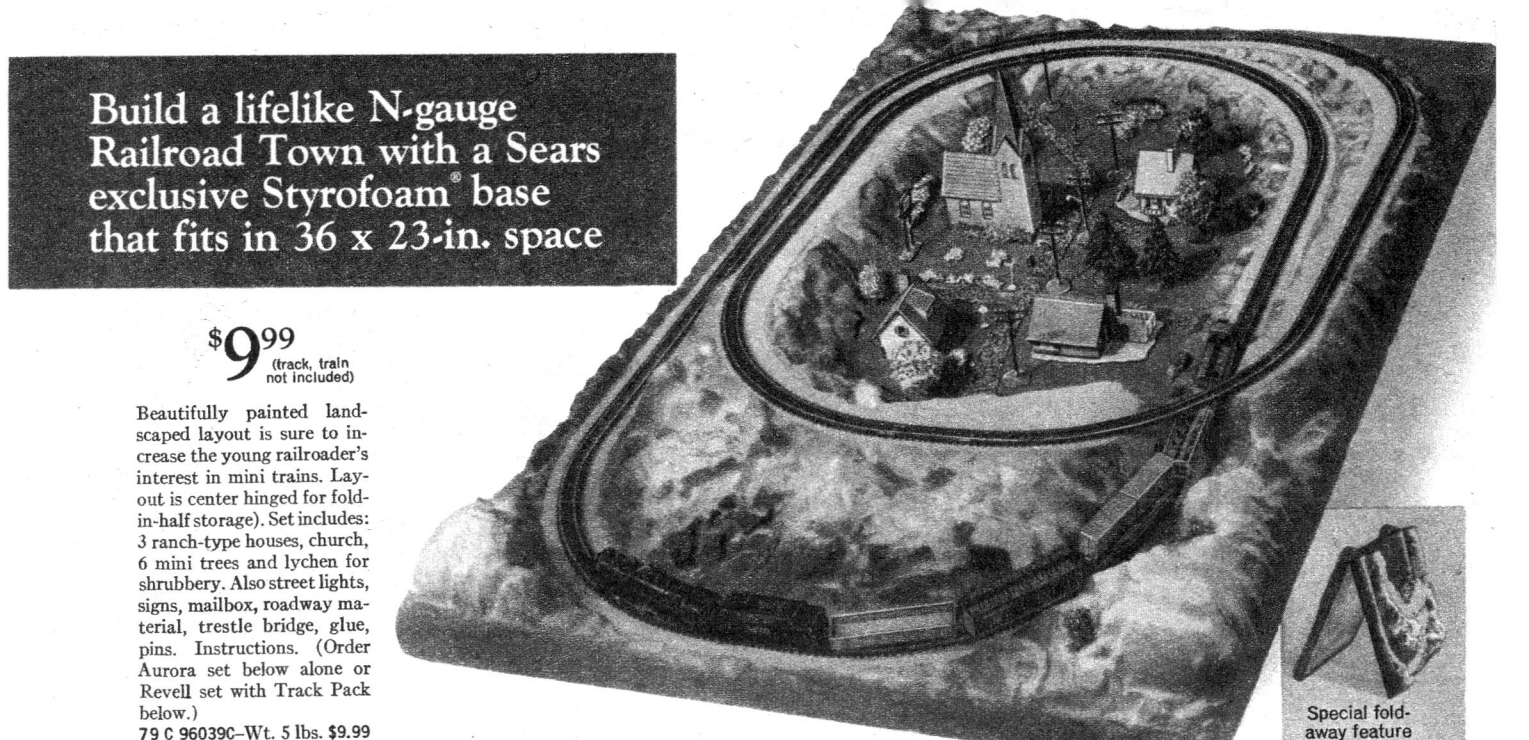

Build a lifelike N-gauge Railroad Town with a Sears exclusive Styrofoam® base that fits in 36 x 23-in. space

$9.99 (track, train not included)

Beautifully painted landscaped layout is sure to increase the young railroader's interest in mini trains. Layout is center hinged for fold-in-half storage). Set includes: 3 ranch-type houses, church, 6 mini trees and lychen for shrubbery. Also street lights, signs, mailbox, roadway material, trestle bridge, glue, pins. Instructions. (Order Aurora set below alone or Revell set with Track Pack below.)
79 C 96039C—Wt. 5 lbs. $9.99

Special fold-away feature

N-gauge Electric Train Outfits with Power Pack

N-gauge trains use about ¼ the space needed for HO

Aurora Sets fit N-gauge layout above

6-unit Double Diesel Set $26.99

7-unit Steam Freight Set $34.99

1 Santa Fe diesel locomotive with dummy diesel. Cars include hopper, tank car, piggyback flatcar with two trailers, caboose. Straight, curved track . . 68x23-inch layout (fits base above). UL listed, 16-volt DC power pack* has 18-v. AC accessory terminal.
49 C 96015—Shpg. wt. 3 lbs. 1 oz. $26.99

2 Mighty 4-6-2 Pacific steam locomotive and tender. Freight cars incl. hopper, piggyback car with 2 trailers, cattle car, gondola car, and caboose. Metal, plastic. 39 track sections forms 68x23-in. layout (fits above base). UL listed, 16-v. DC power pack* with 18-v. AC accessory terminal.
79 C 96016C—Shpg. wt. 3 lbs. $34.99

*NOTE: Power packs operate on 110–120-volt, 60-cycle AC.

AURORA

Revell Sets with 41-inch Oval track

"Load King" 4-unit Set $15.99

"Rail Master" 6-unit Set $19.99

3 Sleek cab-type New York Central diesel locomotive, 2 freight cars and caboose. Includes billboard refrigerator car, tank car. Ready to go . . UL listed .6-amp power pack,* 4 pieces 90° curved track, 1 straight, rerailer. Track adapts to any N-gauge system.
49 C 96041—Wt. 2 lbs. 10 oz. $15.99

4 Speedy Alco cab-type Southern Pacific diesel loco with detailed cars. Hopper, boxcar, flatcar, tanker, caboose. 4 curved tracks, 1 straight and rerailer. Two adapter sections make any N-gauge track useable. Power pack,* .6-amp, UL listed.
49 C 96042—Wt. 3 lbs. 1 oz. $19.99

Revell

Track expander sets increase layout size

Revell Track Pack. More than 75 inches of curved and straight track. 13 pieces; 4 curved, 9 straight. Combine with Revell sets for use with above Styrofoam base.
49 C 96043—Shipping weight 4 ounces. . . . . Set $2.99

Track Extender Set by Revell. Incl. 2 manual switches, 8 straight tracks, 2 curved . . over 100 in. of extra track.
49 C 96044—Shipping weight 4 ounces. $6.99

Sears 517

Eldon Bi-level Rally Race

1/32-scale Porsche and Ferrari compete on 25 feet of rugged track..around a banked curve with speed to spare!

THAT REMINDS ME... DID MOM TELL YA WHAT HAPPENED TO OUR CAR TODAY?

Rambling roadway has enough track to make many different layouts

$24.99

Cars flash down the straightaway, around a 180° banked turn close to full speed without spinning out. Zip over, under, up and down the tricky roadway. 1/32-scale set includes 2 molded plastic cars, each about 5½ inches long, 2 six-volt plug-in rheostats with pistol-grip controllers. Six-volt power pack, 38 pieces of plastic and metal roadway, lap counter track, bridge set, fence, nylon supports, decals, screwdriver. Layout about 5x9 feet. UL listed for 110-120-volt, 60-cycle AC.
49 C 95012—Shipping weight 11 lbs. 4 oz. $24.99

Lap Counter in track keeps official score

Eldon Over 'n Under Road Race Set

Look to Sears for UNCOMMON VALUE

You get 14 feet of 1/32-scale track, 2 pistol-grip controllers and 2 speedy sportsters

All for only **$13.99**

Pick your favorite, the Porsche or Ferrari. They're both trim and really fast. 5½ inches long, lightweight vacuum-formed plastic. Each has a completely assembled chassis equipped with high-rpm. Dyna Mite® motor. Rheostat speed controllers with speedometers showing scale speeds up to 160 mph. 6-volt power pack, UL listed, 110-120-v., 60-c. AC. 28-piece plastic and metal roadway, bridge set. Extra track sold at right.
79 C 95019C—Shipping weight 8 pounds..........$13.99

Eldon 1/32-scale Racing Accessories

(1 thru 4) **Cars for sets on this page.** All cars are about 5½ inches long. Plastic and metal construction.
(1) 49 C 95021—Chaparral   (3) 49 C 95022—Camaro
(2) 49 C 95024—Sting Ray   (4) 49 C 95023—Ford "J"
Shipping weight 14 ounces................Each $4.99

Track and Accessories for sets on this page. Plastic and metal. Straight and curved sold in pkg. of 2.
49 C 9926—Straight Track. 6½ in. Wt. 7 oz......Pkg. $1.29
49 C 9927—Curved Track. 45° curve. Wt. 7 oz....Pkg. 1.49
49 C 9925—Speed Controller. Shows mph. Wt. 4 oz. 1.99
6-volt Power Pack. UL listed. 110-120-v., 60-c. AC.
49 C 9952—Shipping weight 1 lb. 10 oz............$5.49

Want to know more?

Suggested Reading about Electric Trains

The Lionel Train Book
Written by Robert Schleicher
Published by Lionel Trains, Inc., Mt. Clemens, MI

Toy Train Collecting and Operating
Written by John Grams
Published by Kalmbach Publishing Co., Waukesha, WI

Lionel: A Collectors Guide & History, Vols. 1-6
Written by Tom McComas and James Tuohy
Published by Chilton Book Co., Radnor, PA

How To Build Your First Lionel Layout
Written by Stan Trzoniec
Published by Kalmbach Publishing Co., Waukesha, WI

Suggested Reading about Sears, Roebuck and Co.

Sears, Roebuck U.S.A.
Written by Gordon L. Weil
Published by Stein and Day, New York, NY

Shaping An American Institution
Written by James C. Worthy
University of Illinois Press, Chicago, IL

The Great Merchants
Written by Leonard Sloane and Tom Mahoney
Curtis Publishing Co., Philadelphia, PA

Electric Train Associations and Clubs

THE LIONEL COLLECTOR'S CLUB OF AMERICA (LCCA)
6355 Westland Drive, Westland MI 48185

THE LIONEL OPERATING TRAIN SOCIETY (LOTS)
135 76th Street, Boulder, CO 80303

THE LIONEL RAILROADER CLUB
Post Office Box 748, Mount Clemens, MI 48046

NATIONAL MODEL RAILROAD ASSOCIATION (NMRA)
4121 Cromwell Road, Chattanooga, TN 37421

THE TINPLATE TRACKERS SOCIETY
1701 Grandview Avenue, Glendale, CA 91201-1207

THE TOY TRAIN OPERATING SOCIETY (TTOS)
25 Walnut Street, Pasadena, CA 91103

THE TRAIN COLLECTORS ASSOCIATION (TCA)
Post Office Box 248, Strasburg, PA 17579

Suggested Magazines and Periodicals

CLASSIC TOY TRAINS
Published 8 times per year by Kalmbach Publishing Co.
(800) 533-6644

O GAUGE RAILROADING
Published 6 times per year by Myron J. Bigger Group
(610) 759-0406

MODEL RAILROADER
Published 12 times per year by Kalmbach Publishing Co.
(800) 533-6644

THE TOY TRAIN DEPARTMENT

Please send me _____ copies of THE TOY TRAIN DEPARTMENT at $19.95 each (plus $3.50 Postage and Handling per order.) CA residents add tax. My check or money order is enclosed.

Name: _____

Address: _____

_____

City: _____

State and Zipcode: _____

Mail To: WINDMILL PRESS • P.O. Box 56551 • Sherman Oaks, CA 91413

Would you or a friend like more copies of this book?

Mail this handy coupon today.

Would you or a friend like more copies of this book?

Mail this handy coupon today.

THE TOY TRAIN DEPARTMENT

Please send me _____ copies of THE TOY TRAIN DEPARTMENT at $19.95 each (plus $3.50 Postage and Handling per order.)   CA residents add tax. My check or money order is enclosed.

Name: _____

Address: _____

_____

City: _____

State and Zipcode: _____

Mail To: WINDMILL PRESS • P.O. Box 56551 • Sherman Oaks, CA 91413